》 》 》 *The Consuming Myth*

Seen from the café, now, the Woman is more distinct: knee, belly, ribcage, breast (a shallow hemisphere) slung backwards to the long throat; a firm jutting chin, nose ditto; mouth shut, refusal of a kiss.
She gives the landscape an intense dreamlike quality.

the CONSUMING MYTH)))

THE WORK OF JAMES MERRILL

STEPHEN YENSER

HARVARD UNIVERSITY PRESS

CAMBRIDGE, MASSACHUSETTS, AND LONDON, ENGLAND 1987

Copyright © 1987 by the President and Fellows of
Harvard College
All rights reserved
Printed in the United States of America
10 9 8 7 6 5 4 3 2 1

Publication of this book has been aided by a grant from
the Andrew W. Mellon Foundation

This book is printed on acid-free paper, and its binding
materials have been chosen for strength and durability.

Library of Congress Cataloging-in-Publication Data

Yenser, Stephen.
  The consuming myth.

  "Works by James Merrill": p.
  Bibliography: p.
  Includes index.
  1. Merrill, James Ingram—Criticism and interpreta-
tion. 2. Myth in literature. I. Title.
PS3525.E6645Z97 1987   811'.54   86-14886
ISBN 0-674-16615-9 (alk. paper)

Designed by Gwen Frankfeldt

To Elizabeth Bramblett Yenser and Willard Yenser

Always a knit of identity, always distinction, always a breed of life.
    Walt Whitman, *Song of Myself*

Contents

Illustrations

› › › *The Consuming Myth*

BACKWARD-LOOKING FIGURES
A Recent Poem through Some Early Work

Small beyond great swaying glooms
Over driveway gravel strewn
With golden acorns and shed plumes
From the pigeon-lariat
Twirled of a long afternoon
Stands the house of fifty rooms.

>)))

The friends that have it I do wrong
When ever I remake a song,
Should know what issue is at stake:
It is myself that I remake.

    W. B. Yeats, untitled poem

A force de construire, me fit-il, en souriant, je crois bien que je me suis construit
moi-même.

    Paul Valéry, "Eupalinos, ou l'architecte"

In my house the weaving is always going on.
I weave on and on and I myself am the cloth.

    Kabir, quoted by Grazia Marchianò

L I F E magazine produced a colorful spread several years ago entitled
"Eleven American Poets." Those of us who saw the article will long remember most of the pictures, taken by an enterprising photographer. One of the
poets, a man, has been snapped at an excruciating moment during a set of
exercises in a Birmingham gymnasium. Another, a woman, holding a long-
handled costume ball mask fringed with feathers, and wearing a silver-scaled
gown, is stretched out along the back of a palomino. One of the poets not
enticed into a glamorous pose is James Merrill. Fully and ordinarily clothed,
he sits in his dining room in Stonington, Connecticut, his hands on the edge
of the round table with its milk glass top, where he and his friend David
Jackson, fiction writer and essayist, have so often sat with their Ouija board,
made contact with the other world, and taken notes on those seminar sessions, picnics, masques, and fêtes which, along with the brilliant set pieces,
have gone into *The Changing Light at Sandover,* the epic work completed in
1982 that was immediately recognizable as a landmark in American literature.
    It is a modest, almost unremarkable photograph. But there is some-
thing a little odd about it, beyond the wraparound look lent by the wide-
angle lens, at least if the reader has seen the poet in the flesh or in other

photographs. Eventually one realizes that the printer has reversed the image, so that to see Merrill as he is, one would have to hold the picture to a mirror. A mistake in the layout, no doubt. But still in some sense "NO ACCIDENT," in the stern phrase favored by certain spirits on the other end of JM's and DJ's wireless. From the beginning—now two novels, two plays, and twelve books of poems ago, not to mention assorted playlets, essays, and translations, during which stretch he has received the Bollingen Prize, the Pulitzer Prize, and two National Book Awards—Merrill has been a writer uncannily alert to reversals and doublings. The duplicate and the didymous, the obverse and the inverse, the geminate and the specular are part and parcel of his art. Pun, paradox, alter ego, chiasmus, spoonerism, and all kinds of literary double-stopping and counterpointing are his stock in trade, as essential to his writing, to his "poem's world," as perhaps they are to what he thinks of, at least at times, as "the world's poem," where Mother Nature herself "sets meaning spinning like a coin." "Anything worth having's had both ways," he offers in *Sandover*, where he also proposes that we live in "One nature dual to the end."[1]

This last phrase succinctly formulates what I take to be two opposing principles in Merrill's work. I say "two opposing principles" even though the second is that opposing principles must be one, because the first is that any single principle will double. By which I mean to say, in the first place, that Merrill—predisposed, he might suggest, by the double *r* and the double *l* in his last name—is an inveterate dualist. Throughout his career, as a result of some epistemological application of the physicist's "pair production," whatever he has looked at hard has yielded up its contraries. He has discovered, all about him, divisions and dichotomies. All about him—and within him. He does not read much philosophy, it appears, but it is not impossible to imagine him sitting one sunny afternoon on the terrace of that Stonington house he has told us so much about, leafing through *The Philosophy of Language*, and coming with a start of recognition on the speculations at the end of the second lecture. Schlegel has been mulling over the entanglements of thinking and speaking, and "as speech must be regarded as a thinking outwardly projected and manifested," he decides, "so, too, thinking itself is but an inward speaking and a never-ending dialogue with oneself." A page later, he elaborates: "So profound, moreover, and lasting is this our intrinsic dualism and duplicity . . . so deeply is this dualism rooted in our consciousness, that even when we are, or at least think ourselves alone, we still think as two, and are constrained . . . to recognise our inmost . . . being as essentially dramatic."[2] One might venture that Merrill's most characteristic work began in earnest when he incorporated in a poem such a dramatic duplicity. I have in mind the first poem in *Water Street*, "An Urban Convalescence," especially its turning point—the point at which Merrill

4

suddenly turns on himself, or turns, perhaps in a double sense, into himself. Having just confronted a disillusioning instance of the "ugliness and waste" in the world, he vows that he will learn whatever he can from it, from its "soiled gusts" and its "shrieking" winds, which he swears he will face "Full into, eyes astream with cold"—and then comes the sharp change in tone, the interruption by another, more realistic self, who knows that to look outward can be to see inward: "With cold? / All right then. With self-knowledge."

Merrill's internal divisions have manifested themselves in any number of ways. From the many examples to be taken up later, I might single out here as emblematic his decision to live in two worlds, the American and the Mediterranean. He has spoken of the appeal to him of the experience of an acquaintance who vanished one day and reappeared some time later in another place with another name and another life altogether: "Now it may sound—it may *be*—childish, but haven't we all dreamed of doing exactly that? To disappear and re-emerge as a new person without any ties, the slate wiped clean. Sometimes one even puts the dream into action . . . In my own case I began going to Greece—over ten years ago [about 1959]—very much in the spirit of one who embarks on a double life. The life I lived there seemed I can't tell you how different from life in America."[3] As time went on, Merrill ruefully continues, his two lives, the one in Stonington and the other in Athens, grew more and more the same. But even as this similarity was growing, he and David Jackson, who shared both houses, were increasingly living another double life, for they had become involved with the Ouija board and thus with the *au-delà*.

Such longings for a double life correspond, in Merrill's view, to an ambivalence in the nature of poetic language and even in nature itself. He has summed up his dualism in this way:

> I suppose that early on I began to understand the relativity, even the reversibility, of truths . . . There was truth on both sides [of a typical issue]. And maybe having arrived at *that* explained my delight in setting down a phrase like, oh, "the pillow's dense white dark" or "Au fond each summit is a cul-de-sac," but the explanation as such neither delights nor convinces me. I believe the secret lies primarily in the nature of poetry—and of science too, for that matter—and that the ability to see both ways at once isn't merely an idiosyncrasy but corresponds to how the world needs to be seen: cheerful *and* awful, opaque *and* transparent. The plus and minus signs of a vast evolving formula.[4]

While the second of the phrases he quotes is from "Up and Down," a poem in *Braving the Elements* (1972), the first phrase comes from "Hotel de l'Univers et de Portugal," in *The Country of a Thousand Years of Peace* (1959), his second full-length book of poems. The same "ability to see both ways at once," however, was present long before that—before even *The Black Swan*, a collection published in Athens (in an edition of only one hundred copies) in 1946. I am thinking of Merrill's first publication in book form, a curious gathering of precocious poems, stories, translations, and prose pieces entitled *Jim's Book*, whose limited printing was sponsored, without the knowledge of its sixteen-year-old author (then a student at Lawrenceville School in New Jersey), by his father in 1942.[5]

In this book's essay on Elinor Wylie, "Angel or Earthly Creature," an extraordinary foreshadowing of his later fascinations, Merrill writes sympathetically of that poet's connection with the other world. He observes that Wylie "felt that, in some way, she was psychic." Indeed, she sometimes thought that Percy Bysshe Shelley was her "closest friend" and her "celestial guide," that she was "by an archangel befriended." The young Merrill also analyzes the dichotomies implicit in Wylie's spiritualism. He discusses the struggle "between mind and flesh" that preoccupied her once Shelley had given way to a new mentor, John Donne, and he senses that "there is an eternal fight raging inside her—her intellectual thinking self as opposed to the desires and impulses of her body." The same conflict drives many of Merrill's poems, and related polarities abound in his work. Often one can imagine him echoing Blake's fervently prayerful lines in his letter to Thomas Butts: "And twofold Always. May God us keep / From Single vision & Newtons sleep."[6] At other times he makes one think of the troubled Emerson: "A believer in Unity, a seer of Unity, I yet behold two . . . Cannot I conceive the Universe without a contradiction?"[7] The science of our time, with which Merrill has recently been preoccupied, would seem to say not. "Contemporary physics lives off paradox," Lewis Thomas reminds us. "Niels Bohr said that a great truth is one for which the opposite is also a great truth."[8]

Which returns us to the other principle: it is, Merrill insists, "*One* nature dual to the end." It is as though he were such a dualist that he must also be a monist. Throughout his work one senses either a yearning for oneness or, more often, an intuition of it. This attraction to unity motivates many of the paradoxes that riddle his writing, as well as his characteristic moot questions ("Good? Evil? Was it all the same?") and his framing of alternatives so that they seem to be aspects of one another. He surmises that his earliest literary efforts sprang from a need to reconcile the influences of his mother and his father, whose marriage ended just before his twelfth birthday, when he glosses a phrase he wrote in his diary, some time after the divorce, about Silver Springs, Florida:

6

"Heavenly colors and swell fish." What is that phrase but an attempt to bring my parents together, to remarry on the page their characteristic inflections—the ladylike gush and the regular-guy terseness? In reality my parents have tones more personal and complex than these, but the time is still far off when [the boy he was then] can dream of echoing them . . . By then, too, surrogate parents will enter the scene . . . Proust and Elizabeth Bishop, Maria [Mitsotáki, a Greek friend] and Auden in the Sandover books. The unities of home and world, and world and page, will be observed through the very act of transition from one to the other.[9]

The subtle slipping from one set of paired terms to another and the implicit agonistic engagement throughout of the basic pair, division and unity, are Merrillian. Time and again he seeks to combine his apprehension of the irreducible contrariness of things with his sense of unicity. "The magician," he has said in regard to a figure in "Yánnina," "performs the essential act. He heals what he has divided. A double-edged action, like his sword. It's what one comes to feel that life keeps doing."[10] Life and his art both, to name the other edge of *that* sword—and what is "sword" but "words" rewritten? He persistently seeks means analogous to the image at the end of "Yánnina," where, after musing on the sawing in half of the magician's assistant ("Done by mirrors? Just one woman? Two?"), he envisions Ali Pasha afloat in a barge that keeps "Scissoring and mending" the still water.

It is an appealing coincidence that Merrill's primary home for more than two decades has been in Connecticut, whose name puts the relevant antithetical imperatives on either side of the *I* that separates and joins them. This is a linguistic circumstance that must have occurred long ago to this poet so charmed by logograph that, for instance, he has discovered in the two words "Begin. Carnation" the command to "beg incarnation" and thus the occasion for a poem ("Komboloi"). The same cast of mind leads him to see in the word "Ibis" the quasi-French address for a second self, "I *bis*" ("The Will"), and persuades him to include in his "Autumn Elegy" (in *The Yellow Pages*) a reference to a certain showy shrub, all too often the subject of "bad seasonal verse," on the grounds that its name spells, "In the mind's mirror," the name of "the young demi-god Camus." His comments on the magician's "double-edged action" and on "what life keeps doing" recall another text about cutting and connecting that he would know well:

Certes, s'il s'agit uniquement de nos coeurs, le poète a eu raison de parler des "fils mystérieux" que la vie brise. Mais il est encore plus vrai qu'elle en tisse sans cesse entre les êtres, entre les événements, qu'elle entre-croise ces fils, qu'elle les redouble pour épaissir la trame, si bien qu'entre le moindre point de notre passé et tous les autres un riche réseau de souvenirs ne laisse que le choix des communications.

Certainly, if he was thinking purely of the human heart, the poet was right when he spoke of the "mysterious threads" which are broken by life. But the truth, even more, is that life is perpetually weaving fresh threads which link one individual and one event to another, and that these threads are crossed and recrossed, doubled and redoubled to thicken the web, so that between any slightest point of our past and all the others a rich network of memories gives us an almost infinite variety of communicating paths to choose from.[11]

Proust is writing, it seems, not about writing but about actual events and the ways in which our memories and imaginations weave them together, even though the people involved drift apart or never meet. Yet it is clear enough on reflection that the writer, or at least Proust's kind of writer, operates on the premise set out here. Proust's huge novel, as Roland Barthes puts it, is "among other things, a tremendous intrigue, a farce network," in which "everything ends by coinciding." It takes its texture from the mental life that produced it. Or is it the other way around?[12]

Proust himself takes the line of thought that crucial step further when he argues, earlier in his final volume, that one's essential life comes into being only because of or in the course of the creative process:

> La grandeur de l'art véritable . . . c'était de retrouver, de ressaisir, de nous faire connaître cette réalité loin de laquelle nous vivons, de laquelle nous nous écartons de plus en plus au fur et à mesure que prend plus d'épaisseur et d'imperméabilité la connaissance conventionelle que nous lui substituons, cette réalité que nous risquerions fort de mourir sans avoir connue, et qui est tout simplement notre vie. La vraie vie, la vie enfin découverte et éclaircie, la seule vie par conséquent réellement vécue, c'est la littérature; cette vie qui, en un sens, habite à chaque instant chez tous les hommes aussi bien que chez l'artiste. Mais ils ne la voient pas, parce qu'ils ne cherchent pas à l'éclaircir. Et ainsi leur passé est encombré d'innombrables clichés qui restent inutiles parce que l'intelligence ne les a pas "développés."

The greatness . . . of true art . . . lay, I had come to see, elsewhere: we have to rediscover, to reapprehend, to make ourselves fully aware of that reality, remote from our daily preoccupations, from which we separate ourselves by an ever greater gulf as the conventional knowledge which we substitute for it grows thicker and more impermeable, that reality which it is very easy for us to die without ever having known and which is, quite simply, our life. Real life, life at last laid bare and illuminated— the only life in consequence which can be said to be really lived—is literature, and life thus defined is in a sense all the time immanent in ordinary men no less than in the artist. But most men do not see it because they do not seek to shed light upon it. And therefore their past is like a photographic dark-room encumbered with innumerable negatives which remain useless because the intellect has not developed them.[13]

"La vraie vie . . . c'est la littérature," and literature is the tissue of connections the artist discovers in life. The paradox would be dear to the heart of the Amherst student who wrote an honors thesis on Proust for his professor Reuben Brower.[14] Later he would write that "life was fiction in disguise." And in that magazine article mentioned earlier, where as though in an attempt at a peremptory stroke *Life* itself reversed the poet's image, he maintains his balance by declaring, "As for myself, I can't imagine my own life without poetry. It created me." Now that statement means in part that the poems he knows have shaped his view of things.[15] But it means too that the process of writing made him what he is, partly because of the disciplines it entailed, but surely also because of the memories that had to be "developed," in the metaphor of Proust—who, Merrill confirms, has influenced him more than any other writer.[16]

> > >

Being committed to duality, like Yeats, Merrill has been sharply aware of the divergent demands that art and life make; and like Yeats, being dedicated to unity, he has devoted himself to confounding the dichotomy. When he defines the poet as a person "choosing the words he lives by," he chooses his words with care. Eupalinos, Valéry's architect and spokesman, could speak for him as well: "I truly believe that, by dint of building, I have built myself."[17] His work strives to embody a process epitomized in the transformations traced near the end of section S in *The Book of Ephraim*, the first of the *Sandover* volumes, where JM addresses a Russian character named Sergei, whom he figures as a plant and whose lineage he traces to a former neighbor in Stonington:

When he was cut down I took slips of him
To set in tidy ballad stanza-boxes
Made, one winter, about Stonington.
His pliant manners and sharp-scented death
Came up Japanese. You came up Russian
—Next to a showy hybrid "Mrs. Smith."
Here you are now, old self in a new form.
Some of those roots look stronger, some have died.
Tell me, tell me, as I turn to you . . .

The actual old man became Ken, the Japanese houseman in "The Summer People," then turned into Sergei in *Ephraim*, and then—by what means and to what ends I shall detail later—into the poet himself. The process appears at a different level in the *Sandover* trilogy at large, which habitually revisits its earlier incidents and figures and discovers in them its later ones. There, one often has the impression, as in dialectic, whether Hegel's or Dante's, of "a single process growing in subtlety and comprehensiveness, not different senses, but different intensities or wider contexts of a continuous sense, unfolding like a plant out of a seed" (though I do not mean to invoke a simple emanationist view of poetic creation).[18]

Such a process is one thing Merrill means by "translation" in "Lost in Translation," which seems to me more completely expressive of "the unities of home and world, and world and page" than any of his poems of a comparable length. It is at once a memoir and a poetics with metaphysical and epistemological aspects. Ripe and full at every turn, it is the kind of venture that "Tintern Abbey" is—and "Mont Blanc," "Fra Lippo Lippi," "When Lilacs Last in the Dooryard Bloom'd," "Sunday Morning." A poem with structural integrity—Merrill has always been a writer of poems, not of poetry—it is nonetheless absorbent and reflective and anticipatory of his other work. It all comes to *this*, the poem seems to say. Merrill altered its position in the sequence of poems from *Divine Comedies* included in *From the First Nine: Poems 1946–1976*, his selected poems excluding the *Sandover* trilogy.[19] He decided to make it the last poem from these first nine volumes, and he did so, I think, because it is a consummation—and thus a place to begin.

Written in 1972, probably not long before the first inklings of *The Book of Ephraim*, and published first in *The New Yorker* and then in *Divine Comedies*, "Lost in Translation" reaches back to 1937, shortly before Germany's aggressions would "shake / This world . . . to its foundations." In 1937, James Merrill was about to have his family world shaken to its own foundations. He had been born on March 3, 1926, in New York City, the only child of Hellen Ingram Merrill, whose maiden name is her son's middle name,

10

and Charles Edward Merrill, the founder of the brokerage firm Merrill Lynch, Pierce, Fenner and Smith. Charles Merrill had been married once before, to Eliza Church, with whom he had had two children: Doris, the older, who was to marry Robert Magowan and become a benefactor of the arts, and Charles, writer and founder of the Commonwealth School in Boston, whose experiences as an educator are set down in *The Walled Garden*.[20] The marriage to Hellen Ingram was of about the same length as the first marriage—and as far as that goes of the third marriage, which was already casting its shadow over the summer of 1937. Merrill wryly summarizes his father's adult life in the second poem in the sonnet sequence "The Broken Home":

> My father, who had flown in World War I,
> Might have continued to invest his life
> In cloud banks well above Wall Street and wife.
> But the race was run below, and the point was to win.
>
> Too late now, I make out in his blue gaze
> (Through the smoked glass of being thirty-six)
> The soul eclipsed by twin black pupils, sex
> And business; time was money in those days.
>
> Each thirteenth year he married. When he died
> There were already several chilled wives
> In sable orbit—rings, cars, permanent waves.
> We'd felt him warming up for a green bride.
>
> He could afford it. He was "in his prime"
> At three score ten. But money was not time.

The poet, who identifies himself by a circuitous route with another "flyer" in *Ephraim,* would eventually decide precisely "to invest his life / In cloud banks well above Wall Street and wife."

Having lived almost exactly that span allotted to us by the Psalmist, Charles Merrill died in 1956. That was the year after his son's play, *The Immortal Husband,* opened off-Broadway on Valentine's Day, and the year before the publication of his first novel, *The Seraglio,* in which (we are told in *Ephraim*) his nearly quadrigamist father served as a "Model / For 'Benjamin Tanning,'" the novel's sultan, whose last name has overtones of his hardiness and his severity alike. In 1937, at fifty-two, Charles was on the verge of his second divorce, an event that would occur in February 1938 and that was to be a turning point in his son's life. We might infer something of the boy's feeling during the summer of "Lost in Translation" from his response to his

11

parents' inadequately explained absences and his corresponding obsession with an enormous jigsaw puzzle, rented from a New York shop and late in arriving, which he and his governess, "His French Mademoiselle," have planned to assemble during the school vacation: "A summer without parents is the puzzle, / Or should be. But the boy, day after day, / Writes in his Line-a-Day *No puzzle*." Isn't there something of the determined or fearful disregard about that way of putting it? Even though to work at the one puzzle, when it finally arrives, is to work at the other, the family crisis is never explicitly acknowledged. (One reason it need not be acknowledged is that by this point in his career Merrill has written about it so often that he can take for granted his reader's acquaintance with it. And a more important reason is that he has come to write *as though* he could rely on the reader's acquaintance. His allusions conjure the familiarity they seem to presume.)

"Lost in Translation" calls into play three autobiographical situations. In the most recent one, which the poem outlines last, the setting is Athens, where Merrill had his second home, on Athinaion Efivon Street at the foot of Mount Lykabettos, from 1959 until the late 1970s, and the subject is his rereading of Valéry's magnificent lyric, "Palme," and his subsequent search through the city's libraries for Rilke's translation of that poem into German. Merrill half-recalls having seen the translation years earlier, but when he cannot turn up a copy, he wonders whether he hasn't imagined it. That the translation does exist, and that he eventually finds it, his epigraph—an excerpt from Rilke's version—attests. The memory of the French and the German poems, and the memory in particular of the exhortation to "Patience," calls up "His French Mademoiselle," in whose care he spent that summer in the family's home in Southampton and on whom he had a crush, though she must have been a good thirty years older than he, since "In real life" she had been "a widow since Verdun." That summer is the second situation in the poem. It occupies sections one, three, and four of five unmarked sections. The moment at which this memory of 1937 begins to unfold in the poet's mind, one of his variations on the celebrated madeleine passage in *A la Recherche du temps perdu*, comes at the end of his second verse paragraph:

> Noon coffee. Mail. The watch that also waited
> Pinned to her heart, poor gold, throws up its hands—
> No puzzle! Steaming bitterness
> Her sugars draw pops back into his mouth, translated:
> "Patience, chéri. Geduld, mein Schatz."
> (Thus, reading Valéry the other evening
> And seeming to recall a Rilke version of "Palme,"

That sunlit paradigm whereby the tree
Taps a sweet wellspring of authority,
The hour came back. Patience dans l'azur.
Geduld im . . . Himmelblau? Mademoiselle.)

By setting out first the remembered experience and only then, in the parenthesis, exposing the cause of the memory, the rereading of Valéry's poem,
Merrill's narrative sequence reverses Proust's. One result is that we are reminded of the elusiveness of a "source." Is the poem's real source the relationship with Mademoiselle? Or is it indeed Valéry's lyric? Life or literature?
To whose soft, imperative "Patience" is it finally traceable? Or is the source
better represented by Rilke's translation? Merrill foreshadows the answer
formulated at poem's end in this passage's little vortex of metamorphoses,
where the sugar cubes translate the coffee's taste, the coffee's bitterness
renders the boy's disappointment, that disappointment is sweetened by
Mademoiselle's counsel, and her words accidentally predict his knowledge of
Valéry's lines—which antedate them. Through it all, the past moment of
bittersweet anticipation and the present moment of nostalgia figure each
other.

Given such density, it is remarkable that the poem's five parts make up
such a clearly structured, nearly symmetrical arrangement. The first part,
about the wait for and the arrival of the puzzle, is in a flexible mode that
Merrill devised for poems in *Water Street* and has been refining ever since:
verse paragraphs of occasionally rhymed iambic pentameter lines. This part
concludes when, after the puzzle's pieces have all been spread out face up on
a card table in the library, "The plot thickens / As all at once two pieces
interlock." Because the "plot" is the poem's in addition to the puzzle's, the
page's as well as the home's, the first section interlocks just here with the
second, where Merrill gives up the blank verse for a line that is shorter and
more and more insistently accentual and alliterative. The situation changes
too, to the third situation mentioned earlier, as the poem records an experience that "lay years ahead" of the boy—in London, where the poet witnesses a demonstration by a medium. Ostensibly an afterthought, this second section fits with the first partly because it too takes place in a library and
partly because it involves a piece of a puzzle—though there are also fundamental congruences. Merrill shifts back into blank verse for the central section's two paragraphs, where he describes the progress made on the puzzle
by the boy and his Mademoiselle even as he reveals the latter's background,
which is a good deal more complex than he had realized when he was
eleven. Like the second section, the fourth has its own distinctive prosody,

in this case *Rubaiyat* quatrains. This section describes the completed puzzle, which takes its picture from a painting allegedly done by a disciple of J.-L. Gérôme that has an "Oriental" subject. It breaks off in the middle of a stanza, after not quite two lines, and the last section, which returns to the verse paragraph, tells of the dismantling of the puzzle and the poet's search for the Rilke translation.

Merrill's five-part organization, with its prosodically similar odd-numbered sections and unique even-numbered sections, might also have been modeled on the musical scheme known as rondo form (or second rondo form), which often follows an ABACA pattern. And if it were not, perhaps he would not object to the comparison, since he has commented more than once over the years on the potential usefulness of musical forms to the poet. He has said, for instance, that "whenever I reach an impasse, working on a poem, I try to imagine an analogy with musical form," and he tells us that he solved a certain problem in "The Thousand and Second Night" by "a stroke I associated quite arbitrarily with that moment at the end of the Rondo of the 'Waldstein' sonata."[21] The ingenious structure of the penultimate section of "The Will," in which an entire "sonnet"—seven couplets—intervenes between the octave and the sestet of another sonnet (and thus establishes an 8−7−6 progression that mends even as the inter-polation scissors), derives from the Mozart Concerto in E flat (K. 271), whose presto Finale embraces as its middle section a minuet.[22] Music, in the form of opera, was "the first art that came [his] way." As it happens, he be-gan going to the opera in New York—an experience he recalls fondly in "Matinees"—when he was eleven years old, which would have been the year commemorated in "Lost in Translation."

The opening lines of the poem recall the boy's wait for the puzzle, seemingly lost in translation from the puzzle rental shop—and at the same time they conjure that absence, heavy with imminence, that is the matrix of all poems:

A card table in the library stands ready
To receive the puzzle which keeps never coming.
Daylight shines in or lamplight down
Upon the tense oasis of green felt.
Full of unfulfillment, life goes on,
Mirage arisen from time's trickling sands
Or fallen piecemeal into place:
German lesson, picnic, see-saw, walk
With the collie who "did everything but talk"—
Sour windfalls of the orchard back of us.

14

Hardly a line here but that tugs in Merrillian fashion in two directions. If the "library" implies intellectual work—the study of German, under the eye of Mademoiselle, or of "Palme" in Rilke's translation—the card table introduces the element of play, and together they go some way toward defining the experience of assembling a difficult puzzle, or the experience of writing a poem. The more and less insistent oxymorons in the phrases "keeps never coming," "Full of unfulfillment," and "Sour windfalls," and the latent antitheses of "Daylight" and "lamplight" and "arisen" and "fallen" embody Merrill's special knotty grain of thought. While the rhyme near the end of this quotation, "talk" and "walk," is a little flourish that acknowledges this tour de force of coupling, the term that sums it all up is "see-saw"—which perhaps also slyly extends the reference to the daily language lesson (with its conjugated verbs), itself opposed (as though to iterate the opening line's balance) by "picnic," whose own rhyming reduplication is echoed by "see-saw."

If we do hear a punning allusion to a language lesson in that last term, that is partly because these lines are rich with a sense of time's own richness. The negated continuous construction at the end of Merrill's second line vibrates with possibility. The present tense and the implied passage of time continue to correct each other through the second sentence, while in the third the "trickling sands" suggest both the seeming desolation of the boy's life and the hourglass that the dragging days keep inverting. Unobtrusive but most piquant of all is the fragment between quotation marks, which unexpectedly introduces the past tense. It would be said, years later, by someone affectionately remembering the collie. The single word "'did'" suddenly frames the whole scene, a miniature puzzle of activities, in the past. The following line confirms this point of view on things, for "back of us" has a temporal dimension too, so that the phrase "Sour windfalls" summarizes that entire little world, full of love and absence, good fortune and disaster.

This scene will not *stay* past, however. As "The clock that also waited / Pinned to her heart, poor gold, throws up its hands," Merrill again resorts to the past tense. Waited—throws, see—saw. No wonder the watch, which ought to be able to tell exactly what time it is, throws up its hands. As the hands meet at noon, so past and present keep converging in the poem. Though these early conjunctions, if noticed at all, are likely to seem merely quirky, they indicate the profound relationship between past and present implicit in the poem's wizard initial sentence—as transfixing in its way as "Longtemps, je me suis couché de bonne heure." And make no mistake: Proust is behind this poem as much as Valéry and Rilke are, as he is behind so much of Merrill's work. If Marcel solves his long-standing problem and embarks on his "vocation" in the Guermantes's library at the end of *A la Recherche du temps perdu,* Merrill assembles his puzzle in the family library, and then in the London library, and finally in the unnamed library that presumably yields the Rilke translation. And it is Proust who adopts the relevant stereoscopic view of his youthful experience, and who uses "translation" as a further metaphor for the elucidation of the artwork:

> . . . ce livre essentiel, le seul livre vrai, un grand écrivain n'a pas, dans le sens courant, à l'inventer, puisqu'il existe déjà en chacun de nous, mais à le traduire. Le devoir et la tâche d'un écrivain sont ceux d'un traducteur.

> . . . the essential, the only true book, though in the ordinary sense of the word it does not have to be "invented" by a great writer—for it exists already in each one of us—has to be translated by him. The function and the task of a writer are those of a translator.[23]

In such a passage as the opening verse paragraph of "Lost in Translation," the smallest pieces fall into place partly because of the poet's tolerance for perfecting. One recalls that Marcel notes how some stitching done on the inside of Madame de Guermantes's cloak is finished as nicely as the ordinarily visible stitching. That detail speaks volumes about Proust's work—as Reuben Brower's student might well have noticed, since Brower himself had such an appreciation for seeming trifles. "The failure of much eighteenth-century poetry," in his eyes, "is not due to over-generality but to the lack of a metaphorical sense which connects and gives meaning to detail."[24] It would be hard to make too much of Merrill's concern with detail, for it has as much as anything to do with the kind of writer he is. Take his evocation of Rilke's translation of "Palme," with its sacrificing of many a Gallic nuance "in order to render [Valéry's] underlying sense":

> that ground plan left
> Sublime and barren, where the warm Romance
> Stone by stone faded, cooled; the fluted nouns
> Made taller, lonelier than life
> By leaf-carved capitals in the afterglow.
> The owlet umlaut peeps and hoots
> Above the open vowel.

Only a poet of the fiercest concentration would find in the stark translation a whole miniature acropolis, discover the pun on "capitals," and not only make us see in the umlaut the eyes of an owl but also let us hear its hoots in his assonance ("owlet," "umlaut," "vowel"). When the boy's puzzle arrives, we learn in the third verse paragraph, it turns out to be "A superior one, containing a thousand hand-sawn, / Sandal-scented pieces." These last words, with their lovely run of sounds ("thousand," "hand-sawn," "sandal"), are the exact analogy to those pieces.

From one angle, then, "Lost in Translation" is itself an intricate puzzle. It is a confirmation of this intricacy that there are several other dimensions to the relationship between puzzle and poem. For example, the puzzle's scene, when it finally takes shape, implicitly stages the situation in the boy's family. Again, the puzzle's composition reflects the poet's material. If much of Merrill's life has been devoted to writing and reading, so that the new poem will avail itself of forms tested before by him and by others, the cutter of the puzzle's pieces has his tradition:

> Many take
> Shapes known already—the craftsman's repertoire
> Nice in its limitation—from other puzzles:
> Witch on broomstick, ostrich, hourglass,
> Even (surely not just in retrospect)
> An inchling, innocently branching palm.
> These can be put aside, made stories of
> While Mademoiselle spreads out the rest face up.

These specific shapes have their own immediate relevance; Merrill invites us to put them aside and make stories of them that will suit "Lost in Translation." Thus we might say that the ostrich figures the boy's state of mind and the poem's manner. Left to his own devices, fearful of what he might see, the young Merrill has hidden his head in the puzzle's diverting desert—repeated here in the hourglass's recovery of the first verse paragraph's "trickling sands" and "tense oasis." Of course the oasis has also given the "inchling, innocently branching palm" a place to take root. It is as though these two were opposing impulses in the same life, responding to different sides of one experience: the cheerful and the awful.

The "Witch on broomstick" has a place in this story too, for she is a crucial element in what the boy has been overlooking. Although the original witch never appears here, she is represented in the puzzle, which pictures a sheik's new consort, who threatens his "old wives." This shadowy figure, who appears in *Ephraim* in the lead role in the unwritten drama of Merrill's youth that he thinks of as *The Other Woman*, will be one reason for the divorce. She also shows up in *Ephraim* in the guise of a character named Joanna, who flies into the poem carrying a Ouija board. Like her, the hourglass has figured in Merrill's other work: he has poems called "Hourglass" and "Hour Glass II," and the hourglass is an important motif in *Scripts for the Pageant*, the last of the *Sandover* books. The palm comes up in a number

17

of his poems and of course in Valéry's lyric. Merrill has absorbed much of "Palme" in "Lost in Translation," and lines especially relevant to this constellation of puzzle pieces occur in Valéry's seventh stanza:

Ces jours qui te semblent vides
Et perdus pour l'univers
Ont des racines avides
Qui travaillent les déserts.

Merrill quotes Rilke's translation as his epigraph:

Diese Tage, die leer dir scheinen
und wertlos für das All,
haben Wurzeln zwischen den Steinen
und trinken dort überall.

And here finally is Merrill's own rendering, published several years after "Lost in Translation":

These days which, like yourself,
Seem empty and effaced
Have avid roots that delve
To work deep in the waste.[25]

So beneath Merrill's "inchling, innocently branching palm" lies an untold, virtually untellable story. In addition to his own pain and regret, and his years of language study, of reading Proust and others, of writing and of waiting (for the puzzle to arrive, for the angel to descend, for the right word, the right moment for this poem or story or translation), there is Valéry's poem, with all the experience stored in it and implied in his superb address to the tree:

Patience, patience,
Patience dans l'azur!
Chaque atome de silence
Est la chance d'un fruit mûr.
Viendra l'heureuse surprise:
Une colombe, la brise,
L'ébranlement le plus doux,
Une femme qui s'appuie,
Feront tomber cette pluie
Où l'on se jette à genoux!

In Merrill's translation:

Patience and still patience,
Patience beneath the blue!
Each atom of the silence
Knows what it ripens to.
The happy shock will come:
A dove alighting, some
Gentlest nudge, the breeze,
A woman's touch—before
You know it, the downpour
Has brought you to your knees!

And there is Rilke's experience and his writing, which Merrill knows well and which contains its own eloquent apologies for patience—including the passage in the third of the *Letters to a Young Poet:*

Allow your judgments their own silent, undisturbed development, which, like all progress, must come from deep within and cannot be forced or hastened. *Everything* is gestation and then birthing. To let each impression and each embryo of a feeling come to completion, entirely in itself, in the dark, in the unsayable, the unconscious, beyond the reach of one's own understanding, and with deep humility and patience to wait for the hour when a new clarity is born: this alone is what it means to live as an artist: in understanding as in creating.

In this there is no measuring with time, a year doesn't matter, and ten years are nothing. Being an artist means: not numbering and counting, but ripening like a tree, which doesn't force its sap, and stands confidently in the storms of spring, not afraid that afterward summer may not come. It does come. But it comes only to those who are patient, who are there as if eternity lay before them, so unconcernedly silent and vast. I learn it every day of my life, learn it with pain I am grateful for: *patience* is everything![26]

Proust too has his version of this faith:

Alors, moins éclatante sans doute que celle qui m'avait fait apercevoir que l'oeuvre d'art était le seul moyen de retrouver le Temps perdu, une nouvelle lumière se fit en moi. Et je compris que tous ces matériaux de l'oeuvre littéraire, c'était ma vie passée; je compris qu'ils étaient venus à moi, dans les plaisirs frivoles, dans la paresse, dans la tendresse, dans la douleur, emmagasinés par moi, sans que je devinasse plus leur destina-

19

tion, leur survivance même, que la graine mettant en réserve tous les aliments qui nourriront la plante. Comme la graine, je pourrais mourir quand la plante se serait développée, et je me trouvais avoir vécu pour elle sans le savoir, sans que ma vie me parût devoir entrer jamais en contact avec ces livres que j'aurais voulu écrire et pour lesquels, quand je me mettais autrefois à ma table, je ne trouvais pas de sujet.

And then a new light, less dazzling, no doubt, than that other illumination which had made me perceive that the work of art was the sole means of rediscovering Lost Time, shone suddenly within me. And I understood that all these materials for a work of literature were simply my past life; I understood that they had come to me, in frivolous pleasures, in indolence, in tenderness, in unhappiness, and that I had stored them up without divining the purpose for which they were destined or even their continued existence any more than a seed does when it forms within itself a reserve of all the nutritious substances from which it will feed a plant. Like the seed, I should be able to die once the plant had developed and I began to perceive that I had lived for the sake of the plant without knowing it, without ever realising that my life needed to come into contact with those books which I had wanted to write and for which, when in the past I had sat down at my table to begin, I had been unable to find a subject.[27]

Although Proust had "pas de sujet"—in effect, "*No puzzle*"—when he sat down at *his* table, it was all the while ripening within, eventually to be "translated" into a form that would also nourish others, including Merrill.

And then beneath each writer's experience is his mother tongue, with its incalculable depths. This heritage is one subject of the poem's second section, the parenthetical digression in which Merrill recalls the medium's performance. This last consists of solving another kind of puzzle, of identifying without seeing it an object that has been shown to an audience, then "planted in a plain tole / Casket." Merrill's translation of the man's musings aloud "Through shut eyes" moves back in time, as the medium hears in his mind's ear "'a dry saw-shriek, / Some loud machinery—a lumber mill? / Far uphill in the fir forest / Trees tower, tense with shock, / Groaning and cracking as they crash groundward.'" As the medium tunes in that episode earlier in the object's history, the reader begins to hear the poet's own machinery. Rather like Pound in his first Canto's palimpsest, Merrill turns to a quasi–Anglo-Saxon verse to remind us again how the present translates the past. The transformations in a poem like this one, Merrill implies as the medium identifies the hidden object, are nothing compared to those of the forces that have produced its materials:

"But hidden here is a freak fragment
Of a pattern complex in appearance only.
What it seems to show is superficial
Next to that long-term lamination
Of hazard and craft, the karma that has
Made it matter in the first place.
Plywood. Piece of a puzzle." Applause
Acknowledged by an opening of lids
Upon the thing itself. A sudden dread—
But to go back. All this lay years ahead.

The real marvel is the ogygian linguistic and historical process, which, like the poem, and indeed like the life, involves plan and accident. Such are the unities of world and page.

While that thought has its reassuring side, it also holds a certain "dread." To have one's eyes opened to this karmic process is not only to see how one's present uses one's past days, however "vides / Et perdus" they might have seemed, but also to see that one is but an ephemeral form of this always economizing flux. The "opening of lids" on "the thing itself" causes a *frisson* because in addition to the medium's eyelids, the "lids" include the one on the "tole / Casket." When the poet tells us that "All this lay years ahead," we hear not only a reason for breaking off this divagation on the medium but also relief at the thought that he can avoid for some time yet Henry James's "distinguished thing." In other words, "this" lies in the future from the point of view of the boy and in either the past or the future, depending on the referent, from the point of view of the man writing the poem. He has characteristically gone ahead and back at once. Somewhere the poor gold watch will be throwing up its hands again—while Proust will be clapping his.

"But to go back. All this lay years ahead": Merrill's use of the past tense in connection with the future event has much to do with the line's allure. We return to it because it rises above time so, and as we return, it takes still other forms. While "All this" is the evening in the London library, as well as the truncated vision of death, the phrase refers us also to this poem's account of that evening and of everything else. "All *this*." Furthermore, since this account that is the poem lies years ahead of the boy, there is a strong sense in which his youth itself lies years ahead of him, to be found in "translation." The poem is a heuristic instrument, a way of discovering the self and knowing it.

But then who is to distinguish between discovery and creation in this area? It is only in view of what he has since become that Merrill can appear *then*—in the form of a figure in the puzzle, which in the third section begins

21

to take shape—as "a small backward-looking slave or page-boy." He finds this figure in the puzzle exactly because in the middle of his own puzzle of a life he is looking backward. In looking backward, that is—and by "backward" I mean "over the shoulder" and "to the past," but not "shy," though Merrill means the latter too—the figure in the puzzle looks forward to the poet who will create him. His "backward-looking" figure prefigures and calls into being the artist, whose work (in Proust's words again) "exprime pour les autres et nous fait voir à nous-même[s] notre propre vie, cette vie qui ne peut pas s' 'observer', dont les apparences qu'on observe ont besoin d'être traduites et souvent lues à rebours et péniblement déchiffrées" ("expresses for others and renders visible to ourselves that life of ours which cannot effectually observe itself and of which the observable manifestations need to be translated and, often, to be read backwards and laboriously deciphered").[28] This is one reason that to speculate as to whether Merrill has imagined this figure (or the whole puzzle) or has remembered him would only be to cloud the issue. One cannot say which is the case in the same way that one cannot say whether the poem began forty years ago, or in the "present" deciphering, or in the medium's performance. It "begins" in several places at once—as this account does, and as a puzzle does: "Mademoiselle does borders. Straight-edge pieces / Align themselves with earth or sky / In twos and threes, naive cosmogonists / Whose views clash."

The "small backward-looking slave or page-boy," "whose feet have not been found" yet, appears beside "Most of a dark-eyed woman veiled in mauve" whom he helps down from her kneeling camel. Mademoiselle perhaps thinks the boy is the veiled woman's son, and if so she might be swayed by her own maternal feelings or by her keen awareness of her employers' domestic plight. We know that she knows a divorce is in the offing, because the boy sneaks a look at her letter to a curé in Alsace, where he reads "'cette innocente mère, / Ce pauvre enfant, que deviendront-ils?'" The boy assumes that these are the figures in the puzzle, but Merrill lets us understand, as we fit together our own pieces, that she is worried about him and his mother. This is pure Merrill, this casting of the poem's one direct reference to its emotional and dramatic center in French and the misinterpreting of it. The principle of restraint is honored even as the imminent trauma is specified and authenticating detail is provided. These lines tell us that Mademoiselle, contrary to the boy's superior observation about what she "thinks mistakenly," would not be all that wrong to believe that the "slave or page-boy" is the veiled woman's son. Although he is not literally her son, this pair mirror the young Merrill and his mother—as we know partly because the veiled woman looks "across the green abyss" at another figure: "a Sheik with beard / And flashing sword hilt (he is all but finished) / Steps forward on a tiger skin. A piece / Snaps shut, and fangs gnash out at us!" And we associate the Sheik with the father—what a delicate house of cards this is!—not only because of the pun on "finished" but also because, as we learn in the poem's last section, the boy's home has its own "mangy tiger safe on his bared hearth." These last words might stand for much of this poem's paradoxical quality, for Merrill's "hearth" hides his "heart" and the heart of the family's crisis, even as the adjective "bared" discloses their presence.

"One should be as clear as one's natural reticence allows one to be": Marianne Moore's dictum might have been the guiding light in this as in many another poem by Merrill.[29]

Mademoiselle has her own family matters to conceal. Years later, speaking French to a French friend, the poet discovers that he has a German accent. Thus he finds out that Mademoiselle's first language was German. French by marriage, she finds it practical, in the prewar atmosphere, to pass. The poem's ubiquitous dichotomizing takes the form in her of "French hopes" set against "German fears." But her heritage is jigsaw-complicated itself, since she is the "Child of an English mother . . . And Prussian father" and was evidently raised in Alsace. No wonder she likes to do the borders of puzzles. No wonder either that her nephew turns out to be a "UN / Interpreter." That last detail is one of several that indicate the relationship between her and the poet, who, in his capacity as translator of Valéry and Rilke and the others, has an analogous occupation. He after all learned French and German from her—not to mention much else that would help make him the kind of poet he is. (Might not that be why Merrill tells us that she is a "remote / Descendant of the great explorer Speke"? Though in fact she seems to have descended from the American explorer Edmund Fanning, John Hanning Speke fits into the puzzle better.[30] Just as Speke discovered the source of the Victoria Nile, so we might find in him, with his convenient name, an emblem of Merrill's own fluent explorations.)

A partner in the boy's creative enterprises, Mademoiselle is muse as well as substitute mother. When we hear that the UN interpreter's account of her background has "Touched old strings," those strings are not only those that sound a metaphorical chord. Besides helping him with puzzles, she "Sews costumes for his marionettes, / Helps him to keep behind the scene / Whose sidelit goosegirl, speaking with his voice, / Plays Guinevere as well as Gunmoll Jean." Indeed there exists a program, dated August 11, 1937, which advertises "*The Magic Fishbone,* by Charles Dickens, as interpreted by the Jimmy Merrill Marionettes. Given for the Southampton Fresh Air Home for Crippled Children." According to the program, "The action takes place in 'The Land of Make Believe,' and Jimmy Merrill himself will play King Watkins, I, the Queen, and Jerry, the Announcer."[31] Just as Jerry, the Announcer, looks forward to that other Master of Ceremonies, Ephraim, so the goosegirl will one day emerge as Psyche in "From the Cupola" and Jean in "Days of 1935." (As for the King and Queen: one cannot but think of God Biology and Mother Nature in *Sandover*.)

Perhaps he would recognize, years later, something of Mademoiselle's manner and their mutual interests in the operas of Bernard de Zogheb— "not operas so much as librettos set to popular tunes of variable vintage and familiarity," as Merrill defines them in his "Foreword" to the text of Zogheb's *Phaedra*.[32] These mischievous, enchanting productions—"designed for that small red theatre in the soul where alone the games of childhood are relived and applauded," acted out by puppets, the music sung by men and women "in the wings"—are sui generis, though as Merrill hints, their melding of heroic emotions and frivolous tunes has precedents in Verdi and elsewhere. (Phaedra drinks poison and she and Thésée part forever to the strains of "I'll Be Seeing You" and "It Had To Be You.") The language of the librettos, "so richly macaronic, so poorly construed and spelt," derives in part from Zogheb's growing up in Alexandria and his acquaintance there with "the bad Italian cultivated by the *gratin,* and a kind of lingua franca used by their domestics." Merrill's fondness for Zogheb's puppet theater, especially its salad of the hilarious and the "exalted and terrible," attests to his belief that "the world needs to be seen [as] cheerful *and* awful, transparent *and* opaque." The light at Sandover is a changing one.

The boy and Mademoiselle are so close as to shade off into each other. If she is "Herself excited as a child" when they get the puzzle, her "world where 'each was the enemy, each the friend'" has its equivalent too in his family life. By the beginning of the fourth section, everything seems to fit:

> This World that shifts like sand, its unforeseen
> Consolidations and elate routine,
> Whose Potentate had lacked a retinue?
> Lo! it assembles on the shrinking Green.

"This World" is at once the political world of the 1930s and the puzzle's world, the Sheik's, with its unanchored sections that combine in surprising ways. It is also the world of the poem as poem, its languages and forms and diverse resources—the poem which exemplifies *its* "elate routine" in the interlacing of "routine" and "retinue" and the internal rhyme of "Potentate" and "elate" and its "consolidations" in the shift at just this point into *Rubaiyat* quatrains, so that the puzzle's exotic form conforms to its matter. The puzzle's subject, the arrival of the new favorite in the Sheik's harem, is said to be "Hardly a proper subject for the Home," but it is the inevitable subject for *this* home. Even the progressive clarification of the puzzle's scene, which also suggests the boy's increasing understanding of his circumstances, parallels the development of the actual domestic situation. As we are first allowed to interpret the Sheik and the veiled woman, they stand in for the boy's father and mother. At this juncture, however, as though to trace the change in the father's affections, the veiled woman has become the mother's rival. Not for nothing is the woman veiled.

After some further shifting of its pieces, the puzzle represents more clearly than ever the boy's world:

> While, thick as Thebes whose presently complete
> Gates close behind them, Houri and Afreet
> Both claim the Page. He wonders whom to serve,
> And what his duties are, and where his feet,
>
> And if we'll find, as some before us did,
> That piece of Distance deep in which lies hid
> Your tiny apex sugary with sun,
> Eternal Triangle, Great Pyramid!

The Page transparently corresponds to the boy, on the verge of having loyalties divided between mother and father and of losing his footing—as the precarious shift in mid-sentence across the stanza break from third person to first person brilliantly confirms. Even as the identification is made, however, the poet retains a significant detachment, since the puzzle so wittily translates his story. Even to be able to see the family in terms of such archetypal patterns as the Oedipal triangle is partly to answer the boy's silent question as to whether he will find a "piece of Distance," for that is also a peace that comes with distance on an emotionally trying situation.

As Merrill moves his units about, they take on the polysemy of allegorical elements; as one's mental focus changes, now the subject is the puzzle proper, now the domestic microcosm, now the political alliances of 1938–1939, now the composition of the poem. The poem even makes a gesture or two in the direction of *Sandover*'s macrocosmic and metaphysical concerns. The "shrinking Green" of the card table reminds us of the world's expanding deserts and the possible death of the planet, while the remark that it is "Quite a task / Putting together Heaven, yet we do" touches on the theme of the creation of God. It begins to seem that there is no subject "Lost in Translation" cannot handle as it shifts among home and world, world and page, often by virtue of the manifold richness of its particulars. At the end of the fourth section, in a bit of bravura, Merrill slips the last piece of the puzzle into place, as he recalls finding the Page's missing feet where they had fallen:

> It's done. Here under the table all along
> Were those missing feet. It's done.

But then whose should those feet be, "under the table," if not the boy's? And if the boy's, then the poet's, "*Here* under the table" on which the poem is being written. The poet is the boy is the Page. Or he is the page on which the poem's words reconstitute him, "a backward-looking slave" to his own needs. Thanks to such "under the table" transactions, it all comes right, it seems. "The correction of prose, because it has no fixed laws, is endless," Yeats wrote to Dorothy Wellesley, whereas "a poem comes right with a click like a closing box."[33] The solution of the last outstanding mystery and the reiteration of "It's done" make just such a "click."

Or is this case closed so easily? We need to notice that this fourth section does not come out even. These two lines on the feet, which seem to conclude it, are a kind of remainder. It is not even clear that they are part of a quatrain; they stand alone and fit neither with the preceding stanzas nor with the following verse paragraphs. In another moment, Merrill would have had to commit himself, for had the second line been carried to its end, it would have had to rhyme with "along," in which event these lines would have been a fragment of a *Rubaiyat* stanza, or not, in which event they would have been a short paragraph. It is a matter of "missing feet"—and of a missing metrical foot or two. A closure that is an opening, this passage is irrevocably in transition.

As the one form comes apart, so does the puzzle—as though *this* UN interpreter were an *un*interpreter:

> The dog's tail thumping. Mademoiselle sketching
> Costumes for a coming harem drama
> To star the goosegirl. All too soon the swift
> Dismantling. Lifted by two corners,
> The puzzle hung together—and did not.
> Irresistibly a populace
> Unstitched of its attachments, rattled down.
> Power went to pieces as the witch
> Slithered easily from Virtue's gown.
> The blue held out for time, but crumbled, too.
> The city had long fallen, and the tent,

A separating sauce mousseline,
Been swept away. Remained the green
On which the grown-ups gambled. A green dusk.
First lightning bugs. Last glow of west
Green in the false eyes of (coincidence)
Our mangy tiger safe on his bared hearth.

Because Rilke looms so large in this poem, one is likely to recall his adumbration of the poetic process in the eighth *Duino Elegy:* "Uns überfüllts. Wir ordnens. Es zerfällt. / Wir ordnens wieder und zerfallen selbst" ("It fills us. We arrange it. It breaks down. / We rearrange it, then break down ourselves").[34] But in Merrill's lines, along with the sense of an ineluctable cycle, there is the sense of synchronic events. Even as there are certain threads "que la vie brise," life is ceaselessly making new connections. The very same words that describe the breaking up of the puzzle create in themselves a subtle pattern. They begin to weave one of the new "costumes"—a mantle or a mantilla, say—with "Dismantling" itself. The "lace" in "populace," the more evident for "Unstitched" and "gown," takes the form of the attachments among "Unstitched" and "witch," "down" and "gown," "blue" and "too," "mousseline" and "green." The disintegration of the one narrative is part of another—to be specific, a little apocalypse. For if we are responsible for "Putting together Heaven," we are also responsible for destroying it along with our cities. These lines trace out in lyric form the story of much of *Sandover.* The underset of retrogression in this passage, the drift (reminiscent of the medium's reverse construction of the puzzle piece's history) from its "populace" and "city" back through "tent" to a virtually Edenic "Green" ("gambled" is also "gamboled"): this is a movement found also at a pivotal moment in *Scripts for the Pageant.* Before that, and before "Lost in Translation," Merrill ran his poetic film backward at the end of "18 West 11th Street," another poem about a childhood home that was destroyed, which concludes with an "Original vacancy" and a "deepening spring." As he puts the adage at the beginning of yet another poem about the partial destruction and rebuilding of a house, "Everything changes; nothing does."

Nothing does: nothing changes. And nothing will *do:* no thing or poem or theory will finally suffice. Nothing will do, partly because something is always missing:

Something tells me that one piece contrived
To stay in the boy's pocket. How do I know?
I know because so many later puzzles
Had missing pieces—Maggie Teyte's high notes

Gone at the war's end, end of the vogue for collies,
A house torn down; and hadn't Mademoiselle
Kept back her pitiful bit of truth as well?
I've spent the last days, furthermore,
Ransacking Athens for that translation of "Palme."

Not finding that translation is comparable to Rilke's not finding equivalences for Valéry's phrases. Having translated Valéry's poem—as well as a variety of other works ranging from maxims by Chamfort through poems by Montale to stories by Cavafy and Vassilikós—James Merrill knows all too well "How much of the sun-ripe original / Felicity Rilke made himself forego / (Who loved French words—verger, mûr, parfumer) / In order to render its underlying sense."[35] But the plight is not just that of the literary translator. The lines just quoted pertain also to the unrealizable vision that motivates any poem, not to mention other projects. As Helen Vendler has seen, Rilke's rendering of Valéry "mimics the translation—by Merrill himself, among others—of life into art."[36] Not that "life" here need mean sensuous or concrete experience alone, whatever that might be. Rilke's passion for Valéry's poems, for the French language, for language—these were part of his "life."

To fail to translate exactly, or rather to have to translate and thus to be inexact, to create a difference between the putatively original and the necessarily substitutive: this might be thought of as our very condition. It is no coincidence that Merrill's felicitous "Felicity"—meaning "bliss" and "good fortune" as well as the very "stylistic aptness" that the line break highlights—and the echo, by way of "sun-ripe" and the French words, of the "orchard back of us" call into play again the concept of Eden. The parenthesis itself, with its untranslated and by implication untranslatable words ("orchard," "ripe," and "to sweeten" or "to scent," respectively), is almost a tiny, tantalizing paradise, an enclosed orchard or *hortus conclusus* (as "paradise" means in its remote Old Persian origins). The orchard and the windfalls are always "back of us." Nothing will ever quite do.

Then one begins to see that for Merrill nothing will not do either. The Rilke translation is found. Mademoiselle, although she "kept back" her bit of truth, was not able to bury it. From one point of view, the piece of puzzle that the boy pocketed was lost, but from another it has been found, by the medium—"This grown man" who is also a translator of sorts, an agent of communication with an extrasensory world, a variation on the JM of the *Sandover* books. The "house torn down" rises again in the form of Sandover. Everything changes. To lose is to create an emptiness that must be operated in, a vacancy that will be filled. "Verger," "mûr," "parfumer": these words are rendered inexactly in German and English, but the approximation is a matrix of possibility. Underlying the phrase "underlying sense," because it comes on the heels of the French words, for example, are the "scents" connoted by them. In that marvelous ruin that Rilke's translation is, "that ground plan left / Sublime and barren, where the warm Romance / Stone by stone faded, cooled," after a rain, "A deep reverberation fills with stars"— and what is such a "reverberation" if not at once an emptiness and a plenishing? "Reverberation": the word means a redounding of sound or repeated reflecting of light (or heat), a re-echoing, as of Merrill's echoing of Rilke's echoing of Valéry (echoing his own sources). "Reverberation" might almost be a translation of "translation," and even though *verberare* is unrelated to *verbum,* Merrill wants us to catch a Cratylean glimpse of "rewording" behind the term, much as Stevens, for instance, means us to see "luminous" shining through his phrase "Voluminous master folded in his fire."[37]

To translate, then, is as much to discover in transference as to lose. Here is Merrill's concluding verse paragraph:

> But nothing's lost. Or else: all is translation
> And every bit of us is lost in it
> (Or found—I wander through the ruin of S
> Now and then, wondering at the peacefulness)
> And in that loss a self-effacing tree,
> Color of context, imperceptibly
> Rustling with its angel, turns the waste
> To shade and fiber, milk and memory.

Two orders of proposition appear here. In the first place, as in "A Fever," Merrill is aspiring, like Henry James, to be one on whom nothing is lost. But when nothing is lost at this level, that is largely because of an original openness to experience and a later strenuousness of memory. Nothing is lost, not because it cannot be lost, for indeed it might be that everything is lost in some sense, but because the possibility always exists that one might recall it in some form—as Proust is said in *Ephraim* "Through superhuman counterpoint to work / The body's resurrection, sense by sense." Nothing is lost in Proust because Proust lost himself in his life's work, or in his work's life, in his own "translation"—his "consuming myth," to adapt a phrase from Merrill's "From the Cupola." In the concluding lines in "Lost in Translation," the Proustian presence is the "self-effacing tree," the palm that appears and disappears as a blue puzzle piece in the blue sky and that conceals the poet's effort; or that gracefully translates his wrestling with his angel into a "Rustling" of fronds and wings, just as the patient palm invisibly "turns the waste" (Rilke's "Steinen," Valéry's "déserts") into the sheltering fronds

29

and the nourishing coconut. As Merrill's poem resurrects his childhood, so its last line recovers, by way of "Palme," its opening lines. As though to prove that nothing is lost, his "milk" translates Valéry's "lait plat," which appears at the beginning of "Palme," along with "le pain tendre" that "Un ange met sur ma table." The table is there in the first line of Merrill's poem, where it has become the card table, while the milk and angel have been kept back until the end. But not lost.

In the second place, this passage concerns the nature of things. All is metamorphosis, it suggests; the world is all "context," its elements are all a fugacity whose interactive events may be either continuations of earlier phases of themselves or ever-new processes. Merrill will make a harder and deeper sense of the idea in *Ephraim*. This poem does not have to decide whether it intends a neo-Hegelian faith in evolution or a neo-Heraclitean hypothesis of flux. It is content to approve, in addition to memory, metamorphosis—rather in the vein of Merrill's recent sonnet "Processional," which sets forth the adventures of a "demotic raindrop" that is first "Translated by a polar wand to keen / Six-pointed Mandarin" and dreams of being further promoted into "a hitherto untold / Flakiness, gemlike, nevermore to melt":

> But melt it would, and—look—become
> Now birdglance, now the gingko leaf's fanlight,
> To that same tune whereby immensely old
> Slabs of dogma and opprobrium,
> Exchanging ions under pressure, bred
> A spar of burnt-black anchorite,
>
> Or in three tidy strokes of word golf LEAD
> Once again turns (LOAD, GOAD) to GOLD.[38]

If that "tune" had a title, it could be "Plus ça change." As early as Merrill's first play, *The Bait* (1953), he had set similar words to it: "our cold virtues, once thought durable, / But now abstract and frail as snowflakes / Alter to lazy water in the sun. / Fluidity is proof against major disasters. / The marbles melt and wink at me." (And Merrill winks at us, since his prose has crystallized to verse within this one speech.)

One remarkable thing about "Processional," really less hymn than scherzando, is its blithe overriding of categories, as in the conversion to "anchorite" of "anthracite." In the translation envisioned here, alchemical, rhetorical, and natural metamorphic processes themselves change into one another. How could we not be somewhat lost in it?

30

❱   ❱   ❱

Like fanlight from snowflake, Merrill's work develops from itself. In this respect he is a different kind of writer from Yeats, with whom he has strong affinities. The latter, in Northrop Frye's clear assessment, "is one of the growing poets: his technique, his ideas, his attitude to life, are in a constant state of revolution and metamorphosis. He belongs with Goethe and Beethoven, not with the artists who simply unfold, like Blake and Mozart."[39] Merrill, however, his own innovations notwithstanding, belongs with Mozart—the subject of two quatrains of alexandrines he wrote when he was fifteen:

> With suavely polished joy, restrained exuberance,
> The violin sings its bland Rococo harmonies,
> Smoothly fashioned phrases soaring to the skies
> In sinuous silver trills of sham insouciance.
>
> Music free from passion, passionately played,
> Plumed with cool perfection, powdered with despair!
> Each delicious flourish daintily debonair,
> Purity on paper, brilliance on brocade!

Merrill perhaps never again used so many modifiers. But in the rhetorical structure and the implicit ambition of that phrase "restrained exuberance" one sees the incipience of the mature style.

When he was choosing poems from *The Black Swan* and *First Poems* (1951) for inclusion in *From the First Nine,* he was struck by such relationships between his early and his recent work:

> It seems to me, reading those poems over—and I've begun to rework a number of them—that the only limitation imposed upon them was my own youth and limited skill . . . Returning to those early poems *now,* obviously in the light of the completed trilogy, I've had to marvel a bit at the resemblances. It's as though after a long lapse or, as you put it, displacement of faith, I'd finally, with the trilogy, reentered the church of those original themes. The colors, the elements, the magical emblems: they were the first subjects I'd found again at last.[40]

One could trace these themes and emblems back even nearer the beginning. The first verse that Merrill can recall having written, when he was seven or eight, a couplet about sneaking with his Irish setter into his mother's room, is the fourth sonnet in "The Broken Home" in embryonic form: "One day while she lay sleeping, / Michael and I went peeping." Furthermore, as Michael, "head / Passionately lowered, led / The child" to his mother, in the sonnet's expansion of the vignette, so the archangel of the same name would bring DJ and JM to Mother Nature in *Scripts for the Pageant.* The other childhood poem that Merrill quotes in this interview is a quatrain, which he tells us was accompanied in *St. Nicholas Magazine,* the monthly children's publication, by a drawing that "showed a little boy on the crest of a hill heading for a schoolhouse far below": "Pushing slowly every day / Autumn finally makes its way. / Now when the days are cool, / We children go to school." We might well think of this verse as a foreglimpse of the poet's further schooling, so much later in his life, at Sandover—a connection facilitated by the rhyme on "day," Michael's identifying mannerism throughout *Scripts* and the "Coda."

What exactly are we to make of such "link-and-bobolink" (John Shade's phrase)? This is the sort of thing that the "no accident clause," formulated in *Mirabell's Books of Number,* purports to explain. Not that we need to lean on cosmological doctrine here; but I think we must acknowledge that the poems have created a field in which such connections occur more often than one would expect. There must be several overlapping causes for this field. For one thing, as I have said, Merrill's development has been extraordinarily gradual and patient, regardless of the large output. As he was to say of Corot in 1960, "His development is very subtle, hardly a development at all. We can see him applying to one period lessons learned from another."[41] Moreover, Merrill has sought out and reinforced unifying strands in his writing. Sometimes a connection is direct, as when in *Ephraim* he adds a light-hearted parenthesis, "(cf. 'The Will')," or as when the figure named Charles surfaces in diverse works, including the very early unpublished play *The Birthday,* "River Poem" (*First Poems*), *The Bait,* "A Narrow Escape" and "Laboratory Poem" (*The Country of a Thousand Years of Peace*), "Charles on Fire" (*Nights and Days*), "Table Talk" (*The Yellow Pages*), and "Ideas" (*Late Settings*). At other times the allusions are tacit or surreptitious. In *The (Diblos) Notebook* a passage in the narrator's draft of a novel in effect glosses a poem called "Swimming by Night" in *Water Street.* The concluding game of hide-and-seek in *The Seraglio*—in which the protagonist, who is "It," is deserted by the children he was to play with—has been prefigured by "Wreath for the Warm-Eyed" in *First Poems.* The same game has been strangely anticipated by the title of Merrill's second play, *The Immortal Husband,* which alludes to Dostoevsky's novella "The Eternal Husband," in which Trusotsky is abandoned by the other participants in two games. It is especially clear in such a case that we are dealing not just with allusions but with a besetting concern—to wit, the solitude that certain kinds of life involve. The game of hide-and-seek in "Wreath for the Warm-Eyed" turns into a game of Patience that the "prisoner" must "play out . . . quite alone." That card game, whose name recalls the salient virtue in Valéry's "Palme," appears a number of times in Merrill's work, and analogues are everywhere, from Psyche's solitary chores in "From the Cupola" to the wrestling with the angel in "Lost in Translation." As we have seen, "wrestling" is there translated into "Rustling," a condensation that echoes the "rustling and wrestling" in the palm tree in "From the Cupola," section four—the same quatrain in which the tree's singular "*shadow . . . never shattered / except to mend back forth.*" "Scissoring and mending," Merrill's work thus moves back and forth itself.

No wonder that he has been sensitive to a kind of literary interaction at a distance. Thus he has written about Dante's *Commedia,* in whose three sections diverse tiny "points" make barely perceptible connections that add up to a "web whose circumference is everywhere," and about Cavafy's historical poems, in which "unexpected strands interconnect"—or in which, "fixed to earth at . . . several points . . . the tent of an entire lost world can be felt to swell and ripple in the air above."[42] His own poems increasingly make a comparable fabric.

In his concluding "Note" in *From the First Nine,* Merrill justifies revisions of poems from *The Black Swan* and *First Poems* on the grounds that "they should otherwise have been dropped altogether, and with them the earliest inklings of certain lifelong motifs I hope I may be forgiven for keeping faith with." The inescapable paradox—which he insists on by confessing to sometimes "shamelessly breaking [that faith] with the hollow phrase or plain ineptitude of the beginner"—is that these "earliest inklings" are in part shaped by the older poet. I suppose we could say, to adapt Sartre, that the early poems were the poems that they were to become in the mode of not being them. We now have the peculiar situation in which a poem in *The Black Swan,* "The Broken Bowl," both anticipates and responds to the end of *Scripts.* In the latter, a looking glass is broken into "splinters apt, from now on, to draw blood, / Each with its scimitar or bird-beak shape / Able . . . to rouse / From its deep swoon the undestroyed heartscape" we have seen in it. In the original of "The Broken Bowl,"

> Glass fragments dropped from wholeness to hodgepodge
> > Yet fasten to each edge
> The opal signature of imperfection
> Whose rays, though disarrayed, will postulate

More than a network of cross-angled light
When through the dusk they point unbruised directions
    And chart upon the room
Capacities of fire it must assume.

In recasting this stanza, Merrill will have wanted to omit the opening's awkward prolepsis ("fragments dropped"), to smooth out the *trouvaille* in line four, and to reduce the sonorous redundancies of the last lines. But he has also struck certain notes, already later amplified on, by working in "heart" and "script" and by asking a question that *Scripts* has answered. Here is his reconstructed breakage:

Did also the heart shatter when it slipped?
    Shards flash, becoming script,
Imperfection's opal signature
Whose rays in disarray hallucinate
At dusk so glittering a network that
The plight of reason, ever shakier,
    Is broadcast through the room
Which rocks in sympathy, a pendulum.

In this rereading of the situation, the "glittering . . . network" of light reflected from the shards is in effect Proust's "riche réseau," which (however imperfect it is) replaces the threads that life (imperfect too) breaks. For the "network" in each version is art's mesh. If Merrill's original had to be numinously "More than a network . . . of light" to indicate its significance, his revision obviates that necessity and its wavering import by introducing "script." The later work seems finally to have supplied him with the word he needed to begin with. The last thing we get to know is what should come first, as Pascal has taught us.

    Look too at what happens in the poem's third stanza, which originally began as follows: "The splendid curvings of glass artifice / Informed its flawlessness / With lucid unities. Freed from these now . . ." In its new life, the passage reads thus: "No lucid, self-containing artifice / At last, but fire, ice, / A world in jeopardy." The improvement shows the influence, I suspect, of a superb stanza in "The Emerald" (the second section of "Up and Down"), where the subject is a bracelet his father gave to his mother: "No rhinestone now, no dilute amethyst, / But of the first water, linking star to pang, / Teardrop to fire, my father's kisses hang / In lipless concentration round her wrist." Rather as this stanza itself translates a line in Donne's "The Relic," making that "bracelet of bright hair about the bone" over into a shudder that is Merrillian (though "lipless" seems as if it *should* be in Donne), so the revised lines in "The Broken Bowl" rework it.

Merrill's title for his selected poems intimates the close relationship among his volumes. The phrase "the first nine" refers in the first place to his first nine volumes and in the second to the other world's lower levels, about which the Ouija board tells DJ and JM and to which, we understand, the volumes before *Sandover* correspond. Does the phrase also summon up the nine Muses responsible for the poems before the angels take charge in *Sandover*? The title would ring other bells for Merrill, including the camel bells in "Chimes for Yahya," which make up a "graduated brass pendant." At the end of "Chimes for Yahya"—published in *Divine Comedies,* the last of the first nine—the poet reaches up to ring these souvenirs of a sojourn in Isfahan:

> Shake.
> A tingling spine of tone, or waterfall
> Crashing pure and chill, bell within bell,
> Upward to the ninth and mellowest,
> Their changes mingle with the parish best,
> Their told tale with the children's doggerel.

As there are nine volumes, so there are nine bells. And the tale (and tail: it is a sort of shaggy dog story, with a real dog in a central role, as "Shake" and "doggerel" hint) that the bells have told (tolled) in this poem's nine sections repeats that recounted by Merrill's volumes.

Or we might think, for a model, of that "glittering . . . network" in "The Broken Bowl," especially since associated images appear throughout Merrill's work. In a "Little Fanfare for Felix Magowan," his greeting to his newborn great nephew includes a "Welcome to earth, time, others; to / These cool darks, of sense, of language, / Each at once thread and maze." "Amsterdam," identified by way of an epigraph from Baudelaire's "Invitation au voyage" with the "pays qui te ressemble," is also a "maze," "a city whose fair houses wizen / In a strict web of streets, of waterways." In "A Carpet Not Bought," the carpet's pattern is a *"maze shorn / Of depth," "what the falcon / Sees when he soars, / What wasp and oriole / Think when they build."* The man in the poem wants the carpet desperately, but in the end, after a feverish night wrestling with the angel of materialism, his better self wins out ("Merde! / Who wanted *things*?"). In the morning light, he lies next to his wife, whose flush suggests that she embodies that better self, tired by its exertions:

Flushed on the bed's
White, lay a figure whose
Richness he sensed
Dimly. It reached him as
A cave of crimson threads
Spun by her mother against

That morning in their life
When sons with shears
Should set the pattern free
To ripple air's long floors
And bear him safe
Over a small waved sea.

The carpet's design gives way to his wife's body, seen as though in Vesalius, at once "Spun by her mother" and spinner of her sons, whose lives both portend the end of his and his wife's and complete their "pattern," immaterial and figured as a magic carpet. As in "The Broken Bowl," love is the force that generates the significant design. If that design here takes the form of posterity (hence the irony of the reference to the actual carpet as the "Labor of generations"), the two kinds of creativity are linked for Merrill.

It is indicative of his work's closely knit nature that not even with the advantage of hindsight could Merrill pick more fitting words to set at the head of his selected poems than those that begin "The Black Swan." This poem opens *From the First Nine* as it once opened Merrill's first real book:

Black on flat water past the jonquil lawns
    Riding, the black swan draws
A private chaos warbling in its wake,
Assuming, like a fourth dimension, splendor
That calls the child with white ideas of swans
    Nearer to that green lake
    Where every paradox means wonder.

These lines tell us a good deal about the young poet and the poet he would become, beginning with his taste for formal invention, for this stanza ($a_5a_3b_5c_5a_5b_3c_4$) is of his own devising. As he has kept faith with his beginnings by reprinting this stanza in *From the First Nine* without changing it a jot, so he returns to the form, three decades later, in *Mirabell's Books of Number,* on three occasions. There is a satisfying aptness to that recurrence, since Mirabell—a resident of the spirit world who at first takes a frightening bat-like form—is himself a kind of black swan, who draws his own "private chaos" in his wake, and who is in due time installed (though in a different form still) beside a "mirror lake." The stanza appears again in *Scripts,* this time, however, in an inverted form. The occasion is a revelation that astounds and then delights the poet, and the stanza's inversion, he has said, corresponds to his having been "rather *bouleversé*": [43]

> (Beneath my incredulity
>   All at once is flowing
> Joy, the flash of the unbaited hook—
> *Yes, yes, it fits, it's right, it had to be!*
> Intuition weightless and ongoing
>   Like stanzas in a book
> Or golden scales in the melodic brook—).

It is right for other reasons that the prosodic design should be inverted at this juncture in *Scripts.* Shortly after, JM finds himself pondering a strange ideogram. It comprises a schematic hourglass and its reflection, one sense of which is that humanity's time is running out, that the waste lands have begun to invade arable earth, "the shrinking Green" of "Lost in Translation." The overturning of this stanza parallels the turning over of the hourglass. And so it is that the first poem in Merrill's first book contains the grains of *Sandover,* published thirty years later.

The beginning of "The Black Swan" tells us much more about its author—including the detail that he knows how to begin. "The Black Swan" sets out with syntax that cooperates with lineation in such a way that the sentence follows the swan's movement like a shadow: "Black on flat water past the jonquil lawns / Riding, the black swan draws / A private chaos . . ." The trailing participle, the delayed subject, and the heavy run-on in both lines all contribute to the swan's power. These features combine with the enjambment in line four, the indentations of some lines, and the staving off of the full stop until stanza's end to insinuate the swan's distinctive shape— the focus then of the second stanza. The swan is everywhere implicit and imperious, drawing the images forth with something of the reckless power of inspiration itself. (The recklessness is there, for example, in the repetition of "black." The music of the first two lines, a matter of the closely related vowels, is so primary that it is probably only after several readings that the reader notices the redundancy.) In other words, this stanza is in part about the music it makes and wants to make. The "private chaos warbling in its wake" might as well be this poem, traveling on its own flat surface in the tow of the "tall emblem" that "pivots and rides out / To the opposite side, al-

ways." As for "The blond child on / The bank, hands full of difficult mar-
vels," who "stays / Now in bliss, now in doubt," in a phrase (sharpened in
revision) that characteristically points an antithesis, he looks like no one so
much as the student author of *Sandover,* half mystic and half skeptic and altogether occupied by a myth that, like the swan, "outlaws all easy questioning: / A thing in itself, equivocal, foreknown." Precisely: "foreknown," and
partly because of this poem, to which those last adjectives were justly added
in retrospect.

Merrill calls upon "The Black Swan" stanza in three other early poems—
though perhaps it should be called the bird stanza, since these poems,
printed one after another (and on the heels of "Transfigured Bird") are entitled "The Parrot," "The Pelican," and "The Peacock."[44] The *rara avis* that
these poems try again and again to name is the Poet, who obviously shares
qualities with the peacock, which in full-dress syntax "trails / Too much of
itself, like Proust, a long brocade / Along." We can discover him too in "The
Pelican," which like "The Parrot" Merrill has omitted from the selected
poems but which is an ebullient poem that provides its own raison d'être in a
bright, dry description, admirably suited to the stanza:

Always the postures foolish yet severe
    Of Empire furniture
Assist him in a courtesy nowadays
Only among artists fashionable, who like
Being in public each a caricature
    The world may recognize
And still be free to overlook.

If the young poet caricatures himself in the form of the pelican, then his
reasons are not only that the latter is quick to "show off unguessed /
Capacities" and is "all grinning or aghast / At the enormity of his habitat,"
but also that he has good manners, however awkward or stiff. The poet's
projection of himself in this case proves his emulation of such "courtesy."
Like "A myth or work of art" that spares "the watcher as it spares itself / By
an apt gaiety, gay ineptitude," he himself provides entertainment (as with
that playful chiasmus). Returning to this theme in *Scripts,* Merrill will joke
that it is always "Barbarity / To serve uncooked one's bloody tranche de vie."

Here in "The Pelican" he acknowledges the representative poem's source
in a literally "bloody tranche de vie." Noticing that the hungry pelican sometimes snatches the fishermen's flung bait in midair, he imagines that the bird,
however risible he sometimes appears, must be "A creature of desire / As
crude as theirs, involved with them" and "Hurt and embarrassed" at the rev-

elation of his creaturely need. Not satisfied with that rather lugubrious admission, however, he goes on to recall the myth about the pelican's selfless nature and to amend it pointedly:

> Yet, lacking food, this bird must be, to feed
> His offspring flesh and blood,
> Himself his own last supper, and die then
> Fattened upon the sense of how they thrive.
> Almost one fancies charity is not greed,
> Seeing the pelican
> From air to emptier water dive.

Here for once is an instance of unsullied generosity, we "Almost" think. But then the self-sacrifice is a special form of self-perpetuation, if we consider the poem's little allegory. Years later, in "The Emerald," imagining a response to his mother's offer of a gift "'For when you marry,'" he will quip that "*the little feet that patter here are metrical.*" "The Doodler" similarly thinks of his art as "the long race that descends" from him—and extends the metaphor by telling us that the works on his pad will include, say, "a baroque motif / Expressed so forcibly that it indents / A blank horizon generations hence / With signs and pressures." In an interview Merrill has said that "The Doodler" turned out to be about God, and we see that it is, but it also plainly deals with the poet.[45] When its speaker tells us that "This morning's little boy stands (I have learned / To do feet) gazing down a flight of stairs," we have a "sultry foretaste" of the lines quoted above from the later poem "The Emerald"—and of the discovery of the boy's "missing feet" found in "Lost in Translation."

Since the artist's offspring is his art, it is his art that he devotes himself to. To put that the other way around, "Art . . . survives / By feeding on its personages' lives," as JM reminds DJ in *Sandover,* in a passage that looks back to "The Pelican." The idea is central to Merrill's work, to his very life, each of which will merit in its own way the phrase "the consuming myth."

)))

The liking for raveling phrase and reversible truth is one with Merrill's overlooked radicalism. To be sure, there are grounds for the commonplace observation that he began as a Fabergé among the post-Modern American poets. But if he was ever handcuffed by artificiality, he slipped those particular bracelets long ago, and he has been a subversive presence at large for decades. A sampling of his original departures should suggest that this is a writer who will try anything. Consider that, in his first novel, against the background of a highly wrought prose, his young protagonist castrates himself in the bathtub; that, in his second novel, well before Jacques Derrida popularized the term that is for the moment an earmark of subversiveness, much of the writing exists literally "sous rature," "under erasure"; that, in a long narrative poem (written when the narrative seemed all but lost to American poetry), he wrote in appreciative description of pornographic postcards some stanzas that remain as ribald as any in twentieth-century poetry; that, in a poem called "Yam," he made of a bowel movement a visionary occasion. Consider that he has written his major poem on the basis of his experience with, of all things, a Ouija board. He is the only poet I know of who has made a radical sign the center of a lyric poem, and its appearance there might fairly represent his own fondness for drastic measures.

That he has written two fine, utterly different novels as well as his poems is indicative of his eagerness to go to the roots of the matter. The same must be said of his two early experiments with drama, the one a surrealist comedy of manners which takes a very narrow slice of life indeed, the other an updating of a myth, alternately charming and blackly humorous. Moreover, what the plays have in common—and share with the work in general—is his impatience with the unexamined and the simple and his corresponding predilection for undermining ironies.

The Bait begins in Venice with a conversation between John and Julie, his new lover, who has been trying to explain to him an obscure incident of perhaps several months before, which culminated in her leaving her husband, Charles. They are interrupted by Gilbert, her brother (and her companion so steadily that they put one in mind of Maggie Verver and her father), who sweeps Julie off for a gondola trip. John's ensuing monologue sets the scene for the transition back to the peculiar earlier incident, which took place in a fishing boat in the Gulf Stream. The crux of the flashback is a grotesque wager between Charles and Gilbert as to whether the former can hold out for ten minutes in the water in a fishing harness, "At the end of a line, like a hooked dolphin." Merrill stylizes Charles's ensuing struggle, as Gilbert reels him in, into a sestina in which he agonizes over his relationship with Julie. Finally hauled out semiconscious, he seems to have won the bet, but that is of no importance next to the less well-defined issues that the incident has settled. The play ends as it began, in Venice, with John and Julie mulling over the "trial by water" and her desertion of Charles and with John anticipating her desertion of him as well.

The Bait is in part a play about character—about that blend of principle, temperament, and intellect that helps to define the individual. Charles, Gilbert, and Julie are in the first place three distinct types. Julie is careless, attractive, selfish, and delightfully, chillingly superficial:

I want to dive down,
Discover, bring back whatever it is, the black
Pearl, the sense of whatever I am,
But my bones are full of air, my words are larks,
The sun is sparkling on the surface of the water
In all directions except from underneath.

She is the fugitive link between Gilbert and her lovers—and is even, one feels, Gilbert's means of attracting those lovers. Gilbert's name might well come from "The Critic as Artist" (whose own Gilbert will be quoted by Merrill in *Ephraim*), since he has just that combination of acuity, insouciance, manners, and fearlessness that Wilde endorses. He takes nothing on faith and nothing seriously—and it is this quality that finally distinguishes him from Wilde's neo-Socratic figure, who takes art seriously. Merrill's Gilbert does nothing; the extent of his purposeful activity is the testing of Charles, "a deep one," whom he goads into nearly drowning himself in his own depths. Charles himself is a good deal like the Ernest of "The Critic as Artist." He *is* "earnest," and "innocent," a shade "melancholy," and in Gilbert's unanswerable summation, he "strives / Overmuch perhaps for integrity." He is a good man, though humorless, the epitome of the "single-minded" as Gilbert is of the "high-handed."

As the play unfolds, however, one grows aware not only of the differences among these three but also of their reliances upon one another. Just after Gilbert finds himself admiring Charles's "single-mindedness," he tells him, "You are at one with your bait," then goes on to boast, "And I have swallowed it, Charles, I've got you." Charles has the obvious riposte: "It would seem in that case that I had *you*." Again, there is Gilbert's name, which Charles tellingly shortens to "Gilly," so that we can hardly overlook this connection between Gilbert and his friend, who swims like a fish. Finally, in a little trio preceding the bet, Merrill writes in couplets which he splits across the speeches: Charles's speech rhymes with Gilbert's, Gilbert's with Julie's, and so on. Gilbert's comment on Charles's "integrity," then, and John's on Gilbert's, both have ironic dimensions, since each needs the other, as well as Julie, who is also bait.

These three intertwine in a little arabesque of frustration and fulfillment. Charles loves Julie, Julie needs Gilbert, Gilbert admires Charles—though that summary oversimplifies the issues. Gilbert's heartless baiting leads to Charles's trial by water and his proof of himself—which lies not in his ability to keep from drowning, of course, but rather in his moral strength, his ability to recognize Julie's indifference to him and yet to love her. His love for her is her reproach, for she is incapable of devotion. Her shame at her inadequacy in the face of Charles's commitment calls attention to an unexpected side of his nature. If she seems monstrous in her detachment and superciliousness, the very purity of his "serious human" response makes him almost inhuman. He is "incorruptibly" who he is, to use his word; he has "become of permanent value," in Gilbert's phrase. His "conscience *is* clear," and justifiably—and so one begins to sympathize with Julie's need to escape him. His steadfast scrupulousness must in part inspire Gilbert's goading, which seems prompted also by his real feeling for Charles and his desire to chip away what he half hopes, half fears is a moral enamel. Gilbert and his sister "have sought to corrupt" Charles, but the meaning of "to corrupt" in this context is "to humanize." In the end, Charles's loss of Julie, incurred in the course of finding himself, makes him one of us, a defective creature. But then as Julie says, the lover never loses. Her speech to John near the end of the play is one of its most moving moments:

> The one who loves isn't the loser. Charles
> Isn't the loser. By hurting him I have
> Empowered him to unveil within my mind
> As in a public square
> An image tasteless and cheap, which is my own.
> Not even a tourist would stop to look at it
> All thickened as if by dreadful squatting birds.
> But Charles—my dear, I even dream of him.
> I see him continue to act in honest concern
> According to what he feels. I see his face
> Turn beautiful under the pumice of disappointment.
> One could almost pretend I had made him a gift of it.

Never forgetting that Julie has a "vicious self," to borrow Gilbert's cruel term, one must appreciate such clairvoyance and find endearing the discreet refusal to defend herself. How appealing such self-suspicion is in view of Charles's self-confidence! And how touching Julie's location of her defaced image in her own mind. But she cannot sustain such a plunge into the depths of her being. In that she resembles many of us, though few of us have her beguiling lightness.

My point is that this play, written when Merrill was twenty-six and twenty-seven, regardless of its deficiencies as dramatic action, bears witness to a sensibility that continually overturns its nicely turned propositions and habitually resists its most fetching formulations, a mind in love with the black swan and with the "black pearl" Julie conceives herself to be. Julie also thinks—or says—that she cannot simplify because it takes a complicated person to do that. But that claim cannot be produced by a simple mind.

Indeed, she sounds very much like the young novelist in *The (Diblos) Note-book* at a moment in which he seems to speak for Merrill. He is quoting an unnamed source (perhaps T. S. Eliot, whose advice as to critical method is nearly identical) to the effect that "'The only solution is to be very, very intelligent.' Intelligence, it is implied, will dissimulate itself, will *lose itself* in simplicity. By the same token, any extended show of Mind may be taken as the work of some final naiveté."[46] Charles, said to be "a deep one," is "simple and good," yet "extremely difficult." Gilbert tells him that "We wanted proof that you could, like ourselves, / Fail to profit by an occasion / For much self-knowledge," and while it seems true that Charles knows himself better after the wager, Gilbert's observation comes from someone who knows himself only too well.

The Bait implies certain hard questions: How do we distinguish between the "deep" and the "superficial"? Can the truly incorruptible individual be morally sound? What is the relationship between a sense of humor and morality? Do circumstances "make" us do things, or do they facilitate our intentions to do them? I'm reminded of Merrill's "Variations: The Air Is Sweetest That a Thistle Guards" (first version): "Now not the answer, for of course there were / No helpful answers, but the air of questioning / Is what one needs to remember." This play augurs a skeptical mind, whose handicap is more likely to be a hamstringing suspicion than a wrong-headed intensity. There is a sense in which this mind is closer to Gilbert's and even Julie's than to Charles's—although one distinguishing feature of the play is the mercuriality of the author. He is most identifiably present in the *process* of the drama, in its testing of motives and ideas. It makes most sense if seen as a staging of conflicts within the self.

Merrill's second play also probes motivation and proposition. If there is any idea that goes unchallenged in *The Immortal Husband,* it is that "Nature is very economical." *The Immortal Husband*—whose title is a thrifty variation on Dostoevsky's—tells us that certain basic situations repeat themselves time and again. Laomedon responds to Tithonus's view of him as an old bore with perfect understanding: "No matter. That is how I saw my father at your age, and how your son will see you." "Everything's changed, yet everything's the same," as Tithonus, already repeating his father, sees early on. He goes on to call his father "pompous, callous as ever before," and one proof we have of that complaint is Laomedon's habit of mouthing truisms. At the same time, Tithonus himself is egocentric and callow and wholly deserving of his father's contempt.

This play's structure, complex but—like the structures of some of the early poems—mechanical, bears out the principle of economy. Its three acts take place in 1854 (in England), in 1894 (Russia), and in 1954 (the United

States). Of the six actors, three must triple roles and one must double. *Mutatis mutandis,* each of these actors plays one type; the names change, and the characters shade off into one another in a little study in nuance. The two main characters, Tithonus and Aurora, appear in each act. Being a goddess, Aurora cannot change—and perhaps cannot even want to change. She lapses as she must into divine indifference to human concerns. Being mortal, and Aurora's lover, Tithonus yearns to be immortal—or rather to evade change. As in the myth, the goddess persuades Zeus to grant Tithonus's wish, but, owing to a characteristically lazy formulation of that wish on the part of Tithonus, she fails to ask that he be made eternally youthful. Before these two go off to face his terrible future, Tithonus has alienated his sententious father and proved himself incapable of learning anything from Mrs. Mallow, a widow with a certain position in the household. The latter takes the form in Act Two of Olga, a thirty-nine-year-old companion to a young Russian woman, Fanya, engaged to Konstantin, a Nihilist, foreshadowed respectively by the maid and the gardener on Laomedon's household staff. When these three come on a sixty-year-old Tithonus painting in the woods, they all react much as they had in their preceding lives, but differently: the maid's sweet appeal now reveals itself to be mindless; Konstantin is disrespectful where he had only risked impudence; and Olga, fatally ill, combines her warm understanding and cool sensitivity with a certain flirtatiousness. In the last act, Fanya's inanity becomes the self-blinkered hopelessness of a young woman named Enid. Because the gardener and Konstantin were each smitten by Aurora, it is no surprise to find Enid's husband, Mark, on the verge of an affair with the goddess, desperate now to escape her senile husband. By the end of the play, these two have run off together. The babbling Tithonus is left in the company of Enid and an utterly efficient Nurse, Mrs. Mallow's last avatar, whom we understand to be Eternity. Laomedon, meanwhile, has returned here as his grandson, Memnon, who has fulfilled the prediction that he would see his father as an old bore. "Willful waste makes woeful want."

But that is the gaga Tithonus speaking, as is his wont, in clichés. "I have lived longer than anybody, and acquired a profound experience of the human heart," he brags. What are his insights? "You can't teach an old dog new tricks." The play mocks such platitudes even as it suggests that all ideas people have ever had are on more or less the same level—and are even more or less the same few ideas. When Fanya gushes about Konstantin's "ideas, so new, so fascinating," we are inclined to the point of view of the middle-aged Tithonus, appalled to think that "we have advanced to an age in which men are praised for new ideas." Like *The Bait,* this play is a critique of naiveté.

Tithonus cannot believe at first that Aurora has made his dream come true because the process she describes "sounds so easy." She is impatient with him, and for good reason—"You keep complaining about how you hate difficult things, and now that something perfectly simple happens, you're not satisfied"—but he is right. Things are more complicated than that. Tithonus's feeling of loss when his mother dies seems "too beautiful" to John, the gardener; and presently we see that his mourning actually projects his fondness for himself and his fear of death, which before long someone aptly interprets as a fear of life—which is exactly what he will not ever be spared. Or it is exactly what he will *always* be spared, since without death, there is no "life" as we know it. It is because he loves life that Mark asks Aurora only that he be allowed to keep his mortality. Not that Mark is our moral norm—things are not that easy.

Only the Olga figure sees things clearly and acts responsibly. The play opens with Mrs. Mallow's request that Tithonus move from the window, before which she is mending a dress. She sounds like Diogenes talking to Alexander: "You're standing in my light, dear. It's hard enough to see as it is." Amen. Her last words, as the Nurse, and the play's last words, are "You see? You see?" When she enters as Olga, her first words again have to do with seeing, and she goes on to tell Fanya that once the latter is all of thirty-nine, "you will be able to see yourself at a hundred and three, as I do now." What she sees must be some version of a scene in which she takes care of Tithonus forever. As he has the worst fate imaginable, so he is left in the best hands— though to say it like that might seem to trivialize a fearful conclusion. Time is the mercy of eternity, as Blake saw. Although its fearfulness must not be diminished, we need to notice that the play is also wickedly witty—as in the following passage:

TITHONUS.   Listen to me! I'm never going to die! Aurora has given me immortal life!
AURORA.   It's true. I have given Tithonus immortal life.
MRS. MALLOW.   For shame, Aurora!
MAID.   Immortal life!
GARDENER.   I don't know as how I'd enjoy *that*!
LAOMEDON, *to them.*   That will do, both of you.
Takes the tray from the MAID.
Not a word of this in the kitchen, you understand.

As Merrill has said, he began to see early on that "the world needs to be seen [as] cheerful *and* awful, opaque *and* transparent." Tithonus's last words, which follow immediately Enid's anguished cry, "He'll never die!", are "A watched pot never boils."

>)))

At the turning point in *The Seraglio* (1957), Merrill's first novel, the protagonist, Francis Tanning, who is twenty-four years old (seven years younger than the author on publication), has been almost paralyzed with terror of heterosexual sex, and has just slammed the door on the opportunity to sleep with a married woman whom he perhaps loves, returns to the hotel near Boston Common where he and friends and relatives are staying. He undresses, runs a hot bath, sprinkles the water with pine-scented salts, takes out a straight razor, and lies down in the tub. The scene in which he unmans himself is all the more shocking because it is so cleanly done. Not just the act—which has its elements of ritualistic precision—but also the writing, which is as delicate as the work of an expert surgeon. We do not know the extent of the wound, but we know that the loss of blood brings Francis near death and that the mutilation, just as he had planned, will keep him from leading what the discreet doctor calls "a normal life, in the fullest sense." It is an awful thing that Francis does—and yet it has another side. It too is a means of scissoring and mending, of severing certain obligations and thus clearing the way for others.

Francis's act is the second major incident of its kind in *The Seraglio*. There are many related instances in this meticulously written work, but most take place on the smallest scale. Still, they are important and sometimes fascinating—like the tiny figure of the artist reflected in a glass in a seventeenth-century Dutch painting. There is the anecdote about Larry Buchanan, the husband of Francis's half-sister, Enid. During World War II, while a prisoner of the Japanese and a senior officer responsible for his men's condition, which was ignored by the captors, Larry found it expedient to borrow an ancient Japanese means of petition: he chopped off the end of his little finger and flung it in the camp General's face while calling out the prisoner's needs. This "strange poetic gesture" anticipates Francis's act and helps us to understand it. For Francis's act too turns out to be the desperate act of a prisoner—in what the novel's conceit makes a seraglio—and it also turns out to impress with its version of heroism the man in charge: Francis's father, Benjamin Tanning, whose Zeus-like promiscuities his son could hardly rival even if he were so inclined. Francis, who until then has been wanly ineffectual, meets his father's passion with an equal and opposite passion. He destroys once and for all his father's oppressive image of what he could be—

just as, in an action meant to be instructive to his ten-year-old niece, Lily, he tears up his father's photo of him holding a blacksnake.

Lily's life and Francis's touch and touch again through the novel, sometimes without the awareness of either character. When Lily and her parents are on vacation in Rome, she sells a gold ring that Francis has given her to an antique and junk dealer, who must be the very man Francis bought it from several months earlier at the end of his year's sojourn abroad. As Lily and her mother start to leave the shop, the shopkeeper tries to sell them "an intaglio mounted in pale gold, blood-red as he held it to the light. It showed the profile of a fattish young man. *'Bello, eh?'*" They turn their noses up at it because it's "'cracked clean through'"—and at that instant, their paths and Francis's diverge. In a sense, that is, the intaglio portrait depicts Francis. We know this because of the shop, the blood-red stone that recalls the red bath water (and that Francis's "blood-red" tie in a later scene recalls in turn), and the Italian adjective, the French cognate of which has been applied to Francis by his friend Xenia, the morning after their lovemaking, his second and last experience of intercourse. But "fattish"? Hasn't our impression of Francis been of a man rather on the frail side? Before long we learn in passing that since his self-mutilation Francis is "'getting fat.'" Such miniature representations succeed marvelously in working out Merrill's themes.

Which brings us back to Lily and to the other major incident, which also involves a scissoring and a mending. As *The Immortal Husband* begins with Mrs. Mallow sewing up a tear in a dress, so *The Seraglio* opens with the repair of a cut canvas: "Exactly a year later Francis learned the truth about the slashed portrait—by then, of course, restored with expert care. The gash running from the outer corner of his sister's eye to her Adam's apple had been patched, sewn, smoothed, painted over, until he really had to hunt for the scar. Enid was posed against a cultivated landscape." It begins as though it were a mystery story, and so it is, in part. Though the reader knows within a few pages who has slashed Lily's mother's portrait, the characters do not know—or rather most of them do not know, including Francis, and others do not seem to know. The network among characters in this novel is in large measure a matter of the secrets they keep from one another. Lily (who has slashed the portrait) and Enid (who knows within hours who is guilty) hide their respective knowledge until nearly the end of the novel. Xenia lets Francis think that he is the father of her child—and Francis lets Xenia think that he *thinks* that he's the father. "As for secrets they might be keeping from *him*—for no doubt it worked both ways—he felt at once incurious and complacent. Of course he was being spared something . . ." So the novel is also a sort of anti-mystery. Exactly unlike the prototypical mystery, it is quite like the puzzles with the missing pieces in "Lost in Translation." Its first sentence resounds with ironies: this novel tells "the truth," but never the whole truth.

The opening tells us too the length of time covered by the novel: "Exactly a year." The smaller circuit made by the pure gold ring returned to the shop by the Spanish Steps is enclosed by the circle made by the narrative. Francis knows that it has been "exactly a year" because there is a significant event to date it by: Lily's birthday. On the day before her tenth birthday, having been punished for misbehavior, Lily has walked from the Buchanan house, on Long Island, to the Cottage, the nearby Tanning house, which is vacant for the moment. Some carefully managed business brings her, with a silver paper knife in her hand, face to face with the portrait—whose canvas she accidentally rips. Or is it accidental? The evidence suggests that, while intent could never be proved, the child wanted to punish her mother. The reference to the "Adam's apple" almost imperceptibly shades the opening in this direction. The landscape in the painting might be cultivated, as Lily's family is cultivated, but its essential nature is untamed. However expertly restored, the portrait is still scarred, as later Francis is, though he too has the best of care and his wound is not ordinarily visible.

The two slashings are central to the two plots, which Merrill intertwines to interpret each other. If Lily's damaging of the portrait is a sublimated attack on her mother, Francis's self-mutilation has a comparable purpose. At one point after his wounding, Francis leaps at the chance to recite from *Macbeth,* apparently in a daffy attempt to see what effect the "unsex me here" speech will have on his auditors, Xenia and Lily, and proceeds to misquote Lady Macbeth's excuse for not killing the King. In Francis's version: "Had he not resembled / My father as he slept, I had not done it." As Lily, who has played Fleance in a school production, points out to him, he has interpolated the second negative. The burden of this Freudian slip is that in wounding himself he has killed his father in him—as of course he has done to the extent that he has cut himself off irrevocably from that kind of life. After his wounding, Francis's hitherto latent homosexuality appears unmistakably. So does an obsession with the other world, which the Ouija board has put him in touch with.

Merrill mines *Macbeth* not only for knife images but also for references to children. Another bit of Lady Macbeth's dialogue becomes a motif: "the sleeping and the dead / Are but as pictures; 'tis the eye of childhood / That fears a painted devil." Francis quotes these lines to Lily, who might well see in them a reflection of her own fear of her mother. Lily is there too at the font during the christening ceremony for Tanning Burr Buchanan, her new brother, near the end of the novel: "'Dost thou, therefore, in the name of this Child,' asked the rector, a fine amateur athlete, 'renounce the devil and all his works, the vain pomp and glory of the world . . . ?'" The echoes of Lady Macbeth's speech encourage us to think that Lily's attack on her mother's painted image was in effect an attempt to resist her parents' world of opulence and ease. The Child resists the parents' devilish works. But the child has the devil in him, as we say. At the christening, "The baby shook its fists in delight or protest." Or both. Tanning Burr divines that the world is both cheerful and awful. Lily repeats her own protest when she buys for her mother, a lapsed Catholic, with the money got for the returned ring, a three-foot tall icon of the Virgin—at which her mother is aghast. Now Lily begins to learn what her impeccably dressed, knuckle-cracking father calls "the value of things." Embarrassed at having so misunderstood her mother's real interests, she returns the Virgin—and buys for herself "a stunning leather purse . . . a Roman scarf, and the most exquisite doll—a Spanish Señorita wearing a mantilla of real lace. By then, of course, everything had changed." Everything. She has traded her nascent spiritual values in for the purse, and with the scarf she can begin to make herself into the most exquisite doll.

Merrill sums up the war between the generations in a comically gruesome episode following the christening proper, when the cake appears and is discovered to be decorated with "a border of babies—oval candies not an inch long, to each of which had been applied, in sugar, a tiny pink face, three dots for buttons, the frill of a bonnet." After a show of civilized distaste, the guests fall on those liquor-filled treats like cannibals in a nursery: "The music began and didn't stop, though all but drowned out by shrieks and laughter, until every baby in sight had been consumed. Those too squeamish to eat their own saw them gobbled up by their neighbors." Later that evening, the adults watch Lily and her friends play hide-and-seek and notice how quickly they learn. They'll have their dinner soon, Enid says. "'A cake with parents on it,'" Francis replies.

Lily asks Francis about *his* rebellions. Did he ever flush his string beans down the toilet? Did he ever kill a kitten? Eat a doll? Within minutes, Francis will be eating his baby along with the others (or rather a baby given to him by Mrs. Durdee, wife of one of his father's associates, since his slice of cake appropriately has none), but in his case the meaning is double. Eating his baby is tantamount to flushing his string beans down the toilet—an image ingeniously reminiscent of his cutting away at himself, "tougher than a thong of leather," in the bathtub. (This cut leather makes its grim little disconnection with Lily's new stunning leather purse.) He also tells his mother, in response to her inquiry about its health, that his cat has died. By doing the most drastic thing, Francis has done all the things Lily asks about. One result is that he will never grow up. "Why he was a *child*!" Jane thinks to herself, when he insists that they try out the Ouija board together. At the novel's conclusion, his inheritance and his new life in sight, he is "Like a tired child on the eve of his birthday, glimpsing gifts but too drowsy to speculate on them." In the last pages Francis accepts Lily's invitation to play hide-and-seek with the children, and he accepts as well her stipulation: "'If he wants to play he has to be It.'" He hides his eyes, counts, looks up—only to find that the children have run off. "The game had broken like a bubble— or had not, had rather, by ending on terms so incongruous, left him still inside it, sustaining it all by himself."

The last phrase shows us the other side of Francis's position. If he is to be a child, he is also to be independent; the same act has had the two conse- quences. He was wrong to think, before his mutilation, that he and Jane could have no relationship simply because she had married: "The naked sword dangled no longer over their heads," he imagined; "it had fallen, cut- ting him free, and would lie henceforth between them." But his imagery was prophetic. Observing Francis after the sword *has* fallen in his bathtub and he has recovered, one of the characters guesses that he will never again do any- thing against his will. His own radical ritual has made him his own special creature. He is singular, unlike—not he, not she, but It. Unsexed, yes, but utterly individual, and powerful because of his individuality. "'What's the keeper of a seraglio called?'" one of his father's former mistresses muses as he leaves a group of his women in Francis's hands one evening. "'A unique,'" is Francis's telling answer. In the end, he *is* the end—the end of his line of gen- eration. It has all come down to him, and it will all go down with him, and therefore the novel's conclusion is plangent with possibility:

> But only after coming upon the children building castles at the sea's edge, oblivious to him, did Francis stare out over the lulled water and understand. He *was* It. He tentatively said so the first time, then once more with an exquisite tremor of conviction: "I am It."
>
> The words carried with them wondrous notions of selflessness, of permanence. His father coughed behind him in the house. The chil- dren trembled against the sea. He knew the expression on his own face. The entire world was real.

What a difference from his feelings a year before, just after his return from Italy, when he complained to Larry that if one is wealthy, "One's never in a position to find out what's real and what isn't—with the result that *nothing*'s real, nothing in the whole world is real!" His feeling at the novel's end is of the same order as that in "So be it. Welcome, O life! I go to encounter for the millionth time the reality of experience."

In other words, if Francis, unlike Stephen Dedalus, is not explicitly an artist, he is not hard to understand as a refraction of one. Now and again Merrill connects him, subtly but pointedly, with the Orpheus of an opera by Tommy Utter, the real father of Xenia's baby. When Francis goes to a party for Xenia in a penthouse kept by a friend of hers named Adrienne, his eye falls on "an Empire mirror shaped like a lyre," which he admires. There is the hint that Adrienne's own "'dear friend . . . wishes, I *think*, to part with it.'" Next we hear that "Red wine flowed. Later, Tommy played gems from his opera," then still in a preproduction stage. The juxtaposition of the opera and the lyre-shaped mirror is especially interesting when a mirror—I suppose it to be the same one—turns up in Francis's apartment in New York, after his recovery. There it has proved invaluable for the sessions with the Ouija board, because Meno, Francis's contact with the Beyond, can see him and Marcello, his lover and partner in the Ouija experience, only in reflection, so Marcello holds a hall mirror in his lap and Francis holds the lyre-shaped mirror in his—where earlier he has held the razor. As though to clinch this connection among Orpheus, who takes his lyre with him into Hell, Francis, and the other world, when Jane presses Francis as to whether he really believes the nonsense from the Ouija board, he dramatically strikes a single note on his harpsichord: "A tone, dry and vital, sang through the air, surprising Jane, who hadn't supposed so elegant an instrument to be in working order." That could be Orpheus's lyre itself. "'I believe all of it,' he replied . . . 'I tell you, this other world is *real*!'" Having that exclamation in mind when we read the novel's last sentence helps us to give its other adjective its proper force: "The *entire* world was real." If we doubt at first that Francis means to include the spirit world, we should look back at this sentence from the vantage of "Voices from the Other World," in *The Country of a Thousand Years of Peace*, which also treats the Ouija board sessions and which ends on this distinctive note:

> once looked at lit
> By the cold reflections of the dead
> Risen extinct but irresistible,
> Our lives have never seemed more full, more real,
> Nor the full moon more quick to chill.

The last line alone, with its pun on "quick," is a hint of the comprehensive world slowly outlined in *Sandover*—a world reminiscent of the one Rilke came to believe in. But at this early stage in his career Merrill had enough "wit to postpone" that tremendous "commitment," and we should no doubt follow suit here.

What exactly is the nature of the relationship between Francis and Orpheus? The important feature of Tommy Utter's hero, though not unprecedented in the many musical and literary treatments of this myth, is his realization that his singing itself has consigned Eurydice to the underworld. In Utter's opera the set mirrors the theater's seating, and—as in "Orfeo" in *The Country of a Thousand Years of Peace*—the stage and the world and Hell all merge. Eurydice delivers her part of the duet with Orpheus, who has "turned his back on the theatre of Hell," from a central box on stage. As Orpheus listens to her, "beyond the reach of his wooing," he comes to know "that he had placed her there himself, for at her death he had enshrined in his song not Eurydice but her loss, her absence that, growing bearable through his art, had as well grown irrevocable. With sickening force this knowledge was to break upon him by the end of the ensemble." The point is not that he wanted to lose her, but that her loss is his triumph. In the opera house Jane sits alone in her box, for Francis has left her, as was his custom when they would go places together in Italy. She has come to a new understanding of Eurydice's death—and no wonder, since she is a kind of Eurydice herself. Francis has lost Jane, or has had her taken from him, not by Hades but by a force as unopposable: biology or temperament or whatever combination of them has removed as well other women, children, posterity.

Unlike Orpheus, Francis has no art yet to deal with the loss. What he does have, in the first place, is the razor. No accident, perhaps, that between the lyre-shaped mirror on its first mention and the reference to the opera there intervenes that prefiguring sentence "Red wine flowed." I do not mean that the self-mutilation is exactly comparable to Orpheus's music. But to put the figure backward, I do mean that the music, to the extent that it cuts Orpheus off from Eurydice forever, has an effect similar to Francis's act. If the artist welcomes a certain loneliness and uniqueness, the razor has given Francis these things as the lyre has Orpheus. The Ouija board experience is an affirmation of this uniqueness, which is both an awful and a joyous thing, and perhaps a phase in the development of Francis's vocation, as it was to be in Merrill's. The little metrical feet that patter in place of the child's are even anticipated here by the spirit with whom Francis and Jane make contact in their one frustrating séance. The cup they use as a pointer swings back and forth between two letters, spelling out *Amamamamamama,* as though in the control of some mindless spirit "asserting its identity or crying for its mother," Jane scoffs. But the spirits might well be considered surrogate family. The parental need is displaced in Francis's description of a hypothetical "patron," a spirit who has escaped the cycle of reincarnation and whose responsibility it is to oversee the life of a reborn soul. Francis, who is in his last life, looks forward to being a patron himself: "'Far below on earth a tiny savage soul is born, in Naples or the Brazilian jungle. It is yours to care for and lead toward wisdom.'"

As the world opens before Francis at the novel's end, as he watches "the children building castles at the sea's edge," his own "old father and artificer" is there in the background. If Benjamin's cough heralds his end, Francis's sense of conviction and permanence proves his readiness to take over. Shortly before, Larry has asked him whether he knew, as no one else had known previously, that one day the Cottage would be his. Francis says that he knew—but he must have known intuitively, for his father has not told him. It is perhaps his ability to claim the inheritance that proves him worthy of it. Before long the family house will be in his hands, along with the seraglio— and indeed the regime has begun to change even by the novel's end, when he succeeds in getting the seductive Mrs. Durdee to extend her visit to the Cottage and in bringing his mother there for the first time in years.

His name is significant in this respect. If it suggests his sexual status, by virtue of its homophony with Frances, it also suggests a certain relationship with the Saint. Like the latter, Merrill's protagonist is the son of a wealthy man, has had an aimless youth, and even acquires his version of the stigmata that appeared on the Saint's body when he was praying on Monte La Verna. Perhaps most important, it is as though Francis Tanning too had heard the words that St. Francis thought he heard spoken by an icon of Jesus in the church of San Damiano at the beginning of his new life: "Francis, repair my falling house." When the young man took the command literally and stole from his father to help pay for the repair of the church, his father disinherited him, but then when he understood the message's metaphoric force and dedicated himself to the Church and the ascetic life, he came into his rightful inheritance. So Francis Tanning follows his father, not literally but passionately, and comes into the Cottage and attendant obligations. Francis has even taken his version of an ascetic vow: he will wed no woman, and his money, though he has come to enjoy being rich, is not of primary importance. By accepting the child in himself he becomes his own adult, and by accepting his wealth he begins to rise above it. His future is undefined at the novel's end, but it is sure to be dramatically different from that of the Buchanan children—"the little Buchannibals," as they are so aptly called.

It is interesting to remember, in regard to Francis's inheritance, that the territorial possessions of the tribe of Benjamin, who had been led by their eponym into the Promised Land, "melted imperceptibly into the possessions of friendly Ephraim."[47]

So by way of the Cottage the sandcastle melts into Sandover, the one real world into the other.

chapter two

BREAKING AND ENTERING

The Country of a Thousand Years of Peace, Water Street,
and *The (Diblos) Notebook*

(While in Italy Dora & Orestes & Sandy can stop in Urbino to see the Piero
Flagellation *which O. has greatly admired in black & white.)*

> > >

One meets a mind desiring and deferring, both, according to the laws of baroque music, solution and resolution.

Merrill on Francis Ponge

Thus, [metamorphosis is] the whole story from Genesis to Apocalypse in any event; in any metamorphosis. Therefore it is important to keep changing the subject. The subject changes before our very eyes. It is important to keep changing our mind—

The mind, that ocean where each kind
Does straight its own resemblance find.

The mind, or the imagination, the original shape-shifter: Thrice-Greatest Hermes.

Norman O. Brown, "Daphne, or Metamorphosis"

T H E   S E R A G L I O is about taking control of one's life. Francis's father—whom Lily, when very young, thought might be God—sets an example that cannot be repeated in his creation of Tanning Burr. But Francis is his true if surprising successor in his creation of his own world, a world he must "sustain" by himself. These two are the makers in the novel. They are also the destroyers. Benjamin breaks up household after household, his own and others'; and the novel's one touching death, Sir Edward Good's, is probably traceable to Benjamin's philandering. As though in retribution for Benjamin's destructions, Francis ruins his father's dreams of a Tanning dynasty. They are linked by their extravagance and their profligacy: they have both driven out of the ruts and have struck down conventions meant to keep them in line. The conniving, vulgar Charlie Cheek and his wife Irene, one of Benjamin's lovers, are no more their foils than are the established, the maintainers of appearance, the calculating and the passionless. When Francis sits with Enid in "the ocean room" of the Cottage, a room whose appointments she has seen to, he almost pities her for the inviolable "poise" that has produced the combination of "blandness and taste" in which each piece is "so harmonious and so fine." This is a room that has "sustained Enid" and himself and countless others with its imposition of decorum. "Wouldn't it help, he brooded, to leap up, cry out, smash something? But the room met his eye so trustingly; it was easier to do violence to himself." Just so.

Francis is not Merrill, to be sure, but his radical solution to his problem is a sign of the kind of writer Merrill is to become. True, the literary allotropes of good manners—including refinement of perception, attention to form, the refusal to insist on things (a quality Francis admires in Poussin), the predilection for the happy ending—characterize Merrill's work from the beginning. But it is all wrong to think of him as academic or precious. As he grows older he is as daring as Byron and Ponge, as extreme as Mallarmé, and withal as driven as Rilke and Proust. But then he is not far from being this kind of writer at the outset. He unfolds, and there are several stages in the process to which one might apply Alice B. Toklas's circumspect remark to him about "The Wintering Weeds," included in both editions of *The Country of a Thousand Years of Peace* but dropped from *From the First Nine:* "*Enfin* it is a big step forward but a very natural development."[1] This is true especially of *Water Street*.

The Country of a Thousand Years of Peace, on the other hand, is a book of consolidations, though perhaps not at its beginning.[2] Francis Tanning admires in others the ability to set themselves "afloat," to push out into unknown waters and trust their own resources. When that Damoclean sword really does fall in the form of his razor, Francis, right there in the bathtub, sets himself "afloat." The first and title poem in *The Country of a Thousand Years of Peace*—an elegy for Merrill's friend, the Dutch poet Hans Lodeizen, who died in a Lausanne hospital of leukemia at age twenty-six—returns at its climax to the image of the sword. I quote the last three stanzas:

> The glittering neutrality
> Of clock and chocolate and lake and cloud
> Made every morning somewhat
> Less than you could bear;

> And makes me cry aloud
> At the old masters of disease
> Who dangling high above you on a hair
> The sword that, never falling, kills

> Would coax you still back from that starry land
> Under the world, which no one sees
> Without a death, its finish and sharp weight
> Flashing in his own hand.

Merrill once said that this poem, drafted after his visit to Lodeizen's hospital room in 1950, "still surprises me, as much by its clarification of what I was feeling, as by its foreknowledge of where I needed to go next, in my work."[3] Since it is possible that he wrote this poem before drafting the pertinent passage in *The Seraglio,* he might have the novel in mind when he speaks of where he needed to go. But he might be thinking in larger terms. What the poem has in common with the novel, beyond the sword (which looks a good deal like the poet's "glaive nu" in Mallarmé's "Le Tombeau d'Edgar Poe"), is the idea that one can take his life "in his own hand." The gist of these last two stanzas is that regardless of the agonizing, slow inexorability of such a death, the death is one's own to fashion in undergoing it. One might think of Rilke's refusal of morphine, in spite of the excruciating pain that he knew at the end. Lodeizen, in contrast to the German poet, "spoke with carefree relish of the injection they would give him presently" and talked of meeting Merrill in Italy later in the year. That brave face put on things is reflected in the "Flashing" and flourish of the last lines. Although there is all the difference in the world between the fictional Francis's wound and the real Hans Lodeizen's death, they are linked in Merrill's work by means of an image whose import is daring and courage.

In "The Thousand and Second Night" in *Nights and Days* the poet will find himself at the center of the poem joyfully "afloat / Upon the breathing, all-reflecting deep," and one can locate similar moments of adventurous departure in *Water Street.* But in this earlier volume the poems tend to be cultivated, ambagious, poised. Merrill himself suspects that "each of at least the shorter [poems] bites off much less" even than his earlier work.[4] One almost feels that a poem like "Olive Grove"—twenty lines long and all one sentence, a tour de force of dependent clauses and prepositional phrases— wants to be a continuous, soporific, slightly modulated humming. Many of the others have the harmony and fineness of "the ocean room." The thing about Enid's "ceremony of blandness and taste," however, is that on reflection it is not really "a ceremony because it concealed nothing, composed nothing, cost nothing." Merrill's poems usually conceal and compose and cost, even if they are now and then such "ceremonies," in which "The glittering neutrality / Of clock and chocolate and lake and cloud" predominates at the expense of the "cry aloud."

"A Narrow Escape," one of the Charles poems, involves a similar opposition, between a suave surface and dark impulses. It begins irresistibly: "During a lull at dinner the vampire frankly / Confessed herself a symbol of the inner / Adventure." It continues just as brightly through its last line, as the hideous depths of human nature alluded to are beguilingly transformed into "flitterings from within, / Crags and grottos . . . the oubliette of that bland face . . ." or wittily blamed for "ghastly scenes over letters and at meals, / Not to speak of positive evil, those nightly / Drainings of one's life, the blood, the laugh, / The cries for pardon, the indifferences." It ends on a pithy silence:

> It was then Charles thought to wonder, peering over
> The rests of venison, what on earth a vampire
> Means by the inner adventure. Her retort
> Is now a classic in our particular circle.

I have always imagined that the retort, delivered across that venison, must have been in some sense a biting one. Since being bitten by a vampire, even metaphorically, might make one a vampire oneself, the little "circle" would be a "particular" one indeed. Perhaps we should also consider that the insider who speaks in this poem could not disclose the vampire's retort without thereby making the circle less "particular" in another sense. In any case, the poem's reason for being is *not* to reveal the retort. This is an emblematic instance of the poem that conceals and composes; it maintains appearances with its civilities and rules out of order all crying aloud. This is also to say that it is a brilliant exercise in the control of tone, or rather in the controlled tone, for the arch, dry, sophisticated manner is hardly varied—and it is really Charles's tone, not Merrill's. Or it is only one of Merrill's.

Poem after poem here demonstrates its author's fluency. Often Merrill will head off in an oblique direction, so subtly evolving his subject that we hardly notice the great distance traveled. "The Octopus" is one such poem, "The Charioteer of Delphi" another, and "The Wintering Weeds" yet another. "The Lovers" provides a paradigm for this kind of development. It begins by comparing its two lovers to a farmer's hands:

> They met in loving like the hands of one
> Who having worked six days with creature and plant
> Washes his hands before the evening meal.
> Reflected in a basin out-of-doors
> The golden sky receives his hands beneath
> Its coldly wishing surface, washing them . . .

As the poem goes along, the original vehicle nudges the tenor aside and the farmer becomes the subject. But then well before that metamorphosis has been completed, a second has begun, and the farmer begins to change into another figure. After looking over "the young fruit-trees / And lowing beasts," the pasture and lights of the town, "for a last fact he dips his face / And lifts it glistening," and the water golden with the sky's reflection reflects also his face.

> —Except for when each slow slight water-drop
> He sensed on chin and nose accumulate,
> Each tiny world of sky reversed and branches,
> Fell with its pure wealth to mar the image:
> World after world fallen into the sky
>
> And still so much world left when, by the fire
> With fingers clasped, he set in revolution
> Certitude and chance like strong slow thumbs;
> Or read from an illuminated page
> Of harvest, flood, motherhood, mystery:
> These waited, and would issue from his hands.

The graduations are nearly musical, from lovers to farmer, from farmer to God, from God to the universe. And then the return in the last words to the lovers takes the conceit back into itself. It is a lovely work, burnished and urbane as an Arp sculpture, its pastoralism notwithstanding. It neither leaves anything to do in its mode nor suggests anything else that might be done. It is exactly the sort of poem that the author of "Mozart" might have dreamed of writing. Merrill is just over thirty.

What next?

Among the poems in which we can get glimpses of *Water Street* are "Marsyas" and the well-known "Mirror."[5] The first does not really resemble the major poems in the next volume so much as it formulates in overtly symbolic terms an issue that those poems meet at the technical level. "Marsyas" is a sonnet put in the mouth of the Phrygian sailor who challenged Apollo to a musical duel. Marsyas played the flute that he found after Athene had thrown it away, and Apollo used the kithara that he had invented. When the Muses declared Apollo the winner, he invoked his right to have Marsyas flayed alive. In Merrill's monologue, the victim is a cross between a beat poet and the ambitious kid gunslinger who has the bad luck to test himself against the old pro. The meter of the first three lines, heavily counterpointed, reflects the speaker's ill-founded casualness: "I used to write in the café sometimes: / Poems on menus, read all over town / Or talked out before ever written down." This carefree attitude came to an end abruptly:

> One day a girl brought in his latest book.
> I opened it—stiff rhythms, gorgeous rhymes—

61

And made a face. Then crash! my cup upset.
Of twenty upward looks mine only met
His, that gold archaic lion's look . . .

This interruption of the speaker's little act is the kind of event that happens more and more frequently in Merrill's poems—though it is often accompanied by a marked shift in tone. Here the slight change is modulated, as before our eyes the rebellious young café poet takes on the inflections of the god (whose last avatar was perhaps Stevens's modern poet, "twanging a wiry string") even as he reads his end in Apollo's eyes,

Wherein I saw my wiry person skinned
Of every skill it labored to acquire
And heard the plucked nerve's elemental twang.
They found me dangling where his golden wind
Inflicted so much music on the lyre
That no one could have told you what he sang.

Stiff rhythms, gorgeous rhymes. What we have here are two selves of the poet, or versions of them: in Marsyas, a caricature of the dark, hitherto rarely seen self, the new Verlaine who would agree with those of Merrill's critics who think the early verse inordinately ornate; and in Apollo, an idealized form of the self who has written most of the poems before this one, and who wins out here, as the sestet incorporates the rhetoric whose neck Marsyas would wring. There is an important drama latent here, though the poem is a polished piece, an ironic justification of Merrill's golden mode.[6]

Before writing many of the poems in the next book, Merrill seems to have decided, in effect, that Yeats's Crazy Jane is right, that " 'nothing can be sole or whole / That has not been rent.'" The surface needs to be broken, it appears, the eloquence called into question. The poem in *The Country of a Thousand Years of Peace* that comes closest to turning on itself in this way is "Mirror." This poem too is built on contrary forces. The mirror, the poem's speaker, we understand before long, bears a certain relationship first to art in general and second to a particular kind of art. The poem opens by responding, virtually *as* poem, to the reader, here placed among the children:

I grow old under an intensity
Of questioning looks. *Nonsense,*
I try to say, *I cannot teach you children*
How to live. —If not you, who will?

Cries one of them aloud, grasping my gilded
Frame till the world sways. *If not you, who will?*

With its "gilded / Frame . . . [and] perfect silver . . . reflectiveness," its con-
tentment with reproducing as in *nature morte* "the table, its arrangement /
Of Bible, fern and Paisley, all past change," and its distance from the natural
world beheld by the window—in all these ways the mirror evokes the kind
of poetry Merrill has sometimes been charged with writing. This poem,
with its subtle figures and rhymes (the penultimate syllable of one line with
the last syllable of the next), is an instance.

The window, indiscriminate as life itself, can "embrace a whole world
without once caring / To set it in order." Then there are the two grown
grandchildren, whose biases we gauge as soon as we find that they "Sit with
novels face-down on the sill" and gaze out the window at the "clouds, brown
fields, persimmon far / And cypress near." One of them makes the remark
that is the poem's climax: *"How superficial / Appearances are!"* Now the reader
knows better than to take this notion at face value: its tautology is flagrant,
its own shallowness apparent. The mirror, however, is shaken to its core:

Since then, as if a fish
Had broken the perfect silver of my reflectiveness,
I have lapses. I suspect
Looks from behind, where nothing is, cool gazes
Through the blind flaws of my mind.

At this point, even as the mirror begins to sense its inadequacy and its mortality, the poem begins a defense of appearances. While the mirror entertains
the possibility that its "reflectiveness" is a trivial virtue, it is precisely the
reflectiveness that allows it to entertain that possibility. The mirror takes
into account, as the poem takes into itself, the direst objection to it, and in
the course of doing so it attains the depth it is said to lack—the same depth
from which that astounding fish rises. I say the depth from which it rises,
but of course it comes from the "superficial" itself. The "fish" and its depths
are there *in* "superficial" by virtue of the unusual rhyme—one of the features
that might ordinarily encourage us to think of this poem as decorative rather
than profound.

Appearances are superficial? No doubt. And if we subtract them, what
do we have left? Where do those "Looks from behind" come from? "Looks
from behind, where nothing is." Where *nothing is*. What if appearances are
everything? In the poem's touching last lines the mirror, speaking to the
window, foresees its own end:

As days,
As decades lengthen, this vision
Spreads and blackens. I do not know whose it is,
But I think it watches for my last silver
To blister, flake, float leaf by life, each milling-
Downward dumb conceit, to a standstill
From which not even you strike any brilliant
Chord in me, and to a faceless will,
Echo of mine, I am amenable.

The mirror cannot know whose "vision" it is because "it" is what has no appearance. It is what will come to be known in *Sandover* as the Adversary and the Undoer, and it—not the window, not the grandchildren—is the mirror's antithesis, absence itself, the universe without mind—for mind is what the mirror has come to represent by the end of the poem. Thinking (the implicit argument runs) is a matter of representation, a matter of image and rhetoric. If one day the mind must come to nothingness itself, meanwhile it has no choice but to set out even that eventuality in "superficial" terms. The "faceless will" can only be an "Echo of mine"—which last phrase asserts the primacy of mind, even as the poem's concluding three words admit its opposite number's authority. The poem insists on the utility of "appearance" also in its handling of the rhyme in these last lines. For the only time in the several poems that he wrote in this form in *The Country of a Thousand Years of Peace,* Merrill varies the pattern. It would have been easy enough for him to break the fifth line at "mill-" to keep the normal scheme, but instead he chooses to use the extra syllable. If this is a "lapse," it is a calculated one. By next making this rhyme mesh with the following, in which he reverses the usual procedure with syllables by pairing "standstill" with "brilliant," he brings the poem to a formal standstill, dissolved forthwith in the concluding couplet, which uses the same rhyme as the preceding four lines but rhymes on two final syllables. He creates a little vortex in which the two wills meet on the instant of disappearance. How but by some such means, drawn from the realm of "appearances," can any subject be broached? Appearances are what we have.

They—and amenability. "I am amenable," the mirror promises, by which it means "tractable" or "submissive," but the word also means "open or liable to testing, criticism, or judgment." The most significant thing about "Mirror" from the point of view of Merrill's development is that it tests itself, that it questions its own principles, its every description and "dumb conceit." What it teaches those children who demand to know "how to live" is that skepticism begins at home.

)))

Water Street is the first book to assure us that Merrill will write better poems. Whereas the first two volumes fulfilled potential, it creates possibilities. The first poem's title is "An Urban Convalescence," and "convalescence," as this etymologically alert poet would know, derives from roots meaning "to grow stronger." "Out for a walk, after a week in bed," the poem begins, with an insistence on fresh air, and indeed it is in the process of encountering the world anew that he gains strength—and sets about building a new "house," as it turns out. *Water Street:* the very title, which is the name of the street in Stonington where in 1956 Merrill and his friend David Jackson bought the house they still have, signals a determination to bring the poems into brisker weather.

"What manner of building shall we build?" Stevens asks in "Architecture." The features of Merrill's manner in *Water Street* are difficult to disentangle, but we might make them out to be at least four. In the first place, there is the increased technical mastery, by which term I mean to include prosodic finesse, the dowser's instinct for the right word, and a superb command of syntactical stratagems. In this volume, the technique has been extended to accommodate an element new to Merrill's work and at bottom inimical to technique. This element, the second feature, is process. These poems are less stubbornly *objects* than the earlier poems. Less highly buffed, they are less likely to rebuff. "I often begin not knowing what I want to say," he has remarked. "When I've got it right, I know what it was I had wanted to say. Such a devious method."[7] This "process of clarification" does not itself distinguish his composition from other poets', but his increased concern with letting it show in his completed work helps to do so. Or to let it show *as it were,* since he will often have contrived his roughness.

Process often manifests itself in these poems in the form of self-interruption, which usually originates in a challenge to a statement just made or in the process of being made: a tentative reexamination, or a change of mind, or a self-mockery. A reflexive and revisionary movement, such intervention is often related to Romantically ironic tactics. It springs from "amenability," and it often issues in aporia or ambivalence or paradox. The poetry that accommodates such interruptions is more likely to extend itself than to round itself off and more likely to include than to exclude. At a stretch, it is digressive and improvisational. Its dramatic discontinuities are ways of surprising, whether in Byron or Browning or Merrill, a way of keeping things off balance and in question.[8] They are ways of chipping or obviating a "glaze of perfection," to use Merrill's own term for a quality in Elinor Wylie's poems. He has touched on his interruptions when defining the means by which he became "a little looser in terms of form" in *Water Street:* "In 'An Urban Convalescence' I first hit upon this sense of the self-reflexive side of the poem—that you can break up the argument in a very fruitful way. This is probably something learned from working in the theater where you write a line and you can have someone else contradict it. But you can also incorporate that within yourself as poet and stop a certain train of thought and break into something new or criticize what you've done up to that moment."[9] Again, in demurring from the proposition that "the self is the last remaining universal," Merrill—here too the follower of Proust—insists that "the self is extremely ambiguous. There are so many different selves."[10] His appreciation of Elizabeth Bishop's "way of contradicting something she's just said" seems also to have encouraged him in the direction of this rhetorical movement.[11] In any event, these poems raise the curtain on that "inward speaking and never-ending dialogue with oneself" that Schlegel writes about. Henceforth, Merrill's work is less a means of displaying talent and more an instrument of discovery.

In the third place, his internal dialogue often takes the form of a rivalry between two impulses, one ludic or aesthetic and the other heuristic or didactic. Merrill will call the products of these two impulses "rigmarole" and "candor." The contention itself is not unusual, for as Auden puts it, "Art arises out of our desire for both beauty and truth and our knowledge that they are not identical"; but the explicitness of this rivalry in Merrill's work is distinctive. Auden proceeds to describe the two demands that we as readers make of a poem and the corresponding motivations behind its composition:

> We want a poem to be beautiful, that is to say, a verbal earthly paradise, a timeless world of pure play, which gives us delight precisely because of its contrast to our historical existence with all its insoluble problems and inescapable suffering; at the same time we want a poem to be true, that is to say, to provide us with some kind of revelation about our life which will show us what life is really like and free us from self-enchantment and deception, and a poet cannot bring us any truth without introducing into his poetry the problematic, the painful, the disorderly, the ugly. Though every poem involves *some* degree of collaboration between Ariel and Prospero, the role of each varies in importance from one poem to another: it is usually possible to say of a poem and, sometimes, of the whole output of a poet, that it is Ariel-dominated or Prospero-dominated.[12]

If Merrill's poetry was originally Ariel-dominated ("Here where no image sinks to truth," goes the line in "Some Negatives: X at the Château"), Prospero has nearly an equal role in the major poems in *Water Street.*

The relationship between the rivals Prospero and Ariel parallels the encounter between living and writing, which now emerges clearly—this is the
fourth feature mentioned earlier—as one of Merrill's favorite subjects. He
has gone on record as opposing "in principle . . . the persona of the poem
talking about the splendors and miseries of writing; it seems to me far too
many poets today make the act of writing one of their primary subjects."[13]
He goes ahead, however, to note that he is "following the crowd" himself,
though he has "hoped as much as possible to sugar the pill by being a bit
rueful and amusing about having to do so." Why, one might wonder, does
he have to do so? But the answer must be that "the splendors and miseries of
writing" are among the experiences that he feels most deeply. Rilke, one of
his early and enduring guides, takes a similarly conflicted stance on occasion, as in one of the *Letters to Merline,* where the promptness with which he
disregards his own counsel would be comic if the obsession were not so
passionate:

> Do not expect me to talk about my interior effort . . . my struggle
> towards concentration. This reversal of all one's forces, this changed di-
> rection of soul can never be accomplished without a number of crises;
> most artists avoid it by means of diversions, but that is just why they
> never again succeed in touching their centre of production, from which
> they started at the moment of their purest impulse. Always when you
> begin to work you must recreate this first innocence, you must return to
> the ingenuous place where the Angel discovered you when he brought
> you the first binding message; you must find once more the couch be-
> hind the briars where you were then asleep: this time you will not sleep
> there: you will have to pray and groan,—no matter: if the Angel deigns
> to appear, it will be because you have convinced him, not by tears but
> by your humble resolve to be always beginning—to be a Beginner!
> Oh Dear, how many times in my life—and never so much as now—
> have I told myself that Art, as I conceive it, is a movement contrary to
> nature. No doubt God never foresaw that any one of us would turn
> inwards upon himself in this way . . .[14]

This turning "inwards upon himself" is Rilke's version of Schlegel's confrontation with "our inmost profoundest being."
Even though it is itself under the sway of the ludic impulse, "From a
Notebook," this volume's second poem, points the direction that Merrill's
work is taking. It opens with a stanza that evokes memories of both Mallarmé's "vide papier que la blancheur défend" and Valéry's gratitude for the
"vers donné," the single inspired line that is the most the poet should hope

to receive from the Muse in the course of writing a poem. Merrill's hopes are even more modest than Valéry's:

> The whiteness near and far.
> The cold, the hush . . .
> A first word stops
> The blizzard, steps
> Out into fresh
> Candor. You ask no more.

In effect, that first word, separated by the line break as by a wishful pause from its adjective, *is* "Candor," whose power in this case, ironically enough, is its duplicity, its meaning of both "whiteness" or "brightness" and "frankness." The term has a special, auspicious force for Merrill—he puns on it again in "From the Cupola" and on "candid heart" in "Scenes from Childhood"—and it signifies his commitment in this volume to both artifice (beauty) and frankness (truth). To step "into fresh / Candor" is both to participate in and to mar its purity.

If openness is one of the intentions in this volume, "From a Notebook" attempts it by charting its own supposed composition, in which even steps not taken are advances made:

> Each never taken stride
> Leads onward, though
> In circles ever
> Smaller, smaller.
> The vertigo
> Upholds you. And now to glide . . .

While Merrill's rhyme scheme, with its successively enclosed sounds, makes its own ever-tightening circle, and the repetition of "smaller" emphasizes the tightness of the inner circles, the sentence begun at this stanza's end pushes off into the second half of the poem, which, with its comparative syntactical complication and figures of speech and silence, mirrors the arabesques cut into the ice:

> And now to glide
>
> Across the frozen pond,
> Steelshod, to chase
> Its dreamless oval
> With loop and spiral

Until (your face
Downshining, lidded, drained

Of any need to know
What hid, what called,
Wisdom or error,
Beneath that mirror)
The page you scrawled
Turns. A new day. Fresh snow.

With that last judicious line break, Merrill pulls up with a flair, almost like that of a skater turning his blades sideways, and the poem, having chased its "dreamless oval" (having pursued its pure form, that is, and having engraved its figures on the pond), ends with a beginning like its own. The poem ends, whiteness returns, as Mallarmé says somewhere.

Its title notwithstanding, "From a Notebook" belongs with Merrill's earlier work as far as its polished manner is concerned. Especially when coupled with its nominal emphasis on "Candor," however, this poem's attention to the process of composition augurs a change. The next logical step—if poetic development proceeded logically—would be to embody in the poem the sort of lapse that "Mirror" alludes to.

Largely because it does incorporate something of the process of its writing, "To a Butterfly" is more complex than its tidy quatrains, with their short lines and full rhymes and simple diction, might seem to permit. Indeed Merrill begins by lamenting, ironically, a loss of simplicity. The simplicity lost is the caterpillar's, but we infer before long not only that the "Poor simple creature" bears some relationship to the poet's past self, but also that this very relationship testifies to the vexing complication. This is the poet who aspires to "Candor," after all, and just look what happens as he details the metamorphoses:

Your slender person curled
About an apple twig
Rebounding to the winds' clear jig
Gave up the world

In favor of obscene
Gray matter, rode that ark
Until (as at the chance remark
Of Father Sheen)

Shining awake to slough
Your old life. And soon four

Dapper stained glass windows bore
You up—*Enough*.

No sooner has Merrill begun to describe the metamorphoses than the insect's cocoon stage has become a metaphor for reading and writing poems, and the emergence of the butterfly has become the young poet's acquisition of style. But it is that style, precisely because it involves such conceits and such showy imagery as in the last stanza above, that the poet has wearied of. One can hear the desperation in his voice as his invention leads him to adapt seamlessly even an allusion to one of Bishop Fulton J. Sheen's proselytizing tracts. As he had once given up the world and then the ascetic life itself, so now he would shed his hard-earned sophistication, his disgusted "*Enough*" insists.

That overriding of the poet's one voice by another is the important event in this poem. When Merrill decides to resist his gift, to make fun of his own metaphor or to drop a tone gone rhetorical, he interjects a new and henceforth indispensable element into the poetry. The various interpolations and interruptions that David Lehman and Willard Spiegelman have written about can be traced back at least as far as this volume.[15] One might even see in an interjection such as this one in "To a Butterfly" a hint of the great poems to come. "The Thousand and Second Night" begins with a persona divided against himself and concludes with a dialogue of the soul and the senses, while "From the Cupola" sets the poet talking to himself in the guise of speakers named Psyche and James. Moreover, since these two speakers in turn divide and multiply at the same time that the god Eros enters the picture, "From the Cupola" looks forward to *Ephraim* and its successors, with their Protean characters.

After this interception of Ariel by Prospero, "To a Butterfly" becomes a richer poem, as Merrill, elaborating his suspicions of his own facility, seems helplessly to justify them. In that artful flouting of his self-criticism we hear the most distinctive tone yet:

Goodness, how tired one grows
Just looking through a prism:
Allegory, symbolism.
I've tried, Lord knows,

To keep from seeing double,
Blushed for whenever I did,
Prayed like a boy my cheek be hid
By manly stubble.

Such reservations occur frequently from now on. But the misgiving can recur only because the transgression is inveterate. In the passage just quoted,
immediately after Merrill has "Blushed" in embarrassment, we catch him
again *in flagrante delicto,* eliciting two meanings from "cheek." In spite of
himself, or because of his two selves, the Ariel who makes the pun and the
Prospero who deplores it, he still sees double. The conclusion owes something to each point of view:

> I caught you in a net
> And first pierced your disguise
> How many years ago? Time flies,
> I am not yet
>
> Proof against rigmarole.
> Those frail wings, those antennae!
> The day you hover without any
> Tincture of soul,
>
> Red monarch, swallowtail,
> Will be the day my own
> Wiles gather dust. Each will have flown
> The other's jail.

On the one hand, he implies, he has known at least since he was a child
mounting his first butterfly in a display case that beauty (either the insect's
or the poem's) disguises mortality. On the other hand, even as time continues to fly, he cannot avoid being enchanted by beauty or interpreting life
in terms of trope ("rigmarole")—any more than the "Mirror" can avoid its
"silver reflectiveness." Indeed it is trope (the linking of the butterfly to the
psyche) that allows him to expound the truth of the matter in the last
stanzas. Ariel and Prospero, at odds at the center of the poem, arrive at
an uneasy arrangement here at the end like that between the butterfly and
the poet.

"To a Butterfly" defines its attitude toward writing in the process of
being written: one voice vies with another and then combines with it in
propositions attuned to the claims of both. "Prism" turns on a similar intervention and dialogue. This poem shares with "*a paperweight,*" as the epigraph labels the particular prism, weight and density, but the title misleads if
it prepares us for a poem perfectly shaped and finished. "Prism" discovers its
own complexities and frustrations as it develops, though it begins on a note
of self-assurance:

Having lately taken up residence
In a suite of chambers
Windless, compact and sunny, ideal
Lodging for the pituitary gland of Euclid
If not for a "single gentleman (references),"
You have grown used to the playful inconveniences . . .

This is a poem confident of its destination, the periodic syntax implies—
as does the jaunty quote, with its allusion to the preceding "reference" to
Euclid, whose geometry comports with the prism's. So far, so good: this
will be a stylish comparison of this "suite of chambers" (a phrase that has
musical overtones that might confuse matters, it is true, but never mind, for
now) to a crystal paperweight.

As Merrill amplifies on the "playful inconveniences," however, they become graver; the speaker seems not so much enprismed as imprisoned; the
syntax and the metaphor grow ominously vagarious and involved:

>   the playful inconveniences,
> The floors that slide from under you helter-skelter,
> Invisible walls put up in mid-
> Stride, leaving you warped for the rest of the day,
> A spoon in water; also that pounce
> Of wild color from corner to page,
> Straightway consuming the latter
> Down to your very signature,
> After which there is nothing to do but retire,
> Licking the burn, into—into—
> Look . . .

Living in the apartment prism is like writing poems, then, or so the invisible
wall put up in the middle of the word "midstride" insinuates, while the
lionish "pounce / Of wild color" has the effect of an unredactable insight.
Thus the poem bears out its own observations about this "suite of chambers" as it abruptly shifts levels and subjects. At this juncture, as the relin-
quishing of that promising opening sentence admits, Merrill seems tram-
meled up in what he would set down. The poem's elements have become so
inextricable by virtue of its tropes that he cannot say exactly what he might
retire as in defeat "into." Another part of the apartment? But it is a funhouse
inseparable from the prism it contains; the prism is the house that houses it.
His thoughts? But his mind is also one with the prism. ("How tired one
grows / Just looking through a prism," he complains in "To a Butterfly," but

the vantage is inescapable there and here alike.) Synecdoche and metaphor have gotten out of hand, and his resulting vision of unity has overwhelmed his executive power, he suggests in the following lines, where a tone so different as to amount to a second voice interrupts:

> into—into—
> Look: (Heretofore
> One could have said where one was looking,
> In or out. But now it almost—) Look,
> You dreamed of this:
> To fuse in borrowed fires, to drown
> In depths that were not there. You meant
> To rest your bones in a maroon plush box,
> Doze the old vaudeville out, of mind and object,
> Little foreseeing their effect on you,
> Those dagger-eyed insatiate performers
> Who from the first false insight
> To the most recent betrayal of outlook,
> Crystal, hypnotic atom,
> Have held you rapt, the proof, the child
> Wanted by neither.

Actually, this other voice interrupts and then reinterrupts, after the first voice has broken back in to state as clearly as possible the essence of his puzzle: the inner and the outer (the mind and its object, the prism, the prism and the suite, the part and the whole) contain each other. Hence the repetitions through this passage, beginning with the iterated "into," which in this context of contrapositions will be heard as "in two." But one point here is that the division is apparent only, that the two are fundamentally one—and this point the doubled "one" makes in the parenthesis's central line. "Look" too occurs twice in this little local symmetry, once for "in" and once for "out" as it were, and frames the parenthesis.

If the sense of fusion with his work is what our "single gentleman," who begins to seem double, once "dreamed of," he did not anticipate his obsession with certain contingent paradoxes, for which all terms seem inadequate sooner or later. No "insight" or "outlook" can suffice, since words by their nature make the distinctions (as these perfectly balanced terms vividly demonstrate) that they lead him to want to see through. He imagined dealing as efficiently as a prism with his various illuminations or relaxing and enjoying the dramas among his poetic cast and never envisioned his fascination with such difficulties as the poem has embroiled him in. The "performers" are "insatiate" in part because they are he, "held . . . rapt" by this play of mind and object. Here is the poet as addict, hooked on paradox:

> Now and then
> It is given to see clearly. There
> Is what remains of you, a body
> Unshaven, flung on the sofa. Stains of egg
> Harden about the mouth, smoke still
> Rises between fingers or from nostrils.
> The eyes deflect the stars through years of vacancy.

Addict—or battlefield corpse, his obsession has reduced him so. At the same time, at such a revelatory, nearly manic moment, his own power seems superhuman: "You and the stars / Seem both endangered, each / At the other's utter mercy." Having spent the night wrestling with his angel, he is at once fearfully fragile and omnipotent. When the moment passes, and "the vision shuttles off," he returns to his occupation, which has as much in common with listening to music after all as with crystal-gazing: "A toneless waltz glints through the pea-sized funhouse. / The day is breaking someone else's heart." No doubt—but he has his consuming interest.

The chief subject of "Prism" is its own enmeshing process, its rigmarole, but its latent subject, nowhere so near the surface as in the surprising last line, is the relationship between writing and living in the world. It is a passionate poem, but its passion is not of the rakish sort that we might expect of a "'single gentleman (references).'" What *of* the life, we might well ask, in view of this evidently single-minded devotion to the task, implied also by "From a Notebook" and "To a Butterfly"? A stubborn concern in Merrill's poetry and fiction, it gets more specific attention here in *Water Street* in "Angel," "For Proust," "After Greece," and the two longest and richest poems, "An Urban Convalescence" and "A Tenancy."

"Angel" sets out the basic situation as crisply as any of these poems. In this genial vignette, the whole of which purports to be an interruption of the poet at work, an angel, "whirring and self-important / (Though not much larger than a hummingbird) / In finely woven robes, school of Van Eyck," hovers above the poet's desk. This gorgeous visitor points with one hand through the window to a winter landscape and with the other to "the piano / Where the Sarabande No. 1 lies open / At a passage I shall never master":

> He drops his jaw as if to say, or sing,
> "Between the world God made

And this music of Satie,
Each glimpsed through veils, but whole,
Radiant and willed,
Demanding praise, demanding surrender,
How can you sit there with your notebook?
What do you think you are doing?"
However he says nothing—wisely: I could mention
Flaws in God's world, or Satie's; and for that matter
How did he come by *his* taste for Satie?

Merrill's fine ironic twist—"However he says nothing"—highlights this further demonstration of the self's duplicity. While the angel's taste for Satie
is Merrill's, so is some version of the admonition not to keep scribbling.
Merrill's angel, who "does not want even these few lines written," is a negative of Rilke's, who is swayed *only* by the poet's willingness to be a beginner.
If there is something about the unsmiling, "round, hairless face" that even
suggests the angel of death in the guise of a tempter to pleasure and cuncta-
tion, he is no less part of the poet for that. Although Merrill seems to elect
perfection of the work over perfection of the life (to import Yeats's famous
distinction), "Angel" implies throughout that the two are bound up together. For one thing, if the poem pays its own tribute to Satie, it praises
also "'the world God made'" in its description of "winter snatching to its
heart, / To crystal vacancy, the misty / Exhalations of houses and of people
running home / From the cold sun pounding on the sea." For another
thing, the messenger himself, this otherworldly spokesman for the worldly,
seems to be a postcard reproduction of a detail in a Flemish painting. Finally, the sarabande whose beauties the angel urges on the poet will have
gone through a phase in its composition comparable to that which the notebook page is nominally in, "Its phrases thus far clotted, unconnected."
     This last line is intriguing in context. The poem's present tense and
these adjectives conflict, since "Angel" more closely resembles the meticulous art of the early Flemish painters than it does a rough draft. An early
example of Merrill's fondness for "rips & ripples & cracks which [stress] the
fabric of illusion," as he puts it in his next novel, this line inverts the practice
in "To a Butterfly." In that poem we see through the broken surface to the
carefully worked piece; in "Angel" we are invited to see through a pellucid
surface to the antecedent chaos. In both instances we are asked to ponder
the embranglements of the finished and the unfinished. Merrill does not
dwell on the point here, but that interaction is part and parcel of the relationship between art and life.
     Word and world are the subjects also of the cryptic "After Greece,"

though that is not clear at the outset. This too is a poem that blazes its own trail and that makes significant changes of direction at those points at which the speaker catches himself up. It opens with a quasi-biblical flourish and an elliptical rhetoric that evokes the essential luminosity—the candor—of Greece:

> Light into the olive entered
> And was oil. Rain made the huge pale stones
> Shine from within. The moon turned his hair white
> Who next stepped from between the columns,
> Shielding his eyes.

That first sentence would make an Imagist poem, with its small but endless circle of associations: sunlight produces the olive, whose oil has been used to yield light. Or perhaps the Imagist poem is two sentences long, or even three. If light has been translated into oil in the first, light and oil together turn into rain in the second. And those stones shining from within mediate between the olive and the moon of the third sentence. The three sentences interlock right down to the way in which each of the last two begins further along in the line than the preceding, so that they are steps down which we walk into the poem.

We are not told who the man is, but he could be the poet, thrust suddenly onto classical Greece's dilapidated stage and thus into the center of his own little drama. The question is, what to do with, or how to respond to, the awesome shambles?

> All through
> The countryside were old ideas
> Found lying open to the elements.
> Of the gods' houses only
> A minor premise here and there
> Would be balancing the heaven of fixed stars
> Upon a Doric capital.

Such imposing reminders of a glorious culture might well haunt him when he "sailed for home." They might even make him reconsider his true origins and proper domicile. From some such dissatisfaction comes the poem's first disjunction:

> The next week . . . I sailed for home.
> But where is home—these walls?

These limbs? The very spaniel underfoot
Races in sleep, toward what?
It is autumn. I did not invite
Those guests, windy and brittle, who drink my liquor.

Not that he can disown his actual home easily. Rather like Goethe's Mignon
(whom he will quote in "The Thousand and Second Night"), he "flee[s] in
dream," in this case back to the Acropolis, to the Erectheum—only to find
(as though he had been granted in 1962 a preview of the recent preservation
work) that his "great-great-grandmothers" have replaced the caryatids. Nor
can he feel, on reflection, passionate about the "old ideas" that, unlike the
ideas of the gods and goddesses, *have* endured from classical Greece until
today. By continuing the "dream" section of the poem, he allows the "Graces,
Furies, Fates" to speak, indirectly, and thus extends the dialogue with the
self:

They seem anxious to know
What holds up heaven nowadays.
I start explaining how in that vast fire
Were other irons—well, Art, Public Spirit,
Ignorance, Economics, Love of Self,
Hatred of Self, a hundred more,
Each burning to be felt, each dedicated
To sparing us the worst; how I distrust them
As I should have done those ladies . . .

As his "explaining" continues, it discloses Merrill's uneasiness in the presence of mere ideas. The same uneasiness has led him to quote with approval
Francis Ponge's verdict: "If ideas disappoint me, give me no pleasure, it is
because I offer them my approval too easily, seeing how they solicit it, are
only made for that . . . This offering, this consent, produces no pleasure in
me but rather a kind of queasiness, a nausea."[16] "How one agrees," Merrill
adds warmly. One problem with ideas such as those presented in "After
Greece," as the self-conscious capitalization admits, is their abstractness. In
the case of the earlier "capitals"—architectural rather than alphabetical—the
"ideas" took concrete forms. And the concrete is what the poet yearns for.
But even to say so is to defeat one's ends:

how I want
Essentials: salt, wine, olive, the light, the scream—
No! I have scarcely named you,

And look, in a flash you stand full-grown before me,
Row upon row, Essentials
Dressed like your sister caryatids
Or tombstone angels jealous of their dead,
With undulant coiffures, lips weathered, cracked by grime,
And faultless eyes gone blank beneath the immense
Zinc and gunmetal northern sky . . .

It is in this dazzling passage that the poem arrives at its true subject, the relationship between things and names, "Essentials" (the word is symptomatically ambiguous) and ideas of them. The point is the old paradoxical one: to specify by naming is to abstract. Merrill's very words indicate an instant before he seems to see it the impossibility of particularizing: the capital *E* in the first appearance of "Essentials," demanded by the line break, nonetheless ranges that word with the preceding abstractions, Art and Public Spirit and so on (as the second, clearly intentional capitalization confirms). The essences of "salt, wine, olive" escape in language, so that in effect all words are capitalized. Hence the marvelous transition to the repugnant "tombstone angels," themselves dead. In that transition we see a metamorphosis comparable to that of essential thing into word for that thing—or so the poet feels at this point.

Meanwhile, in a distinctively Merrillian reversal of a reversal, what has happened is that the "Essentials" have grown more and more specific as the metaphor has extended itself. The "tombstone angels" are repugnant because they are so vividly particularized.[17] Although language cannot ever be absolutely specific, this passage seems to say, it can nonetheless be strikingly so. All English letters are more or less equally abstract, though we might think we catch a glimpse of the original Sinaitic ox or house, but not all words are—or they are abstract in different ways. This passage moves between the comparatively abstract and the comparatively concrete, and its power derives from that movement. The poem's conclusion knowingly, wittily phrases the realization:

Stay then. Perhaps the system
Calls for spirits. This first glass I down
To the last time
I ate and drank in that old world. May I
Also survive its meanings, and my own.

The "system" is the cosmic system, and the poet's own system of ideas or poems still forming—though he could hardly have seen the extent to which he would rely upon yet other "spirits" in the *Sandover* books—and the physical system, the body, for the "spirits" are not only the Essentials to whom he drinks but also the whiskey with which he drinks to their health and his. Both puns bring together the abstract and the concrete in a configuration that would doubtless be satisfying to the poet who, a decade later, would insist on the interdependence of thoughts and things. "No thoughts, then, but in things? True enough, so long as the notorious phrase argues not for the suppression of thought but for its oneness with whatever in the world—pine woods, spider, cigarette—gave rise to it. Turn the phrase around, you arrive no less at truth: no things but in thoughts." [18]

"Literature is the better part of life," Stevens asserts in *Adagia*, but he hurries on to a qualification that Merrill would surely endorse: "To this it seems inevitably necessary to add, provided life is the better part of literature." [19] Something like this sentiment is at the heart of "For Proust," which follows the novelist on one of the nights when he would leave his cork-lined bedroom to attend a soirée where he might glean some more tiny details from the memories of an old acquaintance. The poem is written with a superbly diffident technique. So prudent are the choices of the key words and so sensitive is the disposition of syntax that one might read much of "For Proust" without realizing that the middle lines in each of these quatrains end in identical rhymes. The form is integral to the poem's plain but complex statement because its rigor answers the scrupulousness of its subject's attempts to get things right in his novel, and because the repetition it involves matches the novel's repetition of events from Proust's life. But the very pairing of terms in lines two and three of each quatrain makes us aware of difference at the same time that we see identity. We are led to consider the interplay between the same but different words and between the world and the literature that reflects it.

In the poem's transparent opening stanzas, all of the parts work together:

Over and over something would remain
Unbalanced in the painful sum of things.
Past midnight you arose, rang for your things.
You had to go into the world again.

You stop for breath outside the lit hotel,
A thin spoon bitter stimulants will stir.
Jean takes your elbow, Jacques your coat. The stir
Spreads—you are known to all the personnel—

As through packed public rooms you press (impending
Palms, chandeliers, orchestras, more palms,

The fracas and the fragrance) until your palms
Are moist with fear that you will miss the friend

Conjured—but she is waiting: a child still
At first glance . . .

Quotation is a tantalizing business here because the poem's nature is to per-
petuate itself by means of unbalancing balances. The first stanza, which has
such a solid feel about it, also includes destabilizing elements. Take the first
line, which begins with a repetition that foreshadows all the identical rhymes
and that implies the endless revisions Proust put his text through. This line
by itself has a relevant sense because so much did remain in Proust's mind to
provide the material for the novel. The tentative integrity of this line gives
way in its end, however, with Merrill's enjambment, and the word "Unbalanced" is a remainder that assures a continuation. The slight inequality of
"something" and "sum of things," an echo we might not hear at all if it were
not for the context, also helps to keep matters unsettled. It is as though the
difference were analogous to the discrepancy haunting Proust.

Perhaps without our understanding exactly what has happened, the
tense has changed from continuous past through simple past to present. The
effect is something like that of a legend fading on the screen ("Paris, rue du
Faubourg-St.-Honoré, 1921") as the camera closes in on the scene, so that
the past merges with the present. And indeed Proust has once more "had
to go into the world again": the poem makes him do so, even as its tense
change makes its oblique comment on the goal of his novel. After a brief
interview with his old friend, Proust returns to his "dim room," where now
"What happened is becoming literature." The final stanza balances the first
by changing out of the present tense into the future and then into the future
perfect. This modulation, along with this quatrain's opening phrase and its
own internal echo ("old, old"), pays tribute to time and the world:

Feverish in time, if you suspend the task,
An old, old woman shuffling in to draw
Curtains, will read a line or two, withdraw.
The world will have put on a thin gold mask.

But art also gets its due, especially in the last line, which draws together the
emphases in the preceding two on "the world" and "literature" respectively.
The phrase "a thin gold mask" offsets "The world" to the extent that it
evokes some perdurable work of art, comparable to Yeats's bird of "hammered gold and gold enamelling," that will have transfigured the world. Yet
if the gold mask makes us think of any specific piece, it would be the so-

called death mask of Agamemnon that Schliemann unearthed at Mycenae. Moreover, if the "thin gold mask" is further a figure for dawn, it is simultaneously a tribute to the imagination's power to renew and a reminder of time's passage.

This moving eulogy is but one of this volume's homages to Proust. The villanelle "The World and the Child" gives us another version—too close to its inspiration, I think—of the child's bedtime trauma at having to separate from a parent. More remarkable and delicate is Merrill's adaptation of Proust in "An Urban Convalescence," *Water Street*'s first poem, which amounts to a declaration of the new directions Merrill's work will take.

Like others of Merrill's poems, "An Urban Convalescence" even begins in a Proustian manner by taking a recent illness as its point of departure. On the way to recovery as the poem opens, the poet must confront a more dramatic example of the frailty of earthly things, the demolition of an old New York building, whose premature passing testifies to "The sickness of our time":

> Out for a walk, after a week in bed,
> I find them tearing up part of my block
> And, chilled through, dazed and lonely, join the dozen
> In meek attitudes, watching a huge crane
> Fumble luxuriously in the filth of years.
> Her jaws dribble rubble. An old man
> Laughs and curses in her brain,
> Bringing to mind the close of *The White Goddess*.

Actually Merrill is playfully conflating two passages at the end of Graves's book, that self-styled "Historical Grammar of Poetic Myth" which purports to reveal "the suppressed desire of the Western races . . . for some practical form of Goddess-worship" and which concludes with two poems that anticipate the goddess's return.[20] The first poem is intended to "placate" the goddess, whose awesome second coming Graves likens with relish to the descent of a murderous, "gaunt, red-wattled crane" on a group of complacent frogs. Hence Merrill's different kind of "crane," I suspect. Graves's other poem, in his own words, is "a satire on the memory of the man who first tilted European civilization off balance, by enthroning the restless and arbitrary male will under the name of Zeus and dethroning the female sense of orderliness, Themis." It ends as "an ignorant pale priest / Rides the beast with a man's head / To her long-omitted feast."

A figure not unlike Graves's "quintuple goddess"—a figure waggishly defined as "ONE QUINTESSENCE CHANEL NO / 5 × 5 × 5 × 5 × 5" and shown to have a taste for the apocalyptic as well—is at the heart of *Sandover*.

81

The mechanical monster of "An Urban Convalescence" has none of the later figure's charm and seems at first glance to lack the other's creative faculty— but perhaps she has a connection with the poet nonetheless. In the face of such common devastation as the rough beast of a crane represents, what manner of building *shall* we build? If Merrill's new manner of building is partly Proustian, that is because it demands that he too "Fumble luxuriously in the filth of years." Remembering and "building" (which term I mean first as a participle and second as a noun, as I think Stevens meant it) come to much the same thing in Merrill as in Proust before him. It is largely out of memory that the "academy" at Sandover is constructed—and constructed in part to replace the broken home. Home is not just a place or a physical structure. In "An Urban Convalescence" and "A Tenancy," even more tellingly than in "Prism" and "After Greece," Merrill answers that nagging question, "But where is home . . . ?", which goes back in some form to a story in *Jim's Book,* "Person to Person," where the heroine loses her long-sought, prospective home to an unscrupulous friend.

As an intrusion that introduced an internal dialogue, that question in "After Greece" is itself an element in Merrill's new manner of building. Here in "An Urban Convalescence," such rents in the poem's surface combine with attempts to call up the past. The whole first half of the poem might well be modeled on the famous section near the end of the Overture where Proust discovers the origin of the "plaisir délicieux" caused by the taste of the tea-dipped madeleine. Merrill's conjuring of the past, perforce less momentous than Proust's, is energetic and vivid:

> Head bowed, at the shrine of noise, let me try to recall
> What building stood here. Was there a building here at all?
> I have lived on this same street for a decade.
>
> Wait. Yes. Vaguely a presence rises
> Some five floors high, of shabby stone
> —Or am I confusing it with another one
> In another part of town, or of the world?—
> And over its lintel into focus vaguely
> Misted with blood (my eyes are shut)
> A single garland sways, stone fruit, stone leaves,
> Which years of grit had etched until it thrust
> Roots down, even into the poor soil of my seeing.

Though it seems that such a building as he sees in his mind's eye did once stand there, he might well be confusing it with "another one"—with, say, Aunt Léonie's in Combray. Marcel tells us how, after some disciplined reflection on the taste of the madeleine, the whole lost scene suddenly unfolds miraculously:

> . . . aussitôt la vieille maison grise sur la rue, où était sa chambre, vint comme un décor de théâtre s'appliquer au petit pavillon donnant sur le jardin, qu'on avait construit pour mes parents sur ses derrières (ce pan tronqué que seul j'avais revu jusque-là); et avec la maison, la ville, depuis le matin jusqu'au soir et par tous les temps, la Place où on m'envoyait avant déjeuner, les rues où j'allais faire des courses, les chemins qu'on prenait si le temps était beau.

> . . . immediately the old grey house upon the street, where her room was, rose up like a stage set to attach itself to the little pavilion opening on to the garden which had been built out behind it for my parents (the isolated segment which until that moment had been all that I could see); and with the house the town, from morning to night and in all weathers, the Square where I used to be sent before lunch, the streets along which I used to run errands, the country roads we took when it was fine.[21]

Not that Merrill's passage is an imitation of Proust's. The startling parenthesis in the excerpt quoted above—"(my eyes are shut)"—which introduces another new voice and assumes the presence of the reader, once more attests to Merrill's liking for "rips & ripples & cracks which [stress] the fabric of illusion." His humorous aside, which is really comparable to someone opening an eye a crack when he is supposed not to peek, reminds us to think of the poem not just as a dialogue with the self but also as a *written* work. By interrupting the mental process, itself the product in part of other interruptions ("Wait. Yes."), the parenthesis invigorates it in a manner altogether Merrill's. Yet one is aware of Proust's presence. Even the "shudder" that Proust felt on first remembering the madeleine ("je tressaillis") has its counterpart in Merrill's "shiver" as his own memories continue to unfold from a further question:

> When did the garland become part of me?
> I ask myself, amused almost,
> Then shiver once from head to toe,
>
> Transfixed by a particular cheap engraving of garlands
> Bought for a few francs long ago,
> All calligraphic tendril and cross-hatched rondure,
> Ten years ago, and crumpled up to stanch

Boughs dripping, whose white gestures filled a cab,
And thought of neither then nor since.
Also, to clasp them, the small, red-nailed hand
Of no one I can place. Wait. No. Her name, her features
Lie toppled underneath that year's fashions.

In the teeth of the earlier reminder of the poem's composed nature, this passage reasserts its meditative process. Merrill's slight waywardness is exact, his technique one with the immediacy of these lines. It would be pointless to wonder, for instance, whether calculation or fidelity to the mental experience lies behind the way "Ten years ago" loops back to revise the less specific "long ago." Merrill's second hesitation ("Wait. No.") is a fine musical touch, as it echoes and reverses his first, but it is nonetheless urgent for that.

This intense, flexible process is a way of accommodating the natural world, which lives on change. The finished product is soon finished indeed; the "garland" is a gloomy irony. "As usual in New York, everything is torn down / Before you have had time to care for it." And we understand "New York" to represent more than that city itself—just as, when Merrill enters his own building later in the poem and "the pages of *Time* are apt / To open, and the illustrated mayor of New York, / Given a glimpse of how and where I work, / To note yet one more house that can be scrapped," we know the mayor to be a proxy figure, a sort of secretary in the employ of Proust's great competitor. Sooner or later one's own experiences "Lie toppled under that year's fashions." When the poet fails to recall his former friend's name or features, an entire edifice of recollections "collapses" as though its keystone had been removed. At the same time, Merrill's varied pentameter gives way to shorter, less regular lines, and then the verse paragraph crumbles before our eyes:

So that I am already on the stair,
As it were, of where I lived,
When the whole structure shudders at my tread
And soundlessly collapses, filling
The air with motes of stone.
Onto the still erect building next door
Are pressed levels and hues—
Pocked rose, streaked greens, brown whites.
Who drained the pousse-café?
Wires and pipes, snapped off at the roots, quiver.

Well, that is what life does. I stare
A moment longer, so. And presently

The massive volume of the world
Closes again.

Upon that book I swear
To abide by what it teaches:
Gospels of ugliness and waste,
Of towering voids, of soiled gusts,
Of a shrieking to be faced
Full into, eyes astream with cold—

With cold?
All right then. With self-knowledge.

This final self-directed question invites him to recognize the truth of the sarcastic vow taken in the preceding passage, to own up to his part in the entropic drift—a part just witnessed by his inability to call up the image of his companion in Paris. That the city *was* Paris we infer from the poem's last stanza, but we might have guessed from the "few francs" paid for the engraving and the pousse-café. It is a masterful touch, this line on the pousse-café, which is the kind on which all of a poem's elements (along with its guiding spirits Ariel and Prospero) converge for an instant.[22] It has the levels and hues of its layered cordial; it brings together the New York scene and the memory of Paris by means of the startling comparison of the discolored building and the emptied glass, and it specifies the common denominator in a question that suddenly seems rhetorical. After Merrill has answered it anyway ("that is what life does"), and Prospero has seemingly taken over, the meditation grinds to a temporary halt in two terse, grim lines.

This is the point Merrill had reached when he thought the poem would be "impossible to finish." Then he "had the idea of letting it go back to a more formal pattern at the end." Modeling his resolution on a musical structure—"a Toccata (or introduction) and Allegro"—he let some "quatrains wind up a poem which threatened to fall away."[23] At the same moment that he enters upon his regular stanzas, he also comes "Indoors"—a correspondence of structures that anticipates the poem's conclusion. As he looks about his rooms and muses on his own "walls weathering," however, he finds himself using a language that threatens his stanzas' continued existence, and in interrupting himself to deal with it he strengthens his work—and enlarges its scope enormously. The subject is the "new buildings" that replace buildings like the one that has just been torn down:

The sickness of our time requires
That these as well be blasted in their prime.

You would think the simple fact of having lasted
Threatened our cities like mysterious fires.

There are certain phrases which to use in a poem
Is like rubbing silver with quicksilver. Bright
But facile, the glamour deadens overnight.
For instance, how "the sickness of our time"

Enhances, then debases, what I feel.

This sudden criticism of his meretricious phrasing parallels the earlier correction of his attribution of his tears to "cold" and confirms his resolution
for candor. The point is to keep Prospero's counsel even if Ariel's lead has
been followed in regard to prosodic matters.

Is his admission of a weakness for the "Bright / But facile" phrase the
(bitter) "pill" he swallows at poem's end? Or is that pill no more or less than
a medication, assigned an effect similar to that of Marcel's petite madeleine,
not only in its resurrection of an experience but also in its power to an-
nounce to the writer his calling? There is a sense here at the end of his
having set himself "afloat":

At my desk I swallow in a glass of water
No longer cordial, scarcely wet, a pill
They had told me not to take until much later.

With the result that back into my imagination
The city glides, like cities seen from the air,
Mere smoke and sparkle to the passenger
Having in mind another destination

Which now is not that honey-slow descent
Of the Champs-Elysées, her hand in his,
But the dull need to make some kind of house
Out of the life lived, out of the love spent.

The gist of this passage seems at first that henceforth his concern is not romantic experience but rather the quotidian labor of turning that experience
into poems. That descent of the Champs-Elysées retraces the journey down
from Eden into the fallen world. Work is Adam's curse. But while the need
and much of the occupation might be "dull," one could not tell that from
this writing. On the contrary, the confident suspension of the concluding
sentence, the glissade of a transition from the descent of the airplane to that
of the taxi going down the avenue, and the last line's triumphant, redoubled

echo of the poem's first word are inspired touches, romantic in their way. Whatever love has been spent on passionate affairs, much remains to be spent on writing.

The conclusion of "An Urban Convalescence" understands life and poetry, to adopt a phrase from Stevens just once more, as "the things that in each other are included." Merrill might seem to distinguish the two by renouncing a glamorous life in favor of the "dull need" to write. But the tentative distinction cannot survive a complete reading of this passage, with its treatment of projected oeuvre as house.[24] The metaphor is so apt and full that the relationship cannot justly be called figurative. Consider Gaston Bachelard's description of the house as "one of the greatest powers of integration for the thoughts, memories and dreams of mankind . . . In the life of a man, the house thrusts aside contingencies, its [counsels] of continuity are unceasing. Without it, man would be a dispersed being."[25] He could be describing someone's body of poetry. Nor will it confuse matters if the phrase "body of poetry" recalls that Freud thought "the dwelling-house was [in its origin] a substitute for the mother's womb, the first lodging, for which in all likelihood man still longs, and in which he was safe and felt at ease."[26] For we will remember how Merrill has described his relationship to his poetry: "I can't imagine my own life without poetry. It created me." His need to make some kind of house is no less than his need to make his life, to reshape it in his work. Poetic work and house merge a few pages later in Bachelard's meditation:

> The great function of poetry is to give us back the situations of our dreams. The house we were born in is more than an embodiment of home, it is also an embodiment of dreams. Each one of its nooks and corners was a resting-place for daydreaming. And often the resting place particularized the daydream. Our habits of a particular daydream were acquired there. The house, the bedroom, the garret in which we were alone, furnished the framework for an interminable dream, one that poetry alone, through the creation of a poetic work, could succeed in achieving completely.[27]

Merrill made similar associations when he sat down to compose the opening for his contribution to a series called "The Making of a Writer":

> Interior spaces, the shape and correlation of rooms in a house, have always appealed to me. Trying for a blank mind, I catch myself instead revisiting a childhood bedroom on Long Island. Recently, on giving up the house in Greece where I'd lived for much of the previous

15 years, it wasn't so much the fine view it commanded or the human
comedies it had witnessed that I felt deprived of; rather, I missed the
hairpin turn of the staircase underfoot, the height of our kitchen ceiling, the low door ducked through in order to enter a rooftop laundry
room that had become my study. This fondness for given arrangements
might explain how instinctively I took to quatrains, to octaves and ses-
tets, when I began to write poems. "Stanza" is after all the Italian word
for "room."[28]

Placed at the other end of *Water Street,* "A Tenancy" too involves a vow,
and its central images also have to do with buildings. It further resembles
"An Urban Convalescence" in prosodic structure; it moves from verse paragraphs to expediently rhymed quintets, so that once again the tighter form
interrupts and supersedes the looser. Merrill could not have written whichever came second ("A Tenancy," surely) without thinking often of its predecessor. They differ in the stance he takes toward the material, "A Tenancy"
seeming more certain of its direction, and in the point of view he has on the
commitment to writing—for whereas "An Urban Convalescence" is largely
prospective, "A Tenancy" is chiefly retrospective.

"A Tenancy" ends in the present tense, and ends implicitly looking to
the future, but it hinges on a much earlier scene, when Merrill would have
been on the threshold of his twentieth year—the year that saw the publication of *The Black Swan:*

Something in the light of this March afternoon
Recalls that first and dazzling one
Of 1946. I sat elated
In my old clothes, in the first of several
Furnished rooms, head cocked for the kind of sound
That is recognized only when heard.
A fresh snowfall muffled the road, unplowed
To leave blanker and brighter
The bright, blank page turned overnight.

The sound that the former self awaited was the kind that "light" makes next
to "elated" or the related kind that the rhyme makes at the stanza's close—
the kind that begins a poem. But that sound, that invitation, as Valéry
noted, might be all that is given the poet. The young man recalled here must
have expected more. The "old clothes" he wore as he sat down to *work* betray
a certain naiveté, as does his intention "to seize the Real / Old-Fashioned

Winter of my landlord's phrase." If he imagined (like Francis Tanning, who once thought there was "'something magical in fine old things, that would have helped [him] *be*'") that he might extract poetry from the period pieces in his room, from "the ponderous idées reçues / Of oak, velour, crochet," he was bound to discover that "the objects . . . The more I looked grew shallower." The real "stereoscope" in this poem is formed not by "The 9 and 6" of the date, but by the views of the two selves. Where that young man saw only shallow objects, the poet writing about him sees that the objects reflect the young man's own shallowness and inexperience and therefore have the depth he was unable to discover before.

A sense of the frustration in that early experience with "clotted, unconnected" phrases reaches us by way of the furnishings that "Pined under a luminous plaid robe / Thrown over" them by shadows of mullions and sashes, the "rage" of a previous storm, and the sudden disgust with the wallpaper. But Merrill's emphasis is not on the difficulty of composition but on the determination to compose:

> [The windows,]
> Washed in a rage, then left to dry unpolished,
> Projected onto the inmost wall
> Ghosts of the storm, like pebbles under water.
>
> And indeed, from within, ripples
> Of heat had begun visibly bearing up and away
> The bouquets and wreathes of a quarter century.
> Let them go, what did I want with them?
> It was time to change that wallpaper!
> Brittle, sallow in the new radiance,
> Time to set the last wreath floating out
> Above the dead, to sweep up flowers. The dance
> Had ended, it was light; the men looked tired
> And awkward in their uniforms.
> I sat, head thrown back, and with the dried stains
> Of light on my own cheeks, proposed
> This bargain with—say with the source of light:
> That given a few years more
> (Seven or ten or, what seemed vast, fifteen)
> To spend in love, in a country not at war,
> I would give in return
> All I had. All? A little sun
> Rose in my throat. The lease was drawn.

Time to change that wallpaper indeed! And before we know it, Merrill has changed its flowers to funeral wreaths and abandoned corsages and boutonnieres and has sketched in a setting appropriate to the latter two. Insubstantial, volatile, his images through here have the quality of things seen through water. From the earlier reference to the "shallower" objects through the "ripples" of heat, the poem has been preparing to free the wreaths and bouquets from their enchantment in the wallpaper, to slip them off like decals, so that they could mark different ends, which coincide with the end of a period in the poet's life. These images are still surprising and almost oneiric, however, and they tell us indirectly of the young poet's frame of mind. Where the men in uniform come from is something of a mystery, but I imagine that Merrill is remembering a wartime dance (he had been in the army a year or so before)—though it is possible, if we presume that the "first of several / Furnished rooms" was in the city, that he is remembering looking out his window at the last couples to leave a postwar party.

It is essential only that we see that the dance enacts the process of composition and that the "source of light" is the creative power itself—whatever that means. If it is inspiration, it is also inseparable from the passionate rigors of writing, as those "dried stains" of light (ghosts of the "Stains of egg" in "Prism") must hint. It also seems (as though we were in *Ephraim* already) to be one with time, since the poem brings us, by way of the line "I did not even feel the time expire" (where fifteen years disappear in a blink), to the present tense and situation, in which "A changing light is deepening, is changing / To a gilt ballroom chair a chair / Bound to break under someone before long." "I let the light change also me," he adds—as he lets the meter change the expected word order—though he has his tongue in his cheek, since to the extent that the light of this world is time, he cannot but let it change him as well.

Because the light is time, and because it is the creative power with which Merrill has made a bargain, and because "the dance" has been a way of figuring writing, the chair's transformation during the fifteen years since 1946 has other implications as well. These are lines written with confidence—lines written by a man who has lived up to his bargain. He has given what he could, he has changed, and therefore he himself has changed that chair to a ballroom chair. If in a sense the light has done it, well, a "little sun / Rose" in his throat a long time before. Whether the passage of time or his commitment is primarily responsible, the "body" of those earlier years has itself been transfigured. "Would it be called a soul?" he wonders:

It knows, at any rate,
That when the light dies and the bell rings

Its leaner veteran will rise to face
Partners not recognized
Until drunk young again and gowned in changing
Flushes; and strains will rise,
The bone-tipped baton beating, rapid, faint,
From the street below, from my depressions—

From the doorbell which rings.

Before the world intervenes to dispel the mystery, this poem turns somewhat esoteric. The dying light and the "Partners" will recall that afternoon and long night fifteen years earlier—but what of the bell and the
"leaner veteran" who must "rise to face" those partners? To see this passage
whole we must understand the encounter also as one of Merrill's wrestling
matches—a match, like Jacob's, between the poet and his Angel. At the same
time, as the blending of dance and wrestling match demands, this passage's
"changing / Flushes," "bone-tipped baton" (an unambiguous "index" in the
magazine version), and repeated "rise" have sexual overtones.[29] The "body"
nearly lost in "soul" returns here, albeit in the poem's most dreamlike passage. (When the doorbell breaks into his reverie, and he gets up to let his
friends enter, he finds "One foot asleep.") We are not far, it seems to me,
from the long poems in *Nights and Days,* where inspiration and erotic yearning come together. I am reminded too of a theme in William Gass's work. As
Gass expresses it in an essay, "Painting and poetry (to name just two [arts])
are sexual acts. The artist is a lover, and he must woo his medium till she
opens to him; until the richness in her rises to the surface like a blush." [30]

To think hard is to feel, to write is to make love, to make a poem or a
book of poems is "to make some kind of house." This kind of house must be
broken into in order to be sound, and this poem gains its integrity with an
interruption (which gives a plainer if incomplete meaning to the "bell" and
the "Partners"). When the poet answers the doorbell, here at the book's end,
three friends enter and "stamp / Themselves free of the spring's / Last snow."
What a difference from "In the Hall of Mirrors," the last major poem in *The
Country of a Thousand Years of Peace,* which concludes with a couple's departure from a sort of Eden which immediately recovers its cold, pristine
perfection: "From glass to glass an interval / Widens like moonrise over
frost / No tracks have ever crossed." Here the friends bring the world in
with them:

One has brought violets in a pot;
The second, wine; the best,

91

His open, empty hand. Now in the room
The sun is shining like a lamp.
I put the flowers where I need them most

And then, not asking why they come,
Invite the visitors to sit.
If I am host at last
It is of little more than my own past.
May others be at home in it.

The self-effacing simplicity indicates the change in Merrill's poetry. He will rarely be as plain as he is here, to the disappointment of some readers, but he will always honor the claims of the world. The light has changed a bit more. His early poems, Louise Bogan lamented, "are impeccably written, but everything about them smells of the lamp."[31] Here the lamp has combined with the sun, the study has been opened to friends and flowers. Not that Merrill has given up "art" for "life." On the contrary, as we shall learn in a later poem in which he takes up Bogan's stinging criticism. Meanwhile, where he needs those flowers most is in this poem.

"But where is home?" For the nonce, it is right here, in this homeliest of language.

> > >

As for *The (Diblos) Notebook* (1965), it cannot even begin before it interrupts itself. A second thought is its first word. Ariel and Prospero strike a perfect discord at once.

"~~Orestes~~": From this singular duple opening, at once a word and its cancellation, *The (Diblos) Notebook* unfolds, rather as Liszt thought his Preludes unfolded from a simple five-note theme. It concerns itself throughout with the kinds of parallels and counterparts, oppositions and complements that often engaged Merrill in *Water Street*. Not for nothing does the title's parenthetical word, which names the island where the novel is set, sound like the Greek word for "double." When Atheneum published the novel in 1965, the dust jacket (like the cover of the paperbound edition) bore a photograph of two statues, which stand in the courtyard of a villa on Delos known as the House of Cleopatra. The statues represent the house's two Athenian owners, Cleopatra and Dioscourides, and thus foreshadow the novel's domestic themes. Gown and tunic make it clear that the damaged figures—standing side by side on the same base, each with the right arm bent across the waist—are female and male, but their heads have been knocked off, a feature that further unites them, that bears on issues of identity raised in the text, and that comports with the revisionary mode that Merrill has devised for this novel, whose virtuosity almost conceals its intelligence.

This mode has affinities with the work of Francis Ponge, whose distinction Merrill has defined in pertinent terms: "Ponge may be the first poet ever to expose so openly the machinery of a poem, to present his revisions, blind alleys, critical asides, and accidental felicities as part of a text perfected, as it were, without 'finish' . . . One meets a mind desiring and deferring, both, according to the laws of baroque music, solution and resolution."[32] Merrill's book too is a daring piece of openwork that fills its margins with comments on itself. It presents itself as a notebook kept by an American, about twenty-seven years old, who has returned to a Greek island, never given an actual name but identifiable as Poros because of its vantage on a mainland geological formation called the Sleeping Woman, whose "intense, dreamlike" presence, one with "'the mother country'" herself, is felt throughout the book until, at the end, she "has veered & reshifted into new non-representational masses." The narrator had visited the island some seven years before and become involved in events he means to use as a springboard for a novel, his "1st *long* piece of work."[33] His notebook consists on the one hand of the incomplete draft of this novel, with its cancellations, breakings off, lists of options, revisions, and one thirty-two page "finished" section in "fair copy," and on the other hand of his journal, with its record of encounters, dreams (one printed upside down), and reflections on the novel and its sources, one of which is this journal.

We need a paraphrase of the information given us piecemeal and by implication through the book. The narrator's mother, Eleni, a Greek merchant's daughter, married a Greek goatherd, with whom she had a son, Yannis, later to be known as Orson. The family emigrated from Asia Minor to New York, where—with the help of an American named Arthur Orson, whose life the Greek man had saved during World War II and who was to be the child's godfather—they took up a new life. Before long, however, the father died, and Eleni married a second time; her second husband is a Texas oilman named John, the narrator's father, with whom she still lives in Houston. Seven years before the present, Orson, the narrator's half-brother, a thirty-five-year-old professor in search of his roots, revisited Greece. On board a boat to Diblos, he met a man we know as Mr. N., who in turn introduced him to Dora, the island's doyenne. Fifty-six years old, the daughter of a Greek ambassador and one of the Queen's ladies-in-waiting, Dora was born in Russia, where her father was posted, and grew up there and in England (perhaps because her family was exiled after the overthrow of the monarchy). As a child she spoke English and French, and she later added

Greek and then Italian. She married an Italophone Greek painter, Tassos, considerably older than she, with whom she had a son, Byron, who is about Orson's age. Tassos, by then a neurasthenic invalid, died six weeks after Orson came to Diblos, and Dora invited Orson, whose exuberant romanticism charmed her, to live in her cottage, behind the main house, where he could do his translations and reviews in peace. In love with Greece, or with his idea of Greece, and enthralled by Dora, he leapt at the chance and in short order renovated the cottage.

The narrator, whose name is John, after his father, then twenty years old, came to Greece in the spring following the summer in which Orson arrived. He warmed to Dora immediately, as she to him, while Orson, effusive and opinionated and doting, inspired an embarrassed awe. One evening they attended a panegyri, a festival, where Orson and the narrator, the latter spectacularly drunk, danced together. Orson spent that night with someone else, an event that unexpectedly made Dora jealous. Because of her manners and self-control, the scene between them seemed little more than a contretemps, but Orson's "betrayal" would eventually help end their relationship. Not long after this incident Orson and Dora went to the United States, where he was to begin teaching in New York City. They made a marriage of convenience so that Dora could remain in America, but after four hard years, during which she had to take work as a governess and suffered an amnesiac breakdown, they decided to separate. In the three years since the separation the narrator has maintained his relationship with Dora, thriving in her "narrow New York flat," and has occasionally been in touch with Orson, but he has done nothing to encourage their reunion and has thus hurt his half-brother.

Now, seven years after that initial visit to Diblos, the narrator has returned to work on a novel based on the relationship between Orson and Dora. His visit this time, the notebook entries tell us, covers the period between June 15, 1961, and August 6, 1961. He moves into the local hotel— and forthwith inspires a "galloping passion" in its maid, one Chryssoula, who has six children and a black cat. He runs into an American girl, Lucine, a painter, whom he has met briefly at a luncheon in Athens with the N's, Dora's old friends, and meets an aging, pudgy, all too plausible type who calls himself, after the Parisian boutique, L'Enfant Chic. One day, when the narrator has meant to take a look at Dora's house, now in Byron's charge, events lead him instead to discover the island's slaughterhouse, near which he is seized by an attack of dysentery. After he has recovered, the N's turn up unannounced to sweep him and Lucine away on their caïque to Epidauros, where they see the *Oresteia* performed—and where he learns, to his great surprise, that Orson too has returned to Greece. When the N's invite him and Lucine to join them on a tour of the islands, Lucine accepts, but he declines and thereby puts an end to their little affair. He has his novel to get on with. (Except for that last detail, which gives his life a specific direction, his relationship with Lucine reminds one strongly of Francis's with Jane.)

He finally sees "the House" from a distance, tries writing the novel from Orson's point of view and abandons the attempt, and visits the site of the panegyri. Though Byron behaves well enough when the narrator meets him, the latter turns down an invitation to have a drink at Dora's house. He writes out the fair copy of that section of his novel which deals with the period that his two main characters spend together in New York. Just after he has finished copying out that section, fiction and reality intersect, as Orson—whom we have seen only as the unfinished novel's Orestes—appears on Diblos. Although he has earlier harbored hopes that he could make a legal claim on Dora's cottage, Orson seems to have relinquished them now, and he evidently goes to Dora's house simply to look one last time at the place where he has been happiest and to collect personal belongings. Once there, however (and this we learn from report, since as in the tradition Orson reveres, the climactic violence takes place offstage), he meets Byron, whose injured pride provokes him to drive Orson off the property with a riding crop. Bleeding from the head, Orson walks back to town in a euphoria of suffering, aware through the pain that his fantasies of emulating a tragic hero have somehow been realized. He meets his brother and the N's, who have put in at Diblos on the last leg of their cruise. As *The (Diblos) Notebook* ends, Orson and the N's have sailed for Athens, and the narrator, having decided to give up his novel and return to the United States, is following on another boat.

The narrator's novel, as far as we can tell, owes a good deal to what we can perhaps still call reality. Some figures get fictional names (the narrator becomes Sandy, and Orson becomes Orestes, a name the character significantly chooses for himself), but others (Arthur Orson, Byron, Tassos, Eleni, Dora) retain their "real" ones. There is a comparable relationship between the "actual" events and the narrator's reshaping of them in his fiction. Some discrepancies are more or less explicit: in the narrator's novel, instead of being introduced by Mr. N., Orestes and Dora meet by accident when he is searching for the Sleeping Woman; Sandy's father is a cattleman rather than an oilman; the actual four years in New York are compressed into eight months; Sandy's hepatitis might be an invention. None of these differences is significant as such, however. What counts is that it is often impossible to separate the actual from the fictional. Indeed, one of the chief advantages of the notebook form is that the actual and the fictional can be made to blend in a hundred ways. Thus it is the narrator's custom simply to enclose in parentheses the actual names he has not yet found substitutes for and to continue by fits and starts his novel's story. As he observes with some chagrin late in the notebook, it is telling that he can never rechristen several of his characters. Merrill himself has disclaimed any novelistic talent and ambition on the grounds that he cannot invent, and there is that much of him (and more) in his young writer—who I suppose thereby bears out his inventor's point.[34] The parentheses hover around "(Diblos)" as though to remind us of the special bubble of a world in which it exists. That "Diblos" is in fact a made-up name passing as a real name in need of a fictional equivalent is representative of the issues that this novel worries.

The conception of a novel involving a notebook incites Merrill to many different techniques. In fact, one is tempted to find in the narrator's catalogue of the waves' movements as they break on the rocks at his feet (a catalogue he assigns to his fictive projection) analogies for the movements in the notebook:

> (Sandy, feverish) tried to name their different movements: the ~~swirl~~ pirouette, the recoil, the beat missed on purpose, the upward hurl of white nets, the pounce, the pause for reflection; but no two were ever accomplished with quite the same motive or, for that matter, success. Again & again an ornate sequence would inexplicably break down; the sea would shrug, collapse, retire into a slot, a coulisse prudently hollowed out of rock beforehand. For an instant the stage would be empty; one felt a sad kinship with the effaced gesture. Then a new star a crash of harps! A new, staggeringly assured star, all mist & fretted crystal, had leapt and "frozen" . . .

Use this to complement description on p. 17

It is as a novelist whose own ornate sequences break down that Merrill's narrator can feel "a sad kinship with the effaced gesture." From Merrill's point of view, however, even the effacing can be a permanent flourish; his own ornate sequence consists in part of such collapses as that following "a new star" above. The rougher the form, the more refined the possibilities.

For once, or so it seems, a novelist can have his words and eat them too. The realization might well have overwhelmed Merrill, as the waves' endless permutations do Sandy. Here after all was a poet who had schooled himself in *le mot juste*, who had reconciled himself to the fact that writing poetry is in large part a matter of making choices, of concentration and excision. Imagine, then, finding a "form" that allowed, nay, demanded inclusion of alternatives rather than exclusion. The prospect must have been at once exhilarating and fatiguing. If he wanted "swirl" because of its rhyme with "hurl" but wanted also the superior specificity of "pirouette," he could have both. Is he uncertain whether a particular placidity is more that of the doctor or that of the patient? Then he can prefer one and admit the merit of the alternative as well: "Her face is moonlight gray & mild, as if about to ~~administer~~ receive an anesthetic." A page later, that idea and others can be broken down like the raw material in the alembic and suddenly be reborn in a lyric outburst:

> Neither cold nor hot, the moonlight had the flimsiness of gauze,
> the intensity of frost. It was a gas inhaled
> Holding my hand for comfort
> inhale this gas
> made by the cricket's voice
> Acting on ~~dark bl~~ indigo oxygen
> blind I go!

Of the various recombinations in Merrill's work, few are more satisfying than that last discovery above, an example, if you will, of a "new, staggeringly assured star" who has "leapt" onto the empty stage. Its full significance will not appear until the novel's end, however.

The waves' repertoire includes other movements reminiscent of some of Merrill's techniques. The "pause for reflection" might well send us back to the panegyri:

> Then this simple dance would end, another kind of tune begin, a single young fisherman spin, dip, snap, leap his way through it, eyes always on the earth; or an older dancer, closer to earth in another sense, allude
> execute slow allusions to the passion & agility he no longer commanded.

Or perhaps it is more helpful to think of that hesitation, revision, and resumption as a dip in the *zeybékiko* itself. A little further along in the memory of the panegyri comes a passage that one cannot help but connect with "the recoil, the beat missed on purpose" in Sandy's amazed catalogue of special effects. Orestes is dancing with a man named Kosta:

> ~~H~~hissing like serpents . . . they circled one another until, suddenly, on an emphatic beat
> The very hissing is sexual—sssss! It's of course the consonant missing from a married woman's name (put in the genitive: Mr Pappas, Mrs Pappa, etc.) and so commends itself to the dancer as a tiny linguis-

tic feature related to moustache & phallus, one more fine feather of virility—

beat, Kosta jumped & landed not on the ground but in midair, with legs wrapped about O.'s waist, head fallen back, shoulders still undulating.

The parenthesis in the intervening central paragraph is an amusing example of Merrill's liking for reversible truths. Even as the subtracted consonant makes the Greek name feminine, the name Merrill has his narrator choose becomes a bilingual pun with a masculine sense, while the allegedly male sibilant returns in "Mrs." It is as though language itself were effortlessly subverting the narrator's supersubtle attempts to interpret it. The most striking thing about the passage, however, is the syncopation that the donnée has fostered.

The notebook format opens a dozen other doors for Merrill. He can omit potentially tedious exposition altogether while pretending that the narrator has deferred it until some future draft: "He fetches clothes & books from Athens. The cottage needs a new roof. He sleeps the 1st weeks in the big house." How easy, how expeditious a novel is after all! He can act as his own exegete: "Dora's amnesia—which comes off as well as anything—is largely my experience at the slaughterhouse (p. 17) transformed." He can make the text reflect or embody an action reported in it—as when a thought strikes the narrator and one of his characters at virtually the same moment:

They nodded civilly. An artisan O. sup
On a proprietary impulse, Orestes turned and called after him.

Who needs the pun, which depends so upon the reader's piercing of its disguise, when you can write two things, delete one, and then let it stand? "'Arrived where?' cried his ~~friends~~ tormentors." A more dialectical use of superficial deletion occurs near the end of the novel: "I had a sense of other less personal elements, beauty, joy, truth, splendor—~~things ideas~~ all whose ebbing over the years had been so gradual . . ."

Things and ideas. Life and art. The novel is built on the dichotomy as on a fault, since the narrator's notebook is half diary, half draft. The characters—whether in Merrill's novel or in the narrator's draft—tend to side either with life or with art. The maid Chryssoula—a profane translation of Merrill's "Angel"—tries continually to seduce the narrator, to take him away from his work. Lucine too, though a painter herself, reproaches him for devoting himself selfishly to his fiction. The narrator, for his part, sees the women as distractions or material. He knows that he is "cold to people" and fancies that "it's that, the coldness, the remoteness, that attracts them. If I were warmer, talked more, showed more interest, *felt* more interest—." Even on the foreign island, he is "not lonely enough." He would seem to agree with the Yeats of "The Circus Animals' Desertion," who admits that "Players and painted stage took all my love, / And not those things that they were emblems of." He realizes that he is "playing with [Orson and Dora] in effigy, loving the effigies alone." [35]

The tension between Dora and Orestes is that between the impulses toward life and art. Not that Orestes has much of the artist proper in him: "O. valued the creative act too highly to perform it." If that aperçu reminds us that it is Orestes whose talk is said to pop "like a fire with allusion and paradox," it will be salutary to remember that the narrator and he have much in common, not least their reservations about quotidian living. Orestes too—who does not sweat even when performing the Greek dances he has taken so much care to learn—has a definite coldness about him. He speaks more truly than he knows when he claims, in response to Dora's early oblique invitation to play cards with her, "I have no talent for such things. I would play a diamond instead of a heart." Much later, after he and Dora have become involved and he has stunned her by sleeping with someone else, he tells Sandy that Dora means too much to him for him "'to risk the ambiguities, the tensions of a sexual relationship. She sees it, she agrees with me.'" That, surely, is to play the diamond instead of the heart. Although the narrator tells us that after his arrival in Diblos "Orestes' Latinate vocabulary (his emotions) now gave way to authentic, simple forms: sea, sky, vine, house, plate, stone, woman :rock sea sun wine goat sky," he treats these things with a repellent, vitiating romanticism. He recites stanzas of poetry over flowers seen on walks with Dora. On the occasion of his final evening with Dora, he plans "'to let art have the last word,'" and he takes her to see *Othello*. As tears well in his eyes at the play's end, Dora falls asleep.

The narrator means to sum up the tension between Orestes and Dora in a "Dialogue on the Acropolis," an "organ-point in the book." Orestes' taste runs to "Shakespeare, Flowers, The ~~Monumental~~ Sublime," while Dora prefers "Racine, Herbs, The Subtle," so it stands to reason that they would admire the Parthenon and the Erectheum respectively. The one is "honey-colored," "a lyre the sun fingered," and is "marvelous for its bigness, its openness: a sire, a seer. The father in a novel about a happy childhood." "The other," with the symbolic balcony that Orestes (quick with his Freud as usual) points out,

by comparison seems dangerously complex & arbitrary
Japanese   a small-boned woman

a dressing-table at which somebody has assembled the various elements—powder, eye-shadow, a pleated ~~robe~~ teagown—of a "je ne sais quoi" & vanished, for no more than a moment, surely, into another room.

From the narrator's point of view, "they represent, with a purity & clarity far from mortal,* the two modes of being. The moon, the sun; the earth, the soul; the wife, the god." A carefully worked up set piece, this passage reveals how illusory is the rough quality of the narrator's draft. It brings together in its different styles the characters of the two buildings: just as there is something "complex & arbitrary" about the comparisons of the Erectheum to a Japanese woman and her dressing table, so there is something "noble, simple" and "Sublime" about the perfectly balanced contrast.

But the clarity of that contrast, which dominates this passage as Winckelmann's interpretation of the Greek architects' virtues does our view of them, is the problem, as the narrator's pendant to this passage, the footnote designated by the asterisk, admits:

*far from mortal—here's my mistake. My Dialogue pits 2 dreams against each other, instead of living antagonists. Life, Art—they are words. It's on a lower level that the mongoose closes with the cobra. In a footnote. In the dust.

"Over and over something would remain / Unbalanced in the painful sum of things," Proust found, and the narrator, who comes as close here to merging with Merrill as he ever does, wants to keep from deceiving himself with antithesis and symmetry. The footnote is to the page what the balcony is to the Erectheum—an unsettling element. Its gist is very near Yeats's summation: "Man can embody truth but he cannot know it."[36] The difficulty is that to write so abstractly about life and art is to sort them out misleadingly. The real dialogue here—for the footnote is yet another way Merrill has discovered to interrupt himself—is between the text and the gloss. The note engages the text, breaks up its teeter-totter logic. With the footnote, the thought begins to emulate mongoose and cobra; it becomes the counterpart of the wrestling match with the angel, or of the *zeybékiko* as it is danced by practiced Greeks, "a meditation[,] the body itself thinking, choosing, rejoicing."

If it were not for the footnote, this passage would deteriorate into something as mechanical as Orestes' lecture before the British Council on "The Tragic Dualism of Man," a futile conjuration of polarities: "Body &

Soul, Eros & Death, Time & Eternity . . ." Later he imagines, after a disappointing night at a Greek restaurant in New York, that "the two natures," Greek and American, "absolutely did not mix." This Puritan predilection to declare things immiscible is foreign to Dora, a mixture herself of languages and experiences. When we meet her on the novel's first page we learn that she has "grown used" to a certain "contradiction" in the Greek landscape that at first seems "inconceivable" to the narrator. The novel lives precisely in its own vital contrariety, and the footnote is a microcosm of the novel in that respect. It urges us to consider life and art living antagonists, not "words"— but then "living antagonists" is a phrase, and these "antagonists" clash "In a footnote." Moreover, while the note translates these mere words, life and art, into mongoose and cobra—words too, here—it blandly omits to say which is which. It is just not that pat, this novel keeps admonishing itself. If the narrator's novel takes its models from life, his life seems to have taken its models from literature. The narrator has met Mrs. N., he realizes, in the pages of Proust, where she is the Duchesse de Guermantes. Or is she Madame Verdurin? The cobra and the mongoose.

Merrill consistently undercuts and overrides the art/life dichotomy by reminding us of such relationships. The narrator sees at the end of his notebook that he has been all of his main characters, that they have been "masks behind which lay all too frequently a mind foreign to them . . . *I* was 'Dora,' *I* was 'Orestes.'" "Madame Bovary, c'est moi!" No wonder the narrator's name is a matter of some uncertainty. This passage responds across nearly the length of the novel to the narrator's early problem: "But who he is (Orson/Orestes)—and by the same token, who I am—ah, that I keep on evading." "By the same token" precisely. He discovers who he is in discovering who O. is, who Dora is. Speaking of L'Enfant Chic, the narrator dryly notes that "Actually his name is Yannis, as whose isn't." Yannis, cognate with John, is one of the most common Greek names, but Merrill means more than that. He wants us to hark back to this sentence later, when we discover that Orson was christened Yannis, and when we learn that the narrator's father was John, and that Sandy got his nickname so that he would not have to be John like his father. Merrill repeatedly lets us see through to the tangle of Orestes, Orson, the narrator, and Sandy. "Mrs. N. had given me to understand that he [Orson] & I stood or fell together." "As I saw O., Lucine saw me." Orestes' trip with Dora from Italy to Paris reverses the narrator's own "final trip" with the mysterious "M." "The 2 situations much alike," he notes: "younger man, older woman; monuments, arguments, a love outlived." One begins to feel that *any* two "situations" are much alike.

Merrill hints at such relationships in the section in which the narrator tries to write from Orestes' point of view:

As if in a museum some figure streaked & pocked, a "Roman copy of a lost Greek original," and looked at for decades by none but anatomy students, had suddenly been discovered to *be* the original, ~~Orestes~~ I

Well might he break off. In this little enigma, copy and original, "I" and Orestes—and by implication the prototypical Greek hero and the narrator's fictional character, the narrator's conception of Orson and Orson's conception of himself—weave into one another.

At the novel's center, perhaps its most intense moment, the setting again is the panegyri, where Sandy has watched Orestes and Kosta do their dance. More wine arrives, Sandy gets even tipsier, he and his brother dance. First Orestes has Sandy, who is not so drunk as to have lost all coordination or trepidation, imitate Kosta's role, and in an electrifying moment Sandy leaps as Kosta had:

> He places his hands on O.'s shoulders. "Hup!" cries Orestes, and S., with a last despairing look at the world, springs upwards & backwards to lock his thighs around his partner's waist. The rest of him has fallen free, head inches from the ground, arms trailing. Upside-down, trees, tables, (Dora), the colored wool embroidery of her bag, everything exuberantly revolves. O.'s face grins down: the look of the initiator . . . It ends all too soon. "Up!" cried Orestes, & their uncouplement is effected to applause.

To complete this little ritual, Orestes now makes Sandy play the other part:

> . . . and in a flash the whole staggering weight of another body has become *his*. But he's mad, S. thinks, I can't hold him up! as they go reeling towards a group of tables and Orestes, blissful & trusting, smiles up at him. I cannot! Sandy has opened his mouth to cry—the blood pounding beneath his sunburn—he cannot—yet within seconds it appears that he can; he can, he can. Power & joy fill him. His eyes fill. He can dance under his brother's weight. Then it is over, & the music, too.

It is here that these two unite, if they ever do. Of Kosta and Orestes, joined in their dance, the narrator has noted that "something was there of Narcissus & his image, something of the Jack of Clubs," and we are to think of Orestes and Sandy in that light too. Each, from the other's point of view, is his own image: O., the inveterate teacher, has initiated Sandy in this as in all things Greek; and the narrator, Sandy's original, has refashioned O. in his novel. In short, Jack is a nickname for John, everyone's name. "Clubs" opens a new suit, after Orestes' talk of hearts and diamonds, and reminds us how these two are opposed and hurt each other, even though momentarily and fundamentally joined. In the background the instruments are "wrangling happily together."

"~~Orestes~~ I": as Merrill repeats the narrative *coup* with which the novel begins, he also anticipates the blow with which it ends. While Orestes and the narrator meet in these words, so do the fictive and the actual. Merrill has regretted that his novel's innovative "technique" does not have more to do with its "action," but he cannot have been thinking of this particular component, since in this case the two are one—or will be, as soon as Orson, like the word, is struck.[37] I mean simply that the line that the narrator strikes through Orestes' name prefigures the stripe that Byron's *cravache* leaves on Orson's face. Chekhov laid it down as a principle that the gun on the wall at the beginning of the play must go off by the play's end. That blow struck by Byron—"administered," one wants to say—is the "beat" that has been "missing" since the novel's first word, which is also its last act: "~~Orestes~~."

One reason that name is struck is that it is unsuitable for Orson, at least at the beginning. By the end he has earned the right to be called either by his own name or by the name of the tragic hero. Paradoxically, though we have known O. chiefly as the half-fictive Orestes until the climactic encounter with Byron, and though we have not seen the narrator's half-brother until after that encounter, it is *with* that encounter that he becomes Orestes, a version of the tragic figure he has dreamed of being. But he becomes Orestes just when he appears in his own person for the first time, as Orson, the romantic, nostalgic intellectual in search of his fate. As he returns, "calm & exalted," from the House, face streaming blood, he seems to the narrator not to need to know where he is headed because he has "*become* his destination." As the narrator puts it later, "O. had found a currency in which to pay the full price for what he believed. His view of things, his 'tragic' view, would never be wholly an illusion, once having interlocked so perfectly with his suffering."

At first the narrator is reluctant to think of the result of Orson's visit to the House as tragic. Instead, he is quick to imagine that he is somehow responsible—either because he failed to warn him or because he somehow magically drew Orson to the island—for his brother's suffering. Before long, however, he contradicts this interpretation:

> No one had drawn him here but himself, his life. Betrayal & rejection are what he has always needed in his dealings with people. When Dora didn't answer his letters, what could he do but seek satisfaction at her son's hands? He hadn't deserved his whipping, rather he had made it all

but happen, acting, as he had, in good faith as in bad taste, out of his own ~~blind~~ hopeless allegiance to this country of his dreams. And he had carried it off, made it seem like justice. Even I, in the notebook's blackest depths, would never have dared to construct such a denouement—coincidence, melodrama, every earmark of life's (the rival's) style. Il miglior fabbro!

One can hardly argue with that rhetoric of paradox. Except that no sooner do we assent to the proposition that life is the greater artist than we realize that the novel's "life" is fiction.

But perhaps we may forestall that realization long enough to wonder about Orson's "secret name," which is more complicated than Orestes. The narrator's character thinks of himself as a sort of "composite literary hero" whose traits and duties owe something to figures as diverse as Hamlet, Don Quixote, Houdini, and Oedipus; and Orson himself might be a similar blend. His "actual" name must be a coding of one aspect of his secret name. As the variations on John suggest, this novel, like *The Seraglio,* is full of play with names. Dora's fits her not only because, like her namesake Theodora, she is "Byzantine," but also because she is a stronger person than her husband. Sandy's name derives from the narrator's view of his own dispassionate and therefore "sandy heart." Arthur Orson exemplifies modern chivalry (and his godson, named for him, though in part a Quixote, undertakes his own quest and sets up a "round table" on the terrace at the House). So Orson's name also invites attention. Dora's husband Orson. Husband, that is, or son? In view of his conduct in regard to Dora, Orson might also be thought a whoreson—or so he would be called in an Elizabethan play. Too much is made of the Freudian union between Orson and Dora for us not to think of O. also as Oedipus, especially when he has come to his own Colonnus. "Blind I go": that "I" was in the first place the narrator, in regard to his novel, but at the end the same phrase could be applied to Orson, walking as though without seeing down the quai, his fate fulfilled, since he has come to the "violence to which all the words had been leading." That last phrase, coming as it does from the narrator's description of the climax of *Othello,* reminds us that O. includes qualities of this other tragic hero too. "Betrayal & rejection are what [O.] has always needed in his dealings with people." Indeed if we were to take seriously the narrator's initial thought that he had summoned Orson to his fate, we could see the narrator—in this novel in which deletion is so important—as a "blind I[a]go" to Orson's blind Othello, that other O. The thought grows less resistible when we recall that in Shakespeare's play these two mirror as well as complement each other. Both are too quick to identify "betrayal" in those close to them, for example.

Whether such eagerness for rejection characterizes Merrill's narrator is harder to say, though we learn early on that he needs to make up a *rebétika* song on the theme of "Love & betrayal," apparently central to his novel.

If we are to invoke Shakespeare, we should think also of *The Tempest*, for if the narrator has not brought O. to the island, Merrill assuredly has. On other occasions the narrator implicitly compares himself to Prospero— as when he notes after he has recorded the event at the House, "I will (figuratively) drown my book"—but the more plausible Prospero here is the one who does not appear. Merrill is Dora in the first place, as Dora is Prospero. (It is she who, in the narrow flat in Manhattan, having taken up Chinese, shows Sandy the ideograms for power, language, and island—as though these three had magical bonds, as they have in *The Tempest*.) And Merrill is Byron. Perhaps the narrator cannot be said to cause Orson's whipping, but the author must be held responsible, and so it is that he puts the *cravache* in the hand of the character named for a poet he admires—a poet who, like Merrill, had a second life in Greece:

> In my head he raised his beautiful clenched hand. The riding-crop descended, once, twice, again, upon my
> once, twice, again, inscribed its madder penstroke upon my brother's face, at the tempo of a ~~slowly pounding tempo of a giant's drugged pulse~~
> of the dolphin's progress through glittering foam
> at the tempo of those 3 blows whereupon the curtain of the Comédie rises to reveal, as foreseen, that universe of classical unity whose suns blaze & seas glitter & whose every action however brutal is nobly, inflexibly ordered & the best of each of us steps forth in his profound dark spotlight with poetry on his lips.

Mongoose and cobra. Crop and pen.

An extravagant prose? No question at all. As the allusion to the Comédie Française signifies, this diamond in the rough draft answers the desideratum set down early in the notebook, when the narrator urges himself to imitate Racine's *Phèdre*, "where the overlay of prismatic verse deflects a brutal, horrible action." From its recherché pun on "madder" to its oxymoronic "dark spotlight," this passage is painstakingly overwritten. The narrator presently admits its excesses when he mocks his own "myth-making apparatus" and warns himself that "*That* orgy must never be repeated." Yet it is a marvelous exercise. It epitomizes the paradox that he recognizes after completing his fair copy of the one section: at first his "'finished pages'" are "often believable" to him; then they seem to have "become fiction, which is to say merely life*like*"; but finally they appear "less artful" than the rough pages "with all their indecisions, pentimenti, glimpses of bare canvas, rips & ripples & cracks which, by stressing the fabric of illusion, required a greater attention to what was being represented."

Like so many other key passages in this novel, this one has its redressing counterpart. Merrill has praised Elizabeth Bishop because her work is "on the scale of a human life; there is no oracular amplification."[38] Having allowed himself such amplification in the climactic scene, he now puts his luxury in perspective with the narrator's last stab at his novel, which comprises two sentences on Piero della Francesca's famous painting:

> (While in Italy Dora & Orestes & Sandy can stop in Urbino to see the Piero *Flagellation* which O. has greatly admired in black & white.)
> Orestes' disappointment was keen to discover that the punishment of the god, for all its monumental aspect in reproduction, was in fact quite small, and ~~unexpectedly~~ subtly, vividly colored.
> I must be mad. I've given up this novel.

Seemingly a last-minute jotting for a novel that won't pan out, this brief passage bears very importantly on the rest of the book. In its "subtly, vividly colored" figures and buildings, the painting recalls the basic style of Merrill's novel. The restraint characteristic of the painting, where the nominal subject is backgrounded; the cool surface; the arrangement of structures that on reflection gives us the impression, recently justified by scholars, that Piero was calculating to the millimeter; the primary importance of architectural features, especially the house in which the flagellation takes place: these all have their parallels in Merrill's novel.

Merrill would be especially interested in Piero's combination of qualities that we often think of as opposites. For all its subtlety, the narrator notices, the painting has, in reproduction, a "monumental aspect." Although this aspect is not so evident when the thing itself is viewed, it will not be lost altogether. Orestes' characteristic admiration of things "in black & white" should serve to remind us that the Monumental and the Sublime, those terms from the "Dialogue on the Acropolis," do not exclude one another. Nor do tragedy and comedy, in the broad sense—a point Merrill must mean to make when, in the passage quoted above, he calls up an unnamed drama, tragic in its overtones, and imagines its performance in the Comédie. Again, if Merrill's hand is on the riding crop along with that of Byron, named for the comic Romantic poet, he is present no less in the figure of Orson, renamed for the Greek tragic figure. Orson is "O" partly because he is a cipher, a placeholder for any one of us, everyone's half-brother. His "secret name" is the reader's, just as it is the narrator's. If Orson dissipates concrete experience in his aesthetic theories, the narrator tells us at the end "how little [he himself] cared for [Orson], how much for the idea of him." And if Orson rises to the occasion at the House, we can know that he does because the narrator's prose follows suit, as he demonstrates that "the best in each of us" can sometimes step forth "with poetry on his lips." As John H. Finley, Jr., puts it in a sentence that Merrill would cull as an epigraph to "Up and Down," "The heart that leaps to the invitation of sparkling appearances is the heart that would itself perform as handsomely."[39] Orson's heart has leapt in response to great literary works, and the narrator's leaps in response to Orson's action, just as Sandy has leapt literally in response to Orestes' command.

Piero's painting brings together what the art historian Marilyn Aronberg Lavin calls two different worlds, each with its source of light.[40] Lavin proceeds to offer a fascinating explanation of compositional elements that Philip Guston has memorably defined. Although many of the details of Lavin's account are not immediately relevant to the novel, Guston's formulation of Piero's achievement will suggest further why the painting might have captivated Merrill: "[The flagellation proper is] the only 'disturbance' in the painting, but placed in the rear, as if in memory . . . The picture is sliced almost in half, yet both parts act on each other, repel and attract, absorb and enlarge one another. At times there seems to be no structure at all. No direction. We can move spatially everywhere, as in life."[41] It is easy enough to imagine that the heart of the writer of *The (Diblos) Notebook* would leap in response to such a work, with its scrupulous plans underlying its randomness and its bifurcation giving rise to a maze of interactions. Guston's verbs cannot be improved upon. Throughout *The (Diblos) Notebook,* life and art, no less than Orson and the narrator, "repel and attract, absorb and enlarge one another," until the dichotomy loses itself in the process, in the "numberless half-tones between frankness and artifice" that human experience is.

chapter three

DOUBLE BURDENS
Nights and Days

*. . . a towering mother
smooth as stone and thousandbreasted . . .*

the melting hand-in-hand or mere
desirers single, heavy-footed, rapt . . .

John Berryman, *Homage to Mistress Bradstreet*

Etre humain, c'est sentir vaguement qu'il y a de tous dans chacun, et de
chacun dans tous.

Rien ne me prouve que je ne serais jamais du parti ou de l'opinion adverse. Il
y a de la victime dans le bourreau et du bourreau dans la victime, du croyant dans
l'incroyant, et de l'incroyant dans le croyant. Il y a de quoi passer de l'un à l'autre;
et c'est peut-être cette puissance de transformation qui est l'essence même du véri-
table Moi.

Paul Valéry, *Mauvaises pensées*

I THINK that Merrill would affirm with feeling the credo that Cyril
Connolly's Palinurus announces in *The Unquiet Grave:* "I believe in two-faced
truth, in the Either, the Or and the Holy Both. I believe that if a statement is
true, then its opposite must be true."[1] Connolly's persona, *his* other face,
goes on to assert that "to attain two-faced truth we must be able to resolve
all our dualities, simultaneously to perceive life as comedy and tragedy, to
see the mental side of the physical and the reverse." He quotes with approval
Albert Thibaudet's phrase, "la pleine logique artistique de la vision binocu-
laire," and he refers us enthusiastically to Auden's description of "double
focus" in *New Year Letter* (or *The Double Man,* as it was called in the American edition). In the latter, at the end of Part II, Auden maintains that the
devil "controls . . . the either-ors, the mongrel halves" and that he tries to
get us to be uncompromising and monomaniacal. But the diabolical strategy
has its limitations by its nature:

> For he may never tell us lies,
> Just half-truths we can synthesize.
> So, hidden in his hocus-pocus,
> There lies the gift of double focus,
> That magic lamp which looks so dull
> And utterly impractical

Yet, if Aladdin use it right,
Can be a sesame to light.[2]

It might as well be this lamp whose "rubbed brass" produces "From the Cupola," which at over 400 lines is the longest poem in Merrill's fifth volume, *Nights and Days,* and his major achievement through 1966. From its first word through its concluding dialogue, the other long poem in this volume, "The Thousand and Second Night," is similarly a fantasia on two-faced truth. The very title of the volume suggests Merrill's interest in the Janusian.

That title bears on "The Current," which has something of the fairy tale about it and something of the riddle. It begins with a gypsylike charcoal peddler:

Down the dawn-brown
River the charcoal woman
Swept in a boat thin
As the old moon.
White tremblings darted and broke
Under her hat's crown.
A paddle-stroke
And she was gone, in her wake
Only miniature
Whirlpools, her faint
Ritualistic cries.

How fragile she is, with her "thin" boat and the breakings of the "White tremblings." The paring away of all but the *n* sound in the terminal rhymes of the first four lines puts an even finer edge on the opening image. Our sense of her frailty owes something also to our sense of things passing, of a force pulling the charcoal woman along—this is a matter of syntax and enjambment (the opening adverbial phrase seems to hurry the subject into the verb and on "down" the river as down the thin stanza)—and to the uncertainty of her status. For all its particulars, the image is not determinate, and the situation is dreamlike. We are free to think of her as a kind of woman in the moon and to see wisps of clouds in the "White tremblings," but the image changes before our eyes. The other figure, the sun to her moon, is all that she is not—youthful, vigorous, even brutal:

Now up the stream,
Urging an unwilling

Arc of melon rind
Painted red to match
His wares, appeared
The meat vendor.
The young, scarred face
Under the white brim
Glowed with strain
And flamelike ripplings.
He sat in a cloud of flies.

Whereas syntax and prosody sweep her along, he works his way through them and does not even pull himself fully into view until the sixth line, long after his boat's prow and his wares. The end of her stanza could be marked *verschwindend*, but he is never more solidly there than in the last line of his. His "cloud of flies" rhymes crudely with her "Ritualistic cries." If she is a fleeting impression, a charcoal sketch, he is all garish sensuousness, meat and heat, done in Fauvist colors.

As "The Current" keeps us from simply labeling its two main figures, it also refuses to resolve itself neatly. In a sense it deals with twoness and threeness. Its line varies from two beats to three with the latter predominant, and its opposing figures seem to call for some sort of union or tertium quid. But in the third stanza, though he toys with such a conclusion, Merrill resists its appeal:

If, further on,
Someone was waiting to thread
Morsels of beef
Onto a green
Bamboo sliver
And pose the lean brochette
Above already glowing
Embers, the river,
Flowing in one direction
By moon, by sun,
Would not be going
To let it happen yet.

This stanza snubs the idea of ending—seems to suggest, even, that the idea is unnatural. "Flowing in one direction," the river begins to look like time itself, which knows only transformation. The flow of time is implicit too in the "already glowing / Embers" of the intercepted vision, since, after the dawn and noon of the first two stanzas, the embers suggest evening. This is a poem that shies from finalities (the smart little barbecue indefinitely fore-stalled looks like a stylish translation of an apocalypse) and values the gen-erative difference between, say, imagination and actuality, or soul and body, other names we might give the two principles here.

And yet . . . The last word *is* "yet." Perhaps we should feel uneasy about even such a summation of a poem written against summation. The final "yet," the adverb denoting postponement rather than obviation, has just a *soupçon* of its conjunctional sense too. There is an *under*current here in the direction of closure and fixity. Merrill allows for that alternative in "further on," and the penultimate line formulates exactly its effect. I think of the end of Stevens's "Notes toward a Supreme Fiction," a poem Merrill has said he "teethed on":

> They will get it straight one day at the Sorbonne.
> We shall return at twilight from the lecture
> Pleased that the irrational is rational,
>
> Until flicked by feeling, in a gildered street,
> I call you by name, my green, my fluent mundo.
> You will have stopped revolving except in crystal.[3]

In Stevens's lines the end of the process is doubly postponed, by the future tense and by the final phrase, which gives the thought a shove and sets it revolving again, although in crystal. In Merrill's conclusion the insistence on fluency, on "Flowing" and "going," is qualified by "yet" and "further on" and especially by the finality of the language. The rhymes are so carefully threaded themselves, the syntax so poised, the images so sharp, that the poem concludes in spite of itself. If it prevents factitious pyramidal dialectic, it still resists its own dualism. One understands anew the force of Jonathan Bishop's remark that "Merrill is that rare and valuable individual, the poet who thinks *in* poetry."[4]

"Days of 1964," which concludes *Nights and Days*, recapitulates the volume's central issue, the nature of love. The poem's title alludes to the me-morial titles that C. P. Cavafy gave to five of his poems: "Days of 1903," "Days of 1896," and so on. In a note to their translations of Cavafy's poems, Edmund Keeley and Philip Sherrard point out that all five poems are "ob-viously related to his 'secret life'";[5] that is, each gives a portrait of a young man with whom Cavafy had an affair. Merrill's first "Days" poem commem-orates a love relationship that took place in Athens, and although the other person is not identified as to sex, the title's allusion is a means of broaching the subject, which Merrill treats more openly in "The Thousand and Second Night." He must also have felt that his poem had specific relationships with at least four of Cavafy's poems. In those recalling 1896, 1901, 1909–1911, and 1908, the young men combine divergent attributes: they are either shabby and neglected but beautiful, or debauched yet somehow virginal. The divided figure in Merrill's poem, however, is not the lover but the Greek housekeeper. On the one hand, Kyria Kleo "wore brown, was fat, past fifty, / And looked like a Palmyra matron / Copied in lard and horsehair." On the other hand, she is Aphrodite herself:

> How she loved
> You, me, loved us all, the bird, the cat!
> I think now she *was* love. She sighed and glistened
> All day with it, or pain, or both.
> (We did not notably communicate.)
> She lived nearby with her pious mother
> And wastrel son. She called me her real son.

Lightly but unmistakably Merrill teases out his allegory in that last line— and later, in the detail drawn from his love affair: "your touch, quick, merciful, / Blindfolded me. A god breathed from my lips."

The balance of Eros and Anteros is characteristic by now (compare "pious" and "wastrel," the bird and the cat), but Merrill is no more interested in tidy antithesis than in facile synthesis. In *The Unquiet Grave,* Connolly also enjoins his reader to "Beware . . . false dualities: classical and romantic, real and ideal, reason and instinct, mind and matter, male and female." While "it does not follow that dualism is in itself a worthless process," he urges that such dualities "be regarded as two aspects of the same idea."[6] By adroitly shuffling his terms, Merrill presents a single emotional complex at odds with itself. Thus he modifies his reference in the lines above to "[love], or pain, or both" when he remembers his lover "gasping in my arms / With love, or laughter, or both"; then he restates the original alternative in the glimpse he gives us of Kleo "Cleaning and watering, sighing with love or pain"; and he arrives at the full statement of the matter in the last lines: "But you were everywhere beside me, masked, / As who was not, in laughter, pain, and love." Those last lines apply also to Kleo, who had her own "secret life," as the poet learned one day when he happened to see her walking "into the pines" on Mount Lykabettos to a tryst of some sort. As though to reiterate the poem's use of the motif just mentioned, he tells us that he "Called three times before she turned." What he saw was a poignantly lurid version of the mask his last lines refer to:

Above a tight, skyblue sweater, her face
Was painted. Yes. Her face was painted
Clown-white, white of the moon by daylight,
Lidded with pearl, mouth a poinsettia leaf,
Eat me, pay me—the erotic mask
Worn the world over by illusion
To weddings of itself and simple need.

A "mask," he calls this ludicrous face she has put on, but at the same time it is her heart laid bare, evidence of romantic hopes and physical and perhaps financial exigencies alike.

The implications for Kleo's "real son" appear at about the time this phrase's ironies snare us. Merrill has written the verse paragraph set in the Athens market with admirable finesse. By blurring together the actual and the oneiric as though they were need and illusion themselves, he evokes his shock both at seeing Kleo in such get-up and at seeing himself in her—the daze of 1964:

> Next, I was crossing a square
> In which a moveable outdoor market's
> Vegetables, chickens, pottery kept materializing
> Through a dream-press of hagglers each at heart
> Leery lest he be taken, plucked,
> The bird, the flower of that November mildness,
> Self lost up soft clay paths, or found, foothold,
> Where the bud throbs awake
> The better to be nipped, self on its knees in mud—
> Here I stopped cold, for both our sakes;
>
> And calmer on my way home bought us fruit.

"Leery" is an ingenious choice, since it serves as a nonce adjective indicating "simple need" even as it signifies awareness of "illusion." The whole passage is nearly giddy with its bargains and balances—between need and suspicion, between the wish to be taken and the dread of being taken in. To lose oneself is to find oneself—or is it to risk finding oneself alone? The "plucked" flower, stripped of its petals one by one, can never tell us whether we are loved or not. The speaker fears, in a phrase that compresses sexual hunger, romantic yearning, and skepticism, that "the bud throbs awake / The better to be nipped." Chilled by the applications to his own love affair, he stops himself in his mental tracks—the walk through the Kolonáki section has been a meditative sortie too—nips *that* image in the bud, and goes back home—where he and his lover can laugh at the gossip he has brought home with his fruit.

"Days of 1964" is both "cheerful *and* awful," to revert to that phrase Merrill adapts from Elizabeth Bishop's "The Bight." It is only after the embarrassing meeting with Kleo, only after she has shown the fierce, pathetic side of herself, that he can say with full justification, "I think now she *was* love." At the same time, since Kleo is love, she reflects him, the lover, who has done his own climbing. The "steep hill" near his house, he recalls in terms with sexual overtones, "could be climbed in twenty minutes / For some literally breathtaking views," and its flowers were "Spangled as with fine sweat among the relics / Of good times had by all." He is necessarily her "wastrel son" as well as his "real" one. He elaborates the paradox at poem's end, when he sums up that year's affair:

If that was illusion, I wanted it to last long;
To dwell, for its daily pittance, with us there,
Cleaning and watering, sighing with love or pain.
I hoped it would climb when it needed to the heights
Even of degradation, as I for one
Seemed, those days, to be always climbing
Into a world of wild
Flowers, feasting, tears—or was I falling, legs
Buckling, heights, depths,
Into a pool of each night's rain?
But you were everywhere beside me, masked,
As who was not, in laughter, pain, and love.

In its concluding lines the poem's narrative past tense is resonant. The tense, the insistent nostalgia, and the allusion to Cavafy's poems (in which relationships are transitory with sickening predictability) make us wonder whether the "illusion," if that is all it was, did "last long." There is also the tiny uncertainty registered by a conditional near the end, where Merrill surprises us by shifting out of the past and reflecting on his own work: "Forgive me, if you read this. (And may Kyria Kleo, / Should someone ever put it into Greek / And read it aloud to her, forgive me, too.)" These are only hints, and he arranges things in any case so that "pain" appears between "laughter" and the final "love," but one cannot quite overlook the personal loss implied.

It is the split tongue that speaks. One need not think that Merrill has the temperament of Rilke, who he has said "made almost a career of enforced loneliness and hopeless passions," to realize that he responds especially quickly to estrangement.[7] Though we might note that he has dryly declined to "go into the effect . . . of the opera on my moral sense. All those passions—illnesses, ecstasies, deceptions—induced for the pure sake of having something to sing beautifully about."[8] Division is the source of many of his characteristic devices, since in breaking up his own discourse, he extends himself and opens up new possibilities. Such discontinuities permit and result from a variety in tone. ("Oh but one has many, many tongues," as the lyric poet turned dramatic puts it in "From the Cupola.") For Merrill, one technique that bears directly on tone (or voice: he suspects that "'Voice' is the democratic word for 'tone'") is prosody. In responding to Donald Sheehan's question as to whether voice is "a function of metrics," he admits that he hears "voice a good deal more in metrical poetry. The line lends itself to shifts of emphasis. If Frost had written free verse, I don't think we'd have heard as much of the voice in it."[9] He goes into the subject at greater length in his conversation with J. D. McClatchy:

> Too much poetry sounds like side after side of modern music, the same serial twitterings, the same barnyard grunts. Just as I love multiple meanings, I try for contrasts and disruptions of tone. Am I wrong—in the old days didn't the various meters imply different modes or situations, like madness, love, war? It's too late, in any event, to rely very much on meter . . . I'm talking from a reader's point of view, you understand. Poets will rediscover as many techniques as they need in order to help them write better. But for a reader who can hardly be trusted to hear the iambics when he opens "The Rape of the Lock," if anything can fill the void left by those obsolete resources, I'd imagine it would have to be diction or "voice." Voice in its fullest tonal range— not just bel canto or passionate speech. From my own point of view, this range would be utterly unattainable without meter and rhyme and those forms we are talking about.[10]

The poems in *Nights and Days* testify to this partnership between "contrasts and disruptions" of tone or voice and prosodic variation. If in *Water Street* he first began to talk to himself even as he put different verse forms together, here he introduces more tones and speakers and further diversifies his forms. The difficult poem called "Time" looks like a transitional work. In profile it has a family resemblance to "An Urban Convalescence" and "A Tenancy": it begins with two verse paragraphs made up of basically iambic lines, ranging from dimeter to pentameter, and it ends in six rhymed quatrains. When one examines it in more detail, however, "Time" is more multi-form, more complexly unified than either of the earlier poems. We have to guess at some of the situation it deals with, but it seems that the poet is thinking about and writing "to" a distraught friend (the poem's "you"), per-haps a poet himself, who is caring for his bedridden, dying father and who is going through his own crisis. While the specifics of the neurasthenia are elusive, the friend's symptoms are pitifully clear: aimlessness, distraction, an inability to complete letters, endless games of patience which help him to kill the time—though in alternate moods he feels time flying. In addition to the poet, we hear this friend and the confused old man, as well as a "hand-book" on meditation. There is nothing like such a cast in any poem in *Water Street,* where the speakers are never more than two and where the dialogue is almost always internal. The speakers in this poem break off and in on one another in a half dozen ways:

Let's say you went
So far as to begin: "It's me! Forgive . . ."
Too late. From the alcove came his cough,
His whimper—the old man whom sunset wakes.
. . . . .
He was so feeble. Feeble!

He grasped your pulse in his big gray-haired hand,
Crevasses opening, numb azure. *Wait*
He breathed and glittered: *You'll regret*
You want to   Read my will first   Don't
Your old father   All he has   Be yours
. . . . .
"You'll get well, you'll be proud of me. Don't smile!
I love you. I'll find work. You'll— I'll—"

It was light and late.
. . . . .
You swiftly wrote:

" . . . this long silence. I don't know what's the matter with me. All winter I have been trying to discipline myself—'Empty the mind,' as they say in the handbooks, 'concentrate on one thing, any thing, the snowflake, the granite it falls upon, the planet risen opposite, etc., etc.'—and failing, failing. Quicksands of leisure! Now summer's here, I *think*! Each morning a fog rolls in from the sea. It would lift, perhaps,

if you were to come and speak to it. Will you? Do! One catches the
ferry at . . ."

The pen reels from your hand.

Such interruptions lift the poem off the page and let it appear in the round.

> ❭ ❭ ❭

Merrill "couldn't foresee the structure" of "The Thousand and Second
Night," he has told us, and he "never dreamed . . . that it would be as long
as it is." It began as several seemingly "rather unrelated" poems in progress,
and then "suddenly an afternoon of patchwork saw them all stitched together."[11] As a result of this origin, and no doubt as a result as well of a
sensibility that delights in protean changes, "The Thousand and Second
Night"—which derives its title from that work in which breaking off is the
repeated object—is a tour de force of interruption. By the same token, it is
an anthology of brilliant connective techniques.

The relationships among the parts are sometimes indirect; the poem
proceeds more by impulse and tangent than by hewing to an argument.
Merrill has said as much in the interview just quoted:

> . . . though I'd never looked at more than a page of *Don Juan* and knew
> about Byron only through Auden's "Letter" to him, I knew that he had
> been an influence on "The Thousand and Second Night." When I
> checked, I found very much the tone that I'd been trying for: that air of
> irrelevance, of running on at the risk of never becoming terribly signifi-
> cant. I see no point, often, in the kind of poem that makes every single
> touch, every syllable, count. It can be a joy to write, but not always to
> read. You can't forego the whole level of entertainment in art. Think of
> Stevens's phrase: "The essential gaudiness of poetry." The inessential
> suddenly felt as essence.

That last riddle will caution us against taking Merrill's cavalier attitude toward his material too seriously. If "To *sound* personal is the point," as he says
in this interview, to *seem* casual is also a goal. An "air of irrelevance" is not
irrelevance. Moreover, the interview proceeds forthwith to his remarks on
his "endless revisions," which usually begin "even before the poem is fully
drafted." One wonders how long that "afternoon" would have been in
which he "stitched together" the different pieces in "The Thousand and Second Night." Still, when all is said, this poem has its share of loose ends and

discontinuities, and it would be perverse to construe such a mélange as a classical machine.

In *On, Romanticism,* Donald Sutherland outlines the kind of poem that I think "The Thousand and Second Night" is. He deals with what he calls "the *galant* style" in the context of poetic narrative in general:

> The great advantage of poetic over prose narrative is that the verse moves as well as the action, so that where prose narrative is committed to a fairly continuous external happening and a rigorously onward movement weighted by suspense, verse can handle a wandering narrative line, varying or interrupting it with passages of description, reflection, or lyric exclamation, which count in verse as varieties of movement and not as the inert stretches they tend to be in prose . . . [The movement of the narrative] can be absorbed into the movement of the verse, which can be the expression of a continually varying motion of spirit, so that the events never crystallize into fact or conclusion on their own, nor into objectivity.[12]

By the end of that passage, Sutherland has himself modulated into his account of the *galant,* which he finds exemplified in one form by the same poem Merrill feels affinities with, *Don Juan,* with its "capricious play of mind," its "wit, rapidity, and swagger," and in a more delicate form by Shelley's *Julian and Maddalo* and *Rosalind and Helen.* In such poems we expect a certain legerity, sudden shifts in tone, plots that seem improvised "and at times mysterious and even enigmatic." This sort of Romantic poem "has a kind of tradition in the satires or conversation pieces of Horace when they run to anecdote or narrative and perhaps in the epyllion." The *galant* style, Sutherland speculates, "might easily reemerge out of the modern epyllion like *The Waste Land* or the satirical or mixed conversation piece such as the *Cantos* of Ezra Pound or even the *Paterson* of W. C. Williams," though it would shed the "ponderousness of fact, citation, and ritual imagery" of those High Modern poems, as well as their "portentousness of moral attitude and *Weltanschauung.*"

I would be very curious to know what Sutherland might have made of the two long poems in *Nights and Days,* since his sketch of the *galant* narrative and its future seems almost to predict them. "The Thousand and Second Night" looks strikingly like a *galant* translation of *The Waste Land.* Both poems meld different prosodic forms, both have five numbered sections (the longest of which is the third), both rely heavily on quotation. Unlike Eliot, in just the way that Sutherland might lead us to expect, Merrill has some fun at his own expense for having quoted Valéry, Hofmannsthal, Goethe, Yeats, and the others. He even quotes T. S. Eliot. Merrill's plot, such as it is, involves a strange ailment, a sort of spiritual impotence, a quest in foreign lands, even a "resurrection"—but Merrill has such a light way with these materials that they are utterly different from their parallels in *The Waste Land*.

Like Eliot's poem, Merrill's begins in spring—not in April, however, but on March 21. The first of its five sections, "Rigor Vitae," discovers the poet in Istanbul, in the middle of a trip that will bring him back to the United States within a few months. He is ill—the victim of a malady that has temporarily paralyzed half his face—and depressed. A visit to Hagia Sophia, intended to cheer him, and another to a Turkish bath, undertaken in hopes of curing the paralysis, both fail; in section two, "The Cure," he is in Athens, where "cortisone, / Diathermy, vitamins, and rest" eliminate the paralysis but leave untouched the ennui. He has returned to the States in the third section, "Carnivals," only to be reproached by friends for having become a "vain / Flippant unfeeling monster." Toward the end of this central section, after unearthing a collection of obscene postcards that had come his way when he was a teenager, but for reasons that are not immediately clear, he overcomes his malaise. The untitled fourth section, quatrains written in a different key, has Merrill, now playing the role of a teacher in a boys' school or men's college, making "Some brief points" about his own poem. (So the *galant* poet might make fun of the Modernist's appended "Notes" and the explication they would coax from critics.) This is a surprising and entertaining interlude, a sort of mock parabasis, a fine example of romantic irony. The fifth section is also untitled and in quatrains, but the effect is quite different. A miniature allegory, it finds Scheherazade and the Sultan (soul and body, muse and poet) worrying the nature of their relationship.

A good place to enter the poem is through the fourth section, the one section whose existence we would not specifically sense the need of if it were not there. Once there, it is indispensable. It puts in perspective the drama near the end of section three, where Death puts in a brief appearance in another one of those passages in which realistic description graduates without a hitch into dream vision, and it throws into relief the fifth section's intense lyricism. Along with "Postcards from Hamburg, Circa 1912," a subsection of part three, it makes "The Thousand and Second Night" the first strong evidence that Merrill will be our most forceful recent example of the writer who can merge light verse and serious verse. Curiously enough, it was Louise Bogan, who criticized *First Poems* so severely, who defined two years after her review (without thinking of him) one "task" that Merrill would have just set himself: "It is still the task of modern poets to bridge the division between serious and light forms; to refresh the drooping and weary rhythms of serious poetry with the varied, crisp, and fresh qualities of light verse. In English, Pound and Eliot have performed miracles of deflation and revivification. Auden, as well, has worked to break down artificial barriers of form and tone, between the lively and the grave subject and treatment."[13] Merrill himself, in an interview shortly after the publication of *Nights and Days,* points out that the gap between light and serious verse is "hardly unbridgeable" and suggests that in fact we should be "used by now to the light poem that has dark touches and the serious poem shot through with lighter ones."[14] "The Thousand and Second Night" is so variously shaded, so much "the expression of a continually varying motion of spirit," to adopt Sutherland's terms, that neither of those alternatives seems quite to do it justice.

The fourth section begins by proving that Merrill has become a virtuoso of intervention:

> Now if the class will turn back to this, er,
> Poem's first section—Istanbul—I shall take
> What little time is left today to make
> Some brief points. So. The rough pentameter
>
> Quatrains give way, you will observe, to three
> Interpolations, prose as well as verse.
> Does it come through how each in turn refers
> To mind, body, and soul (or memory)?
>
> It does? Good. No, I cannot say offhand
> Why this should be. I find it vaguely satis—
> Yes please? The poet quotes too much? Hm. That is
> One way to put it.

The mellifluous conclusion to section three has just called our attention to his "fluent passages of metaphor," so the ironic self-consciousness of the first lines here could hardly be a sharper departure. (Much of the pleasure we take in this section comes from this paradox, that the boldness of the poetic movement is in part the conception of the stumbling circumspection of the persona. Not that this persona is any less "the poet" than the speaker at the beginning of the poem or the Sultan at the end. Or Scheherazade, as far as that goes. On the contrary, these figures are among the "many selves" that Merrill speaks of.) Within this interruptive section, Merrill reflects on previous "interpolations," of which more in a moment, and repeatedly lets himself be interrupted, so that section four is a microcosm of the whole wayward narrative. Each disjunction provides an opportunity for invention and variation. The little snag at the end of the first line contributes its bit to the "rough pentameter / Quatrains" in *this* section. The broken word in the third stanza does so even more noticeably. In addition to giving him the chance to shift his tone, it lets him add a touch to his self-portrait. This interruption brings into focus the difference between the students, so eager to understand, and the poet as teacher, muddling along, doing the best he can, but at a loss to *explain* the poem. The same diffidence has manifested itself in the preceding sections, as he indicates at the class's end when answering the question about his numerous quotations:

> Mightn't he have planned
>
> For his own modest effort to be seen
> Against the yardstick of the "truly great"
> (In Spender's phrase)? Fearing to overstate,
> He lets *them* do it—lets their words, I mean,
>
> Enhance his—Yes, what now?

But his response itself, by quoting Spender's poem beginning "I think continually of those who were truly great," calls on the device whose subtle purpose he defines—and in calling on it, alters its purpose. For Spender's eloquent poem is just not the same kind of "yardstick" as Yeats's "Byzantium." Modesty shades off here into near impertinence. If the poet seems mercurial among his ironies, these apparent changes are the life of this burlesque reflection. Slipperiness is its essence, just as fragmentation is its affirming form:

> Yes, what now? Ah. How and when
> Did he "affirm"? Why, constantly. And how else
> But in the form. Form's what affirms. That's well
> Said if I do—[*Bells ring.*] Go, gentlemen.

Just as the fragment "satis—" in the third stanza becomes the perfect half of a whole when "That is" pairs up with it, as though to suggest that the poet can rise above *any* rudeness, so the bracketed phrase fills out the pentameter line. If it were not for the intervention the verse would be incomplete, to put it that way.

Such fugacity and transformation of fragment characterize the poem from the outset. "Rigor Vitae" begins with a series of quatrains that is broken off, as David Lehman has noticed, just in time to turn the passage into a sonnet.[15] Merrill breaks into the fourth quatrain after one and a half lines, rhymes the last words in these lines with end words in the third quatrain, and thereby laces the last lines up into a sestet (*abbaba*)—though the sestet is hard to pick out as such. The interruption is abrupt, the sonnet's last line is really more a hemistich, and it is in German to boot ("*Dahin! Dahin!*"), so the rhyme is disguised. Moreover, because these last one and a half lines are of unequal length, they modulate the verse into the irregularly metered and rhymed paragraph that follows, the first "interpolation" touched on in section four, whose lines move in and out in accord with some Arabic writing's "wild script of gold whips." This verse paragraph ends with a pair of couplets and gives way to what seems to be a verse paragraph of seven and a half lines. A second look discloses two pentameter quatrains put together. So the couplets concluding the preceding verse paragraph anticipate the *ab-bacddc* rhyme here. This new passage's final *c* rhyme is part of a phrase that is capitalized and centered on its own line, even though it completes the pentameter, because it serves also as the title of the next subsection, "The Hamam." (This use of the foreign word or phrase in a rhyming position, as with "*Dahin*," will become Merrill's cachet. Like Auden and Byron and few others, he has expanded the frontiers of English rhyme. He must often arrange to get the least likely words at the ends of lines simply in order to find out where the rhyme might take him—as Byron, having got "Euxine" at the end of a line, could not resist making it a place his passenger "pukes in.")

"The Hamam," then, is another term that leads a double life, as a conclusion and as a beginning. The new section opens with a quatrain that assonates *abba* and thus might seem a continuation of the normative form, except that the lines are tetrameter instead of pentameter. When the second quatrain shuffles its assonantal pattern to *abab,* and is followed by two tercets, this second of the three "interpolations" forms itself into a sonnet. It is not until this sonnet ends that Merrill stops for breath and the poem has its first real break; for sixty-two lines it has been a display of metamorphic poetic forms. So there is a certain irony in the pentameter quatrain to which Merrill returns for just long enough to introduce "an infantile / Memory" that "promises to uncramp my style." Besides glancing wryly back at a passage that has been eminently fluid, the phrase presages the prose he uses to set down his memory. After this last "interpolation," he closes off "Rigor Vitae" with three pentameter quatrains—which balance the three with which this section began. For all its metamorphoses, it has a frame as well.

"The problem is / how / to keep shape and flow," as A. R. Ammons has concisely defined it, and Merrill has come up with an assortment of solutions.[16] He was experimenting with means of keeping his poems processive yet shapely in *Water Street,* and his work in *The (Diblos) Notebook* would have been at least as useful. Those moments in the novel in which the prose precipitates into poetry would have helped him see how to turn the kaleidoscope in "The Thousand and Second Night"—and in "From the Cupola." In the latter, a prose paragraph about a painful insight concludes with the phrase

"Piercing her to the brain." The following sentence, set off by itself, reads as follows: "Spelt out in brutal prose, all had been plain." Now that sentence might be more mere prose. But it scans, and it rhymes its "plain" with "brain," and therefore it gives an ironic cast to the term "brutal prose." Then, as though to make sure we hear the couplet, the very next word, at the entrance to a section of verse, is "RAIN." Nothing to do with that one sentence but to call it both prose and poetry, flow and shape—a structural pun.

But to be two things at once is perhaps not the same as to be one thing divided. The latter, which might even be thought of as a parody of the other, is the motivating predicament in this poem. But although it is clear that the poem centers on such a division, the nature of the problem is murky. The overt complaint is an easily identifiable malady, Bell's Palsy:

Istanbul. 21 March. I woke today
With an absurd complaint. The whole right half
Of my face refuses to move. I have to laugh
Watching the rest of it reel about in dismay

Under the double burden, while its twin
Sags on, though sentient, stupefied.
I'm here alone. Not quite—through fog outside
Loom wingèd letters: PAN AMERICAN.

Twenty-five hundred years this city has stood between
The passive Orient and our frantic West.
I see no reason to be depressed;
There are too many other things I haven't seen,

Like Hagia Sophia. Tea drunk, shaved, dressed . . .
Dahin! Dahin!

But it is not just Bell's Palsy that is troubling him. These lines' multiple dichotomies signal some internal conflict, some *Angst*. The "absurd complaint" has its existential side. The poet's face, its one half stiff and expressionless, its other half especially animated, has its reflection in the hemispheres, the "passive Orient" and the "frantic West," and in Istanbul itself, located at the junction of Europe and Asia, and divided by the Golden Horn into old town and modern town. The date (which happens to combine 2 and 1) is that of the spring equinox. There is also a hint of antithesis in this section's title, "Rigor Vitae." While it denotes a deep-seated ennui reminiscent of *The Waste Land,* and comes closer than any of this passage's particulars to defining the fundamental problem, its literal meaning is a near oxymoron. Even the airline's name conceals its divided figure: Pan, half-man and half-goat, who by virtue of his associations with sex and music initiates one of Merrill's main themes (not to be developed until the third section).

In view of this passage's rampant divarications, it is appropriate that it end with its own witty "double burden," its "*Dahin!*", repeated like a call for a taxi. On the one hand, it gestures toward Hagia Sophia, the mosque located "back there" or "over there," and thus propels us across the divisional break into that "house of Heavenly Wisdom." On the other hand, being quoted from the refrain in Mignon's "Kennst du das Land" (in *Wilhelm Meisters Lehrjahre*—or in Charles Ambroise Thomas's comic opera, *Mignon*), it brings that lyric into play. In Goethe's lines what is "dahin" is Mignon's dimly remembered home, lost to her since childhood, which turns out to be a grand estate in Italy where she had a happy childhood until she was kidnapped, and which she describes in idyllic terms. (The parallel in *The Waste Land* is Marie's childhood sojourn at "the arch-duke's": "In the mountains, there you feel free.") Merrill's "*Dahin!*", by inescapable analogy, evokes an existence that preceded and contrasts with his Bell's Palsy, his rigor vitae, and whatever lies behind them.

The "house" that he escapes to, however, has little in common with Mignon's "Haus"—actually a palace. Hagia Sophia is now a shell of itself, "a flame- / less void," as Merrill puts it, brandishing and extinguishing the fire in the same swift movement. The mosque's interior reflects his mind as he conceives of it in his depression. The mosaic's "old profusion's / Hypnotic shimmer, back and forth between / That of the abacus, that of the nebula" has long since crumbled and disappeared. The "abacus" would be the top of a column's capital and the "nebula" the interstellar formation, but in this context they also make us think of two chief operations of the mind, numbers and vision, or "learning and faith," to use related terms further on in this passage. The exterior also reminds the poet of himself:

> The building, desperate for youth, has smeared
> All over its original fine bones
>
> Acres of ochre plaster. A diagram
> Indicates how deep in the mudpack
> The real façade is. I want *my* face back.

In its subversion of the distinction between inner and outer, the inspired phrase "the real façade" hints at the poem's conclusion, but here any implications of resolution are all but lost in the tedium. The poet's problem is that he feels as though he did not *feel* anything, as though his spirit were as paralyzed as half his face. The ministrations at "The Hamam" assuage neither form of the malaise. Indeed, they suggest nothing so much as the laying out of a corpse: "One is addressed in gibberish, shown / Into a marble cell and thrown / On marble," "scrubbed clean," "wrapped in towels and a sheet / And led upstairs to this lean tomb" to sit "effaced by gemlike moods." If at this sonnet's end he "gravely uptilts [his] mask of platinum / Still dripping, in a sign of life," that life seems to be physical only. These lines are curiously detached, their writer "effaced," partly because of Merrill's allegiance through this interpolation to the third person pronoun "one." Meanwhile, the nasal rhymes spread like the numbness. Beginning with "shown" and "thrown," if not with "Hamam" itself, and continuing through "tomb" and "gloom" and "loukoum," they add up to the ghost of a pun on the last syllable of the last of their number, "platinum."

As Hagia Sophia's past sets off its present deterioration, so the poet's personal past represented by the "infantile / Memory" contrasts with the rigor vitae. His warm recollection of sleeping on his grandmother's lap, "lulled to a rhythm easily the whole world's then," is a nostalgic image of unity that the following passage throws into relief, for these three quatrains picture a man utterly alienated. "Cold" is the first word, and there follows a surrealistic version of "The 'death-in-life and life-in-death' of Yeats' Byzantium": "crowds, a magic-lantern beam— / Belgians on bicycles, housewives with red hair, / Masts, cries of crows blown high in the rose-blue air." *These* are hardly such forms "as Grecian goldsmiths make / Of hammered gold and gold enamelling / To keep a drowsy emperor awake" or forms of the "superhuman," to quote two poems that Merrill's might be written "against."[17] For Merrill, Istanbul has been a place not of unification but divisions, and he leaves the holy city, which has proved closer to Eliot's "Unreal City," for the worldly one: "Alone in the sleepwalking scene, my flesh has woken / And sailed for the fixed shore beyond the straits."

Once the physical complaint has been successfully treated, the poet's malaise looks more and more like a severe case of pococurantism. Like the narrator in *The (Diblos) Notebook,* he worries about being "cold and withdrawn. / The day I went up to the Parthenon / Its humane splendor made me think *So what?*" In the present, in this second section, he is in Athens, and he recalls meeting a Greek in the Royal Park in May. It is a symptom of his indifference that we cannot tell whether their relationship was eventually romantic. The man introduces himself by naming some trees and flowers in Greek:

I thanked him; he thanked me, sat down. Peacocks
Trailed by, hard gray feet mashing overripe

But bitter oranges. I knew the type:
Superb, male, raucous, unclean, Orthodox

Ikon of appetite feathered to the eyes
With the electric blue of days that will
Not come again.

Just as "overripe" and "bitter" take some of their color from the poet's attitude, so the fourth line's adjectives apply to both the peacock and the man.
The implicit comparison betrays a disconcerting objectivity addressed later
in a passage powered by Merrill's characteristic internal dialogue:

> I am afraid
> I was not human either—ah, who is?

> He is, or was; had brothers and a wife;
> Chauffeured a truck; last Friday broke his neck
> Against a tree. We have no way to check
> These headlong emigrations out of life.

The wan wit, the disinterested account, the calculating choice of "headlong," so that one even suspects that "The Cure" of the title refers flippantly
to death: these are meant to justify a fear of a creeping carelessness. That
fear, as well as the self-derisive overtones of these lines, runs counter to the
indifference, but the latter—as in the strikingly similar incident in *The
Seraglio,* where Francis reports Sir Edward Good's death to Xenia—ostensibly has the upper hand.

> Try, I suppose, we must, as even Valéry said,
> And said more grandly than I ever shall—
> Turning shut lids to the August sun, and all
> Such neon figments (amber, green, and red)

> Of incommunicable energy
> As in my blindness wake, and at a blink
> Vanish, and were the clearest hint, I think,
> Of what I have been, am, and care to be.

We have to try to live, Valéry instructs us in "Le Cimetière marin": "il faut
tenter de vivre."[18] Merrill is careful, however, to keep any sense of urgency
in check by means of the lackadaisical phrasing, the lassitude implied by the
sunbathing, and the last line that echoes with wistful irony the passionate
conclusion of "Sailing to Byzantium."

The present in "Carnivals" is the winter of the same year, but this third section is a patchwork itself. It might be divided, like the poem as a whole, into five parts. The first, in brisk quatrains, alludes to recent meetings with three old friends, perhaps those in "A Tenancy," now disappointed in him, who confirm the poet's fear that he has become a "vain / Flippant unfeeling monster." He then recalls a fall evening in the middle of World War II, when enlistment would have been imminent for Merrill, and a "walk with M., / To die in whose presence seemed the highest good," and records a dinner with "M. and his new wife last New Year's." Seemingly prompted by his memories of the war years, he describes in the second part the clutch of postcards that his Aunt Alix's divorced husband, "Morose Great-Uncle Alastair," had brought back from a trip to Europe some thirty years earlier and had hidden away for his private amusement. Merrill sets down his adolescent discovery of the cards in the third part along with two prose quotations, one attributed to his friend Germaine Nahman, the other to a mythical book by a mythical author, *Psyche's Sisters* by A. H. Clarendon. The fourth part, which Merrill has said was the hardest to write until he hit upon his six-line stanza, is the poem's turning point—or his reflection on it, since we might put that point there in the space after the citation of Clarendon and before this part's surprisingly triumphant first words: "Love. Warmth." As this fourth part of "Carnivals" continues, it reaches out into "Scenes not lived through yet," which include a Mardi Gras in Rio de Janeiro. This part breaks off in the middle of a sentence, and the fifth part, in pentameter quatrains after an introductory line and a half, brings us to the poem's present: winter in what seems to be Stonington, a cat called Scheherazade "Eight-ninths asleep" on the "unmade / Brass bed," the poet at his desk and apparently recovered from his "absurd complaint."

But what has happened to cure him? The remedy must begin with the memory of M. and his "new wife." This little group at "a corner table" seem to have overcome through their civilities any tensions created by the former relationship between M. and the poet, and the poem reaches a nadir of politeness. "It was understood / Our war was over. We had made our peace / With—everything," he realizes with disgust. "The heads of animals / Gazed in forebearance from the velvet walls. / Great drifts of damask cleaned our lips of grease." But there's more here than meets the eye—the human eye, anyway. Those mounted heads know something basic about the human animal. One glimpses the "mask" in "damask" and hears the second meaning of "forebearance": if the animal heads look on with tolerance, it is partly because they are our forebears. And because they are, we cannot so easily wipe away the vestiges of the animal meat—which is to say the sensual past. Wipe as they might, M. and the poet are the same people who had whatever relationship they had, which certainly looks to have been sexual. Their wiping the grease from their lips brings to mind that "carnival" comes from roots meaning literally "to raise flesh." At the end of Carnival, the meat is raised and removed from the table to comply with the strictures of Lent, but in "The Thousand and Second Night" meat is first of all raised in one way and another to one set of lips and another. The first occasion is here at the restaurant, and it foreshadows the fellatio and the fornication in "Postcards from Hamburg, Circa 1912."

This "light verse," as Merrill calls it, is remarkable for its combination of elegance and "Shamelessness":

> The ocelot's yawn, a sepia-dim
> Shamelessness from nun's coif to spike heels,
> She strokes his handlebar who kneels
> To do for her what a dwarf does for him.
> The properties are grim . . .
>
> > . . . The next
> Shows him with muscle flexed
>
> In resurrection from his underwear,
> Gaining an underworld to harrow.
> He steers her ankles like—like a wheelbarrow.
> The dwarf has slipped out for a breath of air,
> Leaving the monstrous pair.
>
> Who are they? What does their charade convey?
> Maker and Muse? Demon and Doll?

Who are they? Well, if they are a "monstrous pair," the poet has been judged a "monster" himself, and from the sly allusion to Pan through the animal forebears we have had other inklings of his monstrousness. As soon as we answer "Yes" to the penultimate question above, this section begins to respond to "Rigor Vitae," for with its outrageous pun on "resurrection," the description of the cards burlesques the poet's own renewed sense of wholeness or identity. It is not only burlesque, however, since it is precisely the relationship between the sensual and the spiritual that he means to address.

That is one reason Merrill draws out the religious motif in the last stanzas here, where the photographer closes up shop for the day:

> Sighing, "The death of sin is wages,"
> He paid his models, bade them dress and go,

Earthlings once more, incognito
Down swarming boulevards, the contagious-
ly easy, final stages,

Dodged even by the faithful, one of whom
(Morose Great-Uncle Alastair)
Brought back these effigies and would shortly bear
Their doctrine unconfessed, we may assume,
Into his brazen tomb.

The poet is to be distinguished from his uncle in the point of confession, as we are about to learn. But as far as basics go, they are not so different. Both have disguised a sensual longing—but then who has not, Merrill seems to ask, when the models merge with the crowds in the "swarming boulevards." That swarm itself testifies to the ubiquity of the pertinent appetite. Hence one of the ironies of Aunt Alix's remark to the poet as adolescent: "'Ah, they're all the same— / Men, I mean.' A pause. 'Not you, of course.'" Perhaps *she* is not the same—but if not, that is because she is a different kind of figure altogether from the poet's point of view. She is to Alastair, from whom she is divorced, as the spirit is to the senses it is detached from. Merrill's working out of a cure for his "absurd complaint" involves remembering his kinship with his uncle and his other forebears. After Aunt Alix directed him to "Light the fire" and help her burn the postcards, he "must / Meanwhile have tucked a few into [his] shirt" and subsequently "spent the night rekindling with expert / Fingers—but that phase needn't be discussed." What more could he say?

It is the memory of this fire (which might make us think of Eliot's allusions in *his* third part to St. Augustine's confession to sexual desire in terms of "burning") that warms the heretofore "cold and withdrawn" poet. That memory also summons up the involuted quotation from Germaine Nahman.[19] The core of this paragraph is Nahman's proposition that "All irony aside, the libertine *was* 'in search of his soul'; nightly he labored to regain those firelit lodgings." Nahman means not that her libertine wants to transcend nature by exhausting all avenues of experience (as the Gnostic libertine would), but rather that he seeks experiences comparable to those he had in the womb, at which period "The soul could not be told from the body" and his "transports went far beyond" any sensations known since. Her libertine's baroque logic seems to be that to regain that original sensual experience would be to regain the unity of soul and body. Nahman herself demurs: "Likewise, upon the Earth's mature body we inflict a wealth of gross experience—drugs, drills, bombardments"—which involves us in "a waste of resources all too analogous to our own." Mother Nature responds, she argues, in the form of "Natural calamities (tumor and apoplexy no less than flood and volcano)," which "may at last be hailed as positive reassurances, perverse if you like, of life in the old girl yet." The poet's palsy, an apoplectic condition, appears in this light less a sign of spiritual paralysis than a perverse indication of spiritual life. Soul and body are already and still closely related then. That is the oblique message of the coy excerpt attributed to Clarendon: ". . . faced with such constant bickering, Cynthia would have to pinch herself to recall how warmly and deeply those two did, in fact, love one another." Those "two," if Cynthia is one of *Psyche's Sisters,* will be Eros and Psyche themselves, body and soul. That Cynthia must "pinch herself to recall" is itself cleverly suggestive of their relationship. While the body would feel the pinch, the memory, which Merrill claims in section four is equatable with soul, reacts. (And Cynthia's little "pinch" is very likely an example of the expertness of her own fingers.)

We could formulate this reciprocity in Wildean terms: one can cure the soul by means of the senses and the senses by means of the soul. In "The Thousand and Second Night" the recollection of "A thousand and one nights" of sensual experience leads almost directly (the prose excerpts intervene) to the poet's own resurrection. "Sensual experience," or "love, if love's the word / On the foxed spine of the long-mislaid book." "Love" *is* the word, or a suitable word, he decides when he begins part four of section three with it. It is right, since "Love" has sprung from the memory of desire, that the opening lines of this part also allude to masturbation:

> Love. Warmth. Fist of sunlight at last
> Pounding emphatic on the gulf. High wails
> From your white ship: The heart prevails!
> Affirm it! Simple decency rides the blast!—
> Phrases that, quick to smell blood, lurk like sharks
> Within a style's transparent lights and darks.

It will not be surprising to see onanism and writing coming together, in view of the relations between body and soul and maker and muse. Jacques Derrida, in his well-known discussion of Rousseau in *Of Grammatology,* has mused on the connections among language, masturbation, auto-affection, and imagination. In the course of his discussion he argues that "the movement of language" or "the supplementary menace of writing" is in some respects "totally indistinguishable" from "'sexual' auto-affection" and that imagination is "pure auto-affection. It is the other name of différance as auto-affection."[20] "Could we adore one another the way the poet adores his words or the painter his colors," William Gass asks, "what would be the astonishing result?"[21] To the extent that they are *his* words the poet adores, the act of writing clearly entails a certain autoeroticism. The relationship is more complicated than that, as Merrill amply demonstrates in "From the Cupola," but he is not concerned with exploring it here. Here the point is that because body and soul are inextricable, carnal experience or the memory of it can restore the spirit.

The tone through these first two sextains and more is exultant, the imagery at one point almost mystical: "The lips part. The plume trembles. You're afloat / Upon the breathing, all-reflecting deep." But as soon as the exuberant tone has established itself, in the third stanza, the meter changes to trochaic, and in its wake the poem's direction alters once again:

> O skimmer of deep blue
> Volumes fraught with rhyme and reason,
> Once the phosphorescent meshes loosen
> And the objects of your quest slip through,
> Almost you can overlook a risen
> Brow, a thin, black dawn on the horizon.

From the "Almost," from the "thin" edge of the oxymoron, the last two stanzas emerge. He might overlook that "black dawn," we learn, "Except that . . . One city calls you—towers, drums, conches, bells / Tolling each year's more sumptuous farewells / To flesh." This city is not only Rio, at Carnival, in preparation for Lent. Merrill, having been born on March 3, would associate Carnival with growing older, one bitter subject in "Rigor Vitae," so that "each year's more sumptuous farewells" would have a special meaning for him. From this point of view, the "one city" would counterpoise Yeats's city of artifice and eternity—reservations about which have appeared in the section on Istanbul. Rio is the city that is this world. And in this world, a "thin, black dawn" keeps coming on:

> Among the dancers on the pier
> Glides one figure in a suit of bones,
> Whose savage grace alerts the chaperones.

> He picks you out from thousands. He intends
> Perhaps no mischief. Yet the dog-brown eyes
> In the chalk face that stiffens as it dries
> Pierce you with the eyes of those three friends.

The mask begins to melt upon your face.
A hush has fallen in the market place,

And now the long adventure

And there he catches himself up one last time: "Let that wait. / I'm tired, it's late at night." Which is a fine gallant touch, that postponement of a rendezvous with Death on the grounds of weariness.

He has more fun at Death's expense a few lines later, when he promises that "Tomorrow . . . the few final lines / Will lie on the page and the whole ride at anchor" if only he can find the wherewithal to write "Scenes not lived through yet." Meanwhile, he can begin to round off the poem, since it has virtually come to its conclusion in his intuition of the integrity of body and soul. The end of the third section contrasts directly with the first. Whereas there he wore a "mask of platinum" that might as well have been a death mask, here he refers to a face "bronzed and lined" by experience. He was in frantic pursuit then of "so many other things I haven't seen," but he now finds that "There's so little left to see!" It is as though Merrill, who was forty when this book appeared, had come to welcome the change designated by Schopenhauer when he declared that the first forty years of life give us the text and the next thirty provide the commentary. Rather like the Ancient Mariner after the critical point in his voyage, Merrill can now exclaim, "Voyages, I bless you." Unlike "Sailing to Byzantium," Merrill's voyage brings the speaker back "home" to "winter" and "Real / Snow." It is here, in the world, if anywhere, he seems to insist to Yeats, that body and soul can combine. His cat, whose name makes her a stand-in for the muse this maker deals with, is "Eight-ninths asleep" on his bed, but her tail is awake and "twitching to the steel / Band of the steam heat's dissonant calypso," and that twitching, we can make no mistake, is sensual.

The lovely fifth section formulates as parable the poem's main drift. At the end of "the long adventure," which we understand to be the poet's life or this poem, "the Sultan . . . grown old," and Scheherazade, "her tales all told," who correspond to "'senses'" and "'soul,'" ask for release from each other and go their ways. I say "go their ways," but my tense is a conventional narrative present that misrepresents the poem, which ends with an inspired stroke in the past tense. I quote the last stanza only:

They wept, then tenderly embraced and went
Their ways. She and her fictions soon were one.
He slept through moonset, woke in blinding sun,
Too late to question what the tale had meant.

We may take this parting as an embellished version of the separation imagined in "To a Butterfly," when the self and the butterfly or soul "each will have flown / The other's jail." When the Sultan wakes "Too late to question what the tale had meant," Merrill identifies the Sultan's life by way of that "tale" with the soul's "fictions," and the conclusion is a final tying of the knot of physical and spiritual. Yet I think we must feel that something of the enigma confronting the Sultan as he wakes—to what? where?—confronts us too, when this poem that has worked out so arduously the entanglings of body and soul ends with the one alone. Indeed, doesn't the reader who looks up from the last line—and blinks—take the Sultan's place?

Looked at in some lights, the poem undoes its resolution with a single clean yank of that loose end, and we are plunged back into the real world of blindness and befuddlement and loneliness. For the Sultan becomes the poet at the beginning, who is also alone, waking, in the Orient, and divided from himself. In the end, Merrill accords the intuited unity of soul and body no higher status than the sense of the divided self. This is one of the beauties of the past tense here, that it puts the poem and its resolution definitely behind us even as it puts the motivating problem before. In doing so, it recapitulates our experience of such a work, whose meaning exists in its process, and whose process, overseen by Scheherazade, is so fraught with paradox that it will be somewhat different each time through.

If someone is waiting to skewer this poem's morsels on his Ticonderoga #$2\frac{5}{10}$ and cook it once and for all, she is not going to let it happen yet.

> > >

"The really Romantic individual," Donald Sutherland thinks, "is 'divid-ual.'"[22] The Transcendentalists are Romantic in this as in much else. Here is the *locus classicus* from Thoreau's chapter on "Solitude":

> I only know myself as a human entity . . . and am sensible of a certain doubleness by which I can stand as remote from myself as from another. However intense my experience, I am conscious of the presence and criticism of a part of me, which, as it were, is not a part of me, but spectator, sharing no experience, but taking note of it; and that is no more I than it is you. When the play, it may be the tragedy, of life is over, the spectator goes his way. It was a kind of fiction, a work of the imagination only, so far as he was concerned. This doubleness may easily make us poor neighbors and friends sometimes.[23]

136

This *dédoublement* is at once one of the great virtues of Merrill's work from *Water Street* on and one of the generative problems. If the "spectator" guarantees dialectic and irony, he also tends to make one "cold and withdrawn." Thoreau's last sentence helps to explain the relationship between Orson and the narrator in *The (Diblos) Notebook* and the poet and his "three friends" in "The Thousand and Second Night."

"From the Cupola" is a larger, more daedalian treatment of the divided self than that last poem. It too is a sequence comprising diverse forms including prose and "quotations." One droll happenstance is that the prose excerpts incorporated in "From the Cupola" could have come from the source Merrill cites in the other poem, A. H. Clarendon's *Psyche's Sisters*—except of course that book does not exist, and one must presume that Merrill has invented the passages of narrative prose in this poem's seventh section. "From the Cupola" has ten sections, unnumbered, distinguished from the second through the ninth by the setting of a section's first word in small caps. The first and tenth sections, in matching *abba* quatrains, serve as nearly symmetrical prologue and epilogue; they are set apart visually by the use of extra leads and tonally by the shifts in voice, in the first instance from the poet's to Psyche's and in the second from hers to his. Not that the demarcation between the two voices is that clear for much of the poem.

"From the Cupola" tells three stories, the most immediately apparent of which is Apuleius's tale of Psyche and Cupid—or Eros, to use the Greek name. Merrill's use of the Greek rather than Apuleius's Amor or Cupid is one of several details that suggests that he read Erich Neumann's *Amor and Psyche,* which includes a translation of the tale and a psychological commentary on it.[24] But the most succinct, unflavored summary of the tale is to be found in H. J. Rose's classic *Handbook of Greek Mythology:*

> A certain king had three daughters, the youngest of whom, by name Psyche, was so lovely that she was adored as Venus herself. The goddess became jealous, and sent Cupid to make Psyche fall in love with some unsightly wretch. But he fell in love with her himself, and persuaded Apollo to tell her father that she must be dressed as a bride and abandoned on the top of a mountain. Thence, by the agency of the West Wind, he had her transferred to a fairy palace built in a hidden valley, and here he visited her, but always in the dark. After a time, she begged to be allowed to bring her sisters to see her, and this he reluctantly granted. On the first visit, they became madly jealous, and on a second visit they discovered that she had never seen her mysterious husband. Coming again, they assured her that he was a cannibal monster,

and gave her a lantern to discover him and a sharp knife to kill him. Waiting till he slept, Psyche turned the light on him, and was awestruck by his beauty. But a drop of oil falling on him awoke him, and he left her, upbraiding her disobedience. She set out to look for him, contriving to avenge herself on her sisters. After many adventures, she came to the dwelling of Venus, who received her harshly and set her to perform impossible tasks,—first to sort out a mingled heap of various grains, then to fetch water from an inaccessible fountain, finally to go down to Hades and fetch a supply of beauty from Persephone. The first tasks were accomplished by the unexpected help of ants and an eagle; the third, by following the good advice given by a tower from which she was minded to throw herself in despair, was nearly completed when, having almost returned to the upper world, she had a curiosity to examine the supposed casket of beauty which she carried. It contained, however, not beauty but a deathly sleep, which at once overcame her. Now Cupid interfered in person, having at last won the consent of Iuppiter to the marriage, and she was revived and united to him.[25]

As Joseph Campbell notes, Psyche's quest is "one of the best known and most charming examples of the 'difficult tasks' motif." It is characteristic of Merrill that he would be drawn to a tale in which "all the principal roles are reversed: instead of the lover trying to win his bride, it is the bride trying to win her lover; and instead of a cruel father withholding his daughter from the lover, it is the jealous mother, Venus, hiding her son, Cupid, from his bride."[26]

In Merrill's hands, to turn to the second story, the princess becomes a young woman, still called Psyche, who was raised in the twentieth century in an arcadian Palm Beach ("A city named for palms half desert and half dream") and has moved with her two sisters, Alice and Gertrude, to a New England coastal town modeled on Stonington. There she recalls the South nostalgically and pines over Eros, on whom she had a crush when they were children in Florida and from whom she has been separated, perhaps not until some time after her arrival in the North. The two prose passages in the seventh section are flashbacks to a time when these two were still seeing each other—though that is exactly the wrong word, since Merrill's Psyche too, until the decisive act reported in the second prose passage, did not *see* her lover. When we meet her, she is less Apuleius's heroine performing Aphrodite's tasks than Cinderella, laboring as a virtual domestic in her own home under the baleful eyes of her disagreeable sisters.

The poem's third story is partly secret and autobiographical. In an interview Merrill has touched on the oddest of the contributing incidents.[27] He once received, out of the blue, from a person whose name he "didn't recognize," a "love-letter." Though a stranger, the other person seemed to know everything about Merrill's past. This letter was followed by others, and "That seed"

> Has since become a world of blossom and bark.
> The letters fill a drawer, the gifts a room.
> No hollow of your day is hidden from
> His warm concern. Still you are in the dark.

The second person here and throughout the first section is the poet, talking to himself. Even to offer that clarification, however, is to embroil us, because the "you," we soon realize, is also Psyche. No sooner have we made that discovery than we further understand that the "you" is the reader, who is certainly as much "in the dark" about the poem's subject here at the obscure outset as Merrill/Psyche is about the letter writer's identity. As this section develops we gather that the poet, while receiving these letters, has found himself in a position Merrill's speakers often find themselves in. The phrase "the ash of something I survive" hints at the breakup of a love affair, as does his remark to Psyche about Eros, when he invites her to tell him about the god: "Him I have known too little (or, of late, / Too well) to trust my own view of your lover." He also implies that Psyche's story disguises his own:

> The point won't be to stage
> One of our torchlit hunts for truth. Truth asks
> Just this once to sleep with fiction, masks
> Of tears and laughter on the moonstruck page;
>
> To cauterize what babbles to be healed—
> Just this once not by candor. Here and now,
> Psyche, I quench that iron lest it outglow
> A hovering radiance your fingers shield.

A love affair has ended, then, and as though in compensation, he has begun to get letters and gifts from an unknown correspondent; but this autobiography is to take a back seat to Psyche's story. In upending the procedure he had seemed to advocate in *Water Street* and seeking a remedy not by means of a white-hot "candor" but by means of the shaded oil lamp of fiction, he rejects the manner of the so-called confessional poetry so vital in the sixties. He even sets out, with admirable gall, to devise a contrary style—and to do what Louise Bogan had accused him of doing in *First Poems*. How pleased he must have been to find a new use for that old criticism! That he did make the connection there can be no doubt, since he all but quotes Bogan's arch stricture in this poem's last section, where he reflects on the preceding tale and "The lamp I smell in every other line."

But he does not quote Bogan exactly: "in every *other* line," he says. This is preeminently a poem of doubles and alternates. In the lines quoted above he foresees a union of truth and fiction, tears and laughter—pairs we come to associate, along with reality's "blackmail" and romance's "rosy veil," with Eros and Psyche respectively. It is characteristic of him to see that his town's finest houses have "Renaissance features grafted onto Greek / Revival" and to let that architectural contrivance represent his poem, with its own re-working of a Greek myth revived by Apuleius. Characteristic too is the entertaining of opposites by the town's cupolas, in the passage that introduces the other main voice: "By day or night, cloud, sunbeam, lunatic streak, / They alternately ravish and disown / Earth, sky, and water—Are you with me? Speak." And speak Psyche does—though it is not only Psyche to whom he speaks.

The ambiguous pronoun, the female persona, and the adaptation of a received framework all suggest that Merrill read with interest another long poem, published a decade before he wrote "From the Cupola": John Berryman's "Homage to Mistress Bradstreet."[28] But those similarities are superficial, and there are superficial dissimilarities too. Whereas Berryman uses an eight-line stanza that varies only slightly, Merrill changes his prosody from section to section—a modus operandi that goes back as far as *First Poems'* "Variations: White Stag, Black Bear," whose last section contains Merrill's first experiment with the Psyche and Eros tale. Moreover, the most distinctive feature of Berryman's poem, its vigorous syntactical distortion, seems to have had little effect on Merrill, whose syntax is sometimes hermetically complicated but rarely fractured. Merrill does find a means of achieving some of the effects of Berryman's syntax, however: by omitting punctuation from the second section through the ninth, he helps to create a context of interlaced, mostly definable ambiguities, an end served also by his extravagant punning (which recalls Berryman's). In this context, the male poet and the female persona keep merging and separating. It is at this level that the two poems have strong affinities.

By the tenth stanza of Berryman's "Homage," the poet's voice has modulated into Bradstreet's, and she is musing on her isolation in the New World:

vellum I palm, and dream. Their forest dies
to greensward, privets, elms & towers, whence
a nightingale is throbbing.
Women sleep sound. I was happy once . .
(Something keeps on not happening; I shrink?)
These minutes all their passions & powers sink
and I am not one chance
for an unknown cry or a flicker of unknown eyes.

She thinks back longingly on a civilized land, with its tended lawns and its
carefree women. She does not "sleep sound" herself, partly because of the
barbaric country she has emigrated to, partly because she has not become
pregnant. Her countrywomen back home have passions and powers that
seem beyond her. Something like that is one way we must read this stanza;
but at the same time we hear the poet, pondering his poem on Anne Bradstreet. *He* shrinks from dealing with the problems and opportunities his
poem has presented; it is he, lonely and impotent, who lacks the power to
give birth, to bring his lonely, unpregnant character to life. Berryman's feelings of failure in regard to Bradstreet, when translated into her feelings,
make her a vivid, sympathetic figure. "We are on each other's hands / who
care," he has insisted earlier, and indeed because of their respective estrange-
ments they are made for each other. It is a subtle touch, and funny, that in
the stanza following Bradstreet's remark that "Simon [her husband] is much
away" she is at last and suddenly pregnant, a state she describes in terms that
will do also for Berryman's feelings at finally having succeeded in imagining what she would feel—his feelings, in short, at getting her pregnant:
"My world is strange / and merciful, ingrown months, blessing a swelling
trance."

There follow those stanzas of which Berryman was said to be especially
proud, in which she gives birth to her first child. These are the stanzas that
Merrill mimeographed and distributed to a writing workshop at the University of Wisconsin in the spring of 1967, not long after *Nights and Days* was
published:

19

So squeezed, wince you I scream? I love you & hate
off with you. Ages! *Useless.* Below my waist
he has me in Hell's vise.
Stalling. He let go. Come back: brace
me somewhere. No. No. Yes! everything down
hardens I press with horrible joy down

my back cracks like a wrist
shame I am voiding oh behind it is too late

20

hide me forever I work thrust I must free
now I all muscles & bones concentrate
what is living from dying?
Simon I must leave you so untidy
Monster you are killing me Be sure
I'll have you later Women do endure
I can *can* no longer
and it passes the wretched trap whelming and I am me

21

drencht & powerful, I did it with my body!
One proud tug greens Heaven. Marvellous,
unforbidding Majesty.
Swell, imperious bells. I fly.
Mountainous, woman not breaks and will bend:
sways God nearby: anguish comes to an end.
Blossomed Sarah, and I
blossom. Is that thing alive? I hear a famisht howl.

Just as surely as this is the birth of Samuel to Anne Bradstreet, it is the rebirth of her to John Berryman. What a long labor these stanzas must have entailed. *Redolet lucernam!* The lines in 19 and 20 gasp, grit their teeth, double up with the work of the poet imagining the mother's experience and describing his own experience of imagining it. With "I am me," Berryman becomes himself by virtue of having become Bradstreet, even as she fulfills herself by giving birth. Having thus brought her forth, he can regard her as another person, the relationship between them is so intense. In a touching passage in her memoir, *Poets in Their Youth,* Eileen Simpson, Berryman's first wife, recounts his distress when he found that his poem was demanding that he try to seduce Bradstreet—and his relief when his wife gave him permission to do so.[29] If the attempt does not succeed, the reason is that the "Homage" is about desire—not *a* desire, really, but longing—trying to fulfill itself through words. But one might as well expect Ulysses to return home in Stevens's "The World as Meditation," or the poet to remain in the rose garden in "Burnt Norton"—or Eros to materialize in section five of "From the Cupola."

The "Homage" must end as it began with the separation of the two lovers—an almost intolerable business for Berryman to manage, Simpson has told us.[30] Or we might say that it ends with the reabsorption into the poet of that part of himself that Bradstreet has almost been. We may think of this poem, as of "From the Cupola," as a representation of the process of intense thought—thought as Friedrich Schlegel defines it: "an inward speaking and a never-ending dialogue with oneself." Even when we are alone, we think as two—or especially when we are alone.

Schlegel goes on, in *The Philosophy of Language*, to write about internal dialogue in the most isolated people: "This colloquy with self, or generally, this internal dialogue, is so perfectly the natural form of human thinking, that even the saintly solitaries of bygone centuries, who in the Egyptian deserts or the Alpine hermitages devoted a half-life to meditation on divine things and mysteries, were often not able otherwise to indicate the result of such meditations, to invest it in another dress, to bring it into any other form of exposition than that of a dialogue of the soul with God."[31] Schlegel's last phrase might make us look again at Berryman's last four stanzas, where first the poet's voice takes over from Anne's; then her voice comes back to speak in unison with his; and finally these voices blend with another:

> O all your ages at the mercy of my loves
> together lie at once, forever or
> so long as I happen.
> In the rain of pain & departure, still
> Love has no body and presides the sun,
> and elfs from silence melody. I run.
> Hover, utter, still,
> a sourcing   whom my lost candle like the firefly loves.

Even as the poet and his subject part, Love speaks through them and even joins them. "Love has no body" must mean that the lover is inescapably alone. Yet these two are one with that "sourcing," which we identify with the "I" even though we read it as an object of "utter"—just as we understand "Hover" and "utter" as verbs parallel to "run" and governed by "I" even as we hear them as imperatives addressed to the reader. These different readings force us to see "Love has no body" as a statement that it cannot be localized or limited or destroyed. The "sourcing" is supreme and ubiquitous—a "hovering radiance," to lift a term from Merrill's poem.

Schlegel's phrase "a dialogue of the soul with God" and Berryman's ultimate conjunction of the human and the divine can help us read "From the Cupola" as well as later poems by Merrill. It is instructive to find Erich Neumann, in glossing the eventual deification of Apuleius's Psyche, arguing that it "means that the human is itself divine and equal to the gods . . . The psychic turn of the divine, the inward journey of the gods into what we call the human psyche . . . has its archetypal beginning in this apotheosis of Psyche."[32] Perhaps Merrill's Psyche's ironic surmise, "I may already be part god," has another side. We must notice, moreover, that Merrill's Eros turns out to speak through the poet—and, surprisingly, through Psyche. Either might say, with the speaker in "Days of 1964," "A god breathed from my lips." Then too Merrill has said, in regard to the unknown letter writer who becomes a model for Eros, that "a stranger who knows one very well is practically a metaphor for God."[33] I shall come back to this issue.

Because "From the Cupola" dramatizes the process of thought at its most intense, it will not surprise us that it is shot through with contradictions. Psyche's first words indicate the poem's density: "SUNLIGHT Crossfire / of rays and shadows each / glancing off a windowpane a stone." They indicate and simultaneously embody it, for "Crossfire" glances back across the section break to "Earth, sky, and water" and supplies the fourth element. Such interlacing prevails at the level of character also, although at the outset Merrill's framework looks fairly simple. Having appropriated Apuleius's narrative, he makes some modifications in it so that it will accommodate his experiences with the letter writer. "Was the time always wrong for you to meet?" he asks Psyche in his first section. Then he sees what she must say: "Not that he ever once proposed as much. / Your sisters joke about it. 'It's too rich! / Somebody Up There loves you, Psyche sweet.'" The second section also lets us read it as simply reflective of the episode in which, having fallen in love with Psyche, Eros has installed her at his palace and visits her under cover of dark. Thus her "correspondent" remains "sheer / projection" because she never sees him, and like Apuleius's heroine she has her curiosity piqued, though she knows to her apparent regret that he "will not come / to the porch at noon" in either his own form, whatever that might be, or even "masked as crone or youth." Merrill manages all this with such deftness that we see Psyche and through her himself. When Psyche speaks of having been "utterly . . . undressed" after the "last red" (lipstick? wine?) has been wiped from her lips, we think both of her affair with Eros and Merrill's use of her. For just as Eros is Psyche's "sheer / projection," so Psyche is Merrill's transparent device; she is his "correspondent" because she corresponds to him. This is one way in which "truth" (the poet's isolation, the "tears") can "sleep with fiction" (the Psyche myth, the laughter). And with that fine figure of speech we get a glimpse of the enormous complications, for it implies a parallel between the poet and Eros. To make matters more convoluted, it soon appears that Psyche and Eros are part and parcel of each other. Psyche, looking through the window panes of the cupola "lookout" for Eros, for instance, would also see herself reflected in the glass.

Because of this maze of metaphor and these nested synecdoches, Merrill cannot follow limpid Apuleius so closely after all. Psyche's life in the New England village seems at first parallel to the tale's cohabitation in Eros's palace, but then the present turns out to be a time of trial for her and thus more like her stay with Aphrodite. The period that best answers to the tale's honeymoon is instead Psyche's youth in Palm Beach, where Eros fell in love with her at first sight. In the myth Aphrodite lives at the beach, and in the third section Merrill's figure imagines Eros, an indefatigable surfer, still there:

> You daylong in the saddles of foaming opal
> ride   I am glad   Come dusk lime juice and gin
> deepen the sunset under your salt skin
> I've tasted that side of the apple
> A city named for palms half desert and half dream
> its dry gold settles on my mouth

The first part of this memory is lightly erotically charged, from the allusion to the birth of Aphrodite (the combers she emerged from, on some accounts, resulted from Zeus's having severed and flung Kronos's spurting penis into the sea) through the riding image and the phantom pun on "Come" to the tasting of the apple. The sensual, however, is just one element in Psyche's Palm Beach, which is less Apuleius's palace than a sort of Arcadia. Psyche recalls a "world where nothing changed or died / unless to be reborn on the next tide," a "City half dream half desert where at dawn / the sprinkler dervish whirled and all was crystalline" and each house was "half brothel and half shrine." The description echoes in its rhapsodic repetition Yeats's vision in "Vacillation": "A tree there is that from its topmost bough / Is half all glittering flame and half all green / Abounding foliage moistened with the dew; / And half is half and yet is all the scene." Like Yeats's vision, Psyche's memory is of a world in which opposites such as the spiritual and the sensual unite.

Like many such places, Psyche's Palm Beach has an uncertain ontological status. Although she locates it in her past, it has the feel of an ideal world, Ariel's as distinct from Prospero's—and that I take it is the point of Alice's "*long but kindly meant harangue,*" as she herself too charitably describes it, in the fourth section, which Merrill has professed not to understand entirely.[34] It might help to remember that the poem is still a dialogue within the self. According to Neumann, the Hellenistic tale dramatizes an internal conflict, since at bottom Apuleius's female figure is "far from being merely 'gentle' and 'simple-hearted'; on the contrary, the attitude of the sisters, their protest and hostility, correspond[s] to a current in Psyche herself."[35] It is not the "man-hating matriarchal powers" Neumann discerns in Psyche that Alice projects, however, but rather a realistic streak that runs sourly into cynicism. Alice is a sort of Anteros; she is an exaggeration of that side of the poet that lets him claim to be "Not a believer" in love. From the point of view of this inversion of Lewis Carroll's Alice, Palm Beach was "*a cruel impossible wonderland*" where the whole family was miserable. She compulsively pours out a bizarre little allegory that she certainly means (her disclaimer notwithstanding) to be a comment on Psyche and her "*mysterious friend,*" from whom she is getting those letters.

In Alice's rendering of life in Palm Beach, their old sidewalk plays an important role. "*Like somebody I shall not name it lacked / perspective,*" she says with a significant look at Psyche, and laments how "*the poor dumb thing lay . . . / under a dark spell cast*" by "*the shadow of a towering mother / smooth as stone and thousandbreasted though / her milk was watery scant so much for love.*" This is a palm tree, whose coconuts persuade the ingenious Alice to identify it, by way of the statue of the many-breasted Artemis of Ephesus (another aspect of the Great Mother, whose contradictions preoccupied Merrill as early as "Scenes from Childhood" and would get extended attention in *Sandover*), with Aphrodite.[36] (Hence Eros's punning reference to "*A city . . . half mummy and half myth.*") As for the shadow the fronds cast on the sidewalk, Alice interprets it as "*the batwing offspring of her ladyship*" or Eros himself. These two also take the forms, in this fickle allegory, of a neighbor, a "*veiled and hatted / tanagra,*" and her "*little boy with water wings.*" Now and then, Alice recalls, there would be a cloudy morning when the "*sidewalk*" would have a "*respite*"—"*And yet by ten o'clock / the phantom struck again in a first sunshaft.*" While Alice is unclear about the nature of the suffering, we can presume that she has in mind unrequited love. In Alice's version of things, the weeds were "*hoarse green tongues*" that "*begged from each new crack*" in the tormented sidewalk for the barest scrap of the real life that Eros seemed to promise: "GIVE ME THE SNAPPED SHOELACE / LIZARDS ANTS SCRAPS OF SILVER FOIL." But it was "*No use,*" so they have "*moved here where gray skies are the rule*"—where there are no sunshafts, no shadows, no pain, no drama. No love. Which is just fine with Alice, who is allergic to all affection. Psyche shocks her sister with her suggestion for eliminating the grief that Alice has just described—"*Why not simply have cut down the tree / Psyche I can't believe my   Hush*"—but she is perhaps more moved by the saucy hyperextension of her allegory than by the prospective consequences of somehow doing away with "*the root of all that evil,*" the goddess of love herself.

Psyche is being facetious, to be sure—yet there is an element of seriousness in her suggestion, which recalls Francis's radical solution in *The Seraglio*. She knows only too well about the grief caused by love, as we see more clearly when Alice withdraws and leaves Psyche alone in the "cupola glassed / entirely with panes some tinted amethyst / it is my task to clean":

> Up here among
>
> spatterings and reflections wipe as I will
> these six horizons still the rain's dry ghost
> and my own features haunt the roofs the coast
> How does one get to know a landscape well
>
> When did we leave the South   Why do we live indoors
> I wonder sweating to the cadence   Even
> on sunless days the cupola is an oven
> Views blur   This thing we see them through endures

The poet's farewell to her in section ten—"Thank you, Psyche. I should think those panes / Were just about as clear as they can be"—helps us to read this passage, though even without the later passage one would perhaps hear "pains" as well as "panes" and sense in those "spatterings and reflections" and (fine phrase) "the rain's dry ghost" some sad recollections. And even without the expression of gratitude, which lets us identify Psyche with the Muse, one might associate her indoor labor and her "cadence" with the composition of the poem, which like the cupola is "This thing" through which we watch "Views blur": the poet's into Psyche's, Psyche's into Alice's, and so on.

"Views blur" in the poem's fifth section, in the purest example to this point in his career of a kind of metamorphosis almost unique to Merrill. This section has been foreshadowed by one of Alice's quatrains, where a metaphor leads her back to her obsessive subject:

> *Nights after a windstorm great yellow paper*
> *dry branches lying on the curb in heaps*
> *like fancy dress don't ask me whose someone who steps*
> *forth and is changed by the harsh moonlight to vapor*

The ghostly figure will be Eros, leaving Psyche's side and vanishing before dawn. That evaporation reverses itself in section five, where the god's materialization is so gradual that punctuation is unthinkable:

MIDNIGHT   I dream I dream   The slow moon eludes
one stilled cloud   Din of shimmerings   From across the Sound
what may have begun as no more
than a willow's sleepwalking outline quickens detaches
comes to itself in the cupola
panics from pane to pane and then impulsively
surrendering fluttering by now the sixteenfold
wings of the cherubim unclipped by faith or reason
stands there my dream made whole
over whose walls again
a red vine black in moonlight crawls
made habitable   Each cell of the concrete
fills with sweet light   The wave breaks
into tears   Come if its you   Step down
to where I   Stop   For at your touch the dream

cracks the angel tenses flees

When the metamorphoses begin, the willow becomes its silhouette, a form that looks like that of a creature with wings furled, which then emerges as a moth beating at the cupola's glass, which finally turns into an angelic figure, Psyche's "dream made whole"—Eros himself. And yet, as she begs him to come closer, and he does so, at the instant he touches her, she stops him, and the moment passes.

What exactly has happened here, at the poem's center? Why does Psyche, whom we suppose to be the seeker after Eros, first invite and then stop him? Why does the angel flee?

We can begin to come to grips with this passage by looking a second time at the "angel." Although it must be Eros who comes to her and transforms "Each cell of the concrete" (we think of the sidewalk Psyche has been compared to), this angel, who brings a "sweet light" and who by touching wakes the dreamer, must also be Psyche, if connections are to count for anything, since these are the acts of Apuleius's heroine. By the same token, then, the speaker has to be Eros. This crux in the poem discovers the intersection of these two within the poet's self. To the extent that Psyche is Eros, that "half is half and yet is all," Psyche's dream, which is *of* wholeness, seems to be realized here for an instant. As Neumann tells us in his euhemeristic view of this tale about "the psychic development of the feminine," there is an Eros within Psyche as well as an Eros without; indeed "Eros . . . is the foundation of her own development."[37] This coexistence within the self of Eros and Psyche is not the same, however, as a union of the self with the Eros without; the integration of sensuality and spirit within the self does not assure—though it might facilitate—a close relationship between self and other. Furthermore, the imagined union and the real thing can converge only in the permanently passing split second between "I" and "Stop." The "touch" of the actual always cracks the mold of the dream. In Neumann's terms, "This inner Eros that is the image of [Psyche's] love is in truth a higher and invisible form of the Eros who lies sleeping before her . . . This greater, invisible Eros within Psyche must necessarily come into conflict with his small, visible incarnation." [38] If, as Neumann observes in a note, "it is essential that she unify the dual structure of Eros . . . and transform the lower into the higher," that transformation is not easily effected or sustained. "The tragedy of sexual intercourse," Yeats told John Sparrow, "is the perpetual virginity of the soul." [39]

As Anne Bradstreet and the poet separate in the aftermath of the near seduction in the "Homage," so Psyche and Eros part after this encounter. The sixth section, "NOON," helps to explain that parting. Both Eve and Adam were tempted at noon, Milton tells us, and here Psyche's five senses (one has "many, many tongues") tempt her, as they react bitterly to being forbidden to see to her pleasure. In effect it is they who have invited Eros and she who has commanded him to stop. (That their frustrated desire is fundamentally erotic, there can be little doubt: the palm tree, which was earlier a "*towering mother*," appears here in stunted form as a potted "dwarf.") Putting down their rebellion, Psyche, wickedly witty when she wants to be, proposes that "we think of things to raise our spirits," and she tries to buy them off with doses of bourbon (for Smell and Taste), music, and so on. The reader has begun to understand that Psyche has sworn off love, yes, partly to give herself time to recover from the breakup with Eros, but also to devote herself to the completion of her task—which is not just the cleaning of the windows but also imagining as fully as possible what might be and seeing as clearly as possible what cannot be. Writing the poem about Eros and Psyche, in short. The "principal dilemma" here as in much of his work is what Merrill has identified as Corot's: "loyalty to the senses or to the imagination?" [40] They are "one" only in the dream or in the poem's description of it—and the poem can be written only at the expense of the physical life. When Psyche smiles at the end of this sixth section, where she and Sight and Touch form a little group, she does so because she has just defeated the Eros within:

The pale one with your eyes restively flashing
takes in the dock the ashen Sound the sky

The fingers of the eldest brush my features
But you are smiling she says coldly   *Why*

The transferred epithet, "coldly," tells us exactly why.

In spite of herself, because her senses do have spirits to raise and they are she, Psyche cannot continue to deny the erotic impulse. Her skeptical side knows that any love affair is doomed to fall short of the hopes it inspires; but her romantic self lives always under the sway of section seven's "STAR or candle" (the morning star, Venus). This side insists on seeing the lover in the flesh, which means waking up the Eros within. This is the bind Psyche is in when the poet breaks in to comfort her:

> When as written you have lapsed
>   back into the god
> darts and wings and appetites
> what of him the lover all eclipsed
>   by sheer love
> Shut my eyes it does no good
> Who will ever put to rights
>
> Psyche, hush. This is me, James,
>   Writing lest he think
> Of the reasons why he writes—
> Boredom, fear, mixed vanities and shames;
>   Also love.

What will happen when the Eros within overwhelms Psyche, and the loved one disappoints or disappears? Better not to have opened one's eyes in the first place. But that is not the view of "James," who includes Psyche as she contains Eros and who sees further than she does—though one thing he sees is that all of us must be partly blind:

> Weeping? You must not.
> All our pyrotechnic flights
> Miss the sleeper in the pitch-dark breast.
>   He is love:
> He is everyone's blind spot.
> We see according to our lights.

Eros, the sleeper (in two senses), the blindfold god within, cannot be made to see his inevitable consequences: "He is everyone's blind spot." And yet in the tale Psyche refers to him as the "light of my life," and earlier in this section of the poem it is Eros's emissaries, the eyes, "adamant / for their meal of pinks and whites / . . . who call those various torches in," so there is a sense in which love sheds light and sees after all—a sense in which love is a spotlight. It is a light by which we see some things and are blinded to others. This is the "profound dark spotlight" that Sandy sees Orestes in for a moment; it is the "profound dark spotlight" that "our moments of uncomprehending loneliness," which Merrill identifies in his essay on Corot as "our most true" moments, shine on "the human condition." It is irreducibly "a blind spot."

"We see according to our lights": Merrill demonstrates that truth by recounting in the following prose passage an incident that has two possible readings. Psyche's other sister, Gertrude, who evidently has a bedroom adjoining hers, hears something suspicious after dark one night:

> "What's that sound? Is it you, dear?"
> "Yes. I was just eating something."
> "What?"
> "I don't know—I mean, an apricot . . ."
> "Hadn't you best switch on the light and make sure?"
> "No, thank you, Gertrude."
> A hurt silence ensued.

Is Psyche still weeping? That is one possibility. But more likely the noise betrays a visit by Eros (so that this is either a flashback or a fall from abstinence). Eating something, in that case, but not an apricot. This second possibility is the more plausible as well as the more entertaining. In its light Gertrude's subsequent complaint that Psyche has come to "crave . . . the unfamiliar, the 'transcendental'" and is "turning into the classic New England old maid" is very funny—and I suppose true in a sense Gertrude could never have meant. In either case, the paragraph that follows this exchange provides Merrill's version of what Neumann calls "the Act," Psyche's discovery of Eros (which again we can consider either a past event or a present repetition of it). But what Psyche sees is not the beautiful boy-god that she finds in Apuleius but rather

> a tear-streaked muzzle, the marvelous lashed golds of an iris reflecting her own person backed by ever tinier worlds of moonlight and tossing palms, then, at the center, blackness, a fixed point, a spindle on which everything had begun to turn. Piercing her to the brain.

> Spelt out in brutal prose, all had been plain.

As we have seen, however, this prose is poetry, as Eros is Psyche, or as love (as she has dreadfully foreseen) is "sheer / projection." Looking into Eros's eyes she can find only herself and her romantic vision. That black pupil at the center of her vision is the "blind spot" with a vengeance.

Alice seems further justified when Psyche and her sisters go to a drive-in theater, and the ideal collapses into the real on every hand. The very windshield wipers move with the "automatic coquetry of fans"; Eros takes the form of a teenager who has been making love with his date in the next car and who is evidently faking "Grief" (as is she) at having gone too far, as they used to say; Aphrodite appears as the "love goddess" who stars in the tawdry film. "It's all an act," perfected by professionals and the gods. It even seems to an emotionally drained Psyche that the less one feels, the more godlike one becomes, so that when her own chagrin has abated and she has grown sleepy, she ironically imagines she "may already be part god." Her fading passion is touchingly caught in the softer irony of her drowsy comment on it: "I may even / learn to love it Eros for your sake." Here we have another glimpse of Psyche's blind spot—her inability *not* to love, which is to say the persistence of the god within.

On the surface, however, the dwindling of feeling in Psyche anticipates the next section's opening pronouncement: "MORNING   The task is done." Finishing the task—the purging of the pains, the securing of a clear view of things—betokens Psyche's recovery from her loss even as it does Merrill's completion of the body of the poem. One image that mediates between the two is that of the "red clapboard temple . . . it's a warehouse really" that appears "in the foreground" of a scene that Psyche has metaphorically painted by cleaning the windows. Its colors are red, white, and black:

> Greek colors   An effect I hope
> not too much spoiled by a big yellow legend
> BOAT WORKS on the roof which seagulls helicopters
> the highup living and the happy dead
> are in a position to read
> Outside indeed a boat lies covered with tarpaulin
> Old headlines mend a missing pane

In addition to identifying the building, the "legend" refers to the Psyche-Eros tale and is also, thanks to Merrill's tireless economy, an inscription saying that *this* boat works. Not that everyone is in "a position to read" this particular literary vehicle, perhaps, with all its puns (like those in the last line above), in which case the boat "covered with tarpaulin" might be as apt a comment on it as the roof's "legend."

Whether to be widely read or not, the poem, like the street laid out before Psyche's now spotless windows, is virtually "finished down to the last detail." Even as it draws to a close, however, it keeps putting out little beginnings, like those stirrings of love in the ashes of Psyche's passion. Merrill strikes balance after balance between acceptance of loneliness and scorning of it. On the one hand, Psyche steps out of the house into "spring's first real sun" and finds that a whimsical "baby dock has waded" out into the Sound, where it stands "on stilts in freezing water." On the other, she imagines that the "little dock . . . must know by now / that no one is coming after it," and in her evocation of the spring day she emphasizes not "*apple blossom* and *sun*" but "the dance of darker undertones / on pavement or white wall." Toward the end of this ninth section, the balance tips. When Psyche, uprooting "the last parsnips for my sisters' dinner," pulls up two that "are tightly interlocked" she decides to "bury them / once more in memory of us"—which is as much as to say that she has decided not to take the "rosy veil."[41] By the time she gets back home, "It's dark," and it is her sisters' moment, "when all else goes black / and what is there but substance to turn to." When, as is their wont, they direct Psyche to "*Light the lamp,*" they seem to demand that she see things as they are. And she lights the lamp.

But somehow it does not have the effect her sisters would want:

My hand is on the switch   I have done this
faithfully each night since the first
Tonight I think will not be different
Then soft light lights the room the furniture
a blush invades even the dropped lid
yes and I am here alone
I and my flesh and blood

Although in a sense she is alone, Psyche's last words are not hers alone. For one thing, she and the poet are as inseparable here as Berryman and Bradstreet at the end of the "Homage." Like the two parsnips, they "have grown that way." The "first" night Psyche mentions is the night when she— lighting her lamp, looking Love in the eye—lost Eros, and it is therefore the night when "James"—lighting his lamp, looking at Psyche—began the poem. Both put aside romantic illusions and accepted their tasks and the attendant solitude. But this is not an end of it. "There is no pure deed," Merrill puts it in the final section, and no sooner does Psyche flip the "switch" than a "blush" suffuses the whole room. What are we to make of that surprise, if not that Eros is harder to shake than one might think? Psyche's claim to solitariness, in the last lines above, is a paradox, not just because she is with her sisters, but more significantly because we must identify the "flesh and blood" with Eros. Although to lose the outer Eros, according to Neumann's exegesis, is to discover the inner Eros, the inner Eros drives one out of oneself.[42] This section's last line contains the seed of a new story, though that story would have to resemble this one—or, to call on Merrill's description of the moonlit scene across the street, "Of the warehouse pulverized / one faintest blueprint glimmers by which to build it / on the same spot tomorrow somehow right."

When the poet takes over from Psyche the tone lightens, as he looks forward to finishing this long poem so that he can live a bit. But to turn from the study to the world is to begin the whole cycle anew. I am reminded of the Persian proverb: he who tries to unravel a knot of the universal skein entangles it even more. If Psyche is "alone . . . with her flesh and blood," and that phrase couples her with Eros, its terms call back the moonlight and torch of the opening section. Just as Psyche turns also into Eros, so Eros unfolds into the two of them. In the last section, even as the poet is about to plunge back into life, an ingenious conceit undermines the distinction between writing and living, since it springs from the similarity between his typewriter's bank of type bars and a Roman amphitheater and compares the individual bars striking the page to gladiators sallying forth into the arena. The black print on the page constitutes the poem based on the romantic tale but also represents a criticism of romance, in that it testifies to the poet's loneliness—a condition he is wearying of:

> Damned
> If I don't tire of the dark view of things.
> I think of your "Greek colors" and it rings
> A sweet bell. Time to live! Haven't I dimmed
>
> That portion of the ribbon—whose red glows
> Bright with disuse—sufficiently for a bit?
> Tomorrow mayn't I start to pay my debt,
> In wine, in heart's blood, to la vie en rose?

The "sweet bell" that reminds him of the romantic life, and probably specifically of the doorbell that heralds the arrival of the friends at the end of *Water Street,* is the typewriter's carriage bell (which "rings" appropriately at the end of the line). And it is also the bell that calls him from his corner into the ring for another encounter of the sort that drives him back to writing poems (a wrestling match itself, in his recurrent metaphor), since illusion is as much a part of the world as the "substance" and "fact" adored by Gertrude and Alice (those "realistic" types named ironically for Stein and Toklas).

"There is no pure deed," and by now the plainest statement immediately turns its cheeky other face. As soon as he declares that it is "Time to live," Merrill decides that "This evening it will do to be alone / Here," then enumerates the companions he will be alone *with:* Psyche's "girlish figures: parsnip, Eros, / Shadow, blossom, windowpane. The warehouse. / The lamp I smell in every other line." That lamp, Psyche's, leads him to a thoroughly duplicitous conclusion:

> From its rubbed brass a moth
> Hurtles in motes and tatters of itself
> —Be careful tiny sister, drabbest sylph!—
> Against the hot glare, the consuming myth,
>
> Drops, and is still. My hands move. An intense,
> Slow-paced, erratic dance goes on below.
> I have received from whom I do not know
> These letters. Show me, light, if they make sense.

That is less brassy than polished, I think, and less learned than magical, though one wonders what Louise Bogan would have thought. But of course the primary referent of the moth is Psyche, the resident genie of this poem's lantern. Along with the lamp of learning, however, something else is being metaphorically rubbed here, as the poet's "hands move" in their "erratic dance . . . below" and type out these erotic innuendos. Again, while "the consuming myth" is the life that destroys, it is nevertheless the poetry that absorbs. While the Psyche moth falls and lies quiet, she "is still" in the "hovering radiance" of that lamp.[43]

The "consuming myth," then, is equally life and writing, "tightly interlocked," each at once half and all. They have "grown that way," in both senses of the verb: "become" and "flourished." And it is a myth at once tragic in its insistence on the ultimate loneliness of the lover and comic in its argument that Psyche and the god are always united in the self and that all of us have that union in common. These letters from the cupola are from that copula as well. They "make sense" in two senses of the phrase, Eros's and Psyche's.

chapter four

AT THE WEB'S HEART
The Fire Screen and *Braving the Elements*

(*The smoke cleared
On no real damage, yet I'd wanted changes,
Balcony glassed in, electric range,
And wrote to have them made after the fire.*)

〉 〉 〉

A course in mathematics would not be wasted on a poet, or a reader of poetry, if
he remember no more from it than the geometric principle of the intersection of
loci: from all angles lines converging and crossing establish points. He might carry
it further and say in his imagination that apprehension perforates at places, through
to understanding—as white is at the intersection of blue and green and yellow
and red. It is this white light that is the background of all good work . . .
 Poetry has taken many disguises which by cross reading or intense penetration
it is possible to go through to the core. Through intersection of loci their multiplicity may become revelatory.

 William Carlos Williams, "Marianne Moore"

J'ai voulu te dire simplement que je venais de jeter le plan de mon oeuvre entier,
après avoir trouvé la clef de moi-même, clef de voûte, ou centre, si tu veux, pour ne
pas nous brouiller de métaphores,—centre de moi-même, ou je me tiens comme
une araignée sacrée, sur les principaux fils déjà sortis de mon esprit, et à l'aide
desquels je tisserai *aux points de rencontre* de merveilleuses dentelles, que je devine,
et qui existent déjà dans le sein de la Beauté.

 Mallarmé to Théodore Aubanel

A SEQUENCE of lyrics intermittently narrative, "From the Cupola"
makes it clear that Merrill means to satisfy two aims not easily compatible.
The narrative impulse, which will become epic in *Sandover,* asks that he say
one thing at a time, that he pay attention to cause and effect, and that he
incorporate certain adventitious and repetitious elements, while his lyricism
demands that he say everything at once, that he concentrate on essences, and
that he economize. If the former moves him toward social context and helps
him to become a recorder of conversation and manners without parallel in
American poetry, the latter draws him in the direction of private occasion
and arcane statement. The one makes him say that he thinks it important for
the poem to be entertaining; the other leads him to quote Stevens to the
effect that the poem should resist the intelligence almost successfully.[1] The
narrator within him is responsible for that opening sentence in *The Seraglio:*
"Exactly a year later Francis learned the truth about the slashed portrait—
by then, of course, restored with expert care." The lyric poet, or the poet

159

I am going to call symbolist, writes the opening of *The (Diblos) Notebook:* "~~Orestes~~." Each beginning introduces a "slashed portrait," and each is already full of the story to follow; but whereas the one sketches a symmetrical plot that we can look forward to seeing unfold, the other presents a hieroglyph that sums it all up proleptically.

For one reason and another, these impulses give rise to their purest manifestations in *The Fire Screen* (1969) and *Braving the Elements* (1972), which have similar profiles. *The Fire Screen* contains twenty-six poems in seventy-seven pages, and its longest work is a ballad; *Braving the Elements* consists of twenty-four poems in seventy-three pages, and its longest poem is likewise a ballad. The titles suggest a difference in orientation: as *The Fire Screen* indicates things domestic, cozy, perhaps ornate, *Braving the Elements* points to the great outdoors, discomfort, unruly natural forces. And there is something to this distinction, in that many of the poems in the later volume do involve in one way or another "Nature's book" ("In Nine Sleep Valley"). But even that phrase undermines the difference the titles suggest, and the title of the later volume comes from a poem that is as highly wrought and claustral as anything Merrill has written.

In *The Fire Screen* the narrative impulse predominates. In addition to the ballad, there are occasional poems ("16.ix.65," "Ouzo for Robin," "David's Night in Veliès") and portraits, both in the third person ("Words for Maria") and the first ("Kostas Tympakianákis"), in which anecdote and character are prominent. Then there is the placement of the ballad, "The Summer People," at the volume's end. "Days of 1935," the ballad in *Braving the Elements,* about half as long as "The Summer People," comes fourth in that book, which ends with a closely woven lyric entitled "Syrinx." By putting "Syrinx" last Merrill recognizes even as he helps to define the later volume's quality. He has emphasized a different kind of poem in virtually every volume since *Water Street,* including the multiform sequence in *Nights and Days* and the long ballad in *The Fire Screen,* and there will be the short epic in *Divine Comedies* (*The Book of Ephraim* was originally self-contained), the epic in the *Sandover* books, and the political lyric in *Late Settings.* The comparable venture in *Braving the Elements* is the symbolist lyric.

Not that much rides on this difference in emphasis between these two books. They have a good deal in common, and one thing they share is this unmatched pair of modes, which sometimes strain against each other but which are no more mutually exclusive than teaching and delighting. Both volumes include poems in each mode, and both include poems that call on the two. Not for nothing does the speaker in "Syrinx" say that "X [is] my mark." Like Joey in "The Summer People," who is on his way to MIT to study cybernetics and flute, Merrill aspires to the decussate and the conjugate. It is fitting that the center of "The Friend of the Fourth Decade" is a "crisscrossed" bazaar and that the last words in *Braving the Elements* form a cross on the page.

"Lorelei," the first poem in *The Fire Screen*, has a "crossing" at its heart. In itself, however, it is a poem more or less in the symbolist vein, which recalls Pound's "The Return" in its combination of musical fluency and glyptic precision:

> The stones of kin and friend
> Stretch off into a trembling, sweatlike haze.
>
> They may not after all be stepping-stones
> But you have followed them. Each strands you, then
>
> Does not. Not yet. Not here.
> Is it a crossing? Is there no way back?
>
> Soft gleams lap the base of the one behind you
> On which a black girl sings and combs her hair.
>
> It's she who some day (when your stone is in place)
> Will see that much further into the golden vagueness
>
> Forever about to clear. Love with his chisel
> Deepens the lines begun upon your face.

It is like Pound's poem too in the indeterminacy of its setting. Instead of educing a world already extant, Merrill makes one up out of nothing but that "trembling, sweatlike haze." That last adjective is a powerful word; it not only gives the scene its rich thickness but also implies the dependence of the scene upon the poet's effort to see it. In the end, this is a poem about writing. In the beginning, however, it is a poem about growing older and about seeing oneself in relationship to those who have gone before and those who will come after. The "stones" are at once stepping stones and, "after all," tombstones. And all along they are others' milestones, or the memories of those who have shown the way, left him on the way—though not left him altogether, since he relies on them, as others will on him, for a place to stand.

Finding himself in the middle of the way, in the stream that we all step into and that is never the same one, and wondering whether the stones form "a crossing," he looks behind him to see the "black girl." It is at this juncture, after the third of the six distichs, that the poem does indeed become "a crossing." Because the girl is singing, we must identify her with the title's "Lorelei." But what a surprise that word is now. Imagine the difference if the poem were called "The Stream." As it is, just as the poet has been drawn on into the future by "kin and friend," so he must also be lured into the past. We are forced to consider how the two movements are the same—to consider, for instance, that although the kin and friend are in the poet's past, the trails they have blazed lead him into the future. If the black girl is the past that seduces him, she is by that very token the past that provides the wherewithal to go on.

Her other aspect is inevitably that of the future, of which the past is the matrix. Yet as the poet moves on, he moves deeper into the past, of which all of us become more and more a part each moment. Once entirely past, he will be her stepping stone. There is nothing here *but* "a crossing." To dwell on this crux is to dissolve for a second the stubborn intuition that time is an arrow. It is to get a glimmering of the eternal in Wittgenstein's sense: "If we take eternity to mean not infinite temporal duration but timelessness, then eternal life belongs to those who live in the present."[2] I think that something like that glimmering transforms the "trembling, sweatlike haze" into "the golden vagueness" that is surely neither a sunset nor a sunrise but rather "Forever" itself, always "about to clear." Because for whom—infants and animals possibly excepted—can it ever be truly clear? Even as one squints into the paradox, the lines deepen on his face. (Or hers, since the black girl is also the reader, since the poem is also a mirror.) Here as in "The Current," the absolute gets a mention, but time gets the laurels, as these "lines" deepen. It is love that wears us down, that writes us down, that writes our names and dates on our headstones. But love is also the sculptor whose "chisel" gives the face its shape and character, since the stones here are also busts.

In its location in the penumbra where the actual and the visionary mingle, in its impressionistic atmosphere, and in its fascination with temporal paradox, "Lorelei" approaches Merrill's symbolist mode. Perhaps most important in this regard is the resonance of its key terms—"stones," "lines," "crossing." This resonance is crucial also in "Mornings in a New House," the poem that gives *The Fire Screen* its title. The speaker, in the beginning "a cold man" alone on a frosty dawn in front of the fireplace in his new and sparsely furnished house, thinks about the fire screen, an heirloom of crewel work that his mother made when she was a child and that depicts "giant birds and flowery trees" and "a house, *her* mother's." Having finished the poem, in a flash of insight he adds an intriguing footnote:

> Days later. All framework & embroidery rather than any slower looking into things. Fire screen—screen *of* fire. The Valkyrie's baffle, pulsing at trance pitch, godgiven, elemental. Flames masking that cast-iron

plaque—"contrecoeur" in French—which backs the hearth with charred Loves & Graces. Some such meaning might have caught, only I didn't wait, I settled for the obvious—by lamplight, as it were. Oh well. Our white heats lead us on no less than words do. Both have been devices in their day.

As he has done so often since *Water Street,* Merrill acts here as his own critic, enlarging his framework by getting outside its original boundaries. If he had not been so quick to be ingenious, he supposes, he might have written a deeper poem, a poem that might have put itself in touch with heroic passions, those of Wotan and Brünnhilde, the latter protected by Wotan's magic fire after she has been entranced in the *Ring.* The note itself seems an impetuous afterthought, a little furnace of creative associations.

The more we look into it, however, the more a "baffle" this nearly self-sufficient prose poem of a note becomes—not an insoluble obstacle, as the magic fire is for all but Siegfried in Wagner's opera, but rather a sort of baffle plate, a contrivance built into some stoves and furnaces that allows the operator to redirect the flow of heated air. Like a baffle plate, the note can be flipped back and forth, to say different things. At the same time that Merrill takes himself to task for superficiality, he looks further into his subject. As he speculates on turning the fire screen into a screen of fire, he begins another small design. What is "embroidery," one wonders, if not the sort of wordplay we have in that pivotal chiasmus, that cross-stitch. The "fire" of inspiring emotion is what the poem proper calls a "tamed uprush / (Which to recall alone can make him flush)," and it is in front of that fire too that "Habit arranges the fire screen"—the poem, surely, with its neat rhymes and exact images. But as soon as the fire appears in the note, it becomes part of an intricate structure—in which it is linked by both opposition and affinity to the "lamplight." By opposition, because the latter is at first glance cold and intellectual; and by affinity, because incandescent light is unavoidably one of "Our white heats." In other words, the phrase "Our white heats" turns both ways, and so does the following phrase, "lead us on." Similarly, if Merrill reproaches himself for screening the flames, the flames themselves, once revealed, are "masking" the hearthback with its "charred Loves & Graces." Once that meaning has "caught," and of course it *has* done so here, Merrill must still be dealing with his subject at a distance. The inside has become the outside, and we have come full circle in a wink. Fire screen— screen *of* fire—*screen* of fire.

What began in scorn of artifice and in search of "presence," to use a current term, has revealed itself to be artifice. "Il n'y a pas de hors-texte," in Derrida's notorious phrase, which puts succinctly what many poets have believed. The problem is not a tactical difficulty but a strategic bind, and the issue has only been displaced. The question is, how can the poet treat his subject without "framework & embroidery"? Inasmuch as "any slower looking into things" is undertaken in poetry, it will result in a more elaborate laying out of them. In the note, "white heats" must become "devices," and those "devices" connect inevitably with the plaque's "Loves & Graces." "Devices," which even comes from a root meaning "to divide," reminds us that words necessarily display our distance from their referents, however much they also connect us to those referents. The "white heats" and "words" go together, like the "Loves & Graces" that parallel them. This note's very ampersands, seemingly evidence of haste, are calculated to give us that impression—and to prove withal the inescapable artificiality of the poem, for they are bits of filigree.

In the poem, passion and craft are knotted, crossed, *double*-crossed, partly because the exercise of the art discovers or creates the emotion. The poem proper, at the same time that it follows the process of waking up in the morning, traces the course of such a discovery, the structure of one kind of writing experience—as the note, which begins so enthusiastically and trails off in wry reflection, traces the converse kind. The poem moves from stiffness through routine to emotional perception—and thus sketches in small the arc of experience in many poems by Merrill. Out of "Habit," the "cold man" who "hardly cares" at the beginning "arranges the fire screen," his mother's embroidery and his own, between him and the flames and then stands looking at it,

> stands there wondering until red
> Infraradiance, wave on wave,
> So enters each plume-petal's crazy weave,
> Each worsted brick of the homestead,
>
> That once more, deep indoors, blood's drawn,
> The tiny needlewoman cries,
> And to some faintest creaking shut of eyes
> His pleasure and the doll's are one.

As certainly as this "Infraradiance" is the firelight that brings to life his mother's crewel work, it is the memory that warms the "cold man" from inside. The pendant note notwithstanding, the door to the past opens in the last stanza and allows the poet to see "deep indoors," to when his mother was eight years old, learning to embroider, comforting a doll that she has dropped—and therewith foreshadowing her love for her son. All the poem's elements converge here. The "blood's drawn" figuratively when the doll is dropped and literally when the child sticks her finger with the needle, but also when the poet's pen does its own drawing up of that moment of pain. Craft and passion, cobra and mongoose. Like the making of the screen, the making of the poem causes pain (it is cruel work too), but because the pain is the proof of the emotional life of the poet, it causes pleasure.

For all their close relationship, the verse and the prose gloss are separable in their modes. Whereas the note is a hotbed of puns and paradoxes, the verse gets briskly along and tells its story. The difference is coordinate with that between the symbolist and the narrative powers, which combine more smoothly in "The Friend of the Fourth Decade."

If "Lorelei" is this volume's prefatory poem, "The Friend of the Fourth Decade" is in a sense its opening poem. One advantage of such clearly introductory poems as Merrill likes is that they let him begin again, just as this is one of the advantages of the kind of sequence he writes. "The Friend of the Fourth Decade" itself has eight parts, each comprising seven pairs of lines, predominantly pentameter. The distichs could have attracted Merrill partly because of their similarity to the ghazal, a verse form that might have been in his mind because of the friend's trip to the Middle East. Whereas the true ghazal's lines always have a rhyme, however, Merrill's do so only occasionally—and of course he uses distichs in poems unrelated to things Middle Eastern. In any case, these fourteen-line sections make this poem one of his many variations on the sonnet sequence, a favorite structure ever since "The Broken Home."

This poem's opening lines work just as well as the volume's second beginning as they would have worked as its only beginning:

> When I returned with drinks and nuts my friend
> Had moved to the window seat, back to the view.
>
> The clear central pane around which ran
> Smaller ones stained yellow, crimson, blue,
>
> Framed our country's madly whipping flag,
> Its white pole above roofs, the sea beyond.

They let the poem begin with an entrance, or rather a reentrance, since it begins in the middle of things, and that reentrance meshes with "Lorelei." Because there is no "I" in the preceding poem, the poet has herewith "returned" *in propria persona.* And since he returns he must have been here before—that is, in *Nights and Days,* where Psyche and the poet concerned themselves with various "panes" both "clear" and "stained." Those earlier panes were in a cupola, whereas these are not, and Merrill does not demand that we bring these two poems together in our minds. But if we do we will be more disposed to consider the poet and his "friend" in a certain light.

The first thing we gather about these two is that they are quite different types. The friend is "Tired of understanding . . . The tones, the overtones" of everything he hears, "tired of understanding / The light in people's eyes, the smells, the food." He longs for a new life, a foreign country, a language of which he will know "Barely enough to ask for food and love." This wish to free himself of accumulated experience has led him to relish an odd pastime, to which *his* friend, Karlheinrich, has introduced him; it consists of selecting postcards that he has received over the years from kin and friend, slipping them into a bowl of water, and enjoying the results:

"Each card then soaks for five minutes while its ink

Turns to exactly the slow formal swirls
Through which a phoenix flies on Chinese silk.

These leave the water darker but still clear,
The text unreadable. It's true!

Cards from my mother, my great-uncle, you!
And the used waters deepen the sea's blue."

Chiefly symbolic though it is, this entertainment has an invigorating effect on him, as it expunges souvenirs and clears the way for the rebirth forecast by the phoenix. He resorts to some paradoxical religious imagery to evoke his feelings about "'Scene upon scene's immersion and emergence / Rinsed of the word.'" In spite of such jokes, and some languid mockery of Eliot's "Ash Wednesday," the friend's passion for a new life does have something of the religious about it—something even of the mystical, if not the saintly. He has had a religious aura from the beginning, when the sun shining through the stained glass laid "angry little stripes upon his shoulders" and "flowed positively through / Him in spots" like stigmata. Later, as he loses himself deeper and deeper in the Middle East, he approaches extreme Gnostic libertinism, according to whose teachings (in Hans Jonas's words) "there is a positive duty to perform every kind of action, to leave no deed undone, no possibility of freedom unrealized, in order to render nature its due and exhaust its powers; only in this way can final release from the cycle of reincarnations be obtained."[3]

The last of the friend's postcards to the poet pictures a mysterious "dung-and-emerald oasis." He writes that in this new world

"Individual and type are one.
Do as I please, I *am* the simpleton

Whose last exploit is to have been exploited
Neck and crop. In the usual bazaar,

Darker, more crisscrossed than a beggar's palm,
Smell of money draws them after me,

I answer to whatever name they call,
Drink the sweet black condescending dregs,

Try on their hungers like a shirt of flame
(Well, a sports shirt of flame) whereby I've been

Picked clean, reborn each day increasingly
Conspicuous, increasingly unseen."

It is not easy to think of comparable passages of verse. Robert Lowell's "Words for Hart Crane" comes to mind because of the direct quotation and the mixture of arrogance and humility. Both Merrill's and Lowell's lines are savagely revealing, but Merrill's are more so because the depth of the passion is not quite sounded. The irony in the tailoring of Nessus's shirt into a Hawaiian gabardine is evidence of what has not yet succumbed to the fierce need. These lines are full of other triumphs: the transition in the fifth line, where the "crisscrossed" bazaar becomes the creased palm of the beggar who would be encountered there, and where the "beggar" anticipates the friend—though it is the latter who has the money; the light echo of the creased palm in the repeated "increasingly"; the aptness of the reference to "sweet black condescending dregs," with its murky origin in the cups of Arabic *gaweh* and its restoration of the radical meanings in "condescending"; and the linking of the friend to the poet, who is willy-nilly "trying on" the hunger of the other and thereby becoming "increasingly / Conspicuous" (if also "increasingly unseen").

As I have said, the poet seems to have little in common with his friend at the outset, for whereas the latter is a victim of sophistication, the poet is all ingenuousness. When he tries his hand at the postcard amusement, the results are quite different:

The stamp slid off, of course, and the ink woke.
I watched my mother's *Dearest Son* unfurl

In blue ornate brief plungings-up:
Almost a wild iris taking shape.

I heard oblivion's thin siren singing,
And bore it bravely. At the hour's end

I had my answer. Chances are it was
Some simple matter of what ink she used,

And yet her message remained legible,
The memories it stirred did not elude me.

I put my postcards back upon the shelf.
Certain things die only with oneself.

The poet's relieved acceptance of the past's persistence makes a strong contrast with the friend's desperate attempts to escape it. And yet one senses a reciprocity between these figures. There is the curious repetition of the word "friend" at the end of a line at or near the beginning of most of the sections: the first, third, fifth, sixth, and eighth. In addition to setting up the poem's last phrase—"the perfect *stranger*"—this reiteration asks us to weigh the term and to reassess its applicability to the man it signifies. One thing we might notice is that the friend's attitude during his visit to the speaker is remarkably reminiscent of the rigor vitae in "The Thousand and Second Night." Another is that his language blends with the poet's own. ("Words for Maria" and "Kostas Tympakianákis" indicate how well Merrill is able to mimic others' speech when he is of a mind.) Then we have some loaded phrases here and there. When the friend puts his "back to the view" and the setting sun, rather like those witnesses interviewed on television whose anonymity must be preserved, he loses his individuality and appears as "Anyman with ears aglow, / On a black cushion, gazing inward, mute." The conversion to "Anyman" makes us broaden our conception of him, and his "inward" gaze might associate him with the poet, who could discover the "friend" by "gazing inward" himself. So the creation of this other figure itself looks to be an instance of Merrill's own "tactful disinvolvement." Thinking of the friend as an alter ego helps to explain the specificity of the poem's title: the poem might be read as a farewell to a decade, the last of youth by the usual reckoning, and to certain feelings and possibilities.

It seems to me that "The Friend of the Fourth Decade" conceals and displays an intrapsychic struggle, and that the struggle is a common one. The friend with the ears aglow is indeed Anyman—or any man who knows he is being talked about and is somewhat embarrassed at the gist. He is the universal impulse, perhaps fundamentally erotic, to cut all ties, to free the self to begin anew. If he is hard to conceive of as a person whom any of us might have known (though we will recognize his relationship to Francis

Tanning), that is because of the purity of his motivation, which is to say his essentially allegorical nature. Merrill could be talking about the source of this poem when he tells David Kalstone the anecdote about the son of a friend who had "one day absolutely vanished without a trace." When months later his mother finally found him, she learned that "what he'd wanted was no less than a brand-new life." Sometimes, Merrill imagines, we all want "to disappear and reemerge as a new person without any ties, the slate wiped clean. Sometimes one even puts the dream into action, in a less dramatic way."[4] Writing such a poem as this one would be one "less dramatic way."

Merrill also postulates that such "new" lives as that he'd heard the acquaintance had invented eventually take on the qualities of the old ones. But what if that were not so? What if the slate could be wiped utterly clean? The last section of "The Friend of the Fourth Decade" explores that possibility as it recounts a "dream" the poet has about his "friend." In the dream, "Behind a door marked DANGER," in a process like Yeats's "dreaming back," the friend is stripped not just of his immediate personal identity but of his cultural heritage as well. This passage of especially "fine writing" varies the theme of ink unfurling from postcards, as Merrill begins with incunabula (which "Swaddlings" renders literally) and works his way back through papyrus scrolls to a *tabula rasa:*

> Swaddlings of his whole civilization,
> Prayers, accounts, long priceless scroll,
>
> Whip, hawk, prow, queen, down to some last
> Lost comedy, all that fine writing
>
> Rigid with rains and suns,
> Are being gingerly unwound.
>
> There.

This prodigious unwinding, at once of a mummy's wrappings and a baby's swaddling clothes and history's scroll, keeps before us the idea of life from death. It also suggests the removal of the bandage after a face lift:

> There. Now the mirror. Feel the patient's heart
> Pounding—oh please, this once—
>
> Till nothing moves but to a drum.
> See his eyes darken in bewilderment—

No, in joy—and his lips part
To greet the perfect stranger.

The "perfect stranger"—the hitherto absolutely unknown person, as well as the apparently flawless one—is the ultimate figure in the friend's search for a fresh start in love, so his "lips part" as much to bestow a kiss as to speak. If "the perfect stranger" also has eschatological overtones, this is the result partly of the recurrent religious imagery and partly of the final placement of this charged phrase. Because the poem concludes here, on a note that is breathtaking in more than one sense, the ensuing silence implies something whereof we cannot speak. That is one way to read this passage.

But the command for the mirror will remind us that the friend's quest has been as much for something within himself (his soul, Nahman would say) as for someone else, so the face he sees there, even as he looks into the other's face, is his own. (Yeats says powerfully that lovers hold up mirrors in which each sees not the self as it is but the self as seen by the other.) Though of course the face is not "his own" at all, since the search—or operation—has been successful in the dream, but that of someone new: "the perfect stranger." We need to put that another way: when the friend loses himself he becomes the stranger. And to that we must add that he loses himself, to the extent that they are one, when he parts from his "oldest friend," the speaker. That is, because the poem has been a "mirror" all along, the "stranger" here must be not only a foreign figure the friend meets, with overtones of death personified, and not only the transfigured friend himself, but also the poet, even as he bends over the page to set down these lines. And that is what frightens him.

Nor have we left behind the eschatological dimension of this poem. Think for a moment of Joseph Campbell's summary in *The Hero with a Thousand Faces:* "The two—the hero and his ultimate god, the seeker and the found—are thus understood as the outside and inside of a single, self-mirrored mystery, which is identical with the mystery of the manifest world."[5] This poem brings us to the very threshold of the issues examined in *Sandover.* But first things before last.

So let us retrench and think of "The Friend of the Fourth Decade" in this way: it responds to a desire to escape from routine into a simple life of passion by following out the implications of acting on the impulse and by rejecting the option. The situation repeats that in "From the Cupola" because when the speaker finds himself bound to "the word" and to memory, he is the poet as poet, while the "friend" who would be rinsed of the word is *l'homme sensuel.* "Between extremities / Man runs his course," Yeats proclaims in "Vacillation," and in Merrill's poems as in Yeats's those extremities often take the shape of intellectual satisfaction and sensual pleasure.[6]

)))

Merrill's double allegiance to the senses and the imagination is not the same as his commitment to both the narrative and the lyric. But the two dilemmas overlap to the degree that the lyric, under the auspices of Ariel, separates itself from quotidian life, narrative's province. The ambivalence about poetic mode is evident in the combination of genre and epigraph in "The Summer People." A conventional ballad in its form, it is prefaced by a fragment from Mallarmé: "et l'hiver resterait la saison intellectuelle créatrice." This pronouncement comes from a paragraph that Mallarmé wrote in response to an inquiry, sent to the *Echo de Paris,* by a man who wanted to know how spring affects a writer's creative faculty. For his part, Mallarmé found that winter would continue to be the intellective creator among the seasons.[7]

Mallarmé has his counterpart in Merrill's ballad, but in its manner the poem bears only traces of the symbolist influence. Unlike Merrill's earlier long poems, "The Summer People" is all shipshape. The ballad form as Merrill interprets it and the unnamed town that is the poem's setting suit each other to a T:

> On our New England coast was once
> A village white and neat
> With Greek Revival houses,
> Sailboats, a fishing fleet,
>
> Two churches and two liquor stores,
> An Inn, a Gourmet Shoppe,
> A library, a pharmacy.
> Trains passed but did not stop.

This packed trimness is the poem's home key. Throughout its ten sections it relies on balance and pairing. Each stanza, we see immediately, will have its two unrhymed lines and its two rhymed lines; the poem flies its significant first adjectives like a brace of flags ("white and neat"); and both the churches and the liquor stores are doubled up. These last two pairs, like the library and the pharmacy, set each other off by their muted opposition and thus adumbrate a major antithesis, for just as the summer people are never without their drinks, so the winter person lives in a converted church. Though its antithesis is not as apparent, the fourth line sets the "Sailboats" against the "fishing fleet." Because the poem is in part a rewriting of Aesop's fable of the grasshopper and the ant (and is thus a "Greek Revival" in its own right), this opening allusion pays its way too. The tension here between pleasure and work—between society and privacy, body and soul, summer and winter—is the mainspring of each of the poem's plots.

The subplot covers a longer period—five and a half years—than the main plot, for which it provides a framework. The subplot pits a contingent of the largely Portuguese year-round residents of the village, located a few miles from the (fictional) town of Caustic, Maine, against the supporters of a "Chemical Plant" that would be established in the village harbor. The faction in favor of the Plant, which would bring jobs to an economy increasingly depressed because of a diminishing fish supply, was originally a minority, but as the poem picks up the story it has grown to nearly the size of the group that opposes the Plant. The latter group, which includes Manuel the grocer, argues that the Plant would drive out "the summer people," who, though they live there only a few months of the year, employ villagers as gardeners, handymen, and so on, and who at least do not pollute the harbor, as the Plant is certain to do. By the end of the narrative the Plant has been voted in, and the summer people (or the four we have come to know) have decided to abandon the "ruined" town.

The summer people also come in pairs. On the one hand we have Margaret, a widow with "dawn-colored hair" who has written novels and whose health has begun to fail, and Nora, her divorced daughter. On the other hand there are Andrew, amateur pianist, bon vivant, and incorrigible punster, and his wife Jane, whose rheumatism interferes with her painting and gardening. "These were the Amusing, / The Unconventional ones," the narrator informs us with an arch wit that each of them would appreciate. The main plot emerges from their relationship with Jack Frost, a new arrival who soon becomes the hub of upper-crust village social life. Jack is "years older / Than his twenty-year-old face," and he loves four-hand piano and bridge, croquet, and entertaining. "The happy few" who have been invited to his home—a Baptist church done over and furnished with lanterns, polar bear rugs, bamboo, and such—know him as "a famous host." We are not told what Jack "does." Not that we hear anything of the summer people's vocations either, for their dabblings in the arts cannot be mistaken for callings. But then it is their nature precisely not to be serious. We infer that they are independently wealthy and that their chief struggle is with Demon Boredom.

Jack *is* serious, however, and we are led to think of him as a writer. Until to his consternation the summer people begin to outstay the social season, Jack dedicates his winters to a lonely creative activity that he carries on, like the poet in Yeats's "The Phases of the Moon," late at night in the tower of the former church. "'Jack's sure artistic,' Manuel said / 'But how does he keep warm?'" The epigraph from Mallarmé helps us to see that Manuel puts the answer before the question. When he quits the village for good, Jack leaves behind him papers full of "Unfinished calculation, / Doodle and arabesque" that bear a resemblance to winter's forms: the "white leafage" that the window panes put forth (the term for which is "frostwork"), the "Great lengths of gnarled crystal" that glitter "from porch and eave," and the snowflakes themselves, "Hexagonal, unique." (Merrill's little joke is that the last phrase itself, far from "unique," is a quote from "The Wintering Weeds," a poem in his second book.) If the winter landscape seems to proceed from "a genius / Positively baroque," Jack's name makes him the genius of the season and connects him several times over with poetry.

Grimes, his cat—appropriately white, regardless of his name—plays the familiar to Jack's magician. After Jack's first season in the village, when the others have abandoned their summer homes, he and Grimes gather their forces: "The next days Jack lay drowsing, / Grimes in the bend of his knees. / He woke one dusk to eat a rusk / And smile at the bare trees." This is a little like Psyche smiling at her isolation in "From the Cupola." When, several years later, Margaret and the others decide to stay into the winter, Grimes greets the proposal by digging his claws into Jack's thigh, and when Jack has finally worn himself out between his own hibernal endeavors ("'I didn't sleep a wink / All during last night's blizzard'") and social obligations, it is Grimes who retaliates. Jack has reached his breaking point when Margaret stops by to see what is ailing him:

A white blur sped to meet her—
Was it that ghastly cat?
Grimes spat, crouched, sprang and sank a fang
Into her, just like that!

She screamed. A stern young doctor,
Summoned out of the void,
Dressed her wound, then telephoned
To have the cat destroyed.

So poor Grimes is soon truly a "ghastly cat"—who appears to Jack that night in a dream "in ermine / And coronet of ice" and demands vengeance, which Jack exacts by turning his back on the village forever. Ken, his Japanese "'houseboy'" and gardener left behind, eventually brings his life to a decorous close. Before taking some "small white pills," Ken gets very drunk:

> Nora heard him coughing.
> She stopped her evening stroll
> And went to see. With courtesy
> Both sinister and droll
>
> Ken bowed low, made her welcome,
> Concocted a new drink.
> Darkly hilarious he said,
> "Rong Rife!" and gave a wink.
>
> One didn't need to be Nora
> To see that things weren't right.

But Nora does nothing except bring him some soup and leave him to die. The neglect is typical; it is because the summer people selfishly do nothing that the Chemical Plant's supporters (ants to their grasshopper) succeed in the end.

Not that the summer people are quite as "flat" as they seem at first. The narrator—the heir of the earlier intrusive voices—breaks in in Byronic fashion to draw our attention to a pertinent difference between his poem and most in its genre. His reservations have been prompted by the thought of "Margaret's journal":

> I should perhaps have trusted
> To dry-eyed prose like hers.
> The meter grows misleading,
> Given my characters.
>
> For figures in a ballad
> Lend themselves to acts
> Passionate and simple.
> A bride weeps. A tree cracks.
>
> A young king, an old outlaw
> Whose temperament inclines
> To strife where breakers thunder
> Bleeds between the lines.
>
> But I have no such hero,
> No fearful deeds—unless

We count their quiet performance
By Time or Tenderness.

He's right and he's not. If the dogwood does not crack, in the next section, it breaks into significant speech. If the poem has no "young king" or "old outlaw," Jack and Grimes are reasonable surrogates. Perhaps these people are not "Passionate and simple," yet these words would seem admirably suited to Margaret's decision to have Grimes killed and to Jack's running away from the village in the middle of the night.

We still have no weeping bride? True, but Nora might as well weep because she will not be a bride again. The possibility of a romantic relationship with Jack has been raised discreetly, but whatever faint hope Nora might have nurtured vanishes with Grimes. Merrill writes the key passage with stunning concision:

Nora looked up. The mirror
Struck her a glancing blow.
Her hair once blonde as summer
Was dull and streaked with snow.

"Oh tell me, Mother, tell me
Where do the years go?
I'm old, my life is ending!"
"Baby, I know, I know."

By making us try to think of Nora as "Passionate and simple," Merrill makes us see her complexity. He plumbs the depths of her shallowness, in a phrase from *The (Diblos) Notebook*. She is not just hard and careless but also touching, and in the end one can imagine her reading Austen with feeling. Shortly before the recognition recorded above, however, she has been "rereading *Emma*" and has found herself "Unmoved for once by a daughter's / Soon-to-be solved dilemma." Emma's problem is solved when Mr. Knightley asks for her hand, and Nora now understands that hers can have no such happy outcome. But her mother hits on a solution of sorts, which reveals new sides of each. Margaret recommends "'a clever fairy / Who puts gold back in hair'" and a jet to Rio: "'It will be summer there.'" What would previously have been simply vain, contemptible responses to their situation might now seem realistic, even a touch courageous. Like the houses on Main Street at the poem's end, "faintly crimson" in the sunset, they are "upright in defeat," and one cannot help but admire their cleverness. They are perfectly awful— but cheerful.

Jack Frost is more obviously complicated than these others, who try to reduce him to a simple individual, whereas he is essentially divided. "'Proud Grimes, proud loyal kitty / . . . I love you best,'" he tells his "Gorgeously unimpressed" companion, but he is also genuinely fond of his village friends. Ken objectifies his employer's ambivalence in his party fare: "many a curious hot hors-d'oeuvre / And icy cold cocktail." The thing about Jack is that he needs to lead both lives, the solitary, intellectual life and the convivial, social life.

What then is his relationship to James Merrill? How accurately does he reflect the poet? Because we have no examples of Jack's writing, we cannot be certain of its nature or quality. But details here and there suggest a certain aestheticism, a rarefied sensibility—the kind indulged, say, in some of the poems in Merrill's early volumes, but precisely not in such a poem as this one. Although Jack loves his social life, as long as he can keep it within bounds, we have no evidence that he can draw on it in his writing, as Merrill has done at least since those three friends stamped out of the snow into *Water Street*. It seems likely that Jack Frost is not so much Merrill's Merrill as he is Merrill's Mauberley: an exaggeration of an aspect of himself. There is some confirmation of this view of Jack in the description of one especially beautiful winter morning, when the snow and ice fantasia that we associate with his lucubrations appears as "Invention's breast and plumage, / Flights of the midnight Swan." The phrasing cannot help but call up Mallarmé's sonnet "Le vierge, le vivace et le bel aujourd'hui" with its swan, a captive in the lovely day much as Jack is until he bolts. While it is not clear exactly how Mallarmé sees his swan, we would not be wrong in thinking the latter guilty of not having sung about life ("n'avoir pas chanté la region où vivre"). There must be some Mallarmé in his swan, just as there must be some Merrill in Jack Frost, but I think that John Porter Houston is accurate in his judgment that the bird is "an idealist in the solipsistic fashion expounded by minor symbolists."[8] We might see in Jack's flight to "some Higher Thing— / The Jungfrau, white and tall" a parallel to the swan's useless exile ("exil inutile"), in which case his escape is hardly one at all. Let us imagine that Jack could write poems in imitation of Mallarmé. He could not write this ballad.

It is interesting that the traditional Jack Frost and allusions to "Le vierge, le vivace" also appear in Elizabeth Bishop's "First Death in Nova Scotia," published in *Questions of Travel;* this same volume includes "The Burglar of Babylon," one of the finest of recent ballads and a possible inspiration for Merrill. But what a comparison of the two poems shows is that they are so different as to share only generic resemblances. The difference is partly along the thematic lines sketched by Merrill's self-critical narrator in the Byronic intrusion quoted earlier and partly along the lines of prosody and language. In these areas too Merrill's poem seeks to marry the simple and the complex. The ballad stanza invites straightforwardness and brevity, but it does not preclude linguistic luxury or prosodic subtlety, and to Merrill it is sometimes an opportunity to try out the magnifying glass and the single-hair brushes.

There are signs early in the poem that it will be more highly wrought than the ordinary ballad. For instance, so that the end-rhymed second and fourth lines have a counterpoint, Merrill frequently rhymes the end of a stanza's third line with a word halfway through the same line. A similar mechanism is the basis for the tour de force in the second section of "Flying from Byzantium," which has a slant rhyme in every line. Here is the man in the moon counseling the poet in the course of the night flight that separates him from his lover:

> He then: "Lusters are least
> Dimmed among the damned.
> The point's to live, love,
> Not shake your fist at the feast.
>
> So up from your vain divan,
> The one on which you wane.
> I've shown you how to shine—
> Show me the moon in man!"

The rhymes are less obtrusive in "The Summer People," not only because they are much less frequent but also because they usually occur in tetrameter lines and because Merrill scumbles them over with caesura and enjambment: "Plus Andrew's Jane (she used a cane / And shook it at his puns . . .)"; "'And baby-sit. The benefit / comes home to all of us.'" Another complicating innovation is the inclusion of much repartee and badinage:

> "What can she mean," said Margaret,
> "Speaking to me like that?"
> "I mean you're gaga, Mother."
> "And you, my child, are fat."

In such instances the form's exigencies seem welcome excuses for coming to the point. Similarly, this stanza provides a fine setting for the *mot juste* it sometimes seems to foster: the "Lights of the Chemical Plant / Gloated over water," as though, inspired by the short line, Merrill had found in that verb a portmanteau word ("glowed" plus "floated"). The small stanza also displays conversational gems nicely and moreover necessitates movement onward just when it is most needed, since aphoristic wit is by nature self-contained. So we overhear Andrew irreverently punning on the name of the English monk when he refers to his weakening eyes as "'venerable beads.'" As a tribute to Ken's flowers, Andrew adapts Lincoln Steffens's verdict, upon his return from post-Revolutionary Russia: "Said Andrew gravely, 'I have seen / The fuschia, and it works.'" Even Jane antes up one day when Nora appears "with currant fool / Enough for the whole village," and five of them eat every bite: "'Shame on us every one,' / Jane sighed, 'we've got no fiber.'" (Not that they could see the truth in the censure.)

The most daring of these strokes of brachylogy is given, surprisingly, to Ken, the least duplicitous of them in all senses of the word. It is surprising, but also inevitable, since it depends upon his pronunciation. Merrill sets the stage when he has Ken tell Jack that he wants to return to Japan: "'Dear Jack-san, now am ord, / Dream of my Kyushu virrage / Where nobody catch cord.'" We are ready then to make the necessary phonetic substitutions when Ken, tipsy and on the verge of taking his own life, proposes his toast to Nora: "Darkly hilarious he said, / 'Rong Rife!' and gave a wink." The obscure joke clarifies itself when his "long life" ends a few minutes later. For then we see that the joke has a false bottom, and that Ken's toast was a perfectly pronounced assessment of the village, in which wrong is rife. It might be that this last phrase is an instance in which Merrill breaks through the surface of the poem, since it is hard to imagine that Ken meant the words to be heard two ways—but it is impossible to imagine that the poet does not intend us to hear them that way.

The reckless mood responsible for Ken's phrase is responsible also for the unique witticism in the sixth stanza, which takes us to the town near the village: "Feet still pace the whaler's deck / At the Caustic (Me.) Museum." If the village is Merrill's Stonington, the town with the maritime museum would be Mystic (Conn.), so that transformation itself exemplifies the reason for the town's new name. But the touch I have in mind derives from or more likely necessitates the relocation of the town in Maine, which can then be conveniently abbreviated as above: "Me." The self behind the poem does indeed have his caustic side; while one side that is mostly hidden, though we get glimpses of it in the "Flights of the midnight Swan" and the "harsh white jewel" of the frozen lake, is the mystic side.

)))

By "mystic" I mean to suggest not just that Merrill is concerned with metaphysical or transcendental enigmas, which do appear explicitly in his work in these two volumes, but also that he is an initiate to certain poetic mysteries, for his symbolist poems, like Mallarmé's, are hermetic. I suspect that the two characteristics are closely related in his case.

Merrill's symbolism is first of all an exploitation of language's inveterate multivalence. His symbolist poems are shot through with puns and homophones, equivocations and recoveries of root meaning—all devices that appear throughout his work but not so often or so indispensably as in poems like "Syrinx," "18 West 11th Street," "Under Libra: Weights and Measures," "Under Mars," and "Komboloi." One sees the same streak in other poems in *Braving the Elements,* including "Willowware Cup," "Flèche d'Or," and "Yam," as well as "Dreams about Clothes," which is a virtual parody of this tendency. Merrill would not have been able to avoid thinking of such poems when he wrote an apology for the pun in his essay on Francis Ponge, published in the year that *Braving the Elements* appeared:

> A pity about that lowest form of humor [the pun]. It is suffered, by and large, with groans of aversion, as though one had done an unseemly thing in adult society, like slipping a hand up the hostess's dress. Indeed, the punster has touched, and knows it if only for being so promptly shamed, upon a secret, fecund place in language herself. The pun's *objet trouvé* aspect cheapens it further—why? A Freudian slip is taken seriously: it betrays its maker's hidden wish. The pun (or the rhyme, for that matter) "merely" betrays the hidden wish of words.[9]

The nonchalant tone and the humor in this paragraph vouch for its importance to Merrill, as does its rich phrasing. It is as though he could not help but demonstrate the slipperiness, the lubricity of his words, which as at a large party make all kinds of connections—overt, surreptitious, tentative, flirtatious—among themselves. If we are inclined to hold him responsible for the liaison across the sentences between "slipping" and "slip," we must admit that the mother tongue, our hostess, bears out his last observation by wearing the slip herself.

This idea that puns are made by language is fundamental. Though we must add that it is not just puns that we must be concerned with, but all manner of slippage and linkage, and that language needs the maieutic aid of the poet. Merrill takes up the subject in a recent sonnet entitled "The Parnassians"—where I think it is not the French group he has in mind so much as poets in general, or a certain kind of poet. As the sestet makes clear, it is spoken in effect by common parlance itself, the language used by the servants to whom Villiers de l'Isle-Adam left the task of "living":

> Theirs was a language within ours. A loge
> Hidden by bee-stitched hangings from the herd.
> The mere exchanged glance between word and word
> Took easily the place, the privilege,

Of words themselves. Here therefore all was tact.
Pairs at first blush ill-matched, like *turd* and *monstrance*,
Tracing their cousinage by consonants,
Communed, ecstatic, through the long entr'acte.

Without our common meanings, though, that world
Would have slid headlong to apocalypse.
We'd built the Opera, changed the scenery, trod
Grapes for the bubbling flutes mild fingers twirled;
As footmen, by no eyelid's twitch betrayed
Our scorn and sound investment of their tips.[10]

The Parnassians' language within language recalls in particular Mallarmé, who after all learned much from Gautier, Banville, and the others, who toasted Leconte de l'Isle as a "maître," and who was even published in *Le Parnasse contemporain*. In "Crise de vers" he writes explicitly of Merrill's subject here, "le double état de la parole, brut ou immédiat ici, là essentiel" ("the double state of the word, now raw or immediate, now essential"); and in "Le Mystère dans les lettres" he further characterizes the latter state in a passage that flickeringly exemplifies its matter:

> Les mots, d'eux-mêmes, s'exaltent à mainte facette reconnue la plus rare ou valant pour l'esprit, centre de suspens vibratoire; qui les perçoit indépendamment de la suite ordinaire, projetés, en parois de grottes, tant que dure leur mobilité ou principe, étant ce qui ne se dit pas du discours: prompts tous, avant extinction, à une réciprocité de feux distante ou présentée de biais comme contingence.

> Words, by themselves, kindle in one another many facets known as the most rare or rewarding for the mind, center of vibratory suspense; which perceives them independently of the ordinary sequence, projected, on cave walls, as long as their movement or essence lasts, being that which is not called discourse: all ready, before being extinguished, for a reciprocity of fires that is distant or presented obliquely as though by accident.[11]

So one might say that in Merrill's lines "Communed" and "common" signal each other across the space, and thus link octave and sestet, and that the cryptorhyme of "word" and "*turd*" throws an odd light, whether lurid or mystical is hard to decide, on the relationship between "*turd*" and "*monstrance*." (One thinks of the visionary experience on the toilet in "Yam.") But these are just a couple of the many latent bonds among these words.

In the symbolism of both Mallarmé and Merrill—whose names trace their cousinage by consonants—words are encouraged to generate their own meanings or to converse quietly among one another. One of Mallarmé's finest statements of the idea appears in "Crise de vers":

L'oeuvre pure implique la disparition élocutoire du poëte, qui cède l'initiative aux mots, par le heurt de leur inégalité mobilisés; ils s'allument de reflets réciproques comme une virtuelle traînée de feux sur des pierreries, remplaçant la respiration perceptible en l'ancien souffle lyrique ou la direction personnelle enthousiaste de la phrase.

The pure work implies the elocutionary disappearance of the poet, who grants the initiative to the words, activated by the shock of their difference; they light one another up with reciprocal reflections like a virtual trail of fire over precious stones, taking the place of the perceptible breathing in the old lyric afflatus or the enthusiastic personal control of the sentence.[12]

In Mallarmé's work the withdrawal of the poet before his words sometimes involves the suppression of punctuation, and the same is true in Merrill's. One thinks especially of "From the Cupola" and of "Under Mars" and "Flèche d'Or" in this volume. Merrill's elimination of the poet also takes the form of omission of first-person pronouns. "Under Libra" remarks on its "absent *I* and *you*, / Live, spitting pronouns" that do not appear in the text, and the first person is noticeably absent from "18 West 11th Street," "Under Mars," and "Yam." In these last poems the second person stands in for the first, and the omission might be as much a matter of reticence as of the medium's taking the initiative. Still, when "Syrinx" implicitly likens its own development to "proliferation by metastasis," one recognizes the aptness of the figure. The words in such a poem multiply their meanings by "reflets réciproques," and these reflections are a matter at least partly of the etymological texture of the language. The word "texture" itself is a fascinating swatch of the fabric that language is. It comes from the Indo-European root *teks-*, as the *American Heritage Dictionary* tells us in its invaluable appendix:

teks-. To weave; also to fabricate, especially with an ax, also to make wicker or wattle fabric for (mud-covered) house walls. 1. Latin *texere*, to weave, fabricate: TEXT, TISSUE; CONTEXT, PRETEXT. 2. Suffixed form **teks-lā* in: a. Latin *tēla*, web, net, warp of a fabric, also weaver's beam (to which the warp threads are tied): TELA, TILLER[2], TOIL[2]; b. Latin *subtīlis*, thin, fine, precise, subtle (**sub-tēla*, "thread passing under the

warp," the finest thread; *sub,* under, SUB-): SUBTLE. 3. Suffixed form
*teks-ōn, weaver, maker of wattle for house walls, builder, in Greek *tek-
ton,* carpenter, builder: TECTONIC, ARCHITECT. 4. Suffixed form **teks-
nā,* craft (of weaving or fabricating), in Greek *tekhnē,* art, craft, skill:
TECHNICAL, TECHNOLOGY; PANTECHNICON, POLYTECHNIC. 5. Possi-
bly Germanic **thasu-,* badger ("the animal that builds," referring to its
burrowing skill), in Old High German *dahs,* badger: DACHSHUND.

So a weaver of subtle texts is a builder of houses, an equation especially appropriate in Merrill's case. (And a literary critic, I see, is a dachshund.)

Umberto Eco combines the metaphor of a network with that of a
gymnastic apparatus when he describes language and then culture in general as a web or grid that extends immeasurably beyond the realm of strict
etymology:

> A metaphor can be invented because language, in its process of un-
> limited semiosis, constitutes a multidimensional network of metony-
> mies, each of which is explained by a cultural convention rather than by
> an original resemblance. The imagination would be incapable of in-
> venting (or recognizing) a metaphor if culture, under the form of a pos-
> sible structure of the Global Semantic System, did not provide it with
> the subjacent network of arbitrarily stipulated contiguities. The imagi-
> nation is nothing other than a ratiocination that traverses the paths of
> the semantic rigid structure . . . The 'creative' imagination can perform
> such dangerous exercises only because there exist 'Swedish stall-bars'
> which support it and which suggest movements to it, thanks to their
> grill of parallel and perpendicular bars. The Swedish stall-bars are Lan-
> guage [*langue*]. On them plays Speech [*parole*].[13]

One might think of Merrill's symbolism as an impressive demonstration,
pars pro toto, of this reticulation that the semiotic universe is. Anyone will see
that Eco's phrase "nothing other than" is an understatement that provocatively begs a number of questions, including that of the basis of differences
among imaginations. Writers of Merrill's kind—Mallarmé, Valéry, Ponge,
Joyce, Nabokov, William Gass, even Derrida—have their language dras-
tically affected by their acute awareness of linguistic texture. Looking back
over some of his early literary exercises, in which he sought to perfect individual sentences and even certain sounds without regard for their fictional
frames, Gass deplores (however ironically) the fruitlessness of those undertakings: "These exercises were another idiocy, because I knew that words
were communities made by the repeated crossing of contexts the way tracks

formed towns, and that sentences did not swim indifferently through others like schools of fish of another species, but were like lengths of web within a web, despite one's sense of the stitch and knot of design inside them."[14] "In the Heart of the Heart of the Country" is the sort of story it is exactly because in it Gass exploits these principles.

"The domino effect of equivocation" is what Geoffrey Hartman calls the operation of language in other writers sharply aware that "the screw of language can always be turned further," that "meaning always gets screwed."[15] Because of the "domino effect," it is possible to work by evocation and innuendo alone. This is Mallarmé's ideal (as it is sometimes Merrill's):

> *Nommer* un objet, c'est supprimer les trois quarts de la jouissance du poëme qui est faite de deviner peu à peu: le *suggérer*, voilà le rêve. C'est le parfait usage de ce mystère qui constitue le symbole: évoquer petit à petit un objet pour montrer un état d'âme, ou, inversement, choisir un objet et en dégager un état d'âme, par une série de déchiffrements.

> *To name* an object is to obviate three-fourths of our enjoyment of the poem, which comes from intuiting it little by little: *to suggest* it, that's the dream. This is the right use of the mystery that constitutes the symbol: to evoke bit by bit an object in order to show a state of mind, or, inversely, to choose an object and to extract from it a state of mind, by a series of decipherings.[16]

At this point the poet is back in charge of the metamorphoses—as from one point of view he has been all along. The art I am concerned with here is partly a matter of inducing and guiding forces of equivocation and fusion that threaten always to get out of hand.

"Syrinx," the signature poem in *Braving the Elements,* is a superb example of the symbolist mode. A heavy-hearted love poem that incorporates some inspired *bricolage,* it begins with a version of the pastoral represented by Keats's urn, except that in this case the artifact shatters before our eyes:

> Bug, flower, bird on slipware fired and fluted,
> The summer day breaks everywhere at once.

It opens, that is, as day breaks, and as day breaks into song (we might be reminded of Debussy's "Syrinx"). As the slipware's end is the day's beginning, the one medium turns into the other. A French word with some currency that we might press into service here is *brisure,* which means both a break and a carpenter's folding joint. This is a poem about such antinomies: design and flux, artifice and nature, permanence and transience, unity and division—and their interdependence in love and poetry.

Take the figures on the pottery. At first we are tempted to think something like this: they are no sooner located on the slipware than the slipware shatters. On second thought, however, we see that the sentence will not let us evade its claim that the "slipware" comes into being *with* its destruction. "The summer day" consists of the details in slip that do not exist for the observer until it breaks. Nor is the paradox a result simply of the pun on "breaks," though that turn is crucial; it also owes something to the slide of "slip" into "breaks." Just as important are the participial adjectives, "fired" and "fluted": they nominally modify the "slipware," put in a kiln and grooved, but they also qualify "The summer day," with which the whole first line is in apposition, and indicate its brightness and sounds. In their double application to the pottery that is broken and the day that breaks into being, these two adjectives condense the poem's motivating paradox. The remainder of the poem amplifies this original intuition and recondenses it time after time, since the intention is both to say everything and to say it "at once," exactly. We can detect behind this poem two impulses, elaboration and compression, that we might associate respectively with Merrill's narrative work and his symbolism, even though "Syrinx" itself is as pure an instance as one could cite of the latter mode. There is no limit to synecdoche.

The summer day is "fluted" in yet another sense, as we know from the title, which means "shepherd's pipe" and the vocal organ of a bird. So "fluted" means something like "celebrated"—in a sense somewhere between "sung" and "trumpeted." But of course Merrill also wants us to think of the Arcadian nymph for whom the syrinx is named, who was turned into a reed so that she might be saved from the lecherous Pan, who then made the reed into a flute. Indeed, poor Syrinx is the speaker:

> Worn is the green of things that have known dawns
> Before this, and the darkness before them.
>
> Among the wreckage, bent in Christian weeds,
> Illiterate—X my mark—I tremble, still
>
> A thinking reed. Who puts his mouth to me
> Draws out the scale of love and dread—
>
> O ramify, sole antidote!

The story that the poem coaxes Merrill into is that Syrinx has outlived her time. Plutarch tells us how a mysterious voice proclaimed at the exact moment of Christ's birth that "The great god Pan is dead"—and with Pan went the whole pagan classical world. Yet Merrill's Syrinx has lingered on, the source of a melancholy music, a reed in the Christian weeds that have sprouted among the wreckage of the old culture and the shards of the day that has broken. A reed, but still a "thinking reed," or "un roseau pensant," as Pascal defined humanity. Syrinx has been disguised, or dressed up in the Christian philosopher's phrase as in clothes, since "weeds" also carries its rarer meaning here. She is a cross now between pagan and Christian, and her "mark," once called the christcross, is also the Greek *chi* that begins and abbreviates *christos,* "the anointed one." Whether or not the X is "the letter writer's kiss," as it will be in *Scripts for the Pageant,* Syrinx is the poet as lover at the same time that she is the poet as musical instrument and mourner. The poem becomes a maze here toward the middle as every word leads to every other word. Her very mark means intersection. The antidote she invokes is one with the ailment, dread one with love, and these feelings one with music, heard here in the invocation to it, for in a singular invention Merrill incorporates a muffled solfeggio in the words "O ramify, sole antidote."

"'How much further, James, will you be driven?'" he arranges to ask himself in "Days of 1971" on being presented with a walking stick. It is a question one asks of him several times in this poem alone. Because in its root sense *ramify* means "to branch out," as the poem continues to do, the X also signifies multiplication, the subject of the following passage:

O ramify, sole antidote! Foxglove
Each year, cloud, hornet, fatal growths

Proliferating by metastasis
Rooted their total in the gliding stream.

Some formula not relevant any more
To flower children might express it yet

Like $\sqrt{\left(\dfrac{x}{y}\right)^n} = 1$
—Or equals zero, one forgets—

The *y* standing for you, dear friend . . .

As the ramification produces the "Foxglove," so its leaves provide digitalis, a drug used in heart stimulants and therefore connected with music and love. But music and love are passionate strains in the same experience that kills; in Merrill's paradox, a variation on Yeats's "dying generations," they are "fatal growths." Both sides of the matter are implied by "metastasis," which has both pathological and rhetorical meanings: on the one hand, the transference of malignant cells, and on the other, the rapid skimming of a subject. Metastasis, the flitting figure or the figure of remove, is the rhetorical counterpart to the movement of Eco's implied gymnast.

Within this disseminative language, however, which figures an incorrigibly volatile experience, there is a centripetal pressure, which the "formula" tries to express. An attempt to distill the quintessence of a love story, the formula is at the same time an attempt to frame a summation. Even as it points toward a union, however, its symbols (x, y, and n, plus the small Roman numeral on the right side of the equation and the initials in "$square$ $root$"), as though in an instance of Ferdinand de Saussure's ingeniously proposed hypogram, spell "Syrinx"—whose lonely name is thus what it all comes to, as the name itself is epitomized by the fickle "X."[17] Or we might think of the name the other way around, as one of those "rare single words [that] can imply, like seeds, whole energy systems."[18] In either case, the formula glosses and doubles the doubleness of "breaks," which implicitly equates creation and decreation, for when Merrill turns the "1" into "zero" and then back into "one," he repeats the transformations that we have in the poem's first two lines.

The last lines follow out this opposition between "one" and "zero":

The y standing for you, dear friend, at least
Until that hour he reaches for me, then

Leaves me cold, the great god Pain,
Letting me slide back into my scarred case

Whose silvery breath-tarnished tones
No longer rivet bone and star in place

Or keep from shriveling, leather round a stone,
The sunbather's precocious apricot

Or stop the four winds racing overhead
          Nought
    Waste   Eased
      Sought

The phrasing has the finality, the permanence of the predetermined, as for example "cold," "silvery," "star," and "bone" form a little pattern that extends itself immediately in all directions. "Star" chimes with "scarred" and "tarnished" and "bones" with "tones" and its anagram "stone," while "star" and "rivet" fix each other by virtue of the latent metaphor. One might say of the end of "Syrinx" what Thibaudet said of the end of Mallarmé's "Salut," that it is not a set of phrases but a constellation surrounded by the white page.[19] It is the equivalent in image and sound of the so-called "formula." Yet how tentative any such formula or aesthetic form must be, while the thinking reed is the frailest of instruments, as the delicate *frissons* insist. To be left "cold" by Pain, one aspect of Pan, is to be left flat and unfeeling both. It is therefore also to be left dead: the "scarred case" has funerary overtones, and the shriveling of the "precocious apricot" suggests the final shrinking of flesh. The phrase "precocious apricot" has other shadings as well. The apricot tree is precisely precocious in the botanical sense, because its blossoms begin to appear before its leaves, but that is a minor accuracy. This is a rare instance in which adjacent words form a doublet: they come from the same roots, meaning "early ripe" or "precooked," so that they translate each other almost exactly. The word "precocious" *is* this poem's "early apricot." The etymological discovery overlaps with the sense of the distich as a whole, which reminds us that the shriveling is there in potential in the ripe fruit, the wrinkling in the young, sunburned body. In a word, ripeness is all. Similarly, the "scarred case," which is the body before it is a coffin, harbors within it, as the coffin will, a "carcass." In such lines Mallarmé's desiderata are fulfilled. One strand linking him and Merrill runs through Verlaine, whose "Art poétique" also treats nuance, flute, and union at once:

Car nous voulons la Nuance encor,
Pas la Couleur, rien que la nuance!
Oh! la nuance seule fiance
Le rêve au rêve et la flûte au cor!

For still we want nuance,
Not color, nothing but nuance!
Ah, only nuance betroths
Dream to dream and flute to horn.[20]

Merrill's poem's last "line" circles back to the explosive opening. Formerly shaped temporarily by the flute's "silvery breath-tarnished tones," the "four winds" are flux and chaos, here held in check forever in the moment at the poem's end by Merrill's arrangement of them on the page. His form is continually changing, however, since we cannot tell in which order to read the riveted epitaphic words and must therefore shuffle them about and redraw the various connections among them. True, the most likely order in which to read the words, and the order Merrill adopts when reading to an audience, is "Nought Sought Eased Waste." Nothing sought has eased the waste. Moreover, traced out on the page, this is the order in which Pascal or any Catholic, facing the reader, would cross himself, so that the christcross is indeed the speaker's mark here at the end. Nevertheless, in the absence of syntax, the form these words have must be kaleidoscopic. The poem continues to be, in Hugh Kenner's admirable definition of a poem (though it evolves from a poetics rooted in symbolism and thus applies better to some poems than others), "a controlled transformational process. As the cables of a suspension bridge graph a system of stresses, the words on the page plot stabilized energies."[21] The plotting is especially graphic in Merrill's conclusion, whose energies sweep it past the risk of looking merely ingenious (or too much like Goren on bridge).

Kenner also puts it this way: the symbolist poem is "an effort to anticipate the work of time by aiming directly at the kind of existence a poem may have when a thousand years have deprived it of its dandelions and its mythologies, an existence purely linguistic, determined by the molecular bonds of half-understood words."[22] Although "Syrinx" draws upon our knowledge of mythology, it redefines the myth so radically that it remakes it as time might, while relationships like those among "precocious," "apricot," "fired," and "ramify" exemplify such bonds. By disposing its syntactical elements so that any punctuation would be restrictive, Merrill's "Under Mars," a lyric inspired by a deserted New England barn, stresses these linguistic unions. The poem defines its own ideal operation: "Penknife-pearl-and-steel ripples / Paring nobody's orchard to the bone / Cut both ways the pond believes." Like the ripples from a disturbance of the pond's surface, the words' meanings should move in all directions at once. Thus the ripples themselves (1) pare an orchard that now belongs to nobody by cutting back and forth across its reflection, (2) pare nobody's orchard at all, since they are only ripples, and (3) pair the orchard by mirroring it. Paring and pairing both, the ripples scissor and mend. In addition to being through and through multivalent, "Under Mars" also means to have outlines as sleek as those of "Lorelei" and "Syrinx," to emulate the glimmering vision in its sixth distich: "Our light fantastic fills the barn / Turning the Model A's stripped body gold"—like some relic found in Tut's tomb. But the poem's clever phrasing often fails to meet the standards set by these two excerpts, as Merrill acknowledged by excluding it from *From the First Nine*.

Taking its name from the European passenger train the poet finds himself on, "Flèche d'Or" is an intense meditation on Zeno's paradox of the arrow (since at any point in time the flying arrow occupies a position in space equal to itself, and since to occupy such a position is to be at rest, the arrow in flight cannot move):

euphoria's
Authoritative gliding forth,
The riddle of the rails
Vitally unmoved in flight
However fast
I run racing that arrow
Lodged in my brain
Down the board platform beyond hurt or hope . . .

This arrangement of line and syntax makes first the rails and then the poet "unmoved in flight," and as we grasp the second possibility we look back at the first, so that as we plunge on down the lines we do not move. Merrill reinforces the paradox by letting his mind rerun his race down the platform as the train and the poem race forward. Like "Syrinx," this poem tries to have it both ways, and though it lacks the eye-opening inventions of the other poem, it too hovers on the edge of mystical experience:

now yet
Might somebody
Seeing it all (for once not I or I)
Judge us wisely in whose heart of
Hearts the parallels
Meet and nothing lasts and nothing ends.

A virtuoso demonstration of doubling, these last lines keep folding into themselves. Let us say that the "somebody" who "might" be omniscient and "might" judge wisely is a hypothetical deity, while the poet's two I's are the poet himself and his persona. The "us" then might either be all of us (if the "I" is representative in its doubleness), or it might refer to the two I's, which would parallel each other and might be thought to converge in the poet's "heart of / Hearts." But that "heart" might be in "somebody": the syntax tergiversates. It follows that the parallels—the two I's, figured visually as the rails—are the "somebody" and the "us." In our heart of hearts, we might say, and Merrill does say in *Sandover* if he has not in "From the Cupola," humanity and deity meet. The latter is within us, as the "all" that can be seen is literally at the heart of "par*all*els." The parallels (also implied in the pair of I's) meet to make the poem's point, the point of the golden arrow, which, even as it extends away from the poet in the form of the apparently converging tracks, is lodged in his brain or heart and in any case in his flesh, since he is mortal. But the convergence of flèche and flesh suggests a point not attainable in this life. To bring together the flèche d'or and the heart of hearts is to take the thought to the very door beyond which flesh cannot go as flesh. All one can do is state the alternatives and try to conjure the ineffable one by trying to identify contraries or by following the *via negativa*. Merrill does both in his last two clauses, each of which has two meanings. "Nothing lasts" means both that all temporal things are transitory and that an eternal Nothing (Nirvana) endures. "Nothing ends" means both that all things go on forever and that the virtual nullity of temporal existence ends in absolute nullity. Those last two clauses are perfectly parallel, opposite, and convergent.[23]

Merrill treats the same idea with a sense of humor in "Mandala," whose conclusion echoes that of "Flèche d'Or": "But who needs friends / To remind him that nothing either lasts or ends? / Garrulous as you, dear, time will tell." "Komboloi" opens with the encoding of its subject mentioned in the first chapter: "Begin. Carnation underfoot, tea splashing stars / Onto this mottled slab, amber coherences, / Unmatched string of the habitué / Told and retold, rubbed lucid, quick with scenes . . ." In light of the rest of the poem, in which the speaker clicks off on his string of amber worry-beads several past incarnations, the flower underfoot likely indicates a funeral just attended. The speaker, who recalls the poet in "Mandala," his "cat / Sights" set "on two or three / More flings here in the dark," has become a habitué not just of the café, but also of life, and the "Unmatched string" is both the komboloi with its various beads and his chain of diverse lives, which he wants to extend. But the poem ends with a somber vision:

The wheel

Founders in red rainwater, soul inchdeep in pain,
Charred spokesman of reflections grimly

Sanguine with siftings from the great
Cracked hourglass. Click. Will . . . ? Click.

Will second wind come even to the runners
Out of time? These beads—O marble counter—Done.

Once again Merrill follows the thought as far as possible, but the "runners / Out of time" leave the temporal world. In this case his concluding question has a moral dimension: it asks not whether the worthy will be saved, but whether even those who waste their time might be allowed another life. Or is the café's "marble counter," with its overtones of a mortician's slab, a figure for an implacable deity who coldly counts our allotted days? The speaker who begs incarnation can remain only "grimly / Sanguine."

As linguistic slippage is the means whereby metaphysical concerns merge with image in that last vision ("sanguine" combines the scene's redness with hope, "spokesman" combines the wagon wheel with the soul, and so on), so it provides the infrastructure of "The Black Mesa," in which topographical features figure the relationship between the poet and another person. This poem is complicated by its use of historical incident and of the plot of *Thaïs*—perhaps as much Massenet's opera as France's novel. The speaker is the Black Mesa of San Ildefonso itself, possibly volcanic in origin and located in the desert (near Santa Fe, New Mexico)—circumstances which allow Merrill to make the Mesa a bilious writer by turning "parch" into a noun and by letting idiom and syntax turn "igneous" into an adjective that shares something with "impious" or "odious":

> So much is parchment where I gloom,
> Character still sharp enough to prick
> Into the hide my igneous
> Old spells and canticles of doom.
> The things that shape a person!

Toward the middle of the poem the relationship between the speaker and the "you," figured as the surrounding land, is obscured by Merrill's adaptation of recherché elements,[24] but he revives it powerfully in his concluding aporia, tinged with that knowing wistfulness that is his cachet:

> And we are friends now? Funny friends.
> Glaringly over the years you knit
> A wild green lap robe I shake off in tears.
> I steal past him who next reclaims you, keep
> Our hushed appointments, grain by grain . . .
> Dust of my dust, when will it all be plain?

While *Thaïs* remains in the background (for first the anchorite reclaims her and then God does, and one of the climaxes in the opera is the unison phrase in act 2, scene 2, "Que tout ce qui fut moi retourne à la poussière"), the poem finds its closure in the relationship between the Mesa and the flatland, with its vegetation encroaching on the basalt. The point is not so much that one day the Mesa will be leveled and everything will be "plain" or clear, though the idea of the hourglass's sand running out is as certainly behind this "grain by grain" change as it is behind the end of "Komboloi"; it is rather that things cannot be "plain" this side of such a leveling or reunion. The final question is a semi-ironic gloss on the poem, which suddenly gets even darker here at the end. Rhetorically, the last line could not be more conclusive, but meaning has proliferated. The phrase "Dust of my dust," taken with the earlier reference to "human / Frailties," encourages us to think of "you" and the flatland as Eve and of the speaker as Adam, whose name means "earth." It is when he "falls" for her "lie"—to borrow from the second stanza—that time enters the world, and we have been falling as time has been running out ever since.

If things cannot be plain here and now, that is partly because even words like "plain" keep splitting under pressure. The prefatory poem in *Braving the Elements,* "Log," presents a pertinent case:

> Then when the flame forked like a sudden path
> I gasped and stumbled, and was less.
> Density pulsing upward, gauze of ash,
> Dear light along the way to nothingness,
> What could be made of you but light, and this?

For Merrill this flame is always forking like a sudden path. The flame pulsing "upward" up word after word breaks many of them, as it breaks "Log" into firewood and journal, as it splits "light" into gaiety and illumination. Hence the density here of the light—Merrill's ever-changing light. No wonder that so many of his poems end in knots of paradox and plena of nothingness. Such poems meet us with what Geoffrey Hartman calls (in speaking of Joyce and Derrida) "a rain or ruin of unsummable meanings that seems to scatter us." Hartman goes on to wonder whether modern literature is "sliding toward a Dionysian revel which no longer knows its name." [25] Merrill has wondered the same.

"Dreams about Clothes," from which this volume's title comes, is its most extreme manifestation of Merrill's penchant for finding whole texts in single words. Every phrase is self-consciously aquiver with equivocation, a quiver of points to be variously aimed and shot. The poem mocks its puns as quickly as it makes them and succeeds so utterly in its strategy that from its opening words it is on the verge of concluding in despair at its manifold discoveries. "In some," it begins, in reference to both dreams and clothes, but we also hear "In sum," and to open with such a fissured phrase is to acknowledge "unsummable meanings." Any summation, the implication is, is partial and instigative.

> In some, the man they made
> Penetrates the sunlit fitting room,
> Once more deciding among bolts of dark.
> The tailor kneels to take his measure.

Soon a finished suit will be laid out
By his valet, for him to change into.
Change of clothes? The very clothes of change!
Unchecked blazers women flutter round,
Green coverts, midnight blues . . .
My left hand a pincushion, I dispose,
Till morning, of whole closets full of clues.

"Unchecked blazers" precisely! And with their own "bolts of dark" (shades
of Milton's "darkness visible"), as in the sudden chiasmus, "Change of
clothes? The very clothes of change!" In view of the overtones of "laid out"
and the ominously surgical meaning to a poet of the phrase "to take his measure," the pun on "close" suggests a literal dead end—a consideration that,
however, only provokes Merrill to ring more changes on the subject. Before
he knows it the Muse, masquerading as a gold digger, is taking him and his
clothes (not that there is a difference, since clothes make the man) "to the
cleaners"—specifically, "Arturo's Valet Service, one block East." Once, he
enjoyed nothing more than soaking up the art of those who taught him
technique and texture. "The tempest used to be my cup of tea," as he puts it
when recalling how he would steep himself in Prospero and Proust. Now he
has begun to tire of his art, his habits, many of them riddled anyway with
"holes made by the myth" (or Psyche moth) or given to an old clothes man,
whose disguise as a hunchback does not keep the poet from recognizing in
"his baby face" the Angel of Death. Enough poetry! "For there's more enterprise / In walking naked," as Yeats proclaimed. Merrill turns to the pro-
prietor of Arturo's for help:

Tell me something, Art.
You know what it's like
Awake in your dry hell
Of volatile synthetic solvents.
Won't you help us brave the elements
Once more, of terror, anger, love?
Seeing there's no end to wear and tear
Upon the lawless heart,
Won't you as well forgive
Whoever settles for the immaterial?
Don't you care how we live?

Once nicknamed and placed in his proper surroundings, the cleaner stands
forth as the very Art that presses the poet's diverse suits. Since the poet's life

193

itself causes enough wear and tear to keep Arturo flush, perhaps he will not mind if the poet surrenders his aesthetic concerns and turns instead to common passions? This is Merrill as Ariel, seeking his release from Art—or the kind of art that involves "volatile synthetic solvents." Like "From the Cupola" and "A Tenancy," and like "Days of 1935" in this volume, this poem seems to end by turning away from the word toward the world.

But does it really do so? The answer here, I think, should be the typical Greek response memorialized in "More Enterprise," a poem in *The Fire Screen* that was dropped from the selected poems, which takes its title from Yeats's "A Coat," quoted earlier: "A sideways flicker, half headshake of doubt— / Meaning, confusingly, assent—fills out / The scant wardrobe of gesture" the poet still uses. In "Dreams about Clothes," even as the poet makes his plea to Art, an undercurrent questions its legitimacy. For one thing, the penultimate line identifies life with "the immaterial," and although that label is technically consistent with the poem's basic metaphor (the clothes are made of "material"), its sense conflicts with the idea that life is a matter of the primary emotions. For another thing, while the poet looks forward to braving the elements of life again, the reader cannot avoid thinking back on the fourth verse paragraph, where Merrill remembers having been drenched by those "rainy spells" of art. The whole problem is summed up in a "memory" isolated by parentheses: "(Come in, Mme. de Garments called, / You'll be soaked to the skin! I never woke.)" Was she calling him into the house, to take shelter, after the storm had begun? Or was she calling him earlier into the tempest and the tea? This is not a matter of incoherence, but rather of the poet's—or the language's—assertion that it is only in art that a poet braves his elements.

"The Victor Dog," dedicated to Elizabeth Bishop (and perhaps indebted to her "Cirque d'Hiver"), reopens the issue. "Art is art," it concludes: "The life it asks of us is a dog's life." But the life of the RCA Victor dog as Merrill imagines it is anything but "dry" and "artificial." True, the Victor dog's "work" demands discipline and "forebearance." "He ponders the Schumann Concerto's tall willow hit / By lightning, and stays put," and nothing can make him howl; he "listens long and hard as he is able" to "whatever plays." But such listening, far from cutting him off from life, lets him experience it more intensely. Not only can he surmise "Through one of Bach's eternal boxwood mazes / The oboe pungent as a bitch in heat," he can also smell "Those lemon-gold arpeggios in Ravel's / 'Les jets d'eau du palais de ceux qui s'aiment.'" If Art doesn't care how we live, the implication in these poems is, then no one does.

But "Dreams about Clothes" and "The Victor Dog" are not true symbolist undertakings. Although they rely on a language within language, it is more a matter of simple punning than evocation, of Fancy than Imagination. "18 West 11th Street" is a more substantial, substantially more obscure "controlled transformational process." Like "Syrinx," it sometimes seems just under control; unlike "Syrinx," it has a narrative. Because the narrative is not easily disentangled from the highly charged details, a paraphrase is useful.[26] The narrative actually comprises two strands, one of which splices bits of the history of the Greenwich Village townhouse that used to stand at the address given in the title and that was Merrill's family's New York residence from before his birth until some five years later. In March 1970, almost exactly forty-four years after he was born, the townhouse was blown up when members of the militant radical faction of Students for a Democratic Society known as the Weatherman accidentally set off some dynamite in the building's basement, which, police later determined, had been serving as a bomb factory. Three of the five young people in the building at the time were killed. Two women—Kathy Boudin and Cathlyn Wilkerson, the latter the daughter of the townhouse's owner—escaped the tremendous blast with cuts and bruises, borrowed clothes from a neighbor, and fled the scene (neither to appear again in public until they turned themselves in separately after more than ten years spent underground). The second narrative strand is a recollection of a love affair with a woman the speaker calls B. B broke off the affair in the winter of 1969–70, had an affair with another man, then tried to patch things up in June, when it was too late. In addition to these two sketchy plots, which cross paths to suggest that in the destruction of the building Merrill sees a parallel to the fate of the relationship, the poem's structure involves occasional indirect observations on its composition.

The first of the poem's five sections (eight tercets each) begins in the past perfect tense as though it were to be about the Weatherman, breaks off in relief at sunset, then drops into the present tense and ruminates on the poem's raw material and the immediate setting. The second section consists mostly of the poet's memories of the house's music room and the player piano. The third begins with recollections of the house and then calls up the days after the explosion, when the speaker, laid up with a cold and abandoned by B, reads the newspaper accounts. The love affair dominates the fourth section, which also alludes to the poet's sympathy for the other man, and then, taking things in reverse chronological order, recalls his feelings of anger and grief on the night B left him. The last section, making a marvelous transition, continues the film "Run backwards," except that now it is a newsreel of the explosion. It takes us from the billowing smoke back through the coiling—no, the *re*coiling of the hoses, the unswearing in of a city commissioner, the thinning of the crowd as it once more nears the point at which it began to gather, and then back through the emergence from the wreckage of one of the two women, through her disappearance and the ex-plosion itself, to this vision of the street before the blast and the townhouse as it would have looked when first put on the market:

> a pigeon's throat
> Lifting, the puddle
>
> Healed. To let:
> Cream paint, brown ivy, brickflush. Eye
> Of the old journalist unwavering
>
> Through gauze. Forty-odd years gone by.
> Toy blocks. Church bells. Original vacancy.
> O deepening spring.

These are thrillingly direct lines, the more so for concluding a poem as involved as this one, but they are hardly one-dimensional. The two nar-ratives, which sometimes seem distant from each other, join here, even as the townhouse and the "old journalist" do—for the description of the building is a self-portrait of the poet as war correspondent, as the curtained window turns into a bandaged eye and so on. They meet in the feeling of gratitude not just for the experience preceding the loss but even for the loss itself, which creates the power for transcending it. "All things fall and are built again," Yeats chants, "And those that build them again are gay." Like "Lapis Lazuli," this poem puts tragedy in perspective. That is one point of those "Toy blocks," which are among other things the city blocks of Manhattan. The blooming flame, the moment of terror and death, is immediately trans-lated into the pigeon's lovely throat, and the freshly painted building is an imagined new one as well as the one Merrill lived in. The "forty-odd years gone by" take us back to the time of his birth and forward from then to the near future. He would have played with blocks when a child, but the "Toy blocks" are also blocks of print, the stanzas, or these simple, almost childlike phrases at the end, of which he builds the destroyed townhouse anew. The "Church bells"—which we hear ringing in the rhyme of "unwavering" and "spring"—let the "film" go back as far as his parents' marriage, and the phrase "Original vacancy" gestures toward the beginning of it all (not for nothing has Merrill gleaned from newspaper accounts the riveting de-tail that one woman emerged naked from the rubble moaning the name "Adam"); but no sooner has the last line's "O" been uttered than the "deep-ening spring" returns us to the present.

However direct these lines are, the poem as a whole is rife with diffi-culty. The poet has something in common with "the Aquarians in the basement" who at the poem's opening are pictured "perfecting a device" that would make "sense to us / If only briefly and on pain / Of incommunication ever after." The poem itself is a dangerous device that might lead to a penchant for "in" communication:

> Now look who's here. Our prodigal
> Sunset. Just passing through from Isfahan.
> Filled by him the glass
>
> Disorients. The swallow-flights
> Go word by numbskull word
> —Rebellion . . . Pentagon . . . Black Studies—
>
> Crashing into irreality,
> Plumage and parasites
> Plus who knows what of the reptilian . . .

The turn on the phrase "prodigal son" will put us on the alert for the sleight-of-hand involving the "glass," a windowpane that "Disorients" because it turns the poet's gaze from the Orient to the west (though the sunset there has an Oriental carpet's splendor) and a cocktail glass filled at the appointed hour. The alleged "Disorientation" owes something to alcohol, something to the dizzying connections among the words. Or say that his imagination takes "swallow-flights." So the newspaper's words are birds and vice versa crashing into dusk, the journalistic "irreality." While that "irreality" bears a certain relation to the Kingdom Come that the Weatherman intended to blow the "parasites" to, the poet hears it as a conflation of "eerie" and "reality." It defines this poem's world, in which words light up unexpected facets of one another. The aural connections between "irreality" and "reptilian," the cousinage traced by their consonants—which the winking links among "flights," "parasites," and the next stanza's "lights" help us to register—make just the sort of "rhyme" that this poem's semantic obliquities call for.

This poem's irreality derives in part from Merrill's insistence on writing simultaneously about the explosion, the affair, and the poem's composition, as in the last lines of the first section, where his retrospection takes the form of an address to the man we later understand to be B's other lover: "The point / Was anger, brother? Love? Dear premises / Vainly exploded, vainly dwelt upon." As the motivations are the Weatherman's, and B's, and his own (for writing the poem), so "premises" encompasses the building, the assumptions of the revolutionaries and of B, and Merrill's own points of departure. Just as he is quickly impatient with solutions as "simple" as the

Weatherman's or the typical regime's and with the commensurately distorting language usually invoked to report them, he cannot help but see implications and parallels. For him to focus on such political events is to discover the kind of connection that the brutal acts and language would sever. He cannot read about the Weatherman's inventions and speculate on the revolutionaries' emotions without seeing himself in them; he cannot read the phrase "bullet-pocked columns" without seeing in it "Bulletin-pocked columns" and the whole relationship between journalistic cliché and violence. When he reads the papers' telegraphic jargon, he also sees how little adjustment it needs to become a sort of proto-poem. If his columns of verse are "Bulletin-pocked," however, the bulletins have had a wand passed over them. "NIX ON PEACE BID" reports at once a response and the preceding offer—a response that would have been implicit *in* the offer, since it was extended by the old cold warrior in 1970 in the middle of his first term as President. Merrill has only to create a lacuna to reveal the unbridgeable gulf already there.

As for "PROPHET STONED," that headline with proverbial overtones, it needs merely to be set down in this context for it to yield up a plausible source for *this* prophecy's eerie reality. Back in the first section, after sunset, enter a mysterious figure, "The maid, / Silent, pale as any victim," who resembles both a woman escaped from the blast and the moon, and who as she "Comes in, identifies; / Yet brings new silver, gives rise to the joint, / The presidency's ritual eclipse." In her guise as the maid, the Muse herself might bring new utensils and a joint of meat, just as in her role as moon, having replaced the presiding sun (a trope for the Presidency itself and for a "realistic" way of seeing things), she would make things silvery. To that end she might also suggest a joint of marijuana. A few such might even make the joint jump, in a langorous way. Prophet stoned.

The moon lights the beautiful and strange second section, where Merrill summons up the music room and its player piano:

The piano (three-legged by then like a thing in a riddle)
Fingered itself provocatively. Tones
Jangling whose tuner slept, moon's camphor mist

On the parterre compounding
Chromatic muddles which the limpid trot
Flew to construe. Up from camellias

Sent them by your great-great-grandfather,
Ghosts in dwarf sateen and miniver
Flitted once more askew

Through *Les Sylphides*. The fire was dead. Each summer,
While onto white keys miles from here
Warm salt chords kept breaking, snapping the strings,

The carpet—its days numbered—
Hatched another generation
Of strong-jawed, light-besotted saboteurs.

"Chromatic muddles" exactly: a good definition for one kind of symbolist poem. The "muddles" themselves, in proximity with "mist," get back some of their root liquidity, and the preceding plosives nearly turn them into "puddles." Sounds change through virtual semitones into one another: "Tones"—"tuner"—"moon's," and "Flew"—"construe"—"askew," where the last word remarks on the kind of rhyme it makes. Sense impressions fuse: the moon's light becomes a mist not only felt and seen but also smelled ("camphor" is aromatic, though the word comes from a root that means, appropriately, "chalk"), then the mist precipitates into the piano music. Words even kick over their syntactical traces, so that in the extraordinary phrase "the limpid trot / Flew" a lame Pegasus seems to take off (and thus to provide an emblem for this poetic mode). The first reference, however, must be to the musical score (a "trot" would be a kind of translation) with which the "Smoker inveterate between hot bouts" (and butts) "Of gloating over scrollwork" might modify the music dictated by the piano roll. But then we must also imagine that the "Smoker . . . gloating over scrollwork" is the poet.

This is the kind of passage that makes one know that Merrill also has his readers in mind when he describes the people in the film run backward as a "crowd . . . thinned to a / Coven rigorously chosen from so many / Called." He even seems to find himself in the player piano, which "Fingered itself provocatively." We will recall in this connection the end of "From the Cupola" and the "joint" that the Muse-maid-moon "gives rise to." So he "fingers" himself in another sense also: he identifies himself as the culprit, guilty of writing what some readers see as narcissistic, self-indulgent verse that ignores the world with all its misery. And there is no denying that with Chopin on the piano roll, the garden, the moonlight, and these spirit-like presences undergoing magical metamorphoses, this vignette has its precious side. It is as ephemeral a vision as Fokine's ballet, a dance with no plot. Cyril W. Beaumont's description of *Les Sylphides* (with Alexandre Benois's scenery and costumes) could easily be adapted to Merrill's scene: the dancers, fitted with silvery wings and dressed in skirts *à la* Taglioni, remind Beaumont sometimes "of snowflakes whirled hither and thither by the wind in the moonlight of a winter's eve. At other times they resemble wisps of mist, the surf on a breaking wave, and perhaps best of all [when joined by the single male dancer] a phantom poet and his muses, at play beneath the waning moon in the shadow of a frosted glade."[27] For all its subtlety, however, Merrill's poem is anything but fragile or shrinking. It implicitly addresses the charges that it implicitly raises against itself; it opposes down the line, with its own radicalism, the radicalism that would regard it as self-involved or irrelevant. The moths, wonderful "Ghosts in dwarf sateen and miniver," are later justly transformed into "strong-jawed, light-besotted saboteurs" that figure not only the Weatherman but also the poet—"light-besotted" at least since the bargain made long ago in "A Tenancy" and identified with another moth in "From the Cupola." It is his function, by such means as this poem, to give a purer sense to the words of the tribe (as Mallarmé puts it in "Le Tombeau d'Edgar Poe"), which decay on every hand into political doubletalk and journalistic buzz and blur.

"Under Libra: Weights and Measures" resembles "18 West 11th Street" both in its verse form (five sections have five tercets and a concluding distich while the sixth section has six tercets) and its manner. Mallarmé's "Le vierge, le vivace" is a point of orientation, half-acknowledged by the sixth section's centerpiece in the form of a swan, but this poem's world is even stranger than those in "18 West 11th Street" and "Syrinx." We learn about the events that give rise to the poem by inference and by guess, and in the end we still know only a fraction of what has transpired. From the deliberate transformations at the beginning—"The stones of spring, / Stale rolls or pellets rather, rounded / By a gorgon's fingers, swept to the floor, / Dragged south in crushing folds"—the poem translates its items into its own special terms. Thus those "Stale rolls," part of the till left by a glacier, are also part of the same domestic motif as the swan centerpiece. Mediating between them is the fifth section's "little mesa set for two" from which one evening the poet and his friend overlook Los Alamos, the nuclear research center. (This kind of metaphor, which domesticates a landscape and which is characteristic of Merrill's work from the late sixties on, perhaps owes something to Elizabeth Bishop's "sleights of scale," on which he has commented.[28] The same turn of mind that lets her, while packing, find the room to slip in "one more folded sunset, still quite warm," lets him in "The Black Mesa" see cirrus clouds over the New Mexico desert as "blown shawls / Shining and raveling to this day / Above erosions in [Mother Earth's] pot of rouge" and lets him set the mesa or "table" for two in "Under Libra.")

The poem has a fragmentary plot. Its elements include two visits to the American West, where we would find the spectacular hoodoos of section one: "certain curious formations" that "Dwindle in the red wind like ice in tea." The "present" in the poem seems to be toward the end of the period

"Under Libra" (September 23 to October 23) or a little later. Merrill looks back in the first section on a trip west during a preceding spring, which culminated in his return "Home" with a heavy clutch of glacial debris, probably picked up in northern New Mexico, where a couple of small glaciers grazed during the Pleistocene. That winter these souvenirs served him as door-stops—and also tripped him up on occasion when he moved "in the small hours from room to room." The following five sections give us glimpses of the autumn visit, just ended, to New Mexico: an adobe house where the poet and his friend lived; the ice freezing on a nearby ditch and on a pond where (sonorous lines) "two swans are dozing, swansdown quilts / Drawn over heads"; a drive south into warmer zones (section three) and then the return (section five) by way of Los Alamos to the adobe house; a cemetery with wild peacocks where one Angel Ortiz has recently been laid to rest (section two) after an illness evidently witnessed during that earlier spring (section four); a last talk at the dinner table between poet and friend that goes on until early morning; peacock feathers and swan feathers brought home as souvenirs of this season, as the stones had been souvenirs of the spring.

But these narrative fragments refuse to add up to a story, which is instead diffused in images of things often of tangential importance in themselves. These images frequently have to do with hard, translucent things whose relationships must be entrenched in all languages: ice, glass, jewels. Thus the poem slides from the glacier, with its "Long dirty tablecloth of ice," through an iced stream that is a "blown glass simulacrum," the pond covered with "thin ice," the sun reflected in the ice first as an "opal" and later as a "Gem," and "the 'necklace of death'" that the lights of Los Alamos make at night, to a prism on a windowsill that sows the house "With arcs of spectral seed, a peacock's tail." In this coruscating context, even a scene viewed through a dirty windshield "Glints through . . . blazing dust and wings," and flies on the decrepit Angel Ortiz are remembered as having "cudgeled quarter-carat wits." Meanwhile, the sun's reflection in ice, "Mist and fire," appears also in the form of a steamed bathroom mirror, into which a "dreamer" who must be the poet gazes as "Into the dormant crystal of himself, / A presence oval, vitrified—/ That without warning thaws, trickles, and burns!" The poem as a whole is a lustrous girasol that one turns and turns in order to see how the light and colors fuse and melt into one another.

Yet "Under Libra" is not simply verbal abstract impressionism; it builds its meaning up as it sheathes a secret worry and hope in association after association. It declines to be confessional, but it declines in a special context, so that it ends by being intensely private. What it intimates is an odd condition of suspense. The title, with its Balance and its paired trochees on either side on the colon, gravely weighs itself, and the opening sentence, eleven lines long, defers its verb until the last line. The "dreamer," the poet, sleeps under what is evidently a native American blanket that has a "double-headed bird" woven into it, and his question as to whether it will "keep him warm" much longer signifies an uneasy equipoise. Angel Ortiz, "both quick and dead, / Awaited judgment and suspended it" those afternoons he spent sitting in his son's unused truck. As though in grotesque magnification of the poet's condition in "The Thousand and Second Night," Angel seems to have had paralysis on one side of his body and convulsions on the other. He was both trying to die and clinging to life, and "It seemed / Both sides of the old character knew best."

I think we are very close here, at what seems the poem's least integrated element, to the heart of the matter—as we are again in the fifth section, in another seemingly digressive moment, when we get a glimpse of "Los Alamos' lights where wizards stay up late . . . To save the world or end it, time will tell." Like the hemiplegic Angel, the poet is both awaiting judgment and suspending it, and so perhaps is his friend. It is as though their relationship had evolved an equilibrium it would not be able to maintain. This equilibrium is reflected in Merrill's rhetoric, when he imagines that he will one day look back "through saltwater, through flames" at this period in his life. The language he and his friend speak is a metaphoric Esperanto, which takes its name from its inventor's pseudonym. Is the poet "the hopeful one" in this case? If the poem does not allow us to decide that question, it does let us understand why Merrill includes the table's "Undripping centerpiece, the Swan," which recalls Mallarmé's immobilized bird. This swan and Mallarmé's sum up the dilemma that these two men (with whom we must connect the two swans dozing on the pond and the double-headed bird on the blanket) find themselves in.

This situation helps to account for Merrill's tone, his postponement of inflection. It also helps to explain the initially bewildering treatment of time and tense. In the second section, events that must be past are treated in the present and the future tenses, and then in the third section the incident just treated in the future tense is "Past." Later in the third section, the poet and his friend drive south, "Drive / Until the trees have leaves again / And the tanner's colors change to those of the mint, / Copper, silver, green / Engraved by summer's light, by spring's." But here time does not go backwards, though geography makes it seem to do so, and eventually they reach a riverbend, a place where "time turned round at last, drew rein." As they turn around with the river and head north again, the poet muses that "Yesterday's Gem" "*will* float across" a "frost of stubble" that is both a cut field (when the Gem is "tomorrow's opal") and—no less suggestive—the poet's day's growth of graying beard (when it is a razor). "There was one / Direction only, after all," is the lesson of this little excursion, which cannot cancel the day of reckoning.

Merrill's masterfully equivocal tenses seem to suspend time or to turn it "round" *and* round—as do his odd repetitions of phrases. But when the third section's rhyme of "burns" and "learns" is echoed in the last tercet, the tense has become grimly past. The conclusion, after calling up that late autumn night at the table with its "Undripping centerpiece," insists on the "one direction," the movement forward, inexorable as that of the glacier, which seems frozen but inside flows as surely as the water in the ditch flows beneath its "blown glass simulacrum" (which crystalline term itself might suddenly thaw to yield a fluent *lac* or "saltwater" *lacrimae*):

Days were coming when the real thing
No longer shrugged a wing, dipping its mask

Where any surface thawed and burned.
One learned. The heavy stones of spring.
These autumn feathers. Learned.

In the coming days, as the pond freezes solid, the "real thing" or swan outside (whose "mask" hides also the face of the poet) will continue its migration to Mexico. Things change—and there is even a sense in which "the real thing" *is* change. At the moment at the table, however, the future of the relationship hangs in the balance. Like the nuclear "wizards" who "stay up late . . . To save the world or end it, time will tell," these two at their negotiating table are inevitably deciding the fate of their small world, however invisibly. In this scene whatever "sparks that flew . . . were translated into the windiest / Esperanto," Merrill tells us, as he himself translates the emotional situation into the details of the hearth. The pervasive sense of such translation is this poem's power and drama.

> > >

What then of the poet who so admires Cavafy's candor and Elizabeth Bishop's limpidity? What of the *conteur* of "The Summer People"? He is here in *Braving the Elements* in poems like "After the Fire" and "Strato in Plaster" and "Days of 1935," poems which seem at first quite different from the hermetic ventures.

"After the Fire"—written in sporadically rhymed pentameter flexible enough to accommodate anecdote, conversation in Hellenicized French, epigram, and detailed description—derives from "Days of 1964." It has characters with histories, its usual tense is the simple present, and it has a plot. The poet returns to his Athens home, which has just been redecorated—fresh paint, "Balcony glassed in, electric range"—after a fire of mysterious origin during his absence. He comes back to other changes as well. A love affair with someone in Athens has come to an end. And Kleo, his cleaning woman still, has strange tidings about her mother, "the yiayia" (the Greek word means "grandmother"). Although she is now nearly ninety, her temperament and manner have suddenly altered radically. From the window of the basement apartment she shares with Kleo and Kleo's son Panayióti, she "Hurls invective at the passing scene, / Tea bags as well, the water bill, an egg." Worse, while she seems to have overlooked her daughter's questionable behavior for years, "When Kleo really was a buxom armful," she now screams her tardy reproaches so loudly that the whole neighborhood hears. Moreover, her "terrible gift of hindsight" makes her shriek at Panayióti—"a *Degenerate!* a *Thieving / Faggot!*"—even though "Now he must be forty, / Age at which degeneration takes / Too much of one's time and strength and money." During his second day in the city the poet visits Kleo's apartment, where the family will celebrate a saint's feast day and where he encounters Panayióti, who has spent the preceding evening making love with the priest in the church, who speaks a brutal French, and who immediately bullies the poet into accepting a homecoming gift, a "'Zoli foulard . . . Mais prends-le donc, c'est pas volé— / Ze ne suis plus voleur, seulement volaze.'" It is not clear that he is no longer a thief, however: the apartment is full of items evidently "translated" from the poet's house. It even occurs to Merrill "that P. caused the fire." As they are talking the yiayia suddenly becomes her old self, and at this point the poem ends.

Beneath the gossipy surface, through the cracks between the lines, we get glimpses of something else going on. As in *The (Diblos) Notebook* and "Under Libra," one has the sense that Merrill wants "something to be concealed *by* the story, by the writing." "Some of those embers can't be handled yet," he cryptically explains. Like "The walls' original oldfashioned colors, / Cendre de rose, warm flaking ivory / . . . hidden now forever but not lost" beneath the new paint, and in the very shades of those colors, a certain fire pervades the poem. It is there in the poet's imagining of a "lover's ghost / Stumbling downstairs wound in a sheet of flame," in the candles on the cake, the fever run by the yiayia, the crimson robe Panayióti wears, even in a "ruby glass ashtray."

We can gather something of the motivating events and their effects from the figures and objects around the speaker—or from the way he sees them. Take Kleo, who appears at the beginning:

Everything changes; nothing does. I am back,
The doorbell rings, my heart leaps out of habit,
But it is only Kleo—how thin, how old!—
Trying to smile, lips chill as the fallen dusk.

She has brought a cake "for tomorrow"
As if tomorrows were still memorable.

If tomorrows are no longer memorable, in Merrill's amusing paradox, that must be because of the breakup of his affair. We hear nothing more of it until we are forty lines into the poem, but the juxtaposition of the last two lines above with Kleo's sadness suggests that her feelings mirror his. He too, in view of the expectations that the doorbell arouses, must be "Trying to smile" as he faces Kleo and the dusk behind her. That her lips are "chill" tells us something about his emotional state, as does his choice of a "quiet sensible light gray" color for the new paint, while the "electric range" bespeaks a desire he seems not to recognize to separate himself from the "fire." He is yet another version of the "cold man" who "hardly cares." In this context the description of a photo in Kleo's apartment reveals a good deal about his last relationship: "Upon the sideboard an old me / Scissored from its glossy tavern scene— / I know that bare arm too, flung round my shoulder— / Buckles against a ruby glass ashtray." Once burnt, twice shy.

It is difficult to think that the breakup has simply left the poet mildly sorrowful and wary, however. The poem is surprisingly, not to say suspiciously, quiet and sensible. If Merrill's cool surface hides some other emotion, as the "light gray" paint hides the warmer colors, it does so at the same time that it displays it in the person of the yiayia. When the yiayia does not recognize him at first, mightn't it be that he is not himself—just as she is not herself? It is as though she had taken on herself all the passion—the spitefulness, the anger, the shame—that he might be expected to feel if he had been betrayed. Just as she has her "terrible gift of hindsight," so he remembers "past evenings in this hall" and "candles minutely / Guttering in the love-blinded gaze." In order to console Kleo about her mother's condition, he mentions his "own mother's mother's illness, / Querulous temper, lucid shame," and when "Kleo says weeping that it's not the same," one naturally wants to respond as the first line has primed one to do: "Everything changes; nothing does."

The effect of the latent comparison between the two grandmothers is to make him one of the family—and even to draw a parallel between him and Panayióti. Panayióti wears the poet's crimson robe and his slippers and lives among items spirited away from the poet's house. Moreover, he confesses to being fickle, and the poet, admitting after the fire that "The smoke cleared / On no real damage," nevertheless decided that he had "wanted changes . . . And wrote to have them made." Is that a way of saying that he too has been *volage*? When it strikes him, "as happily it did not / The insurance company, that P. caused the fire," mightn't he be acknowledging his own part in the breakup? Panayióti has a hot temper, and the poet's mother's mother has a "Querulous temper," and "that lover's ghost / Stumbling downstairs wound in a sheet of flame" might have been fleeing the speaker's wrath, however justified it might have been. It is significant that when the poet visits Kleo's family, he is intercepted by Panayióti: before he can embrace the yiayia, according to the poem's implicit myth, he must embrace the grandson. As he does so, we recall that in "Days of 1964" he and Kleo's "wastrel son," then unnamed, were alter egos. Not that Panayióti is a stalking horse for the poet; he is much too individual a figure for that. Besides, we might also regard him as reflective of the former lover, whose own fickleness seems to have been the original problem. Or perhaps we should consider that he, who steals anything else, "caused the fire" in the sense that he had a relationship with the former lover. Or "not to complicate affairs," to borrow Merrill's leading but cautionary phrase, let us think of Panayióti as blurring out into the general condition. If he is a thief, we are told that "Life" itself "like the bandit Somethingopoulos / Gives to others what it takes from us." Which is another way of saying that while everything changes, nothing does.

The poet changes, at the poem's end, as does the yiayia—and they do so at the same instant, as how could they not. As he recovers his feeling (which, having come to terms with himself, he can do), she regains her senses:

> I mean to ask whose feast it is today
> But the room brightens, the yiayia shrieks my name—
> *It's Tzimi! He's returned!*
> —And with that she returns to human form,
> The snuffed-out candle-ends grow tall and shine,
> Dead flames encircle us, which cannot harm,
> The table's spread, she croons, and I
> Am kneeling pressed to her old burning frame.

This is to reach beyond that "quiet sensible light gray" and to feel again what he thought was "hidden now forever but not lost." It is love's feast that he has come to, and as in "Flying from Byzantium," "The point's to live, love, / Not shake your fist at the feast."

The figures in "After the Fire" thus engage in "reflets réciproques" much as the words do in a symbolist poem. What we have, even as the linguistic mesh is somewhat looser, is a tissue of characters. "Strato in Plaster" is a shorter, less intricate, but cleverly turned poem in the same mold. It might well be about the same relationship, though not a fire but a fracture is the focal point. After a separation that has endured for some time, though nothing has changed between them, the poet and his friend have met for a drink in an Athens café. Strato has been a self-confessedly "'bad friend,'" and the poet has decided to make a break. Coincidentally, Strato has recently suffered another bad break; a contractor, he was building a house when he fell from the scaffolding and broke his arm. That is one reason for the title: when he meets the poet, he has his arm in a cast. The other reason is the contrast between Strato, a handsome man, and statues of Apollo in marble. A friend of the poet—"Chester," who is very likely Chester Kallman, who will turn up also in *Sandover*—has sent him "a postcard . . . / Of the Apollo at Olympia, / Its message *Strato as he used to be.*" With the card in mind, Merrill cannot help but allude to Rilke's "Archaïscher Torso Apollos" when he considers what has become of Strato and their relationship:

> Three winters. Trowels of frigid white
> Choke the sugar-celled original
> That once stayed warm all night with its own sun.
> The god in him is a remembered one.
> Inflexibility through which twinges shoot
> Like stars, the fracture's too complex,
> Too long unmended, for us to be friends.

The figure "that once stayed warm all night with its own sun" harks ironically back to the torso in the Louvre, which "glüht noch wie ein Kandelaber" ("still glows like a candelabra"), and the twinges shooting like stars play off Rilke's marble, which also explodes "aus allen seinen Rändern / aus wie ein Stern" ("from all its limits like a star"). The "remembered" god lacks the power of the dismembered marble one. The plaster cast itself is a convenient means of indicating the real reasons for the "fracture": Strato's brittle egotism. The Greek epigraph, a saying which translates as "breast of marble and heart of potato," points to the same "Inflexibility" (as well as to a certain sentimentalism). There seems nothing for the poet to do but end the relationship. Strato—who is on his way to a wedding—accepts the unspoken decision with characteristic *sprezzatura*, though it is clear that he has misgivings. The poem ends with these lines:

> Today at least a cloud of rice and petals
> Aimed at others will envelop him.

207

Risen, he wonders—almost saying what.
I take his swollen hand in both of mine.
No syllable of certain grand tirades
One spent the worse part of a fall composing,
Merely that word in common use
Which means both *foolishness* and *self-abuse*
Coming to mind, I smile:
Was the break caused by too much malakía?
Strato's answer is a final burst
Of laughter: "No such luck!
One day like this the scaffold gave beneath me.
I felt no pain at first."

"One day like this": precisely. He will have put up the scaffold that caused the fall and the "break," and though he seems not fully to realize it yet, he has repeated the catastrophe. It has been a matter of "self-abuse" indeed.

But this poem must be seen from another angle at the same time, lest we turn the page unjustly thinking it self-righteous. In characterizing Strato, Merrill also deals severely with himself—for liking himself too much. It is he, after all, who proves to be "Inflexible" in the end and who forecloses on the relationship. The poem hints at this reflexiveness on several occasions, as when we learn that Strato is "living far from home" and is a "Builder." At the end of the first verse paragraph, after he delivers himself of a smug opinion, Strato's "eyes fairly cross / With self-importance. That, I recognize." As "eyes" and "I" and "recognize" echo among themselves, we see that the two men also "cross" at the point of "self-importance." It follows that the poet too has suffered a "fall," so it is no surprise to recall that Merrill "spent the worse part of a fall composing" those "grand tirades" he chooses not to deliver. Since composing them was a kind of masturbatory act, they represented "the worse part of a fall" he has taken. Because the poem ends with him smiling and joking, we might infer that, like Strato, he feels no pain at first. The poem, however, with this self-indictment, or self-abuse, is evidence of a potato heart within the poet's own marble breast. Not that it would do for him to dwell on that. But one feels that if it were to go on a line longer, this poem would have to end as "A Renewal" ends in *The Country of a Thousand Years of Peace:* "Now I see no way but a clean break," the poet avows in that poem, and his lover nods assent. But then in the last sentence, "When I next speak / Love buries itself in me, up to the hilt."

"Etre humain . . .": what has Valéry said? To be human is to feel dimly that there is something of all of us in each one of us, and of each in all. He continues his counsel thus: "Il y a de la victime dans le bourreau et du bourreau dans la victime."²⁹ "Strato in Plaster" does not concern itself with victim and executioner—though Merrill wants us to hear that other meaning of "scaffold," since Strato has taken enough rope and hanged himself—but the poem exemplifies Valéry's general observation, a variation on Merrill's principle of reversible truths.

As it happens, there is an execution of sorts in "Days of 1935," though the warp and weft of this ballad are not characters so much as concepts or forces—reality and imagination. "Days of 1935," written in a tighter stanza than "The Summer People" (this time Merrill uses *rime croisée*), unfolds in bright, dramatic specifics a fantasy that Merrill tells us he had when he was nine years old. Three years before, in 1932, two days before Merrill's sixth birthday, the infant son of Charles and Anne Morrow Lindbergh, who were by then internationally famous figures, was kidnapped in Hopewell, New Jersey. Although a ransom of $50,000 was paid, the child was found dead in May of that year. Two years later Bruno Hauptman, a German immigrant, was charged with the kidnapping and murder. His trial, held in 1935, ended in his conviction, and he was executed in the electric chair in 1936. The case made for sensational headlines and led to new federal kidnapping laws. As the young son in a wealthy family, Merrill would have been warned of the danger he was in. His vivid impressions of the Lindbergh case, whose horrors he could not fully have comprehended, and his routine at home might well have led him to concoct an elaborate daydream in which he was abducted.

In the child's fantasy a man whose name will turn out to be Floyd climbs into his bedroom window one night and carries him off in an "old jalopy." They drive over back roads until dawn, when they arrive at a "hovel in the treeless / Trembling middle of nowhere," where they are met by Floyd's accomplice, the gunmoll Jean mentioned in "Lost in Translation." As they wait for his parents to respond to their ransom notes, Jean and Floyd fight, make love, and read the newspaper stories about the kidnapping, and the boy develops a strong attachment to them. Eventually his parents make a deal with his captors, and he is returned. But Jean and Floyd, having been double-crossed, are captured by G-men, tried, perhaps executed. The child wakes to find himself on his bedroom floor at home, where he has fallen. The next day, "The child is bored," as life goes on as usual. His father comes home and has his cocktail in the den, while his mother dresses to receive that evening's guests. "She kisses him sweet dreams"—but now that "Floyd and Jean are gone" he feels at a loss: "Who will he dream of? True to life / He's played them false. A golden haze / Past belief, past disbelief. . . / Well. Those were the days."

Though it misses little in terms of plot, such a summary omits most of the poem, whose real story is the nature of "Real stories—but not real, I mean. / Not just dumb things people did," as Jean puts it when describing the kind of story she hopes the boy will tell her that day when *she* is bored. From the outset, the imagined details are rich: "Ladder horned against moonlight, / Window hoisted stealthily— / That's what I'd steel myself at night / To see, or sleep to see."

> It seemed entirely plausible
> For my turn to come soon,
>
> For a masked and crouching form,
> Lithe as tiger, light as moth,
> To glide towards me, clap a firm
> Hand across my mouth,
>
> Then sheer imagination ride
> Off with us in its old jalopy,
> Trailing bedclothes like a bride
> Timorous but happy.
>
> A hundred tenuous dirt roads
> Dew spangles, lead to the web's heart.
> That whole pale night my captor reads
> His brow's unwrinkling chart.

The transition resembles that in Eros's visit to the cupola, but here the transformation from "dream" to "reality" is carried through. The first long sentence and the several similes obscure the action's origin in dream or fantasy, and the switch to the present tense, virtually imperceptible after the participles, the infinitives, and the subjunctive, turns the poem from made-up events to a recounting of real ones.

Even as the imagined situation turns real, it becomes parabolic, for we understand in retrospect Merrill's eagerness for his imagination to run away with him. Cartoon-vivid as Floyd will be—"Lean, sallow, lantern-jawed," equipped with pistol and cartridge belt—he is also the poet's power to lose himself in his work, or to steal himself away, for now that phrase "steel myself . . . To see" shows its other side. As Floyd faces his reflection in the windshield and "reads" all night "His brow's unwrinkling chart," Merrill faces himself in his "captor," whom he also calls "sheer imagination." We are further invited to think of Jean and Floyd, this ballad's Bonnie and Clyde, as the child's versions of the "Maker and muse" of "The Thousand and Second Night." If Floyd is a kind of writer, who each day posts another penciled ransom note, Jean, "A lady out of *Silver Screen*," with her "rosebud chewing gum" and "platinum / Spit curls," is a déclassée Beatrice or Stella. And it is she who inspires the child to tell her his stories of the little mermaid and others.

As the little mermaid and "The beauty [who] slept in her thorn bower" are to Jean, and as "the fisherman's hut [that] became Versailles" is to the "hovel" that seems to the boy "Hidden from the world by palace / Walls of dust and glare," so the boy's fantasy is to the poet's life. In telling the child's story, Merrill rehearses his own situation, as in recounting the tales the child does his. Moreover, if the child's tales, to the extent that they ingratiate him with Jean, save his life, the poet's story about the child saves his life as a poet. The crucial question is asked in the newspaper caption beneath the boy's photo: "*Is This Child Alive Today?*" Just as in the fantasy the child turns out to be alive and well, so the poem itself is proof that the imaginative child lives still inside the man. After that newspaper caption puts the poet's question to himself (along with an ironic response: "*Last Hopes Disappear*"), Jean speaks directly to the boy for the first time: "I couldn't take my eyes away. / Let her meet them! Let her speak! / She put down *Photoplay:* / 'Do you know any stories, Kid?'" In his plea—"Let her speak!"—we hear the poet thinking about his character speak in unison with the boy yearning for intimacy with his captor. It is when his character can "speak" that the poet has a story to tell. And when he has a *story* to tell, he knows that child is alive today.

By the same token, once he has executed his characters, in both senses of that word, his life is the less, whether we think of him as child or as poet. There can be no question but that the boy's dream is a richer life. This is the point of the striking comparison of imagination's "old jalopy," trailing bedclothes, to "a bride / Timorous but happy." Floyd gives the child the opportunity to express his incipient sexual feelings in a way that his father, his den guarded by the butler and his thoughts occupied by the *Wall Street Journal,* does not. As for Jean, "For good or bad" she watches over the boy "As no one ever had." He turns down his chance to escape because his life with Floyd and Jean, with its love-making, quarreling, jokes, seems—*is* more real. With Jean, whose looks and inflections we know so well by the end of the poem, we need to compare his mother, whom we find—or try to find—in a newspaper photo "Hatted, bepearled, chin deep in fur," and who appears at the end in "miles of spangled blue" as she "puts her make-up on." Next to Jean, she seems an actress in character. Next to that imagined hovel, the world his parents live in, populated by "Tel & Tel executives / Heads of Cellophane or Tin, / With their animated wives," is as fantastic as Oz.

Or more fantastic, because it is just such imagined worlds that are to the boy real. The child "knew / That life was fiction in disguise," and so does the poet. The child's malaise after his dream has ended projects the poet's at the end of the poem:

> A rainy day. The child is bored.
> While Emma bakes he sits, half-grown.
> The kitchen dado is of board
> Painted like board. Its grain
>
> Shiny buff on cinnamon
> Mimics the real, the finer grain.
> He watches icing sugar spin
> Its thread. He licks in vain
>
> Heavenly flavors from a spoon.
> Left in the metallic bowl
> Is a twenty-five watt moon.
> Somewhere rings a bell.

That bell in another part of the huge house is also in his mind, since the "twenty-five watt moon"—a phrase that marries cheapness and romance— will remind him of a naked bulb in Floyd and Jean's "hovel." Merrill's repetitions ("bored," "board," "board" is especially telling) emphasize in contrast the deadly luxury of his family's mansion. At the same time, the identical rhymes help to confound the real and the imitation, and that merger is one "thread" that leads back from this passage's spun sugar to the tales spun at "the web's heart," to use Merrill's early phrase for the location of the hovel in the middle of the mazy roads.

There at the web's heart, at the end of the second of five sections, as Jean falls asleep listening to the kid's stories, and before Floyd returns with the news that the ransom demand will be met, Merrill switches into the present tense and uses several variants on the web image:

> Jean's lids have shut. I'm lonely. I
> Am pausing on tiptoe
>
> To marvel at the shimmer breath
> Inspires along your radii,
> Spider lightly running forth
> To kiss the simple fly
>
> Asleep. A chance to slip the net,
> Wiggle down the dry stream bed,

Now or never! This child cannot.
An iridescent thread

Binds him to her slumber . . .

In this intriguing passage the fly stands in for Jean, as well as for the reader, whom Merrill modestly supposes to have nodded off along with her. But then in this poem to sleep is to dream, and to dream is to live intensely. Moreover, as we learn later, the boy at this point might have fallen asleep to dream rather than to fantasize the poem's doings, so the poet could also be speaking to the child he was—even as the child speaks to Jean. It makes sense, then, that the poet would be both the "spider" and the willing captive in the "net," this poem's version of "the consuming myth." If the reader is also asleep, he is therefore a captive, and if he is caught up in the narrative, he is a captive for that reason, so it seems that he can in no way escape the web—which is itself another referent for the "you," since those "radii" are not simply the sleeper's crossed wrists but also, in the context of all this filature, the threads running out from this text's "center" to its periphery.

One begins to wonder what the boundaries might be to the mesh this narrative has become. Certainly we cannot draw them in such a way as to separate it from Merrill's symbolist mode. On the contrary, "Days of 1935" would make us think as quickly as any poem in *Braving the Elements* of Mallarmé's announcement to Théodore Aubanel, the original of which I have quoted as an epigraph to this chapter: "I meant simply that I had just finished planning my entire Work; that I had found the key to myself, the crown, or the center (if you prefer to call it that, so we won't get our metaphors mixed)—the center of myself where, like a sacred spider, I hang on the main threads which I have already spun from my mind. With these— *and at their intersections*—I shall make the miraculous laces which I foresee and which exist already in Beauty's bosom."[30] In much the same spirit that Mallarmé wrote to his friend, Merrill might have paused on the threshold of Sandover.

chapter five

THE FULLNESS OF TIME
The Book of Ephraim

That young man in dark rose, leaning on his staff,
Will be St Theodore, earliest patron
Of Venice, at ease here after rescuing
His mother from a dragon . . .

> > >

This *connection* of all created things with every single one of them and their adaptation to every single one, as well as the connection and adaptation of every single thing to all others, has the result that every single substance stands in relations which express all the others. Whence every single substance is a perpetual living mirror of the universe.

Leibniz, *Monadology* (trans. Paul Schrecker and Anne Martin Schrecker)

. . . between the usual subjects of poetry and "devotional" verse there is a very important field still very unexplored by modern poets—the experience of man in search of God, and trying to explain to himself his intenser human feelings in terms of the divine goal . . .

T. S. Eliot to William Force Stead

The unity of divine and human, or past and present, is as real to him as their disparity.

Merrill on Cavafy

"C E N T R E de moi-même," Mallarmé wrote to Aubanel: center of myself. But in the first place he had written "centre de mon oeuvre."[1] The emendation is one that Yeats might have made with the same rightness, or Rilke. Or Merrill. Still, until very recently we had somehow managed not to see, perhaps to his benefit, that we have been harboring among us a truly extraordinary poet. Even a few years ago, the numerous prizes and the growing reputation notwithstanding, one might have begun a discussion of Merrill's work by playing advocate. With the completion of his trilogy, *The Changing Light at Sandover,* however, that role must seem nothing but a ploy, since it is one of the most ambitious, original, and variously brilliant works written by an American.

He accomplished it in a remarkably short time. The first part, *The Book of Ephraim,* appeared in *Divine Comedies* in 1976, four years after *Braving the Elements* and two years after *The Yellow Pages,* Merrill's selection of earlier work that he had excluded, for one reason and another, from previous books. The second part, *Mirabell: Books of Number* (retitled *Mirabell's Books of Number* in the one-volume edition) came out in 1978 and *Scripts for the Pageant* in 1980. The "Coda" and the title, *The Changing Light at Sandover,* were not added until the one-volume edition, published in 1982, though it had been clear for some time before that the trilogy is a single work, with its successive parts building upon its earlier ones. But it had also been clear that each of the three books has its own integrity. *Ephraim* is the most easily de-tachable of the three because it was conceived first as an independent work. In *Mirabell,* at the same time that he leads us to expect a third volume, Mer-rill implies that the second came as a surprise. In any case, because of its initial position as well as because of its coherence and its density, *Ephraim* should first be read as a separate work.

Running to about 2,500 lines, and thus substantially less than half the length of *Mirabell* or *Scripts for the Pageant, Ephraim* is a good deal longer than *Notes toward a Supreme Fiction* and *Four Quartets,* with both of which it shares certain thematic concerns. Not that it resembles either of those poems, or any other, very much. A sort of eccentric *Essay on Man*—of course any *Essay on Man* would have to be eccentric today—it also conjures up works as different from Pope's and from each other as *A Vision* and *Pale Fire.* As though turning Nabokov's *donnée* inside out, Merrill incorporates in his verse bits of a novel, the unfinished manuscript of which was left in a taxicab in Georgia, as Merrill has told us in "The Will," and never recovered. Like the lost manuscript, although in a more straightforward fashion, the poem sets forth the experiences that Merrill and his friend David Jackson have had with the other world, especially with a spirit named Ephraim, with whom they made contact in one of their first sessions with the Ouija board some twenty-five years earlier and with whom they have been in touch ever since. Like Yeats's communicators, Ephraim provides information about the structure of the universe, but unlike them he has a subtle sense of humor, a predilection for aphorism, and, being at only stage six in an empyrean he imagines to consist mostly of nine stages, a less than complete understand-ing of the nature of things. This last is fortunate, no less for JM and DJ, as our mediums are known, than for the reader:

> —For as it happened I had been half trying
> To make sense of *A Vision*
> When our friend dropped his bombshell: POOR OLD YEATS
> STILL SIMPLIFYING

Ephraim speaks in the board's capitals, of course, and without punctua-tion (although Merrill mercifully uses a double space to indicate a full stop), with the result that his voice sounds more distinct from JM's than it might otherwise. The capitals also provide a clever means of disposition, for the poem is divided into twenty-six sections, each beginning with the appropriate letter of the alphabet. Throughout the poem the normative meter is iambic pentameter, occasionally rhymed, from which other verse forms emerge and into which they then dissolve: couplets, quatrains, sonnets, sonnet sequences, hendecasyllabics, *terza rima,* and other prosodic schemes swirl to the surface to form their own permanently transitory little systems. These are all interlocked by motif as well as by narrative so that the effect is largely musical, and it is hardly surprising to find Mahler, Stravinsky, Beethoven, Mozart, Bach, Haydn, Puccini, Verdi, Satie, and Wagner alluded to. Allusion to Wagner's *Götterdämmerung* is in fact one of the main motifs in *Ephraim,* and the ease with which the poem can absorb such an influence indicates its extensiveness and depth.

But more about motif in a moment. First it will be helpful to summarize the situation—or rather situations, for there are three main plot lines woven together through *Ephraim.* The first of these arises from the relationship between DJ and JM, on the one hand, and Ephraim and the other world, on the other. One night during the summer of 1955, a year after moving into their house in Stonington, Connecticut, DJ and JM sit down to try their hands at the Ouija board, and after a few false starts—contacts with recently disembodied souls who have not yet learned how to use this sort of wireless—they raise Ephraim, a Greek Jew "Born AD 8 at XANTHOS" who "Died / AD 36 on CAPRI," a minion of Tiberius and lover of Caligula.[2] Clever, profound, sybaritic, and moral by turns, and golden-haired, with "*eyes that amazing / blood-washed gold our headlights catch*" (so we learn from the recounting of the one unforgettable glimpse DJ gets of him when under hypnosis), Ephraim—a truer or refictionalized version of Meno in *The Seraglio*—is thenceforth this poem's *buon maestro,* instructing DJ and JM by séance in the ways of the soul after death. Through him they learn that every person on earth is a "representative" of a spirit or "patron," who however has virtually no control over the representative's actions; that regardless of that last limitation, patrons are promoted from stage to heavenly stage partly on the basis of their representatives' representations; that, as in much Oriental philosophy, and as in *A Vision,* a soul can escape the wheel of life—and thus become a patron himself. They also talk on the party line to Stevens, Auden, and others who move in Ephraim's circles. Meanwhile, Ephraim, who can evidently see anything within his mediums' ken that appears in a reflecting surface and who can hear as well as most of us, meets friends and relatives (both living and dead) of JM and DJ, listens to Mahler and Stravinsky for the first time, and accompanies the other two members of the board on trips to the western United States and around the world.

The second plot line, in part a translation of the autobiographical narrative, is that of the novel, which JM summarizes and even extends in the poem. The action takes place in New Mexico, and the chief figures are Eros, a sensual spirit whose character exaggerates one aspect of Ephraim; Sergei Markovich, a Russian emigré who bears a discreet resemblance to JM; Mrs. Rosamund Smith, later the Marchesa Santofior, owner of some property in New Mexico on which Sergei lives; Leo Cade, who served in Vietnam, where he seems to have taken part in the murder of a young Vietnamese whom his outfit made out to be a spy, and who has returned to the United States, where he falls under the spell of Eros and has experiences that recall both DJ (his vision under hypnosis) and JM (his return through hallucination to an earlier self); Leo's helpless wife Ellen; and Joanna, a middle-aged vamp with inscrutable motives and dark designs on the affections of Matt Prentiss, a character modeled on DJ's father. Definitely a subplot, the action in the novel gets extensive treatment only in sections J, N, S, T, X, and the ingenious D, for "Dramatis personae," where Merrill lists several of the novel's characters as well as a number of actual and apparently actual people who figure in the poem. (And one who does not.)

In the third place we have the story of the writing of this poem, always rendered in the present tense. This plot is less related to the first than an element in it, since it covers the last of the reported phases of the association with Ephraim, and is closely allied with the second plot, partly because the history of the poem involves the tale of the lost novel. At this level the action takes exactly one year, from January 1974, when JM begins the poem in Stonington, through December 1974, when, back in Stonington, he completes it. In the interim he takes an autumn trip to Greece, where he and DJ have a second home, and returns to the States by way of Venice, where he chances upon a nephew, Wendell Pincus, who, owing to a certain reprehensible exchange of information between the Ouija boarders and their familiar spirit, is the latter's representative. He is also the son of Betsy Pincus, purportedly the model for the figure of Ellen Prentiss Cade in the unfinishable novel.

But the novel *is* finished, in the form of the poem, for if the novel was a translation into fiction of scenes from real life, the poem is a sort of de-translation of the novel. In A, after admitting his weariness of "Our age's fancy narrative concoctions," of authors "Suckled by Woolf not Mann," JM goes ahead to explain:

> So my narrative
> Wanted to be limpid, unfragmented;
> My characters, conventional stock figures
> Afflicted to a minimal degree

With personality and past experience—
A witch, a hermit, innocent young lovers,
The kinds of beings we recall from Grimm,
Jung, Verdi, and the commedia dell'arte.
That such a project was beyond me merely
Incited further futile stabs at it.

Or so he claims. But although its narrative is not unfragmented, the poem is crowded with precisely the types listed here, not just because he retells much of the novel in verse, but also because his real people often fit into the categories named—as how could they not? The linking of Grimm, Jung, and Verdi will startle us into remembering that conventional figures are conventional because they distill common experience. The real Maya Deren is as much a witch as the fictional Joanna, JM as much a hermit as Sergei, DJ and JM once as much innocent young lovers as Leo and Ellen. (Indeed Ephraim refers to them in C as "MY POOR / INNOCENTS.") It figures, then, that about three-quarters of the way through the poem, in S, Merrill should recapitulate an incident that was to occur "three-quarters through the novel." Again, reflecting on the relationship between truth and fiction in T, he declines to pursue the subject further because what he would have had to say about it comes "Too near the end of the unwritten book," and from one point of view the gist is that we must wait until later sections—especially V and X— for the continuation of the meditation.

One of the oldest and most fertile themes in Merrill's work, the interdependence of reality and fiction takes a dozen different shapes here. In A, JM describes his original quandary as to form:

Also my subject matter
Gave me pause—so intimate, so novel.
Best after all to do it as a novel?
Looking about me, I found characters
Human and otherwise (if the distinction
Meant anything in fiction).

Of course he found the "characters / Human and otherwise" in life as well as in fiction, if the distinction means anything in a realm just possibly overseen by those less human than otherwise. As he puts it in a passage in K that looks forward to one of the trilogy's last revelations:

If we are characters
As now and then strikes us, in some superplot

Of Ephraim's, isn't our prerogative
To run away with its author?

At one juncture in L, JM recalls that he and DJ, after one of the inevitable arguments, vowed never to repeat such "'a scene / From real life'"; and in T he finds that a certain "foreshortening" of time in Proust, which he once took "for an unconvincing / Trick of the teller," now seems to be "truth instead / Babbling through his own astonishment." As he put it in "Days of 1935," "life was fiction in disguise." In V tourists hurry "To sit out the storm in the presence of Giorgione's / *Tempesta*"—which is then described as "nothing less / Than earthly life in all its mystery." It is characteristic that, in S, Stendhal should be referred to, in the context of a discussion of fictional characters, as "H BEYLE," his "real" name.

The poem's basic composition itself, including as it does verifiable autobiography, "Notes for the ill-starred novel," figures from others of Merrill's works, and characters and incidents apparently invented for *Ephraim,* interlaces the realms of reality and fiction. Moreover, since Merrill forces us to make a hypothetical distinction between novel and poem, he is paradoxically able both to imply the literal nature of his poetic account and to remind us that it too might have its fictional elements. What are we to make, for example, of such a figure as Beatrice ("Betsy") Merrill Pincus? We are told in D that she was born in 1937 and is "JM's niece" as well as the "Model / For Ellen Prentiss Cade." Inquiry, however, has disclosed no such conveniently named real person—and it does seem unlikely that, if she were real, Merrill would have confessed to her, let alone in public, that he and DJ were responsible, through their dealings with Ephraim, for the nature of the soul that was slipped into the fetus during the sixth month of her pregnancy. Or *would* he? Where are we?

> Where were we? On unsteady ground. Earth, Heaven;
> Reality, Projection—half-stoned couples
> Doing the Chicken-and-the-Egg till dawn.
> Which came first? And would two never come
> Together, sleep then in each other's arms
> Above the stables rich with dung and hay?

> > >

The deft persistence with which reality and fiction are woven together in *The Book of Ephraim* suggests the poem's density of texture. If it could be charted by a computer—and why not, since bird song can now be graphed and pyramids x-rayed—the result would show something like a system of ley lines, lines of force supposedly traceable in England even today between ancient sacred sights which intersect in quantity at key points and lace the whole island together with their irregular mesh. Since *Ephraim* is so tightly reticulated that almost any passage in it might be considered both a point of intersection and a point of departure, there is no reason not to open a discussion of its designs *in medias res*. The nature of the middle of things even makes it appropriate that we do so.

Near the center of *Ephraim*—in lines 51–52 of the even 100 lines of M—JM paraphrases for us his familiar spirit's explanation of a dream purportedly dreamed by Maya Deren, a friend of the poet and DJ until her death in 1961 and (as we have been told in D) the "doyenne of our / American experimental film": "This dream, [Ephraim] blandly adds, is a low-budget / Remake—imagine—of the *Paradiso*." Now Dante's presence is felt throughout *Ephraim,* from the epigraph (drawn from the *Paradiso*, XV, 61–63), through a documented allusion in K, to the encounter in the Venetian twilight with a figure from the poet's past (related in a *terza rima* as fluent as any since Shelley) in W. Hardly less pervasive is the influence of Maya Deren, who recorded her own fascination with occult deities in her book on Haitian voodoo, *Divine Horsemen* (which, like some of her films, acknowledges a debt of friendship to Merrill and which is excerpted in Q), and whose experiments in film have analogues in Merrill's innovative adaptation of certain cinematic techniques.[3] At the end of L, for example, when JM recalls with Ephraim's coaching his death in the preceding life, the episode is done in reverse chronological order, as one might run film backward—and as Merrill did run his own newsreel backward in "18 West 11th Street." Maya Deren, in short, holds up one of the many mirrors in this poem that reflect JM, and Ephraim's studiedly casual remark—though too much (or too little) could be made too quickly of the relationship—applies to the "book" that bears his name as well as to Maya's dream.

This "dream," related in the first half of M, actually constitutes, according to Ephraim, an instance in which Maya's soul leaves her sleeping body and, in this permutation of the roles of Beatrice and Dante, escorted by Ephraim, attends a *soirée* on the sixth stage ("chandeliers, white orchids, silver trays / Dense with bubbling glassfuls"), where a breathtaking transformation occurs. At first, Maya is the only one in the gathering not resplendent in evening dress—she is indeed in "mourning weeds"—but then:

> [Ephraim] leads
> Her to a spring, or source, oh wonder! in
> Whose shining depths her gown turns white, her jet

To diamonds, and black veil to bridal snow.
Her features are unchanged, yet her pale skin
Is black, with glowing nostrils—a not yet
Printed self . . . Then it is time to go.

Maya's glimpse of her future self, rendered in appropriately photographic
terms, draws together several of the poem's major motifs: water, the mirror, and transformation or rebirth. The first of these motifs runs through
Ephraim like (and often in the form of) a stream, sometimes in evidence
and sometimes not but never far away, so that the reader finds himself in a
position something like that of a visitor to Pope's famous grotto, described
by Peter Quennell, who is quoted (as a number of the poem's seeming ma-
trices are) in Q:

> *Every surface sparkled or shimmered or gleamed with a smooth subaque-
> ous lustre; and, while these coruscating details enchanted the eye, a deli-
> cate water-music had been arranged to please the ear; the 'little dripping
> murmur' of an underground spring—discovered by the workmen during
> their excavations—echoed through the cavern day and night . . . Pope in-
> tended . . . that the visitor, when at length he emerged, should feel that he
> had been reborn into a new existence.*[4]

In other words, even as he lets the "workmen" anticipate his critics,
Merrill implicitly compares his own "folly" (or *folie à deux,* as his analyst and
he, with significantly less conviction, view it in I) to that of Pope—whose
influence, recurrently apparent, JM explicitly notes in D, where it is revealed
that his own patron is one Kinton Ford (1810–1843), a hitherto unknown
editor of the Augustan poet's works. Both poem and cavern, after all, remove us from the quotidian world, as Maya's "dream" removes her—and
sure enough, back in M, she wakes from her dream "in bliss." Later, we learn
in the second half of M, she makes her film, "Ritual in Transfigured Time,"
at the end of which "The young white actress gowned and veiled in black /
Walks out into a calm, shining sea" and as she sinks "Feetfirst in phosphores-
cent negative" becomes "a black bride." In treating in the last part of M an
actual film that is based on a dream, reported in the first part, that is really a
vision of paradise, Merrill sets his own work, with its concern with the inter-
face of reality and fiction—as Ephraim has DJ and JM place the euonymous
Maya in G—between two mirrors.

If the spring in which Maya looks to find herself transformed as in a
magic glass is the same one that flows through Pope's grotto, it is also the
one that is identified with the "voice" of JM's genius, or the creative power.
Recalling Ephraim's *dictée* in C, JM says: "As it flowed on, his stream-of-

consciousness / Deepened." The phrase "stream-of-consciousness" itself suggests how closely allied the spirit and the poet's inspiration are—how tempting is the analyst's argument that Ephraim is "only" a projection—and just as the poem moves from underground depths to glittering surface detail, so Ephraim's profundity sometimes gives way to superficiality: "Observe the easy, grateful way we swim," JM says in P, "Back to his shallows." When the "novel" peters out in T: "Now along crevices inch rivulets / At every turning balked." At the conclusion of T, significantly juxtaposed with the end of that particular endeavor, there occurs this marvelously startling paean to a power at once mundane and transcendent:

> When the urge
> Comes to make water, a thin brass-hot stream
> Sails out into the updraft, spattering
> One impotent old tree that shakes its claws.
> The droplets atomize, evaporate
> To dazzlement a blankness overdusts
> Pale blue, then paler blue. It stops at nothing.

Ephraim finally disappears in X, "Back underground he sinks, a stream," and JM wonders in what mood he will now face a new season, since he wrongly thinks he will be "without a guide," with "nothing along those lines—or these / Whose writing, if not justifies, so mirrors, / So embodies up to now some guiding force." Again, in S, he explains that he wanted the "neutral ground" of the lost novel on which to work out his theme, "so that (when the fall rains fell) would go / Flashing through me a perfected flow, / Landscape and figures once removed."

The "guiding force" or "stream" takes the form also of "a Bach courante / Or brook that running slips into a shawl / Of crystal noise" (N), and as the brilliant puns and metaphor insinuate, the power it seeks to define is mercurial. It is one thing for Ephraim or Dante's ancestor Cacciaguida, the heavenly soul who is the speaker of the lines quoted as an epigraph, to "look in the mirror in which, before you think, you express your thought," and quite another for the mortal poet to set about his task. All too often the latter finds himself in *this* discouraging situation, described in a punning phrase in Z as the "Cost of living high":

> The fire we huddle with our drinks by
> Pops and snaps. Throughout the empty house
> (Tenants away until the New Year) taps
> Glumly trickling keep the pipes from freezing.

Sometimes, in dramatic contrast to that exiguous trickle, the imagination flows unchecked and the poet feels in touch with the source, as in X:

> What I think I feel now, by its own nature
> Remains beyond my power to say outright,
> Short of grasping the naked current where it
> Flows through field and book, dog howling, the firelit
> Glances, the caresses, whatever draws us
> To, and insulates us from, the absolute . . .[5]

The dilemma is familiar enough—we find it, for example, in Eliot's *Quartets,* with their "intolerable wrestle / With words and meanings" in an attempt to say what humankind could hardly bear anyway, and in Stevens's "Prologues to What Is Possible," where the unsayable syllable that lures the voyaging poet on "would shatter the boat" if it were caught up with—but not the more easily resolved for that.

The elusiveness of this "spring, or source" that manifests itself in the dog's howl, as well as in the lover's caress and the poet's book, both keeps us from seizing it and keeps us tracking it. If the source is a "naked current," that current is multiform, being for instance metaphorically electrical as well as fluid, as the preceding reference to insulation suggests. The *anagnorisis* of the novel takes place in New Mexico when, JM says in J, Joanna and Sergei

> "Recognize" each other, or I as author
> Recognize in them the plus and minus
> —Good and evil, let my reader say—
> Vital to the psychic current's flow.

By such means Merrill turns his water into fire, and in doing so, in converting the one current into what might seem to be its opposite, he at least exemplifies the power that it lies beyond his power to define. Time and again he equates the apparently beneficent element with the potentially dangerous one: in C, when Ephraim flows on in his "stream-of-consciousness" and leaves an issue "hanging fire"; in X, where the conventional heroines are "Ringed round by fire or water"; in J, where in a rainstorm the clouds become "sable bulks awince / With fire"; in P, where the poet recalls hearing, when he was a boy, the Rhinemaidens in *Götterdämmerung,* "fettered in chain / Reaction," singing their refrain and thus causing a "spark" to alight on his mind ("so pitifully green" that it did not catch for years). A room in the Stonington house with "Walls of ready-mixed matte 'flame' (a witty / Shade, now watermelon, now sunburn)," is where JM and DJ receive the flood of information—in which fiction is to fact as water is to fire (or as water is to electricity, since the one current conducts the other)—from another changeable, witty shade.

Besides that of the ambiguous current, this force also takes the form, perhaps more surprisingly, of *the* current, or the "current," or the flow of time, as in A, where time "was running out like water," and in a difficult passage in T, where fire and water mix once more:

> "All that we dread by midnight will have burst
> Into a drifting, cooling soot of light,
> Each speck a voodoo bullet dodged in vain
> Or stopped with sangfroid—is the moment now?
> At sunrise? Yet the hangfire talks go on.
> Current events no sooner sped than din . . ."

The speaker, who goes on with what Merrill later calls an "Unrelenting fluency" and who thus reminds us of Cacciaguida's gift and Ephraim's stream of consciousness, is an initially mysterious "figure in the mirror stealing looks"—who must be, as both the ambivalence of "stealing looks" and this section's letter indicate, Time himself, at the same time that he is literally a reflection of Sergei, the person spoken to in this passage.[6]

Time, it turns out, often speaks in spoonerisms and related devices, as the figure in the mirror implies when he conflates the phrase "no sooner said than done" with the name of the popularizer of the rhetorical slip and comes up with "'no sooner sped than din.'" He also observes, in a purer example, that he and Sergei pick their ways toward each other through "'grums of class,'" and—to return to the mainstream—he announces to Sergei that "'You clothe my mowing as I don your flask.'" In donning the mask of Sergei, that is, Time disguises his mowing as a flowing. This inevitable alliance, nay, identity with one whom we are wont to consider the enemy, this complicity with the wrinkles we cannot iron out, is the subject of one of Cavafy's marginalia on Ruskin, which Merrill has quoted in a review of Robert Liddell's book on the Greek poet: "When we say 'Time' we mean ourselves. Most abstractions are simply our pseudonyms. It is superfluous to say 'Time is scytheless and toothless.' We know it. We are Time."[7] When JM, hearing in R the shriek of the crowd at the Athens stadium, likens the noise to that of a "blade / On grindstone," he sets up the same equation, although he restores to Time his traditional implement. Time's remark to Sergei in X that "'One wand hashes the other,'" even as it unmasks the optimistic adage, makes the point just as grimly and more specifically. The artist works hand in glove with Time, in other words, and yet the other hand of the latter, not caring what its partner is doing, wields the scythe.

Time and the imagination, although from one point of view apparently different names for the same absolute but fugitive force, have been provisionally opposed from the beginning. A passage in A that foreshadows T's confrontation contradicts another sanguine commonplace in describing JM's plight after the manuscript of the novel was lost or stolen:

> I alone was left
> To tell my story. For it seemed that Time—
> The grizzled washer of his hands appearing
> To say so in a spectrum-bezeled space
> Above hot water—Time would not . . .

The passage from *The Faerie Queene* included in Q's garland of quotations epitomizes this eternal dilemma:

> *But were it not, that* Time *their troubler is,*
> *All that in this delightful Gardin growes,*
> *Should happy be, and haue immortal blis* . . .[8]

As JM says in another context in K, "There will be no way to fly back in time." Only Time himself, it appears, can be both the "grizzled washer of his hands" of all things and the capricious infant enigmatized by Heraclitus, also quoted (and translated) in Q:

> *Time is a child, playing a board game: the kingdom of the child.*[9]

Nor is art exempt, as the havoc Time plays with venerable phrases in T suggests. Even such a masterpiece as Giorgione's *Tempesta* is slyly said to be "timeless in its fashion."

But "'One wand hashes the other,'" and that the spoonerism cuts both ways is one point obliquely made in the treatment of Giorgione's famously riddling painting in X. Deriving many of his views from an eye-opening essay by Nancy Thompson de Grummond, JM interprets *La Tempesta* as a rendering of the salient incidents in the legend of the life of St. Theodore, the patron saint (before St. Mark) of Venice.[10] On this interpretation, the "young man in dark rose, leaning on his staff"—or wand—is St. Theodore the Recruit, after he has slain the dragon or serpent, thus at one stroke saving the town and rescuing his mother, and after the archangel Gabriel has changed the course of the stream that blocked an exit from the cave in which Theodore and his mother were imprisoned. The young woman nursing a baby, according to Grummond, is St. Theodore's mother, but at an earlier stage in her life—at that stage, in fact, when she was nursing the young Theodore. In the background is the storm from which the painting gets its traditional title and which alludes to the power that St. Theodore was thought to have over the elements—or, as Merrill more pointedly has it, over "electric storms."

As excavation at Pope's grotto revealed the presence of an underground stream, so x-rays of the painting have shown that Giorgione painted out, along with an earlier version of the woman, the image of the dragon—now referred to only by an emblem "above a distant portal" and an unobtrusive lizard in the foreground. (The "mute hermit slithers to his cleft": the sexual twist given the image makes it comport with the Oedipal overtones Merrill finds in the painting and thus provides another explanation for St. Theodore's legendary destruction of "a temple to the Magna Mater.") [11] Giorgione's pentimento is much to Merrill's purpose:

> As for the victim, flood-green, flash-
> Violet coils translated into landscape
> Blocked the cave mouth, till Gabriel himself
> Condescended to divert the stream . . .

There are two translations going on here, for if the painter changed the dragon to landscape, the poet turns him into a reptilian stream that absorbs some of the qualities of the electrical storm, and this conversion, especially when coupled with the blocking of the "cave mouth," suggests that we are dealing here with the old force primarily in its adversary aspect, that of Time.[12] In fact, in T, Time has pictured himself as a "slitherer" with scales of "coalfire-blue." Accordingly, St. Theodore and the archangel Gabriel (his diverting aide as Ephraim is JM's) are the figures emulated by the poet, whose own work, like Giorgione's (which affords a rare example of synchronicity in the Renaissance), seeks to overcome the temporal, or to turn the destructive flow of time into the creative flow of the imagination. Indeed the poem might have been called, after Maya Deren's film, "Ritual in Transfigured Time."

Merrill rings a number of changes on this theme. Here in X he invokes Wagner's Siegfried and "his worm / Slain among rhinestones," and on several occasions he refers fleetingly to Mercury, whose caduceus (or wand) includes two intertwined serpents. The dragon is really "relegated / To a motif above a distant portal" at the beginning of P, where the dollar sign is interpreted as a combination of "Snake and Tree of Life." More directly to the point, in Q, Merrill quotes John Michell's *The View over Atlantis* on the Lord of Lambton, an English folk hero:

He put on a suit of armour set all over with sharp blades and stood on an island in the river. The dragon rushed upon him and tried to crush him in its coils, but the knives on the armour cut it into little pieces which were swept away by the current before the dragon could exercise its traditional power of reassembling its dismembered parts.[13]

"'One wand hashes the other.'" The river in this case, if we see the poem as a whole in the light of this passage, *is* the poem, its flow sweeping along the numerous time segments that result from the narrative lines' continual interruption of one another. To belabor JM's passing pun in U, there are three "stories" in this structure, but none of them is toured all at once; on the contrary, we are continually *de*toured, led by some unexpected stairway or passage concealed by a bookcase down or up a level, discovering as we go that certain features (mirrors, arrangements of flowers, furnaces, and so forth) are repeated with slight variation, so that it is sometimes difficult to say which story we are in, especially since the tenses shift not according to historical time but according to narrative exigency. Imagination hashes chronology, and time's passage is acknowledged only to be transformed by the configuration of events.

It is not just time that is divided so; but then, according to the quotation from Cavafy, it is not just time that is time: at the beginning of T Sergei looks into the mirror and sees Time's visage. But things are a good deal more intricate than that, for Sergei, as his name perhaps intimates (Sergei = Sir Gay?) is a figurative reflection of JM, who at the end of S has himself been addressing Sergei, who turns out to be a "cutting" from a real person. In S, in a passage touched on in Chapter 1, musing over a cut geranium, JM recalls his fictional character's lineage, which can be traced to a man who, years past, lived next door in Stonington. "When he was cut down" by the proverbial reaper, the poet "took slips of him," one of which became the houseman Ken in "The Summer People" and another of which "came up Russian":

Here you are now, old self in a new form.
Some of those roots look stronger, some have died.
Tell me, tell me, as I turn to you,
What every moment does, has done, will do—
Questions one simply cannot face in person.

The figure JM "turns to" then in T—for the poem's characters are almost as volatile as its main current, and we will recall that Maya's source mirrors as it transforms—is Sergei, or Time in the guise of Sergei.

Much of the poem's infrastructure consists of such metamorphoses, as a glance at some of the different embodiments of the female principle will suggest. Repeatedly portrayed as "smoking" or "fuming" (J, S, T), Joanna is also a version of the adversary, a Jungian terrible mother, and is thought in X to be "the last gasp of [JM's] dragon." At the end of J, she "reminds" her creator of his stepmother, once the leading character in a real *tranche de vie* he entitles *The Other Woman,* but then in X she represents an aspect of his real mother when JM finds the latter present in Joanna's "fuming." The poet's mother, in turn, merges with St. Theodore's and suddenly seems to be "here / Throughout, the breath drawn after every line, / Essential to its making as to mine." One reason that she is "Essential" is implied in a passage in R in which JM questions Maya about her Haitian goddess:

How about Erzulie? BUT SHE IS THE QUEEN
OF HEAVEN   Oh, not Mary? Not Kuan Yin?
THEY ARE ALL ONE QUINTESSENCE   CHANEL NO
$5 \times 5 \times 5 \times 5 \times 5$

The relationship among the other women, in short, doubles and overlaps with that among those in heaven, and Joanna, St. Theodore's mother, JM's mother, Maya (whose dream transformed her in Erzulie's image), and Lucy Prentiss (Maya's "BOSS" is St. Lucy) are also among the "COUNTLESS FACES" of the Queen of Heaven.

Mirroring images proliferate. If the poet's mother is "Here . . . in Maya's prodigality" (X), Maya is here in JM's, most notably in R's second sonnet. In the context of a memory of Maya's last days, JM asks himself whether he should revise section P or let it stand, and he finds that he is "divided"—a claim that has other meanings when we come to the recollection that he and DJ "tried to bear / The stroke *for* Maya." Her stroke divided her from him, to be sure, but it also divided him from that part of himself which, since he so loved her, *was* Maya. "What light there was" in the hospital ward "fell sideways from a mind / Half dark," he says, and we see that the "mind" is either his or Maya's. The point is also made by a pun on "eye" in the description of his friend, by now an alter ego, just before her death: "The other eye, the one that saw, remained / Full of wit, affection, and despair."

Joanna is another "old self in a new form," for it is she who flies the Ouija board into the novel, and her name, as we are told in T, is intended to connect her with St. John the Evangelist, the supposed author of the Book of Revelation and the brother of St. James.[14] (James and John were known collectively as the Boanerges, the "Sons of Thunder," because of their impulsiveness. In Luke 9 : 54 they ask Jesus to call down fire on the heads of the Samaritans and have them consumed. Joanna first appears in a terrible thunderstorm, and JM, who through St. Theodore is associated with storms, asks that lightning strike in R and gets caught in his own cloudburst in V.) Because of his relationships with Joanna and Maya, themselves linked to the Queen of Heaven, it is less surprising than it might be to find JM imagining, when confronted with Ephraim's bad news that he and DJ will not be re-born together, "Dressing up as the Blessed Damozel / At Heaven's Bar to intervene" with the powers that govern reincarnation.

In fact, or rather by proxy, JM does more obviously dress himself up, if not in drag, in an unexpected costume to appear before a bar—though of a different kind. Q provides the opportunity, in a quotation that purports to come from a book entitled *Time Was* by one A. H. Clarendon, the same mythical authority Merrill cited in "The Thousand and Second Night," and that is really based on a hilarious anecdote about the flamboyant Brian Howard:

> *One evening late in the war he was at the crowded bar of the then smart Pyramid Club, in uniform, and behaving quite outrageously. Among the observers an elderly American admiral had been growing more and more incensed. He now went over and tapped Teddie on the shoulder: "Lieutenant, you are a disgrace to the Service. I must insist on having your name and squadron." An awful silence fell. Teddie's newly-won wings glinted. He snapped shut his thin gold compact (from Hermès) and narrowed his eyes at the admiral. "My name," he said distinctly, "is Mrs. Smith."* [15]

And the name *is* Smith, just as it is also Theodore ("Teddie" is a "recruit") or JM. He might also be called Ephraim—since he is associated, by way of the compact and the wings, with the messenger of the gods—and Ephraim, that other mercurial envoy, who becomes Eros in the novel and whose counterpart in Maya Deren's experience is Erzulie, is in some sense JM.

We are told early in C that "several facts" in Ephraim's background "coincide" with those in JM's and in I that Ephraim's knowledge of history, geography, and language is virtually coextensive with the combined knowledge of DJ and JM. It is perhaps no more than another coincidence that St. Ephraem (according to the *Penguin Dictionary of Saints*) was a poet who also "wrote commentaries on a considerable number of books of the Bible, and a personal 'Testament' which seems to have been added to by a later hand" and that "even as a theologian he wrote as a poet." [16] But it is not a coincidence that would startle Tom, JM's analyst. Reading the lines in B in which JM says that "even the most fragmentary message" from Ephraim was "Twice

as entertaining, twice as wise / As either of its mediums," Tom would probably say: *exactly* so.

Tom's explanation of Ephraim, however, would be at best a fractional
truth, if only because there is hardly a figure in the poem who is *not* just as
intimately connected with JM—it is not for nothing that his familiar spirit,
a Greek Jew with a converted Christian father born in Asia Minor, is a sort
of Everyman—and it is with this reflection in mind that we must read that
delicately shaded conclusion of Y, in which Merrill touches on some "spells
of odd / Self-effacing balance" induced by the writing of *Ephraim:*

> Better to stop
> While we still can. Already I take up
> Less emotional space than a snowdrop.
> My father in his last illness complained
> Of the effect of medication on
> His real self—today Bluebeard, tomorrow
> Babbitt. Young chameleon, I used to
> Ask how on earth one got sufficiently
> Imbued with otherness. And now I see.

As he remarks in X: "So Time has—but who needs that nom de plume?
I've— / We've modulated," and the plural encompasses a host of characters.

In "The Critic as Artist," in a passage partly paraphrased in I, one of
Wilde's personae contends that "the objective form is the most subjective in
matter. Man is least himself when he talks in his own person. Give him a
mask and he will tell the truth." [17] One has no difficulty applying the observation. If we were to take Ephraim and these other figures simply as projections, however, we would be in danger of compounding Tom's mistake, or
of committing an error analogous to that committed by Dante in the *Paradiso*, III (a comparatively unremarkable phrase of which gets quoted in K),
when he mistakenly takes some faces lambent in the moonlight for reflections rather than real spirits. Merrill is no Narcissus—indeed he is also reflected in the figure of Wendell, who turns up as a cynical portrait artist in
W—and these other figures retain their individuality at the same time that
to varying degrees they represent JM. The point is that, by availing himself
of these different masks—which is really to say, by finding himself in these
different people, real and fictional, "Good and evil"—Merrill, like Proust in
Q, testifies to his *"désir de mener la vie de tout le monde."* By leading that
variegated life, he comes closer to presenting what R calls "The god's own
truth, or fiction." Especially in the context of Wilde's insight, the last term
seems an appositive rather than an alternative.

So we are where we were, on unsteady ground.

>)))

The place is Venice, unsteady a ground as could be found, the time is the fall of 1974 (JM is en route from Athens, his "home away from home," to Stonington), and the weather is stormy. "Let lightning strike," JM has pleaded in R, when in the stifling Athens September he felt short on inspiration, but in that section "stolen thunder dwindle[d] out to sea" and the response was instead the memory of Maya's stroke. Here, in V, within hailing distance of the Accademia, as JM walks across the bridge over the Grand Canal, and as we recall that Proust's manifold desire in Q included a "*désir . . . des tempêtes*" and a "*désir de Venise*," lightning finally (in two senses of the phrase) "strikes the set":

> Gust of sustaining timbers' creosote
> Pungency the abrupt drench releases—
> Cold hissing white—the old man of the Sea
> Who, clung to now, must truthfully reply—
>
> Bellying shirt, sheer windbag wrung to high
> Relief, to needle-keen transparency—
> Air and water blown glass-hard—their blind
> Man's buff with unsurrendering gooseflesh
>
> Streamlined from conception—crack! boom! flash!—
> Glaze soaking inward as it came to mind
> How anybody's monster breathing flames
> Vitrified in metamorphosis
>
> To monstrance clouded then like a blown fuse
> If not a reliquary for St James'
> Vision of life: how Venice, her least stone
> Pure menace at the start, at length became
>
> A window fiery-mild, whose walked-through frame
> Everything else, at sunset, hinged upon—

and then we are in W. Wonderfully evocative of the sudden post-storm calm as well as of the initially furious cloudburst, this passage is still probably as difficult as anything in *Ephraim*, partly because of its chain-lightning puns, partly because of its quasi-Jamesian syntax, but primarily because in it Merrill tries not only to cling to his shapeshifter (who, according to legend, prophesies truthfully if held through all his metamorphoses) but also, immensely concentrating his general strategy, to become him.

Yesterday a young chameleon, today an older Proteus. This symbolist passage in V is in the first place a small ritual in transfigured time, as Merrill's old man of the sea, the very principle of metamorphosis, having first changed from the poet into the recognizably draconic "monster breathing flames," briefly assumes the shape of a monstrance (which since it contains the host after transubstantiation is to this passage what the passage itself is to the poem) before becoming, in the poet's ironic glance at his own virtuoso effort, a blown fuse and thus perhaps another receptacle, a reliquary for the vestiges of a vision that is more James Merrill's than Henry James's or the impetuous apostle's.[18] Here Merrill condenses the vision that energizes much of the poem. We are time, and time is change (we are "Streamlined from conception"), but change is the essence of life and thus sacred, and to recognize that is to see the monster turn to monstrance—the difficulty being that that proposition, once made, tends to fix itself and thus to blow like a fuse. "NOTHING LIVE IS MOTIONLESS HERE," Ephraim says in Q, and what he seems to be saying of the *au-delà* holds true in its converse form of the here and now.

For these lines constitute in the second place a phase of the discovery of the identity of heaven and earth—an idea that will seem especially appropriate to section V, by the way, in light of what we learn about "V work" in *Mirabell*. The phrase "vision of life" itself, in its blurring of the ideal and the actual, tends in this direction, as does the religious terminology. "A whole heavenly city" Venice is called earlier in V, and the appellation is not to be taken lightly. Almost as important to *Ephraim* as to the *Cantos*, in which it is one of the richest images of the "paradiso terrestre" Pound claimed to have tried to create, Venice is here not only a microcosm of a possibly moribund world but also an analogue of the good place. Indeed, V's opening catenation—"Venise, pavane, nirvana, vice, wrote Proust"—recalls in its euphony and sense M's invocation: "Paris—the Piraeus—Paradise." Venice is thus a version of Valhalla; and it is also, this "Palladian / Sculpture maze" (W) built on water, a convenient metaphor for any intricate work of art. So it is that we find the consummate artist, Proust, earlier in V, with his last suppers, his "Passion," and his attempt "Through superhuman counterpoint to work / The body's resurrection, sense by sense." Although he makes more use of the literally superhuman than the earlier visitor to Venice, Merrill's endeavor is the same. "Does it still appear / We'll get our senses somehow purified / Back?" he asks the "powers that be" in P; and although this poem declines to deal unequivocally with eschatology, it is at every point and counterpoint an argument for art's power to resurrect—to resurrect not only one's personal past but also the pasts of friends and the cultural past, to lead at least a significant part of the life of all the world. Hence the comparison of Proust to the god-man, and hence too the "sustaining timbers' creosote / Pungency." The sustaining timber is surely that of the bridge, which links Merrill to Proust, James, and Giorgione, and reality to fiction (JM meets Wendell on the bridge in W), rather than that of the cross, but the bridge also connects earth to heaven, and the pungency released here derives in part from the Greek roots of "creosote," which mean "flesh" and "preserver." The poet's aim, as JM has it in I's transposition, is "Flesh made word." The episode in L in which JM resurrects his former self, Rufus, is emblematic of one part of the task Merrill has set himself.

He dramatically compresses the theme in Z. DJ and JM return one night to their Stonington house to find a "bedroom ransacked, lights on, loud / Tick of alarm, the mirror off its hook / Looking daggers at the ceiling fixture"; but this particular thief in the night—this "burglar . . . in the Enchanted Village" reminiscent of both the Troubler in the Garden and Hermes, patron of thieves ("Mercury dropping" JM has noted earlier in Z), as well as of Ephraim, who was perhaps responsible for the loss of the novel—seems to have taken nothing: "nothing's gone, or nothing we recall." Later, "Nothing we can recollect is missing." Precisely: Time steals to the extent that we fail to recollect, which proposition correlates with that represented by, say, Proust's undertaking—and which is another aspect of the idea that "We are Time."

The problem, which seen aright might be its own resolution, is not so much that even a Proust can only be partially successful in the end, although of course that is true to the degree that we suppose the criterion for success to be a triumph over time; it is rather that the artist-recruit enlists himself also in the service of time. It could hardly be otherwise, since as JM puts it at the beginning of the poem: "Time, it had transpired, was of the essence. / Time, the very attar of the Rose . . ." And the Rose, we learn by tracing a few connections, is for one thing the rose of the world, evident in both Venice's "dull red mazes caked with slime / Bearing some scented drivel of undying / Love and regret" (V) and the lost novel's landscape, its "arroyos— / Each the abraded, vast, baked-rose detail / Of a primeval circulatory system" (S), as well as in the poet's "red flower" (or flow-er) "Not yet in the dread phrase cut-and-dried" (S). Specious etymology could discover the key phrase in the first name of Mrs. Rosamund Smith, who is described in D as "Perennially youthful, worldly, rich, / And out of sight until the close" and who nonetheless reappears as Teddie in Q and, appropriately, as "the resourceful Mrs. Smith" in S (where a photograph of her is torn into "pieces" and where she is also the eponym of "a showy hybrid" flower) before she returns anonymously in Z as "The ancient, ageless woman of the world," a cooler version of Stevens's "Fat girl." Like Spenser's "great Grandmother of all creatures bred . . . Unseene of any, yet of all beheld," and like Ephraim, whose "presence" in H is "Everywhere felt" although he never shows his face, she has been here—*sub rosa*—all along: in JM's mother; in Joanna, whose face is likened to that of the earth in J; in Maya, her "Touches of tart and maiden, muse and wife / Glowing forth once more from an *Etude* / *De Jeune Femme* no longer dimmed by time" (R). In fact, the title of Merrill's picture in memory, like Deren's "Ritual in Transfigured Time," is a shadow title for this poem—although Mahler's *Das Lied von der Erde*, mentioned in G, might be more in keeping, especially since "Ephraim" means "fruitful" in Hebrew and Mrs. Smith appears in D's description of the twilight of the novel (if not of the gods) as one who "will / Have wrinkled soon to purple fruitlessness."

Because *Ephraim* is through and through a song of the earth, it is also a vindication of "the test of time that all things pass" (R), and in the final analysis the poet might be represented less fully by St. Theodore than by yet another James, Joyce, "the great wordsmith" (he is another member of that family too), "Forging a snake that swallows its own tail" (X). To incarnate the monster, as Merrill does in V and X, is not after all to slay it but to make it take a shape; and to make it swallow its tail, as Joyce does in *Finnegans Wake* or Wagner does in his *Ring,* is to keep time from swallowing its own tale. The ouroboros, the Gnostic symbol of time and life's continuity, re-appears in diminished form in Z ("Zero hour": the year's cycle completes itself and the poem comes full circle), when the furnace fails and JM imag-ines, with characteristic wryness, that the furnace man might find "an easy-to-repair / Short circuit." It will either be that, he surmises, or "the failure long foreseen / As total, of our period machine." An alternative description of this poem, as well as of the world it celebrates, the "period machine" frankly gives time its due, and in its capacity as furnace it recalls the means of martyrdom of St. Theodore, who had to do the same. JM decides in Z *not* to burn the transcripts of the hours with Ephraim, and by extension the manuscript of this poem, but he entertains the idea:

> And that (unless it floated, spangled ash,
> Outward, upward, one lone carp aflash
> Languorously through its habitat
> For crumbs that once upon a . . .) would be that.

The word "time" is elided in this formulaic beginning not only because the poem in its end has in a sense overcome the temporal but also because, with the burning of these pages that praise it, time would give away that much more to the awful silence of eternity, represented here by the ellipses JM refers to in X as "black holes." From one point of view, then, and in the very process of recollection that foils the thief, the dragon cut up in Q reassembles itself in the poem, although in a transfigured form. It is no coincidence that in X the dragon-slayer himself is a "young man in dark *rose*."

But—and how often Merrill's conjunctions force us to that conjunction—even as it is on earth and in the fullness of time that "a whole heavenly city" is created, the Rose of which time is the attar is also redolent of Dante's heavenly rose. I am reminded of Eliot's dictum in "Burnt Norton," "Only through time time is conquered," but to the degree that Eliot stresses the *apprehension* of "The point of intersection of the timeless / With time," the saint rather than the swordsman, the efforts of Yeats and Stevens better comport with those of Merrill. Ephraim, in Q, provides this poem's most candid, distinctive, and moving comments on the relationship between earth and heaven, worlds so joined in his view that JM (in F) no longer prays "For the remission of their synthesis":

> & NOW ABOUT DEVOTION   IT IS I AM FORCED TO BELIEVE THE MAIN IMPETUS   DEVOTION TO EACH OTHER TO WORK TO REPRODUCTION TO AN IDEAL   IT IS BOTH THE MOULD & THE CLAY   SO WE ARRIVE AT GOD OR A DEVOTION TO ALL OR MANYS IDEAL OF THE CONTINUUM   SO WE CREATE THE MOULDS OF HEAVENLY PERFECTION & THE ONES ABOVE OF RARER & MORE EXPERT USEFULNESS & AT LAST DEVOTION WITH THE COMBINED FORCES OF FALLING AND WEARING WATER PREPARES A HIGHER MORE FINISHED WORLD OR HEAVEN

The entire poem eulogizes these various facets of "DEVOTION," and one of its chief aims is precisely to help to "CREATE THE MOULDS OF HEAVENLY PERFECTION" and even "THE ONES ABOVE." This idea of a world that has the potential of creating the ideal it might become lies at the heart of *Ephraim*, for it is this idea that ultimately justifies its union of fiction and reality even as it renders futile and superfluous any speculation about the ontological status of Ephraim and his peers.

Just as the configurating *process* implicit in this concept distinguishes this poem's universe from those of other works inevitably called up—from, say, the terraced cosmos of the *Paradiso* or the Escher-like labyrinth of *Pale Fire*—so the temperament disclosed by it distinguishes Merrill's "vision of life" from that of such an obviously kindred spirit as Stevens. The former's "devotion," symbolized by the "heart-emblem" that Maya Deren burns onto the floor in G (an emblem presumably identical with the voodoo *vever* for Erzulie that she illustrates in her book) and embodied in the unselfish services rendered the natives of Kenya by Isak Dinesen in O, is after all closer to

Dante's "love," "l'amor che move il sole e l'altre stelle," than to Stevens's more abstract "imagination." Still, Stevens is a tutelary spirit here, as Merrill testifies in S:

> Stevens imagined the imagination
> And God as one; the imagination, also,
> As that which presses back, in parlous times,
> Against "the pressure of reality."
> Scholia discordant (who could say?)
> Yet coursing with heart's-blood the moment read.[19]

Even as the emphasis upon the heart's assent, the renunciation of even the momentary pose of the savant, sets Merrill apart from his predecessor—not that Stevens would have quarreled with Yeats's summation that man cannot know truth but can embody it—these lines assert a strong affinity.

What attracts Merrill to Stevens's view of the divine power of the imagination attracts him also to Jung, to whom he alludes in U: "Jung says—or if he doesn't, all but does / That God and the Unconscious are one." The theme informs much of Jung's work, but it seems that Merrill has the "Answer to Job" in mind. In that long essay Jung argues against what he considers the "opposition" in orthodox Christianity between God and man, and although he stops short of denying man a certain individuality, the blessed poverty of the "limited ego," he finds it difficult to extricate him from "the One." "It is only through the Psyche that we can establish that God acts upon us, but we are unable to distinguish whether these actions emanate from God or from the unconscious. We cannot tell whether God and the unconscious are two different entities."[20] To the extent that they are one, Ephraim's little lecture on the creation of the moulds of heavenly perfection and Jung's thesis dovetail, for according to Jung the crucial question is "whether man can climb up to a higher moral level, to a higher plane of consciousness, in order to be equal to the superhuman powers" he possesses. If he fails to do so, man has neither excuse nor future, "for the dark God . . . has given him the power to empty out the apocalyptic vials of wrath on his fellow creatures."[21]

Merrill has carefully situated and highlighted this, his theme's grim side, which will get more attention in the subsequent volumes. R begins with the poet's injunction to himself:

> Rewrite P. It was to be the section
> Golden with end-of-summer light. Impossible

So long, at least, as there's no end to summer.
Late September is a choking furnace.

The allusion is to the classical ratio and proportion discerned by Euclid and structurally implemented from time to time by artists, writers, and composers from Virgil through Bartók. In Euclid's *Elements*, the golden section is set forth in these terms: "A straight line is said to have been cut in extreme and mean ratio when, as the whole line is to the greater segment, so is the greater to the less".[22] In its simplest numerical terms, the ratio is $1 : 0.618$. In this poem of twenty-six sections, the division would occur in the sixteenth section, P, and within P, which is 127 lines long, the division would occur at line 78. Without knowing whether Merrill did eventually rewrite P so that it would utilize the golden section, we can observe that there is a division in P at line 78 and that the passage that follows is in a sense "Golden with end of summer light," for it comprises a memory of attending *Götterdämmerung*, and it focuses on the climactic moment when Valhalla goes up in flames, the gods are destroyed, and the Rhine floods, enabling the Rhinemaidens to regain their golden ring at last. This memory of the final act of the *Ring* cycle has been inspired by Ephraim's comments on "the Cosmic Mind" to the effect that the existence of heaven depends upon that of the earth. Should we destroy ourselves by misusing the "Power" celebrated in P, "when the flood ebbed, or the fire burned low, / Heaven, the world no longer at its feet, / Itself would up and vanish." In the light of such information, the two mediums' earlier "swig of . . . no-proof rhetoric"—the insouciant observation that they are content to "Let what would be, be" if an annihilated earth could "Melt like dew into the Cosmic Mind"—is precisely no proof at all. Just as man can create the moulds of heavenly perfection, so he can destroy them. In Jung's terms, there is "antinomy in Deity itself," and the Deity acts through the unconscious.[23]

Jung characterizes God in other pertinent terms: "We can [also] imagine God," he says, "as an eternally flowing current of vital energy that endlessly changes shape." The same as the one that "Flows through field and book," Jung's current further manifests itself in the "Unrelenting fluency" of time and in the flow of the imagination—for in this stream one hand washes the other—and it can be followed back to the "spring, or source" in Maya's dream. As the ultimate power, the "naked current" which is both inside and outside man, it is epitomized in Proteus and implied by all of Merrill's metamorphoses and mirrors, his diverse personae. These figures are all variations on what Jung calls "a few basic principles or archetypes" which collectively represent God and which, "like the psyche itself, or like matter, are unknowable as such." "All we can do," Jung argues, "is to construct models of them which we know to be inadequate, a fact which is confirmed again and again by religious statements."[24] As he proceeds to make clear, however, the inadequacy of these models notwithstanding, our very construction of them serves a maieutic purpose, bringing the unconscious to the light of consciousness, incarnating God in man, creating the moulds of heavenly perfection. "The religious need longs for wholeness, and therefore lays hold of the images of wholeness offered by the unconscious, which, independently of the conscious mind, rise up from the depths of our psychic nature."[25] Merrill's metamorphic stream is just such an image, his "woman of the world" another, and it is the result of the coupling of exactly such a need with devotion that Ephraim speaks of in Q:

> U & YR GUESTS THESE TIMES WE SPEAK ARE WITHIN SIGHT OF & ALL CONNECTED TO EACH OTHER DEAD OR ALIVE   NOW DO U UNDERSTAND WHAT HEAVEN IS   IT IS THE SURROUND OF THE LIVING

Merrill's statement is not Dante's. It could not be, since as Jung avers the mind "manipulates images and ideas which are dependent on human imagination and its temporal and local conditions, and which have therefore changed innumerable times in the course of their long history."[26] At the same time, however, the implicit comparison at the center of this poem, which is where we are still, needs to be there. In their respective ways both the *Paradiso* and *The Book of Ephraim* concern themselves with man's "limited ego" and "the One who dwells within him, whose form has no knowable boundaries, who encompasses him on all sides, fathomless as the abysms of the earth and vast as the sky."[27]

> > >

But where were we? Merrill answers his own earlier question at the same time that he answers one asked in the last lines of his poem by another who receives all manner of guests, everyone's patroness and hostess:

> And look, the stars have wound in filigree
> The ancient, ageless woman of the world.
> She's seen us. She is not particular—
> Everyone gets her injured, musical
> "Why do you no longer come to me?"
> To which there's no reply. For here we are.

Here on Earth, evidently. And yet the filigree of starlight, which seems to presuppose a distant vantage point, as though the planet were seen from space, would be appropriate dress for the Queen of Heaven. If "She is not particular," she must be universal, this figure whose predecessors in Merrill's work go back through the *"towering mother"* of "From the Cupola" at least to a Mrs. Crane in *The Birthday*, the verse playlet written and performed when Merrill was a senior at Amherst in 1947. Mrs. Crane, who sometimes seems to be everyone's mother, is also "nobody in particular."[28] In any case, the scene combines heaven and earth, the "fanciful" and the "real," which are as inextricable as Jung's unconscious and God. In other words, it is *because* Ephraim is primarily spirit that JM and DJ have "reached a / Stage through him that he will never himself reach" (X), for that stage is one in which reality and fiction merge.

There is a passage in *The Necessary Angel* in which Stevens says something that I think this poem means to show: "We have been trying to get at a truth about poetry, to get at one of the principles that compose the theory of poetry. It comes to this, that poetry is a part of the structure of reality. If this has been demonstrated, it pretty much amounts to saying that the structure of poetry and the structure of reality are one or, in effect, that poetry and reality are one, or should be."[29] As the qualifications indicate, however, Stevens had his doubts, and Merrill for his part is far too wise, too aware of the susceptibility of dogma to rigor mortis, to formulate principles or to purge his work of ambiguities. Late in the poem, it is true, in X's conclusion, he conjoins "The world's poem" and "the poem's world," proceeds to describe the universe in terms of his verse, and goes so far as to liken black holes, "Vanishing points," to his ellipses; but even there, by reference to "Gassy expansion and succinct collapse," he includes rather than reduces antipodes, and his concluding suspension points leave us up in the air in regard to poetry and reality, heaven and earth. Indeed they must do so if Merrill is to keep hold of his Proteus, Yeats's simple embodiment of truth, Jung's eternally flowing current. Heraclitus's river flows, and the Venetian canal in V is continuously "Ruining another batch of images."[30] The concern goes back through the many instances discussed earlier at least as far as a short story published when Merrill was twenty-three. Near the beginning of this piece, a young man who has come to dinner turns before the children's eyes into a rabbit. Before they can get used to this transformation, he continues his metamorphoses: "He was alternately a frog, a groundhog, a bird, a goldfish. The children watched each evolution with delight, trying, as the meal progressed, to catch him in the act of change." The name of the short story is "Rose."[31] So in a sense nothing has changed. As Heinrich Zimmer tells us in Q:

The powers have to be consulted again directly—again, again and again. Our primary task is to learn, not so much what they are said to have said, as how to approach them, evoke fresh speech from them, and understand that speech. In the face of such an assignment, we must all remain dilettantes, whether we like it or not.[32]

Or as Rilke reminds us in *Letters to Merline,* the poet must always be willing to be a beginner. Merrill has always been willing. Even he does not seem to have realized, however, how soon he would be consulting "*the powers*" again—let alone what kind of "*fresh speech*" he and DJ would evoke.

chapter six

THE NATURE OF MIND
Mirabell's Books of Number

The new
Wallpaper—field of heavenly dark blue
Blazoned with Hubbell's fans and clouds and bats . . .

❯ ❯ ❯

Let us not forget that Leibniz, proto-inventor of the new science, said in time and against his time that one should listen to old wives' tales.

Michel Serres, *Hermes: Literature, Science, Philosophy* (trans. Josué V. Harari and David F. Bell)

A story is a little knot or complex of that species of connectedness which we call *relevance* . . .

Now I want to show that . . . the fact of thinking in terms of stories does not isolate human beings as something separate from the starfish and the sea anemones, the coconut palms and the primroses. Rather, if the world be connected, if I am at all fundamentally right in what I am saying, then *thinking in terms of stories* must be shared by all mind or minds, whether ours or those of redwood forests and sea anemones.

Gregory Bateson, *Mind and Nature*

I think what's significant is that consciousness doesn't stop with human beings. There is probably a great untapped mind, if you can call it that, in the natural world itself.

Merrill to Ross Labrie

OR DO I MEAN the mind of Nature? In the end perhaps it is all one. But then we live in "One nature dual to the end," Merrill writes in *Mirabell's Books of Number*, and the word he uses to signify duality is itself double, for he means us to hear overtones of "duel" as well. In its fascination with the relationship between "plus" and "minus," *Mirabell* resembles *Ephraim*. But it is also quite a different matter. If the first volume would have been a lyric among epics, had it stood alone, this one is a whole ramshackle, rattle- and claptrapping shebang of a machine—a unique loom, say, weaving a fabric with "Warp of physics, woof of whim," to borrow from "Dreams about Clothes." First, the background.

Ephraim ends with DJ and JM waiting—in Stonington, in December 1974—for "Bob the furnace man," who is on his way through the snow to repair their "period machine." *Mirabell* finds them, several months later, driving "through melting drifts" to the home of a friend named Hubbell, whom they have asked to design a parlor wallpaper that will incorporate motifs from their decade-old Chinese carpet, a field of "ghostly maize in winter sun" bordered with "Overlapping cloudlets that give way / To limber, leotarded, blue-eyed bats / —Symbols of eternity, said the dealer." Before long, having left the execution of the design to Hubbell, they fly off to their home in Athens—and thus put even further behind them, they imagine, their obsession with the other world. Weary of communicating with the dead, and frightened by their brush (section U of *Ephraim*) with certain intimidating spirits who lived on Earth "B4 MANKIND" and who "HAVE WINGS TO WHICH / THE TRAILING SLEEVES OF PALACE ROBES ALLUDE," they have broken off their connection months before and have found reasons not to get back in touch. But Hubbell is not the only one executing a design.

In April 1975, shortly after they arrive in Greece, they decide to summon DJ's infirm parents, Mary and Matt, who can no longer be trusted to live alone in California. Installed in a flat near the Athens house, and provided with a maid, they can live out their last years in comparative security and serenity. But the time remaining to them turns out to be only a matter of weeks. In June Mary dies of the complications of a broken hip, and Matt, deprived of the victim on whom he has come to depend, follows in July. During Mary's illness, DJ and JM turn once again to Ephraim. "Where else," JM asks, "to look for sense, comfort and wit?" Besides, their contacts in the other world can help Mary "through Customs." Especially since they find no evidence of that "peremptory, commanding power" who had so rudely intervened in the earlier session, they soon settle into the old routine—a routine made all the more entertaining by the addition to the party line of two recently dead friends: Maria Mitsotáki, who appeared rather puzzlingly in D of *Ephraim* and to whom Merrill had addressed the tribute "Words for Maria" in *The Fire Screen;* and Chester Kallman, Auden's longtime friend and collaborator. After some disillusioning discoveries about her new environs ("NO PRIVACY NO COFFEE & NO PLANTS"), MM has adapted beautifully. She charms Stevens and the others and even finds a use for her green thumb: she helps St. Agatha plant "FLEURS DE MAUVAISE CONSCIENCE / In politicians' beds." Nor has CK changed all that much. What does he do all day? "READ   BUFF MY NAILS   DO CROSSWORDS   JUST LIKE LIFE / THOSE YEARS WITH WYSTAN   ONCE A BACKSTREET WIFE / ALWAYS A

BACK Stop this! STREET Chester! WIFE." Later, in a state of manic disgust at the revelation that he will be reborn as a heterosexual, unpoetic, black South African, he joins JM in a funny, touching, outrageous duet:

FANCY A NICE JEWISH MS LIKE ME
(Chester after dinner) GETTING T H E
ULTIMATE REJECTION SLIP   IS GOD
CYRIL CONNOLLY? But you're coming back,
It's too exciting! PLEASE   TO SEE MY BLACK
FACE IN A GLASS DARKLY? I WONT BE
WHITE   WONT BE A POET   WONT BE QUEER
CAN YOU CONCEIVE OF LIFE WITHOUT THOSE 3???
Well, frankly, yes. THE MORE FOOL U MY DEAR
You shock us, Chester. After months of idle,
Useless isolation— ALL I HEAR
ARE THESE B MINOR HYMNS TO USEFULNESS:
LITTLE MISS BONAMI OOH SO GLAD
TO FIND ARCADIA IN A BRILLO PAD!
LAUGH CLONE LAUGH   AH LIFE   I FEEL THE LASH
OF THE NEW MASTER   NOTHING NOW BUT CRASH
COURSES   What does Wystan say? TO PLATO?
HAVING DROPPED ME LIKE A HOT   O SHIT
WHAT GOOD IS RHYME NOW   Come, think back, admit
That best of all was to be flesh and blood,
Young, eager, ear cocked for your new name—   MUD

(Confront the writing student who complains about the *constraints* of rhyme and meter with this passage, which has its potato and drops it too, and you could change a life.)

By August 1975 Mary has been reborn in Iceland—a country that the overseers perhaps choose because of the prohibitive distance and climatic difference from Iraq, where Matt will later turn up as "AN ALERT BROWN SUCKLING." Then, toward summer's end, those same mandarin spirits, "whose discipline / Thrills through the nine Stages like long waves / Or whips that crack above the heads of slaves," force themselves anew on DJ and JM. Mincing no words, they make a demand of JM that is as surprising as the glimpse they afford of their own nature:

UNHEEDFULL ONE   3 OF YOUR YEARES MORE WE WANT   WE MUST
   HAVE
POEMS OF SCIENCE   THE WEORK FINISHT IS BUT A PROLOGUE

ABSOLUTES ARE NOW NEEDED YOU MUST MAKE GOD OF SCIENCE
TELL OF POWER MANS IGNORANCE FEARES THE POWER WE ARE
THAT FEAR STOPS PARADISE WE SPEAK FROM WITHIN THE ATOM

Though distrustful of "*Them*" and dismayed by the assignment ("Science meant / Obfuscation, boredom"), JM resigns himself to the task before he flies back to the United States and a teaching commitment in the fall. Having presumed "That inspiration from now on would come / Outright, with no recourse to the Board," he is chagrined when he realizes, by winter, that he must at least prepare the ground. If he could satisfy previous stirrings of curiosity about the relationship between science and art by parodying them (as in Orson's lecture on Darwin in the second novel) or by assigning them to characters he could then wish well and dismiss (Joey in "The Summer People"), this is another matter. But in for a penny, in for a pound: willing as usual to be a beginner, he sits "glumly down to read" a "biophysichemical / Textbook" and other putatively heuristic material. The terminology in part justifies his prejudice, since "Words like 'quarks' or 'mitochondria' / Aren't *words* at all, in the Rilkean sense of / House, Dog, Tree," but it also startles him with its occasional felicities: "through Wave, Ring, Bond, through Spectral Lines / And Resonances blows a breath of life."[1] Still, he has no idea how to construe the confusing assortment of information his reading yields, so when he writes from Stonington to DJ in March 1976 about travel plans, he also suggests that, regardless of misgivings, they might "*have to approach* Them" on their return to the States:

> *And you're dead right, it*
> *is scary. But so, don't forget, was Ephraim*
> *at first. Say we've reached again some relative*
> *point—that of fear—on a spiral forever*
> *widening. Why couldn't the whole adventure,*
> *as before, just graze peril on its outward*
> *curve to insight?*

After spending the spring in Athens, DJ and JM return in June to Stonington, by way of England, where they visit Stonehenge and Avebury. They cannot know it at the time, but the very layout of the latter site confirms JM's suspicion that they will take new risks. Here is his "watercolor" of Avebury:

Within a "greater circle" (the whole myth
Dwarfed by its grass-green skyline) stand

Two lesser, not quite tangent O's
Plotted monolith by monolith.

Two lenses now, whose once outrippling arcs
Draw things back into focus. Round each stone
(As Earth revolves, or a sheepdog barks)
Rumination turns the green to white.

The rest of what "happens" in *Mirabell* "Takes place in the course of the one summer / Of 1976 . . . at the round white table / Under the dome of the red dining room" in the house on Water Street in Stonington.

> > >

The exchanges recorded in *Mirabell* differ from those in *Ephraim* in important ways. For one, Maria Mitsotáki (MM) and Auden (WHA) sit in on these sessions and contribute as much to them as DJ and JM themselves. For another, thanks to the didactic powers that now control the teacup, these sessions become classes, seminars—part of the curriculum in a highly selective academy whose name they will learn in due time. Before and after the meetings, our four students (and their friends) have time for gossip and jokes, but (especially near the beginning) the new instructors permit little fooling around during class. In contrast to Ephraim, a kindred spirit more inclined to chat than to lecture, they have come to DJ and JM to teach them about the nature of the universe, so that JM can write those "POEMS OF SCIENCE" they need to advance their own project, which we first heard about in *Ephraim:* the creation of Paradise on Earth, an undertaking the students now learn to refer to as "V work." Because their teachers have so much to impart, and partly because those teachers prove to be exasperatingly inept organizers of their material, this book is much longer than *Ephraim*—about 6,500 lines as compared to about 2,500. Merrill divides *Mirabell,* like its predecessor, into sections, and just as his former arrangement made use of the board's letters, so his new one draws on its numbers. The "Zero" that begins *Ephraim's* last section and indicates the closing of that volume's circle also initiates the transition to *Mirabell.* Apparently out of half-ironic deference to what we understand to be his mentors' penchant for mathematics, or at least for numbers, he subdivides each of ten main sections or books, 0 through 9, into ten and designates each of these subdivisions after the first by a decimal figure.

The figures behind these figures challenge the imagination. Like Ephraim, they are messengers: "WEATHER IS THE PROVINCE OF NATURE & /

SIGNALS MESSAGES THE TRANSPORTING & DELIVERY / OF SOULS, OURS: WE ARE MERCURY." Unlike Ephraim, who ranks far below them in this scheme of things, they were never human, although they did once live on Earth. They "THINK IN FLASHING TRIGONOMETRIES," go by "formulas" rather than names, and call themselves collectively the "oo BEYOND THE NINE"—that is, the nine stages that Ephraim and his cohorts inhabit. They, or at least the "twin zeroes" that represent them, are "Central to this b00k," as JM tells us in a sonnet located near the volume's center, in section 4.5. They are also its point of departure, since *Mirabell* begins with a double O (and with other allusions to circles), which is the more fitting since the prefix "oo—" means egg or ovum (as in "oogenesis"):

0   Oh very well, then. Let us broach the matter
Of the new wallpaper in Stonington.
Readers in small towns will know the world
Of interest rippling out from such a topic,
Know by their own case that "small town" is
Largely a state of mind, a medium
Wherein suspended, microscopic figments
—Boredom, malice, curiosity—
Catch a steadily more revealing light.

Actually, much of the volume is here *ab ovo*. The 00's "matter," from virtually their first "WOORDS" (1), *is* matter; one of their favorite pedagogical devices is a change of scale from microcosm to macrocosm, a technique foreshadowed here in the deft modulations among "medium," "small town," "state of mind," and "world / Of interest"; and the volume itself catches "a steadily more revealing light." True, its conclusion turns us back to its origin, for just as "Oh" is JM's first word, so its homophone is his last, as he muses in 9.9 on "Birdlife, leafplay, rockface, waterglow / Lending us their being, till the given / Moment comes to render what we owe." But we have not merely returned to the beginning. Even as the reference to DNA's "spiral molecule" in 9.9 echoes JM's speculation at the outset (in .9) that in their adventure he and DJ might be following "*a spiral forever / widening*," the image involves ascent as well as repetition—and at *Mirabell's* end the 00 give way to superior guides, the powers of light, whom we come to know as the angels. One of them, Michael, rounds off this middle volume with an eloquent speech that builds to the following directive, which has its own linked doublings and circles:

LEAVE THIS FIRST OF THE FIRST TWO MEETINGS IN A CYCLE OF
TWINNED MEETINGS IN A CYCLE OF TWELVE MOONS
LOOK! LOOK INTO THE RED EYE OF YOUR GOD!

As that singular "EYE," the steadily more revealing light itself, reminds us once more of the volume's opening, the first and last lines of this "b00k" meet to make the outermost circle rippling out from the topic of "the new wallpaper in Stonington."

Because stones too are important in *Mirabell*, we might ponder the coincidence that the name of DJ and JM's "'small town'" is Stonington—especially since to hear Them tell it, there is "NO ACCIDENT" in the ineffably complicated nature of things. It was no accident, for instance, that DJ's and JM's first contact with the other world, which took place in 1953 before they had even moved to Stonington and which they had forgotten until the transcript turned up in JM's copy of "Gilchrist's *Life of Blake*," was with a spirit named Cabel Stone. (No accident either that JM slipped the page into that book, one supposes. Like the imperious new teachers, Blake saw his work as "an Endeavour to Restore what the Ancients call'd the Golden Age," and like Merrill, Blake freely admitted that he had sometimes written "from immediate Dictation" and that "the Authors are in Eternity.")[2] Nor was it really on a whim that DJ and JM visited Avebury. As we eventually learn, their new teachers once had and still maintain certain connections with that site—and so the "Two . . . not quite tangent O's" of stone that stand within the "'greater circle'" of the horizon declare. Since those O's take other forms in "the round white table" (another "ANCHOR POINT" for the 00) and the "dome of the red dining room," the two elements that dominate the setting for *Mirabell*'s lessons, it even looks as though their new teachers, in the interests of orientation, surreptitiously influenced their choice of home and furnishings long ago. They clearly had a hand in the selection of that Chinese carpet back around 1965 and in the decision, ten years later, to have Hubbell incorporate motifs from the carpet in the wallpaper. For when JM asks the 00 about their appearance, they give him this disconcerting, embarrassed response:

DO YOU IMAGINE YOU CHOSE THAT CARPET THAT WALLPAPER
 Our bats! The gargoyle faces, the umbrella
 Wings—of course, *of course* that's how you look!
 A dash of jitters flavors the reply:
NO WELL PERHAPS JUST A BIT IS IT AN UGLY NOTION

They have also prefaced their arrival by means of an incident recorded near the end of section .6, where CK's discourse is mysteriously interrupted:

& AS FOR INNOCENCE IT HAS
A GENIUS FOR GETTING LOST I FEAR
ONCE THE BABE FINDS PLEASURE WHERE IT SUCKS
THE TRAP IS SET   ALREADY ITS TOO LATE
Excuse me, that's the doorbell— OR THE BAIT

But no one's there. Or only an unfamiliar
Black dog, leg lifted at our iron gate,
Marking his territory. Dusk. The mountain
Rippled by heat, scent of green pine, a star
Delicately remind us where we are.

Now "where we are" at this early juncture is Athens, in the house near Mt. Lykabettos that figures in a number of Merrill's poems—but these lines also put us right back where we were ("For here we are") at the end of *Ephraim*, with a foot in either world. We are still both here and there when DJ and JM return to Stonington, that other world within this one, as Merrill hints when he refers to the dining room table's "white / Theatre in the round" as "The blind bright spot of where we are." By this point, however, the emphasis has shifted from "the outside world," since JM and DJ have got more and more caught up in the "fictive darkness" and their little drama inside. As CK has suggested, DJ and JM have lost their innocence, thanks to Ephraim, and by now there can be little question of their withdrawing from their enterprise. Like the "black poodle" in *Faust*, JM sees later, that "unfamiliar" dog marking his territory must have been a new familiar, or "A kind of feeler" sent out by these new powers, whose identity is perhaps concealed in the not quite tangent o's in "no one" and who waste little time associating themselves (their project for Paradise notwithstanding) with a darkness less "fictive" than ominous. Indeed, it was probably "TOO LATE" (once more the two O's peek out at us) for DJ and JM to save themselves from consorting with these baleful spirits even long before the black dog appeared. After one of their number, resorting to a venerable name whose elements he scrambles into a remarkably Merrillian term, calls himself "BEZELBOB," WHA points out the connection with "Bob the furnace man," whom DJ and JM had summoned at the close of *Ephraim*. (The other part of the name occurs at the other end of *Ephraim*, near the conclusion of A.) Nor is that connection merely verbal. "HUGE SQUEAKING" creatures "QUITE LIKE BATS . . . WITH LITTLE HOT RED EYES," in MM's vivid sketch, they associate themselves with fire and destruction.

254

Especially nuclear destruction. Although they claim to be "NOT EVIL BUT IMPATIENT," these bats with the blazing eyes equate themselves with the atom's "NEGATIVE" potential. Rather confusingly, they also picture themselves as both "THE SONS OF CAIN" and "THE BAD ANGELS":

WE TRIFLED & F E L L   NEGATIVE ENERGY THE BLACK HOLE
WAS BORNE   WE B U R N   YET THERE IS MERCY   & HAVING
   SUFFERD
IT IS OUR DUTY TO WARN MAN AGAINST THE CHAOS ONCE
WORSHIPT BY US   OUR IMAGE IS LITERALLY BLACKEND

Such stuff at first frightens DJ and frustrates JM, who needs hard facts if he is to answer the demand for "POEMS OF SCIENCE." After a while he does get, if not facts—for they must "USE WORDS" to represent "FORMULAS GOVERNING / HUMAN LIFE," since "THE WHOLE REDUCED TO CHEMICAL TABLES WD / BE MEANINGLESS TO U"—at least a more or less coherent story of the bats' origins and purpose. Oddly enough, this story recalls JM's first notions of scientific poetry, which he imagines to involve squinting through "those steel-rimmed / Glasses of the congenitally slug- / Pale boy at school, with his precipitates, / His fruit-flies and his slide rule." For if, according to 4.5, the 00 turn out to be the "lenses" through which he and DJ see in this book (and the "double O," we might recall, is old American slang for a "once over" or a "close scrutiny"), they are also, though not exactly fruit flies, descendants of "MUTANT FLIES NOT A HUMAN FINGERLENGTH," which a prehistorical race of immortal "CENTAURS BRED IN THEIR INCUBATORS." Originally developed in order to serve those centaurs as messengers, they later became architects and then physicists, charged by the younger centaurs with devising atomic weapons powerful enough to blast an increasingly burdensome population of decrepit immortals down to a convenient size. Having dreamed up such weapons, the bats overthrew their masters and created their own civilization—a shimmering network of "SMOOTH PLAINS & LATTICE CITIES" suspended above Earth and anchored to it at fourteen points, one of which was Avebury. (It is because they hold that number sacred that JM decides to arrange the transcriptions of their messages in lines of fourteen syllables.) Encroaching vegetation eventually weakened the moorings, and because they were too proud to lower themselves to repairing them, the bats finally perished with their antigravitational world.

Much of this information (and much, much more) comes from one of the new instructors—741, as he first calls himself, or Mirabell, as JM names him for the character in *The Way of the World* after he astonishingly changes one day, this descendant of a "GREEN GRASS FLY," from a bat into a peacock.

Not the first of these eerie instructors to speak, and not the most powerful of them, he becomes their emissary after he proves to be the most sympatico. One of the last born of the bats and thus comparatively removed from their usurpation and consequent fall, he is more congenial and more adaptable than his "ANCESTORS," for whom he reserves the honorific term "00." Unlike his superiors, who are "UNMANNERD TO THE NTH DEGREE," Mirabell has feelings, a predisposition to courtesy, an incipient sense of humor, and a certain flair for words. He and the two mediums hit it off in 2.1, and thereafter he is this volume's bizarre equivalent of Dante's Virgil.

From time to time Mirabell corrects Ephraim's explanation of things. Thus we learn that Mozart, rather than being reborn as a black rock star, last appeared on Earth as Stravinsky; that the episode involving Rufus Farmetton was "A PARTIAL FICTION TO DRAMATIZE / THE KIND OF FACT U CD AT THAT POINT HAVE BELIEVED"; that the dead do not regain their senses, regardless of the level they achieve. As for the nagging question of "APPEARANCES" in the other world: it seems that the solicitous spirits have been keeping them up so as not to burden DJ and JM with the fearful truth that they inhabit "SHEER EMPTINESS . . . WE DO NOT SEE EACH OTHER, JUST THE LIT / SPACE OF YR GLASS EACH TIME U ENTER IT." Furthermore, far from being the hub of the universe, as Ephraim had let on, the nine-stage hierarchy is a virtual backwater. The presiding power in our sector of creation is one God Biology, at whose right hand sit the white forces, the counterparts of the bats. Also known as "THE 12 PER CENT" or simply "THE 12," these white angels, led by Michael, make only a couple of brief appearances in *Mirabell* (as the bats did in *Ephraim*), but we understand that they will take matters into their own hands in the third volume. "EVERYTHING UP TO THE 12: / SUN STARS MOON ALL NATURE" is "GOD B'S GREENHOUSE," where innumerable experiments, all parts of V work, go on continuously. Mirabell and his kind carry out the crucial, exotic projects in "the *Research Lab*," which is "An EMPTINESS PACKD FULL. No language here / But formulas unspeakably complex / Which change like weather. No raw material / Other than souls." These souls are an elite group of some two million "DOERS & MOVERS"—especially writers, scientists, and musicians—whose avatars labor toward the earthly Paradise. The bats "clone," "mine," and mix these souls in their effort to create a race with the highest possible spiritual "density" (or "Jewishness"). To date, the R/Lab's finest accomplishment has been the creation of "THE 5" (the V in "V work" is the Roman numeral as well as the short form of the French "vie"), notably dense products who, "like those thirty-six Just / Men of the Jews," return to Earth to "PURSUE THEIR LEADERSHIP / UNDER VARIOUS GUISES." While the 00 and their assistants tinker,

toil, and scheme in the R/Lab, the shades in the nine stages, that "GREAT
DULL / BUREAUCRACY OF PATRONS," pass their "time" fretting over the lives
of the 3.5 billion non-Lab souls whose effect on history is negligible.

Much goes on outside Mirabell's ken. He knows little of certain "OTHER
SYSTEMS / & THE SUNS & THE GODS OF EACH   THESE ARE THE PAN-
THEON," to which God B himself belongs. Nor does Mirabell know much
about the white angels, of whom he stands in awe, except that they come
from the "S/O/L" or "SOURCE OF LIGHT"—the origin, we will recall, of poetic inspiration in "A Tenancy." He cannot even enlighten us about "THE
BLACK HOLES" and that terrible darkness they epitomize. Even though he
and his species seem so closely associated with antimatter, it remains an
enigma he can approach only by means of metaphor:

> HOW ELSE DESCRIBE (WITHOUT THE FORMULAS
> EVEN WE LACK) WHAT IS TO US A RIDDLE? IMAGINE
> A WORLD WITHOUT LIGHT   A LEWIS CARROLL WORLD THAT KEEPS
>   PACE
> WITH OURS   A WORLD WHERE WHITE IS BLACK   OF STILLNESS IN
>   THE PLACE
> OF SUCKING WINDS   MORTALITY? DESIRE? WE FIND NO TRACE
> . . . . .
> IS IT THE ORIGINAL? ARE WE ITS CARBON COPY?
> OR: ARE WE IN THE PRESENCE OF A BLACK TWIN P A R A D I S E

This other side of the other world might be either "A BENIGN POLICE
FORCE KEEPING WATCH ON US" or a malevolent power awaiting its chance
to destroy God B's greenhouse. The latter possibility seems the more likely,
however, in view of the caveat issued in 3.7 by "THE ELEMENTS," whom we
suspect to be the white angels and whom the simultaneous focusing of the
energies of DJ, JM, MM, WHA, and Mirabell (another group of five) invokes. Here is the last part of the Elements' address, all of it delivered in the
stanza of "The Black Swan":

> THE MATTER WHICH IS NOT WAS EVER OURS
>   TO GUARD AGAINST. ITS POWERS
> ARE MAGNETIZED BY FOREIGN BEACONS, BLACK
> HANDS TESTING THE GREENHOUSE PANE BY PANE.
> CLING TO YOUR UNION: 5   THRU THE DARK HOURS
>   WE KEEP WATCH   WE PRESS BACK.
> AT ZERO SUMMON US AGAIN.

Given his limited knowledge, then, Mirabell's view must be what he calls Ephraim's, a "SATELLITE TRUTH THAT ORBITS THE ESSENTIAL."

❭ ❭ ❭

Even such a brief summary of this sprawling volume will suggest that it poses certain problems. For one thing, to take the least troubling first, the variety of speakers and points of view, the congeries of tones and attitudes, and the sheer vivid multifariousness of it all render impossible the sleek unity characteristic of *Ephraim*. As JM complains, surely not altogether disingenuously, he finds the foreignness of the material "maddening—it's all by someone else! / In your voice, Wystan, or in Mirabell's." WHA rejoins with a magnificent defense of self-effacement in poetry:

THINK WHAT A MINOR
PART THE SELF PLAYS IN A WORK OF ART
COMPARED TO THOSE GREAT GIVENS   THE ROSEBRICK MANOR
ALL TOPIARY FORMS & METRICAL
MOAT ARIPPLE! FROM ANTHOLOGIZED
PERENNIALS TO HERB GARDEN OF CLICHES
FROM LATIN-LABELED HYBRIDS TO THE FAWN
4 LETTER FUNGI THAT ENRICH THE LAWN,
IS NOT ARCADIA TO DWELL AMONG
GREENWOOD PERSPECTIVES OF THE MOTHER TONGUE
ROOTSYSTEMS UNDERFOOT WHILE OVERHEAD
THE SUN GOD SANG & SHADES OF MEANING SPREAD
& FAR SNOWCAPPED ABSTRACTIONS GLITTERED NEAR
OR FAIRLY MELTED INTO ATMOSPHERE?

But in *Mirabell* humility leads not only to such moments of bravura as this breathtakingly reflexive passage (WHA would be the first to point out that *it* necessitated some self-effacement) but also to the most startling instances of, for example, what JM accurately calls "perfect silliness." When Merrill's customary urbanity absents itself, the poetry can sink immediately from the 00's portentous account of their work to this bathos:

Once more Maria intercedes: REMEMBER
THEY HAVE NO MANNERS   THEY WERE NEVER MEN
THEY KEEP THEIR TAILS BETWEEN THEIR LEGS LIKE PETS
WHO WEEWEED ON THE RUG   ITS ALMOST TOUCHING
Weewee'd on the rug? DESTROYED A WORLD

Giggles break from us, we try to stifle
As in the dormitory after dark.

And here is an exchange between DJ and WHA that comes on the heels of
some moving reflections by Mirabell on his metamorphosis:

Is that you, Marius? COME & GONE MY DEAR
PLATO SAYS ATHENS WAS AT BEST HALF QUEER
What's Plato *like*? O YOU KNOW   TATTLETALE GRAY
NIGHTGOWN OFF ONE SHOULDER   DECLASSEE,
TO QUOTE MM   A GAS, TO QUOTE CK

Such vagaries in mood and tone are disconcerting at first, even if they help
to put the bats' often preposterous notions in perspective and to demonstrate that behind this poem there is a whole complex sensibility at work.[3]
    Mirabell's diversity derives also from the bats' eldritch version of "sci-
ence," a jumble of "MYTH & LEGEND, FACT & LANGUAGE." WHA, more tolerant by nature than JM, attributes this gallimaufry to "URANIA," the recurrently young epic muse of astronomy, now "BABBLING ON THE THRESHOLD
OF / OUR NEW ATOMIC AGE," and from the beginning he finds it enchanting.
At first JM won't have any of it, and he responds to his friend's praise with
inspired invective:

Dear Wystan, VERY BEAUTIFUL all this
Warmed-up Milton, Dante, Genesis?
This great tradition that has come to grief
In volumes by Blavatsky and Gurdjieff?
Von and Torro in their Star Trek capes,
Atlantis, UFOs, God's chosen apes—?
Nobody can transfigure junk like that
Without first turning down the rheostat
To Allegory, in whose gloom the whole
Horror of Popthink fastens on the soul,
Harder to scrape off than bubblegum.

Especially toward the beginning, JM entertains "grave doubts" about his
teachers, whom he sometimes derides to their absent faces, as when he
sneers that "It's too much to be batwing angels *and* / Inside the atom, don't
you understand?" In another session, he reacts scornfully to Mirabell's insistence that flying saucers are scouts for obscure alien powers and that the bats
have verified the UFOs on their "SCREENS": "Dear 741, / That's excellent.

But *your* verification, / While you yourselves remain unverified? / You can't expect us—well, thanks anyhow." Mirabell's funny, mild retort—"CURIOUS THAT U ACCEPT THE CUP & NOT THE SAUCER"—can hardly overcome JM's skepticism. Understandably, he fears for the poetic result, the pudding the proof is in. Late in the volume Mirabell himself, implicitly comparing this bit of V work with "an immense Victorian mirror" that DJ salvaged some twenty years before from a house undergoing renovation in Stonington, acknowledges the difficulty: "OUR GREAT ORNAMENTAL & BIZARRE OBJECT HARDLY / ABLE TO BE GOT THRU THE DOOR IS IF NOT LAUGHABLE / AT THE LEAST ODD TO HOUSE."

At the least. Such a Goldbergian machinery Mirabell and the others reveal! Such cross purposes, lack of economy, and general disorderliness they give us puzzling glimpses and rickety explanations of—as though it were no accident (though it surely is) that "bat" in British English (from the Hindi *bat*) means the vernacular speech of a foreign country. Not that the arrangement they outline is simply incomprehensible or incredible; indeed, at times the universe from their point of view looks alarmingly like what we have grown wearily accustomed to in large corporations, government bureaucracies, and universities. But their system is hardly convincing science. Indeed, if tempted to think along scientific lines at all, we might think of Niels Bohr's immortal response to Wolfgang Pauli, after the latter's lecture in New York in 1958: "We are all agreed that your theory is crazy. The question which divides us is whether it is crazy enough to have a chance of being correct. My own feeling is that it is not crazy enough."[4]

And yet, if rarely so crazy as to have the ring of absolute truth, these notions are whacky enough to save JM from himself—or rather from that part of himself that seeks, with a convert's energy, hard facts and streamlined theories. It is doubtful that a poetry based on fact and theory alone would be at all interesting. Donald Sutherland's observations on science and the Romantic temperament speak to the point:

> Much is said of the "elegance" and "rigor" of [science's] demonstrations, but these qualities almost exhaust its style. Gaiety, affection, malice, or melancholy scarcely enter it, largely because Science is serious about the universe. Romanticism cannot be so, or not long. Even classicism can see the absurdity and asymmetry of taking seriously a universe which does not take you seriously. But science has inherited both the position and the tone of theology, so its companionability for Romanticism is limited. Shelley's science was mixed up with practical jokes like electrified doorknobs, with alchemy and magic—thus enlarging the stylistics of science though corrupting the purity of its intentions.[5]

This seems to me brilliant and helpful, though we must acknowledge that *Mirabell* far surpasses anything Shelley wrote in terms of eclecticism and whimsy. Here we must entertain the old Cabalist theory that "NUMERICAL VIBES . . . RESOUND IN CERTAIN LETTERS" (the word "JEW RINGS WITH THE COMBIND FORCES OF THE DECAD / & OF THE 5" because of the positions that J and E occupy in the English alphabet), the notion that Nefertiti and Akhnaton devised a huge pyramid of quartz that generated so much pyramid power that it destroyed Minoan culture and caused the eruption on Thera, and so on. This volume takes us into the garage of civilization, where all the outmoded, charming, gimcracky devices of our ancestors and our own childhood lie about among a variety of recent half-finished inventions in a baffling confusion: a centaur for a hobby horse, an old hand-sawn puzzle of an Edenic landscape, a defunct model of the atom, a pyramid . . . It is not so much that the poem augments science's stylistics as that its stylistics overwhelms its science.

In order to account more fully for this apparent shambles, this positivist's nightmare, we have to meditate on the source of its weirdly assorted information. Who "are" the bats, anyway—and what is the grounds of their authority? While they claim to live at the heart of matter and to "SPEAK FROM WITHIN THE ATOM," and thus seem part of the natural world, they also encourage DJ and JM to identify them with mind. They pride themselves on being guardians of "THE EMBERS WHICH ARE MIND"; they applaud JM's speculation that their network of suspended cities is really a metaphor for "the brain's evolving cortex"; and Mirabell tells DJ and JM that "WE / ACCUMULATE THRU YOU A KNOWLEDGE THAT MUST HENCEFORTH BE / PART OF US." Moreover, in addition to identifying themselves with subatomic forces and with the evolving mind, the bats dissolve as readily as Ephraim into other members of the cast. In fact, it is when JM wonders whether the 00 might *be* Ephraim that they tell him (as though they were thinking of Chuang Tzu and his butterfly) that "WE ARE U   YOU ARE WE   EACH OTHERS DREAM." The Elements too, defining the relationship between Mirabell and his seminar students, tell the latter that "YOUR MINDS COALESCED / TO FORM HIS: HE IS YOURS." Mirabell likes his new name because it "HAS SOMETHING / OF THE MIRACLE? THE MIRAGE? & SURELY OF THE PLUM!" But just as surely it has something of Merrill. And something of the mirror. So it is no surprise to find JM, as he mulls over Mirabell's excited reaction to being freed by the metamorphosis "TO SPECULATE," musing *sotto voce* on the etymological pun: "If only we were less free to reflect; / If diametrics of the mirror didn't / Confirm the antiface there as one's own."

No wonder then that the bats, at least in the beginning, seem to be desperately ad libbing and beg to be taught how to speak effectively (see 1.6).

No wonder that they must use metaphor, even though they claim to regard it as "VULGAR," and that they find it impossible to prove their existence by some physical token or intervention, some "GLOWING MEDAL STRUCK IN HEAVEN SAYING: TRUE." No wonder either that a voice from the 00 intertwines with JM's in a lyrical duet beginning with these ingeniously bawdy and virtually self-referential lines in 1.4:

> Is DNA, that sinuous molecule,
> The serpent in your version of the myth?
>   Asking, I feel a cool
> Forked flickering, as from my very mouth.
> YES & NO   THE ATOMS APPLE LEANS PERILOUSLY CLOSE
> Drawn by an elation in the genes . . .
> THIS ATOM GLIMPSD IS A NEARLY FATAL CONSUMMATION

The answer itself comes "as from [JM's] very mouth," because he and the bats are as inseparable as the two strands in the double helix or the two halves of the forked tongue—or, as we learn in the next volume, the two parts of the bats' equivocal reply to his question. The bats' confusions reflect—like the Victorian mirror whose appropriation they prompted—those of DJ and JM at this stage in the ascent up their spiral stair. They are teachers who teach only what their students are prepared to know. That often makes them exemplary teachers, but it also often makes them the blind leading the blind.

In other words, I think that one explanation of *Mirabell*'s unsettling, sometimes frustrating disorderliness is that the bats, as their "appearance" testifies, speak primarily for that aspect of "MIND" that we often associate with raw imagination. This volume sets down an essential part of the creative process—the part that *is* process, we might say. Mirabell applies that term to himself in 4.4, shortly after lamenting that he does not have the capacity for "FEELING" that his human contacts have:

> Bon. We will try to remember that you are not
> A person, not a peacock, not a bat;
> A devil least of all—an impulse only
> Here at the crossroads of our four affections.
> OR MAKE OF ME THE PROCESS SOMEWHERE
> OPERATING BETWEEN TREE & PULP & PAGE & POEM

Mirabell's plea puts the matter plainly, it seems to me. Precisely because he and his hotly peering peers embody a process, this volume incorporates false starts, redundancies, conflicting stories, superfluous information, and vagaries. Especially since there is no reason in the world to think that Merrill could not have redacted his material much more clearly and cleanly than he did, we must suppose that he wanted its rawness to be apparent. It is as though he meant to demonstrate in an extreme form what Schiller called those "momentary and transient extravagances which are to be found in all truly creative minds and whose longer or shorter duration distinguishes the thinking artist from the dreamer."[6]

We might think of the bats in yet another way, in terms of a scheme Merrill would know about from the reading that he was doing when completing Mirabell.[7] In *The Origin of Consciousness in the Breakdown of the Bicameral Mind,* Julian Jaynes investigates the different functions of the two hemispheres of the brain in relationship to early "bicameral" man's cognition and especially his idea of the gods. Jaynes concludes in the course of a mazy argument that what bicameral man considered human functions were located in the left hemisphere, while those functions the gods arrogated to themselves were situated in the right hemisphere. He also argues that it is likely that "residuals of these different functions at least are present in the brain organization of contemporary man." I quote his observations on the right brain's predominantly synthetic activities:

> The function of the gods was chiefly the guiding and planning of action in novel situations. The gods size up problems and organize action according to an ongoing pattern or purpose, resulting in intricate bicameral civilizations, fitting all the disparate parts together, planting times, harvest times, the sorting out of commodities, all the vast putting together of things in a grand design, and the giving of the directions to the neurological man in his verbal analytical sanctuary in the left hemisphere. We might thus predict that one residual function of the right hemisphere today would be an organizational one, that of sorting out the experiences of a civilization and fitting them together into a pattern that could "tell" the individual what to do. Perusal of various speeches of gods in the Iliad, the Old Testament, or other ancient literatures is in agreement with this. Different events, past and future, are sorted out, categorized, synthesized into a new picture, often with that ultimate synthesis of metaphor.[8]

This description, *mutatis mutandis,* comports with the didactic bats' ends and means, especially if we keep in mind Jaynes's hypotheses that the right hemisphere is not naturally verbal, that it is responsible for "dark speech," oracles, hallucinations, possessions, and other such experiences, and that it presents its "directions" in the form of "voices" interpreted by bicameral man (or more precisely, by his analytical and verbal left hemisphere, whose functions in the trilogy seem to have devolved on JM) as belonging to the gods. Even as they want to speak on behalf of logic, then, the bats represent vision. Schiller defends such "extravagances" as theirs in his letter to his friend with a costive imagination:

> It seems a bad and detrimental thing to the creative work of the mind if Reason makes too close an examination of the ideas as they come pouring in—at the very gateway, as it were. Looked at in isolation, a thought may seem very trivial or very fantastic; but it may be made important by another thought that comes after it, and, in conjunction with other thoughts that may seem equally absurd, it may turn out to form a most effective link . . . [W]here there is a creative mind, Reason—so it seems to me—relaxes its watch upon the gates, and the ideas rush in pell-mell, and only then does it look them through and examine them in a mass.— You critics . . . complain of your unfruitfulness because you reject too soon and discriminate too severely.[9]

If it is by means of the bats that the trivial and the fantastic rush in pell-mell, it is exactly the kind of precipitate discrimination and rejection that Schiller warns against that JM (who is no more Merrill than Dante the pilgrim is Dante the author) evinces early on in this volume. His impatience with all the 00's falderal would also have provoked Friedrich Schlegel, who wrote so eloquently in praise of the "large inventiveness of Romantic poetry":

> Neither such invention nor any mythology can exist without an original, inimitable, and frankly inexplicable element, which, after all the transformations, still makes it possible for the old nature and power to shine through, and with naive profundity allows a glimpse of the perverse, the crazy, or the silly. For that is the beginning of all poetry, to suspend the course and laws of logically reasoning thought and to transport us back to the fine confusion of the imagination, the original chaos of human nature . . .[10]

So WHA might have said—*does* say, in effect—to the skeptical JM. He does not bother to point out a further advantage of the bats' mode, to wit: by retaining in the poem some of the transcripts' mystifying, frustrating, fantastic elements, Merrill roots his work in the real world, if the Ouija board experience can be thought of in that way. (And after all there is no other way to think of it.)

The bats' kinship with confusion makes sense in light of their revelation in 8.3: "WE ARE MERCURY." "Mercury—of course!" JM exclaims. "How simplewitted / Never, never to have thought of it." He is thinking of their function as psychopomps, but he might also be recalling Ephraim's mercurial nature in the preceding volume. Indeed, for the alchemist, Mercury represents a pervasive, volatile, creative force virtually identical with that which is called the "current" in *Ephraim.* Jung tells us that "When the alchemist speaks of Mercurius, on the face of it he means quicksilver, but inwardly he means the world-creating spirit concealed or imprisoned in matter."[11] When he goes on in *Psychology and Alchemy* to observe that Mercury is, among other manifestations, "the play of colours in the *cauda pavonis* and the division into four elements," one is struck by the similarity to, say, the rhapsodic lyric in 3.6 and 3.7, where the recently transformed Mirabell and the four seminar students pool their psychic energies to summon forth the four Elements and Nature. Here is the first stanza in that set piece:

> Our peacock marks time back and forth from One
>   To Zero: a pavane
> Andante in an alley of green oaks;
> The ostinato ground we each in turn
> Strum a division soundlessly upon;
>   A prayer-wheel whose four spokes
> Flow and crumble, breathe and burn.

These lines themselves flow and crumble and attest to a protean force, as musing and music merge and tone slides off into overtone. (The sward between the oaks turns into the "ground" of the next line, while "pavane" seems almost to derive from *pavo* and the term "Andante" suggests the invisible presence here too of the visionary author of the *Paradiso.*)

The intolerance of stability is related to Mercury's other pertinent meaning. If for the alchemist he is the diversified One, for the poet and mythologist he is the archetypal thief. Thus Pound frames "The Lake Isle," his canny and playful recasting of Yeats, with an invocation that comically lowers its sights, as a ball might bounce down stairs: "O God, O Venus, O Mercury, patron of thieves." As John Armstrong has shown, Mercury's or Hermes' sponsorship of theft is one with his approval of imaginative license. Originally associated, like the bats, with stones—boundary stones—Hermes has the ability to slip through "the set divisions and boundaries on which depends the supremely geometrical institution of property" and is thus "a breaker of these anti-poetic, anti-visionary forms."[12] He or a related figure (snake, child, caduceus) figures frequently in works that explore "the central paradox of imaginative activity"—the paradox that "not only are the forms by which [the imagination] bodies forth the unknown swept into obsolescence, even as they come into being, by form-resistant and anarchic forces . . . but . . . these essentially seditious forces are themselves . . . a vital source of the form-giver's mastery and integrative strength." Just such a *"complicity with the subversive"* or *"collaboration between* [the artist's] *inherited knowledge and beings at enmity with it"* is one of the issues in *Mirabell* and in the whole of *Sandover*—as Armstrong argues it is in *The Tempest,* that play Merrill has so often referred us to, and in "La Tempesta," the painting by Giorgione that is salient in *Ephraim.*

Let me draw these strands together by recalling the mysterious figure who breaks into the Stonington house at the end of *Ephraim.* If he must be Ephraim in one sense and Time in another, he is also and therefore the alchemist's regenerative principle. By the same token, he represents "form-resistant and anarchic forces"—forces who will call themselves Mercury in *Mirabell.* "Mercury dropping," JM notes in Z's cold night, and he speaks more than he seems to know. By opening up *Ephraim* even as that volume is closing—a "form-resistant and anarchic" act that has its exact analogue in the ransacking of JM's bedroom—"the thief" anticipates the bats' characteristic function. For all their strident insistence that they "IMPLEMENT A SYSTEM / OF RULES WHICH GOVERN US & YOU" and which "NOT OBEYD WD GIVE / CHAOS A WEDGE," they oppose symmetry and closure. They are antisystematic too. But it is that subversion of a form that allows the form's subversion, its implicit, inchoate successor, to emerge and begin to take shape itself. The structure that is *Ephraim* (figured as so many poetic works are in Merrill by the house), broken into, breaks down into *Mirabell.* If the systematic tendency encloses the antisystematic in the first volume, the latter prevails in the second, though in both volumes the conflict between these two imaginative forces is central.

In short, I think that Merrill would say that Schlegel had it right: "It's equally fatal for the mind to have a system and to have none. It will simply have to decide to combine the two." [13]

To combine the two. *Mirabell*'s alleged confusion does not preclude structure altogether; JM's gradual acceptance of the bats' mode even provides one of the book's main structural elements. Although at the beginning of this second round of talks he cannot overcome a certain contemptuous doubt, he must before long admit that he has been "hooked" by the adventure and that he continues to resist chiefly "for form's sake." Perhaps he never attains, in this volume, the "FIERCE CREDULITY" that Mirabell identifies as Dante's strength, but he shakes free of an enervating skepticism and a merely willed credulity alike. By the time that WHA extracts from the bats'

history its moral—"BE TRUE TO SOMETHING   TRUE TO ANYTHING"—DJ
and JM have committed themselves again, in spite of its denizens' zaniness,
to the other world. Their promise reaffirms JM's original poetic vows, which
he told us in "A Tenancy" were taken one evening in 1946, when he

> proposed
> This bargain with—say with the source of light:
> That given a few years more
> (Seven or ten or, what seemed vast, fifteen)
> To spend in love, in a country not at war,
> I would give in return
> All I had. All? A little sun
> Rose in my throat.

Now, in response to the 00's "faith" that DJ and JM "will somewhere put /
Everything they tell to brilliant use," the two mediums "promise gravely to
give all we can" to V work. And if the earlier bargain led by way of Ephraim
(who had himself reserved his highest praise for "DEVOTION," which he
called "THE MAIN IMPETUS" and the source of "THE MOULDS OF HEAVENLY
PERFECTION") to the bats, this one leads in turn by way of the transformation of 741 to the angels themselves, "THE SOURCE OF LIGHT" and "THE
VERY POLLEN OF / THE POWER PLANT." One thinks again of that "*spiral forever / widening*" that fitfully defines the shape of the trilogy.

The change in *Mirabell* from doubt to commitment parallels other processes. For one, there is Mirabell's development, which reflects the progress
that DJ and JM make—rather as Beatrice's ever-rarer beauty mirrors Dante's
ascent in the *Paradiso*. As this book unfolds, Mirabell, who became the bats'
spokesman in the first place because of his sensitivity and social presence,
becomes more "human," if that is a possible term for a shade who turns
from a bat into a peacock. This very metamorphosis, which prepares us for
and permits his christening, signifies the development I have in mind, but
even before being given a name, Mirabell begins to use formulas less often
and figurative language correspondingly more. He "likes to signal" his metaphors "With a breezy parenthetic (m)," and before long WHA can see that
"(M) IS HIS MIDDLE NAME." That must be one reason that MM and WHA,
when asked at the end of 6 to suggest names for the peacock, offer "METHU-
SALEH" and "MEHITABEL" respectively—though there are other reasons too.
When JM worries that the poem has "so many M's already," 741 provides
this mellifluous apology for the initial:

> & NOT ACCIDENTALLY   M IS AT ONCE OUR
> METHOD & THE MIDPOINT OF OUR ALPHABET   THE SUMMIT

OF OUR RAINBOW ROOF   IN TIMBRE THE MILD MERIDIAN
BLUE OF MUSE & MUSING & MUSIC   THE HIGH HUM OF MIND

In the *Paradiso* (XVIII, 94–114), as JM remarks in *Scripts for the Pageant,* "Dante saw the letter M / Become an eagle made of ruby souls / Which sang to him." Dante makes use of another traditional interpretation of the letter in the *Purgatorio* (XXIII, 31–33), where the pilgrim encounters shades of gluttons, now hungry and emaciated:

> Parean l'occhiaie anella sanza gemme:
>   chi nel viso de li uomini legge "omo"
>   ben avria quivi conosciuta l'emme.

The sockets of their eyes seemed rings without gems: he who reads OMO in the face of man would there surely have recognized the M.

The allusion is to the belief that the human face, with its eyes as o's and its nose and eye sockets as an uncial M, spells "omo"—that is, "homo."[14] Merrill does not refer to this passage, but the emblem—the OO combined with the M for Man—suggests the dramatic situation of this volume.

In any case, metaphor gradually supersedes number, and even as we move from 0 to 9, we move (as we moved in *Ephraim* toward "Zero") toward 0, at which point the angels manifest themselves and rhetoric replaces formula altogether. As though to highlight the growing insignificance of number for his students, Mirabell numbers the last ten "lessons" (in 7.8 through 9.9) backward, in counterpoint to the sections. A countdown to the angels' entrance, this numbering also amounts to an indication of Mirabell's "encroaching obsolescence." At the same time, it coincides with the "STRIPPING PROCESS," in which all four students but especially the otherworldly contingent divest themselves of selves, and a certain "RECUPERATIVE" process, which has its parallel in the physical world in the aftermath of DJ's hernia operation. Just as "THE EAGER / CONVALESCENT COUNTS THE DAYS THAT SEPARATE HIM FROM HIS / RELEASE INTO LIGHT," so JM and the other principals look forward to their emergence into a higher realm. And this "RESTORATIVE / REVIEW" in turn foreshadows the course that their preceptors would have human history take: "THERE SHALL BE NO ACCIDENT, THE SCRIBE SHALL / SUPPLANT RELIGION, & THE ENTIRE APPARATUS / DEVELOP THE WAY TO P A R A D I S E."

Or so it seems from the sanguine Mirabell's point of view; the antithetical case will be put in *Scripts for the Pageant.* Meanwhile other polarities occupy the foreground in *Mirabell.* It is not so much that Merrill wants to see the crack down the center of things as that he cannot overlook it. Early in these talks he pleads with the 00, whose designation itself is a doubling and who persist in speaking in apparently contradictory ways, to help him to imitate Prospero and "drown the double-entry book / I've kept these fifty years," to purge his work for the nonce of metaphor, myth, and pun. "You want from me / Science at last, instead of tapestry," he points out, and then helplessly exemplifies his dilemma in the following line: "Then tell round what brass tacks the old silk frays." He scolds his teachers and orders them to "Stop trying to have everything both ways." He would have the atom *be* undivided (which is the etymological sense of the term), but he cannot shake the old feeling that "anything worth having's had both ways." His earliest significant experience, after all, which gave rise to his abiding subject, was that of a broken home, a splitting of the so-called nuclear family. The bats' revelations can only confirm his suspicion in 5.3 that division is the origin (and perhaps the end) of the world as we know it:

Eden tells a parable of fission,
Lost world and broken home, the bitten apple
Stripped of its seven veils, nakedness left
With no choice but to sin and multiply.
From then on, genealogical chain reactions
Ape the real thing. Pair by recurrent pair
Behind the waterfall, one dark, one fair,
Siblings pitted each against the other
—Shem and Shaun, Rebekah's twins, whichever
Brother chafes within the Iron Mask—
Enact the deep capacities for good
And evil in the atom.

We live in "One nature dual to the end," and if "THE ATOM IS THE KEY" that is partly because it is divided against itself, because it contains both the "plus" and the "minus" that Sergei and Joanna embodied in *Ephraim*. Those forces take many different forms here, ranging from "ADAM & EVE," who are explicitly "IMAGES / FOR DEVELOPMENTS IN THE VERY NATURE OF MATTER / A WORLD NEGATIVE & POSITIVE DWELLS IN THE ATOM," through matter and antimatter and the bats and the angels, to the rival gods, Biology and Chaos.

As such contraries proliferate and overlap, however, one comes to feel anew that they might be only provisional, that each pair might be different names for the same Whole, as atom and Adam (a recurrent pun) are for a microcosm of it. The atom is also the key because its structure locks nature's opposite numbers together, however unstably, as we learn in that little apocalypse in 1.4, itself a product of a union of two voices, JM's and that of one of the 00 (whose signature frames his last line, itself a concise history, a series of concentric rings rippling out from the nothing of beginning to the all that is and might be):

THIS ATOM GLIMPSD IS A NEARLY FATAL CONSUMMATION
ONE FLOATS IN CLEAR WARM WATER   THE SUN OF IT PULSES GLOWS
   Through eyelids, a veined Rose
A MUSIC OF THE 4 COLORS   TO FLOAT LAPT BY COOL GREEN
   Sun yellow, aquamarine,
   Cradle of pure repose
& OF INTENSE FISSIONABLE ENERGIES BLACK & WHITE
WHICH EITHER JOIN & CREATE OR SEPARATE & DESTROY
   Day and night, day and night
O IT IS SPERM EGG & CELL THE EARTH & PARADISE O

Science and poetry (or myth), which JM often pits against each other, come to seem inseparable. For Dante, "DREAM, FACT & LANGUAGE WERE ONE," and so they sometimes are for JM, almost in spite of himself. His meditation on the possibility of poems of science generates this winsome subatomic pastoral, with its pun in the penultimate line:

               The day will come . . .
The day has never gone. Proton and Neutron
Under a plane tree by the stream repeat
Their eclogue, orbited by twinkling flocks.
And on the dimmest shore of consciousness
Polypeptides—in primeval thrall
To what new moon I wonder—rise and fall.

He ingeniously affirms the union at bottom of these two universal undertakings at the outset of each Book, where the first sound repeats, in one language or another, that Book's number. Just as 0 begins "Oh very well then," Book 1 echoes its number in French (and then English): "UNHEEDFULL ONE." Book 3's opening phrase, "Trials and tremors," draws on Greek and the reader's choice of several other languages, 4's "Fear" on German, 5's "Go" on Japanese, 6's "She stood" on Russian, 7's "CHILDREN" on Chinese, 9's "NO VEIL" on Italian and Portuguese. Books 2 and 8 ring changes on the device, the one beginning with the second letter of the Hebrew alphabet (sometimes used in place of the number) in "Bethinking," the other with "8."

Now fused, now confused, Merrill's facts and fictions seem less and less extricable—which should not surprise us, if only because history teaches that the one may change into the other, as the caterpillar changes into the butterfly, or 741 the bat into Mirabell the peacock. In WHA's joyful pronouncement, "THE ELDER FACTS IN LIVERY OF FABLE / HAVE JOINED THE DANCE FOR FACT IS IS IS FABLE: / THIS IS OUR GIFT FROM MIRABELL MY DEARS." It is as though fable were the afterlife that any good fact could look forward to. In any case, the truth that both fact and fable point to, this poem implies, is a fundamental unity. If at times Merrill's conjunction of science and poetry resembles a double helix less than a hippogriff or a wyvern, he has no honest alternative. As Randall Jarrell once pointed out, "as everyone must realize, it is possible to tell part of the truth about the world in terms that are false, limited, and fantastic—else how should we have told it?"[15]

The identification of fact as fable is just one aspect of a radical paradox, the intuition of which unifies this volume. If in spite of the different progressions it traces *Mirabell* lacks structural elegance, as Robert Morse complains in 8.8, it nonetheless has a center everywhere evident, a sense of the "nuclear Yang and Yin," of unity in duality. "Good? Evil? Is it all the same?" JM wonders. Certainly the bats seem to be both at once. Although Mirabell often takes pains to distinguish himself from the angels or "THE 12," one cannot but notice, since he wants everything to add up, that the digits in his own formula (741) total 12. Similarly, the digits in the bats' sacred number 14 make 5, the number alluded to in the phrase "V work." Their 14 is also, by the way, especially important to numerologists who concentrate on music, among whom Bach is a favorite subject. As such numerologists have observed, if each letter is assigned numerical value according to its alphabetical place (A = 1, B = 2), the letters in BACH add up to 14—and those in J.S. Bach to 14 transposed, 41 (the number incorporated in Mirabell's original designation). Is it "NO ACCIDENT" that in Bach's last work, an organ chorale, the melody's first line has 14 notes, while the melody as a whole has 41? The bats would wholeheartedly approve the project, whose devotional title, "Vor deinen Thron," falls in with their expiatory contributions to V work.[16]

Although the 00 identify themselves with "Cain's sons" and their counterpart with "OUR UNCLE ABEL," they nonetheless do God's bidding—and we might remember that their first messenger called himself "Cabel," a name that suggests not only a firm connection between the two worlds but also a portmanteau blend of the other two names. An overt fusion of these "WARRING ELEMENTS" occurs in 9.9, when the dark powers hand over DJ and JM to the powers of light:

> It's the hour
> When Hell (a syllable identified
> In childhood as the German word for *bright*

> —So that my father's cheerful "Go to Hell",
> Long unheard, and Vaughan's unbeatable
> "They are all gone into a world of light"
> Come, even now at times, to the same thing)—
> The hour when Hell shall render what it owes.

The last line anticipates JM's very last words in *Mirabell*, uttered when "the hour" has passed and "the given / Moment comes to render what we owe." The varied iteration hints that "Hell," in either one or both of the senses, and "we" are interchangeable, so that at this juncture the relationship between the powers of dark and light merges with that between this world and the other one. (JM's final two words, "we owe," which put a *we* on either side of the ambivalent *o*, polish the tip of this point.)

Science and poetry, darkness and brightness, this world and the other one—to these provisional unions we must add another, perhaps the most significant in this volume: that between mind and nature. The first of the bats to make contact with DJ and JM implores them in 1 to "RAISE A SONG TO OUR REAL ORDER   MYND AND NATURE WEDDED," and in 7.3 JM counters some teasing from MM and WHA by arguing that Nature is "Mind's equal. Not a slave / But mother, sister, bride. I think we're meant / To save that marriage." To the extent that he accepts these charges, Merrill puts himself squarely in the Romantic tradition as M. H. Abrams defines it in *Natural Supernaturalism*, for as Abrams vigorously demonstrates, one of the most common and richest metaphors for the Romantic writers is precisely the marriage of mind and nature. This metaphor shows up in vivid form as early as Bacon's *Great Instauration*, which its author considered a "bridal song": "The explanation of which things, and of the true relation between the nature of things and the nature of the mind, is as the strewing and decoration of the bridal chamber of the mind and the universe, the divine goodness assisting, out of which marriage let us hope (and be this the prayer of the bridal song) there may spring helps to man, and a line and race of inventions that may in some degree subdue and overcome the necessities and miseries of humanity."[17] Among later thinkers who adapted the metaphor were Novalis ("the higher philosophy is concerned with the marriage of Nature and Mind"), Hölderlin, Schelling, Coleridge, and Wordsworth ("the discerning intellect of Man, / When wedded to this godly universe / . . . shall find these [versions of Paradise] / A simple produce of the common day"). For these writers and others this marriage metaphor, itself modeled on the Christian metaphor of the marriage of Christ and the soul, is the central trope in an attempt "radically to recast, into terms appropriate to the historical and intellectual circumstances of their own age, the Christian pattern of the fall, the redemption, and the emergence of a new earth which will constitute a restored paradise." Characteristically, a new mythology of this sort will in one way or another try "to naturalize the supernatural and to humanize the divine"—as the translation of Christ and the soul into mind and nature attests.[18]

How exactly does Merrill, in *Mirabell,* understand the relationship between these two forces? In two ways, I think—ways that influence each other but that in their most distinct forms correspond loosely to his alternate leanings to dualism and to monism. On the one hand, mind and nature are originally separate and at odds (aggressor and victim respectively), and although the union of the two must be encouraged, it cannot be assured—or can only be posited at some distant point in the future, when Paradise will have been established. Meanwhile, along with the artist and the other scientists, "THE BIOLOGIST SEEKS THE FRUITFUL UNION" of forces inimical to each other. "MAN," the most apparent vehicle of mind on Earth, "UNKNOWINGLY SAVAGES THE NATURE AROUND HIM / & NATURE RETALIATES BY REPEATING MAN AS IN / A DISTORTING MIRROR." When "THE PHYSICIST IS DRAWN IF UNWITTINGLY TO / FIRE   EXTINCTION," Nature defends herself by urging humanity to overpopulation and lulling us into lassitude, to say nothing of calling into action "TIDAL WAVE & VOLCANO." Thus the bats in their prime, the nuclear physicists divorced from the Earth in their "LATTICE CITIES" until Mother Nature pulled them down, strikingly prefigure the Modern Man whom Lewis Thomas conjures at the beginning of *Lives of a Cell*—a book we know Merrill was reading at the time he wrote this volume: "We are told that the trouble with Modern Man is that he has been trying to detach himself from nature. He sits in the topmost piers of polymer, glass, and steel, dangling his pulsing legs, surveying at a distance the writhing life of the planet. In this scenario, Man comes on as a stupendous lethal force, and the earth is pictured as something delicate."[19]

On the other hand—and this attitude prevails—Merrill thinks of mind and nature as already united, although uneasily—"FRIENDLY RIVALS," as the fallen, wiser bats now think of themselves and Nature. One difficulty with the other point of view, in Thomas's words, is that "it is illusion to think that there is anything fragile about the life of the earth":

> We are the delicate part, transient and vulnerable as cilia. Nor is it a new thing for man to invent an existence that he imagines to be above the rest of life . . . [But] man is embedded in nature.
>   The biologic science of recent years has been making this a more urgent fact of life. The new, hard problem will be to cope with the dawning, intensifying realization of just how interlocked we are.

If that is indeed the problem, a first step toward solving it might be to contribute to the realization. So Thomas implies, anyway, as he proceeds to offer examples of this interlocking. He notes, for instance, that "a good case can be made for our nonexistence as entities," since our very cells are "shared, rented, occupied" by mitochondria, centrioles, basal bodies, and "probably a good many other more obscure tiny beings . . . as foreign, and as essential, as aphids in anthills." This passage (or Thomas's chapter on "Organelles as Organisms") might well be in JM's mind early on, when he recalls his dispirited reflections on all the "bits" of information that his study had yielded:

> I lolled about one winter afternoon
> In Stonington—rather, a whole precarious
> Vocabulary of each different cell,
> Enzyme, ion, what not, millionfold
> (Down to the last bacterial organelle)
> Particles that "show a tendency"
> To form the person and the moods of me,
> Lolled about. We were not feeling well.

Still thinking about man's being "embedded in nature," or its being embedded in us, Thomas tells us how one night, driving through the New England countryside, he was wondering what metaphor would best serve to describe Earth, with its complex interdependencies. "Then, satisfactorily for that moment, it came to me: it is *most* like a single cell." In 6.4 the bats base one of their lectures on the same metaphor: "THE WHOLE GREENHOUSE / IS BUT A CELL, COMPLEX YET MANAGEABLE   ALL MATTER / THERE4 IS PART OF THAT CELL."

Nor can we understand the "CELL" or "GREENHOUSE" apart from mind. On the contrary, mind pervades it, most notably in the form of God Biology himself, whose very name brings together natural and mental processes. Although Mirabell sometimes speaks of God B as though he were transcendent, he also interprets things in terms more Hegelian and Spinozan, as when he announces that "GOD B IS NOT / ONLY HISTORY BUT EARTH ITSELF   HE IS THE GREENHOUSE." The archangel Michael, in this book's concluding communication, defines this immanent and evolving figure more closely: "GOD IS THE ACCUMULATED INTELLIGENCE IN CELLS SINCE THE DEATH OF THE FIRST DISTANT CELL." Such dicta suggest that Merrill has philosophical affinities not only with the German Idealists and the English Romantics but also with recent propounders of emergent evolution—on the one hand with Jung, as we have seen earlier, and on the other hand with Whitehead, in whose formulation "the ultimate metaphysical ground" is "the creative advance into novelty."[20] More recently we have the polymath Gregory Bateson, whose *Mind and Nature: A Necessary Unity* I have excerpted in the epigraph at the start of this chapter, and David Bohm, the British theoretical physicist, who has argued powerfully that nature and mind make a whole, that "the explicate and manifest order of consciousness is not ultimately distinct from that [explicate order] of matter in general."[21] In Bohm's view, the scientific underpinnings of which he explains in great detail, "*what is* is movement," an "enfolding-unfolding universe" in which "the actual *structure, function,* and *activity* of thought is in the implicate order." The corollary is that it would be "wrong to suppose, for example, that each human being is an independent actuality who interacts with other human beings and with nature. Rather, all these are projections of a single totality."[22] In *Scripts for the Pageant* God B and Nature will often appear as distinct coevals—as they do now and then in *Mirabell,* as when he seems to JM to play the Sultan to her Scheherazade—but for the most part here God B seems virtually one with the evolving universe, mind working itself out through nature and vice versa.

Analogues to those interlocked forces inform Merrill's basic dramatic situation itself, since both the individuals in each of the main pairs of speakers and the two pairs themselves complement and require one another much as mind and nature do. Take the two shades. Borrowing a phrase from Spenser, Merrill describes WHA and MM as "Father of forms and matter-of-fact mother," and just as WHA is always off to interview Plato, so MM devotes herself to gardening. In a homologous relationship, while JM's work with "numbers" associates him with form and mind, DJ, the psychic one, is "THE SHAPING HAND OF NATURE." "YOU DJ ARE NATURE," we hear on another day. "WE NEED YOU AS WE DO JMS / MIND & WORDS." At the same time, the other world is related more closely to mind and this one, inevitably, to nature. Here the interlocking takes the negative form of the bats' fall back to Earth, caused by what JM elsewhere alludes to as Mother Nature's "clinging vines," after their effort to suspend their cities above the planet.

The marriage of mind and nature is important to Merrill partly because it affords him the means to think about human evolution and the creation of Paradise on Earth. It also gives him a vocabulary with which to reconcile, however tentatively, the conflicting claims of the physical world and the poetic world. He has always had a healthy fear that his own skein of "LATTICE CITIES" might lose contact with the actual world, that his pursuit of his highly refined art would end in a divorce from life, and the trilogy can only aggravate that fear. "'You're climbing, do you know how high?'" asks Robert Morse in 8.8 after casting a cold eye over the *Mirabell* transcript. "'*Don't look down,'*" he advises. To undertake to write about these bats is to become a little batty, to invite disaster by offending Nature. If poetry draws the poet into the actual world in search of experience, it also drives him back into himself so that he can shape that experience. There are those who enjoy life and those who use it, and the poet—or so it often seems to JM—fits better in the latter category. A part of him—the part DJ speaks on behalf of here in 6.7—vaguely regrets the alienation:

> Each day it grows more fascinating, more . . .
> I don't know. Isn't it like a door
> Shutting us off from living? I've no zest
> For anything else, can't even watch TV.
> This town's full of good friends we hardly see.
> What do you feel? Will that door readmit
> Us to the world? Will we still care for it?

JM's justification of their enterprise must also admit the dilemma: "Art— / The tale that all but shapes itself—survives / By feeding on its personages' lives. / The stripping process, sort of. What to say? / Our lives led *to* this. It's the price we pay." DJ's hernia represents that price in its own way: his injury was caused years before by hauling home and up the stairs of the Stonington house the huge, ornate mirror that Mirabell compares to the transcripts behind this volume.

Merrill resumes the issue in 7.6, a highly wrought, wildly associative lyric in double quatrain stanzas, riddled with Yeatsian vacillations, that ultimately posits the union of mind and nature. The poem begins with the thought that he might, in this free hour, while "half sober," write to his mother, or call her—but then . . .

> Let, instead, the stardeck's otherworldly light
> Call me. Up there's the stratosphere
> Of (how to put it) Mind, that battiness
> Chose over some maternal Nature's less
> Perfectly imagined realm down here . . .

Having set out so clearly the conflicting claims of Mind and Nature, the other world and this one, art and life, and having repeated his tentative election of the one, Merrill complicates the issue in the second stanza:

>   Sent spinning by her kiss,
> Did we *choose* artifice,
> The crust, the mirror meal? Could we devise no better

Than that the argent grub consume us?
That, safe here, where security is vain,
We be delivered from her clinging vine
And the forgiving smother of her humus?

Even as "The crust" recalls the "SHINING CRUST" of a world that the bats built, it looks forward to "the mirror meal," and both phrases imply that while art might image the perfect realm, the artistic life is itself far from satisfactory. The reevaluation of the options continues in the following sentence, where a wonderful pun serves as a turning point. No sooner does "the mirror meal" become "the argent grub" than the seemingly delectable but illusory "grub" becomes itself a devouring worm. What is the point, this stanza asks, in escaping an ordinary, uninspired, unaspiring life if one is going to lose oneself in sterile artifice?

As JM's imagination removes him anew from the natural world, *à la* Yeats, that world becomes more attractive—and less easily distinguished from the poetic one. "Once out of nature," rather like Dante in the *Paradiso*, XXVII, he envisions Earth as though from a satellite, with the different climatic zones alternating "by 'turns' as in a music hall":

So distanced, it could be the way
Of our own world, as the fops in Congreve knew
With their strut and plumage, ah! mightn't Mirabell do
For our peacock's name?—and flowery word play

Based on her wee wild orchid in bumblebee
Motley, her anthology pieces that led
Back through such juicy red
Volumes to seed. All this is eminently me . . .

"[O]ur own world": the Ouija world? the world of the trilogy? DJ and JM's social world? But surely Merrill means to keep these different possibilities revolving, to let them blur into one another. He confounds distinctions between artifice and nature with his own examples of "flowery word play." In addition to singling out as representative of her work one of Nature's colorful puns, the bumblebee orchid, he lets us see through the word "anthology" its "seed" in the Greek term meaning a gathering of flowers (and at the same time traces the way in which famous literary works, like Yeats's "Sailing to Byzantium" and Congreve's play, give rise to new ones). Given such connections, such tangled roots, among which there is also that of "orchid," how can one separate the natural and the artificial worlds? "All this is eminently me," he admits—but "All this" must refer equally to Congreve's wit and to Nature's.

True, he is quick to distinguish his technique from Nature's in at least one regard, since after all "the faint alarm pre-set / In 'Strato's fear of mind'" does not go off upon "Impulses pure as those of the snowflake pun / She utters when *her* mood is zero." Her impulses, in other words, are more innocent than such calculated devices as that double entendre involving Strato in the opening stanza. No sooner has he admired Nature's purity, however, than he allows that her act has "taken [him] in no more than half." Mind still makes its claims on him, especially as he grows older:

> The somber
> Fact is, I remain, like any atom,
> Two-minded. Inklings of autumn
> Awaken a deep voice within the brain's right chamber
> Asking her: "What have you done with
> My books, my watch and compass, my slide rule?
> Will you, whom I married once for real,
> Take back your maiden name now, Mrs. Myth?"

These hard lines must owe something to Julian Jaynes's hypotheses, mentioned earlier, that the gods spoke to bicameral man through the brain's right hemisphere and that in rare circumstances their voices, "vestiges of the ancient divinities," can still be heard there. This particular "deep voice," in view of the peevish dismay expressed at Nature's disregard of the tools of civilization, and in view of the relationship implied, might as well be that of God B himself. As Mirabell has told the class a few pages earlier, whereas God B wants humanity to labor toward "PEACE & PARADISE," "NATURE IS A RUTHLESS FORCE AT ONCE FECUND & LAZY" whose brutally simple tripartite law is "MATE PROPAGATE / & DIE." Having once more mislaid God B's indispensable intellectual instruments (and humanity's: "MAN WANTS IMMORTALITY & NATURE WANTS MANURE"), Nature incurs the patronizing irony of the last two lines in the extract quoted above. When God B speaks *in propria persona* in *Scripts for the Pageant*, he will lack the sort of humor that here reminds her of her original status (in *Ephraim* the since exalted "Mrs. Myth" was known as Mrs. [Rosamund] Smith) and of the airs she has put on.

Her answer is directed as much to JM as to this "voice" partly because the voice is within and in some sense a part of him—as indeed she herself is, as "The mind's ear" (another phrase from Jaynes) intimates:[23]

> She answers with a tug of the old magnet,
> Making me look up from where I sit.

Cocked to those infinite
Spangled thinnesses whose weave gosling and cygnet
Have learned already in the shell,
The mind's ear registers her vocalise.
Flagstad herself had no such notes as these
Of lashing hail and rapturous farewell.

Like the preceding, half-serious invitation to a separation, itself prompted by thoughts of the autumnal years and increasing reliance upon the mental, the punning echo of Catullus's elegiac phrase in the last line helps to prepare for this set piece's conclusion, with its rapprochement. In the last stanza Nature fades into JM's own mother, and it seems at first that she will not or cannot answer the telephone call that he ("Two-minded" as always) has finally put through. The night sky's skeins of stars and nebulas, its "Spangled thinnesses" (which are hers, for she *is* Mother Nature, not just Mother Earth), turn in the mirror, in his mind, into their opposite or negative form, while her "vocalise" degenerates into the staticky emptiness between the telephone's rings:

I've dialed. A humming black dust eats the mirror,
Stardust in negative, between the rings.
Ah God, a thousand things
Could have happened, where is she, my heart contracts in terror
—But no, she answers. And a spate
Of what she still calls news (weddings and weather)
Sweeps me away, bemused, glad to be with her,
Communing where we don't communicate.

So in the end, in spite of his resistance to her objectives and his own dedication to the goals of the bats and God B, Nature remains JM's muse, his own "mother, sister, bride." Although we have learned early on that his alleged "affinities with air" imply an attraction to "MIND & ABSTRACTION   THE REGION / OF STARRY THOUGHT COOLER THAN SWIFTER THAN LIGHTER THAN EARTH," the nature of his mind is such that he cannot abstract himself from the physical world. It is within him, as well as in the drift of the constellations and the behavior of young birds (in their minds? their natures?), that the marriage manifests itself—and it is "NO ACCIDENT" that her news is of "weddings and weather." If *Mirabell* is the "SONG" raised to "OUR REAL ORDER   MYND & NATURE WEDDED," this set piece epitomizes the epithalamion.

❯   ❯   ❯

I have referred to the marriage of mind and nature as the most significant union in *Mirabell,* but I have also called all such unions in this volume provisional, because each is always breaking up into its components. Merrill remains as much a dualist as a monist; he will not rest in either position. As Mirabell says of man, in a passage that *Scripts for the Pageant* amplifies on, he "IS NOT CLONED WITH AN ACCEPTING DENSITY   THEREIN / HIS POWER: HE RESISTS." These are *Books of Number,* and the two chief numbers are 1 and 2, which keep turning impatiently into each other. So perhaps I should say that this volume's basic union—and duel—is between 1 and 2, which combine in different ways at crucial points. While the 00 refer to themselves by one digit doubled, the angels are "THE 12." DJ and JM meet Mirabell in 2.1, and the relationship culminates (and for the purposes of this volume, it ends) on the day of the "picnic" that Mirabell arranges between their last two retronumbered sessions, 2 and 1. This volume's host signs off at the end of that day with "Twelve last words like dry tears / Upon the page," and the one line with his twelve words is double-edged, "kiss / And promise, threat and jeu d'esprit: / I WILL BE THE WOUNDED BLACK HOUND OF HEAVEN AT YR DOOR." Then there is Michael's coda, an overture to the next volume:

> I LEAVE NOW AS THE LIGHT LEAVES AND WIND MY PATH OVER ITS
> TRACK ON EARTH   I AM A GUARDIAN OF THE LIGHT
> LEAVE THIS FIRST OF THE FIRST TWO MEETINGS IN A CYCLE OF
> TWINNED MEETINGS IN A CYCLE OF TWELVE MOONS
> LOOK! LOOK INTO THE RED EYE OF YOUR GOD!

As the phrase "TWELVE MOONS" strikes that note one last time, and as the two O's in the redoubling "LOOK" focus on the setting sun, the 00 themselves resolve into that single O that is God's eye—the fiery color of which nonetheless reminds us of Mirabell's and confirms that particular bond. God is the jewel in the bezel Bob has turned out to be.

It is a sprawling, ungainly volume, it's true, as complex as a cell—or a symphony, with every little system, every sonnet and centriole, villanelle and organelle contributing its notes to the difficult whole. Yet in such moments it is as round as Giotto's O.

chapter seven

THE NAMES OF GOD
Scripts for the Pageant and "Coda: The Higher Keys"

As when the scribe of some ornate
Bismillah *("in the name of Allah")* sees
No doctrine bolder than calligraphy's . . .

At heart the basis of the universe must be as simple as the difference symbolized by 1 and −1, or by yes and no, or (more prosaically) by true and false. The fundamental building blocks of the whole creation must have this simple binary form. Nothing simpler has properties. Only the difference symbolized by 1 and −1, by one and not one, or point and no point, is sufficiently simple to be creatable, but rich enough when sufficiently catenated (as in mathematics and logic) to lead to properties. At root the universe is a dust of binary forms. That is the dust of spacetime.

P. W. Atkins, *The Creation*

Death is the *side of life* that is turned away from us and not illuminated. We must try to achieve the greatest possible consciousness of our existence, which is at home in *both these unlimited realms,* and *inexhaustibly nourished by both.* The true form of life extends through *both* regions, the blood of the mightiest circulation pulses through *both:* there *is neither a this-world nor an other-world, but only the great unity,* in which the "angels," those beings who surpass us, are at home.

Rilke to Witold Hulewicz (trans. Stephen Mitchell)

The poet and the artist who raise the dead cannot be quite trusted, perhaps; they have filled the past with invention and inserted the ardent fictions of their intellect into the ranks of the dead; but we are often drawn even more strongly to these than to any real bony ancestor. The best part of dying, Sokrates thought, would be "to get down there and question the man who led the great army to Troy, or Odysseus, or Sisyphos, or ten thousand others one could name, men and women" (*Apology* 41); true and false, they are waiting for us. The dead are our biggest resource, kept alive by our curiosity and *pothos,* filling our books and paintings and universities and minds. They know what we want to know and cannot discover without them; they made us what we are today and we hope to learn if they are satisfied. In the meantime we keep a place for them, a chair and a book, as a memorial in sun and rain to evoke the past and make solemn the longing of the living for the one we cannot see now.

Emily Vermeule, *Aspects of Death in Early Greek Art and Poetry*

IN *SCRIPTS FOR THE PAGEANT* new students arrive and even more imposing instructors take over at Sandover—the name, we discover, of this little academy founded by God B and his complex twin, Nature/Psyche/

Chaos. ("Sandover" might even be a corruption, we are told, of "Santofior," one of Nature's aliases in *Ephraim*.) From time to time the new teachers, the angels themselves, correct and supplement Mirabell's notions of things. His obsessively applied 12:88 ratio is a "FAULTY READ-OUT," and the Muses, when they appear, remind one less of his "GOLDEN / CONTAINERS" than of petulant dancing girls haled for the visitors' sake into the sheik's tent. As for UFOs, which Mirabell worried might be scouts for alien powers, they are the angels' "TEASPOONS TESTING THE SOUPY ATMOSPHERE." Unlike their chiropteran counterparts, the angels seem infallible in what they know, but they do not know all. "MUCH HERE IS PURE & SIMPLE MYSTERY," one of the new, highly placed sources tells us—and at the same time tells us, although we do not realize it until we get to the "Coda," how some of that "MYSTERY" resolves itself.

Meanwhile, the angels: they turn out to be four brothers, one for each of the elements, but then each of them has three natures, so poor, chagrined Mirabell was not entirely wrong about "THE 12." No one who has followed Merrill's catoptrics this far will be surprised to find that these four, introduced one by one in successive orientation sessions, divide into pairs. Thus we have Michael, "the Angel of Light," and Gabriel, "the Angel of Fire and Death," coupled by a tension born of their equally powerful natures, which call up Vishnu and Shiva respectively. "AIRY MICHAEL," God B's favorite, is the most extroverted and charitable of the four, and it appears at first that he runs this lavish show. Patient, warm, gentle, blessed with a sense of humor, he radiates sublime intelligence unalloyed with mere personality. A stunned WHA describes his entrance:

> WE LOOKED UP:
> A GREAT ORIGINAL IDEA   A TALL
> MELTING SHINING MOBILE PARIAN SHEER
> CUMULUS MODELED BY SUN TO HUMAN LIKENESS.
> IN SUCH A PRESENCE WHO COULD EXERCISE
> THE RIGHTS OF CURIOSITY: HAIR? EYES?
> O IT WAS A FACE MY DEARS OF CALM
> INQUIRING FEATURE   FACE OF THE IDEAL
> PARENT CONFESSOR LOVER READER FRIEND
> & MORE, A MONUMENT TO CIVILIZED
> IMAGINATION . . .

The poet among the angels, Michael shows a suitable fondness for rhyming the word "DAY" (and "JOUR"). His moods run mainly from joviality through playful indulgence. (He teases WHA about the latter's comment on angelic enjambment: "TOO MODERN? EVEN BAD? . . . RUNOVER, HMM. THAT'S A WHOLE NEW DIMENSION.") But he can also speak with grave eloquence, as when he addresses Gabriel as "RED SOLEMN THOUGHT, O DECIMATOR, / CHAOS FROZEN INTO ORDER, WINTER."

The volatile Gabriel perhaps strikes us as more human, which is both fitting and paradoxical, since he is "YOUR BLOOD, YOUR LIFE, AND YES / (Pause, then a volley of cold fire) YOUR DEATH." Evidently kind enough by nature—legend has it that Gabriel diverted the stream to free St. Theodore's mother, we learned when the archangel appeared in a cameo role in section X of *Ephraim*—he must see to both the individuals and the species who have outlived their usefulness, and his dreadful responsibility has bred in him a cynicism that he masks with shyness. He is God B's "SENIOR SON"—Justice, or perhaps Necessity, to the sunny Grace of Michael, who characteristically softens Gabriel's features: "THE SHY BROTHER IS, LIKE HIS FATHER GOD, BENEVOLENT. / BOTH SHIELD THE FLAME OF HUMAN LIFE & WHEN WASTED TALENT / MAKES THE FLAME GUTTER, GOD TURNS AWAY HIS FACE. THE SHY ONE / PUFFS JUST ONCE."[1] If Michael is "A GREAT ORIGINAL IDEA," Gabriel's special province is thought, and thought, MM dialectically observes, destroys ideas. But whether Michael or Gabriel ranks higher remains an unresolved issue—and is, finally, a false one.

Emmanuel (or Elias) and Raphael (or Elijah), the angels of the other two elements, water and earth respectively, are even more closely related, as the similarity between their alternative names suggests. Neither has the distinctiveness or the force of Michael or Gabriel, though each speaks and provides occasions for some of this volume's finest "word-painting." Here is MM on Emmanuel's first appearance:

> FIRST MICHAEL IN HIS GLORY
> THEN HE TURNED & A SHAFT! A RAINBOW SPOKE
> & AS WE KNELT IN WONDER MELTED INTO
> WHITE CLOUD WHICH NEXT GREW SOLID   How baroque!
> A GIANT ALL HOAR & SPIKY ICE   A HISS
> OF HAIL & OUR BLUE ROBES CLUNG WETLY TO US!
> ELIAS ROSE IN A TALL DAZZLING VAPOR
> & MICHAEL'S LAUGHTER MADE ALL HEAVEN QUAKE

The visionary grandeur and brilliance of such passages, along with the new characters introduced, distinguish the mode of *Scripts* from what JM, with a glance at the history of Greek drama, calls "the black / Fustian void of *Mirabell,* against which / At most one actor strutting in costume / Tantalized us with effects to come, / And the technician of the dark switchboard / Tone by tone tried out his rainbow chord." More practiced by now, that "technician" comes up with some of the most breathtaking inventions in recent poetry. JM can set them down the more easily, if I can put it that way, because he discards early in *Scripts* the method used in *Mirabell* and exemplified in the reports just quoted: "why need we—just because / It 'happened' that way— wait till end of scene / For Wystan and Maria's mise en scène?" Instead, he will "now and then incorporate / What David and I don't see (and they do) / Into the script," while "Italics can denote / Their contribution."

What "they" see, in this schoolroom equipped with spectacular teaching aids that project "against nothingness" vividly evanescent environments, makes one speculate on the future of holography:

> *The schoolroom stretches to a line. It breaks*
> *Cleverly into two floating poles*
> *Of color that in dark 'air' glow and pulse,*
> *Undulate and intertwine like snakes.*
> *Whatever road we travel now, this twinned*
> *Emblem lights, and is both distant guide*
> *And craft we're sealed hermetically inside,*
> *Winged as by fever through the shrieking wind.*

"ALL THINGS ARE DONE HERE IF U HAVE TECHNIQUE," MM joked in *Mirabell*. In this instance, technique permits the uncanny vehicle that transports our students to be the same hermetic art that creates it. These two aspects of the "*craft*" can no more be separated than can Mercury's serpents or this passage's import and form. The rhyme scheme, a "*twinned / Emblem*" itself, with its own fusion and fission, its coupled and split rhymes, intertwines with its subject. These quatrains gain a special resonance from WHA's later irreverent reflection on the angels' private name for God, "ABBA," which reminds him of "ONE OF JM'S FAVORITE RHYME SCHEMES"—but more of the metaphysics of Merrill's poetry, or the poetics of his philosophy, soon enough.

Scripts contrasts with *Mirabell* also in its cleaner, classical structure. At one point Plenorios, the architect of the now delapidated Temple of Artemis at Ephesus, outlines his aesthetic for DJ and JM. WHA, forced to paraphrase ideas that yield only "Broad 'visionary' movements of the cup," tells them that Artemis appeared to Plenorios in a dream, offered him her breasts, one of which represented "'PROPORTION'" and another "'SPLENDOR,'" and said that she wanted to be sheltered "'IN GRAND / & SIMPLE BEAUTY.'" Just as Merrill's own work in large part honors Mother Nature, another goddess whose "proper sphere is the earth, and specifically the uncultivated parts, forests and hills" and who is also the twin of a sun god, so his design emulates the Greek architect's.[2] It makes sense, then, both that JM gives his "Full concurrence" to the proposition that *"The House / Is Mother"* and that Gabriel designates the alphabet the "MATERIALS" for a "NEW FAITH" whose "ARCHITECTURE IS THE FLAT WHITE PRINTED PAGE." Its own splendid simplicity notwithstanding, however, Merrill's structure calls little attention to itself, hidden as it is by continual references to day-to-day life.

As in *Ephraim,* the foreground events in *Scripts* take place in about a year. Prominent among them is the composition of *Mirabell,* which goes on at the same time that JM accumulates material for *Scripts.* Early on, during the fall of what must be 1976, while JM is in Stonington, we find him at work on the second volume, quarrying "from the transcript murky blocks / Of revelation, now turning a phrase / To catch the red sunset, now up at dawn / Edging into place a paradox." By February, after he has returned from a month in Athens, "*Mirabell*—by now more Tower of Babel / Than Pyramid—groans upward, step by step," and it occurs to him "to make each Book's first word its number / In a different language." In May he flies back to Athens, where he remains (except for one trip to Samos and Ephesus in the summer and another to Venice in September) until this volume ends, sometime in October. Early in the summer, when we have gotten almost halfway through *Scripts,* he approaches the end of *Mirabell.* This last reference to that volume, occasioned by the death of an old friend, Robert Morse, characteristically entangles past with future and fact with fiction:

> Well, Robert, we'll make room. Your elegy
> Can go in *Mirabell,* Book 8, to be
> Written during the hot weeks ahead;
> It's only fiction, that you're not yet dead.

And of course it was back in 8.8 that Morse made his first and last appearance as a living person in the trilogy. An inspired device, this inclusion of the previous volume's composition among the events in this one decoys the skeptical intelligence (just as JM's dissatisfactions in *Mirabell* anticipated it) and lends an air of immediacy to *Scripts.*

But there is nothing slapdash about the book's fundamental organization. Once more taking his cue from the Ouija board, Merrill divides this volume into three parts, entitled (and beginning) "Yes," "&," and "No." The nearly equal first and third sections enclose a slightly shorter middle section (whose two set pieces, "Samos" and "The House in Athens," neatly frame its conversations with the other world). Merrill enforces this symmetry by giving "Yes" and "No" ten lessons each, while "&" has only five. To describe this structure in one way that has ramifications for the content of this volume, whose central question is whether humanity can save itself from destruction, we could say that "Yes" and "No" mirror each other. In other words, the middle section is a "bridge" that JM suspects "Can . . . be crossed both ways"—or the center of a balance in which "Yes" and "No" are the pans in equipoise. In view of the significance it invests in the image, we might even say that the poem resembles an hourglass, which gets turned over once the sand has run through the neck to one of the interchangeable bulbs. Sandover: in this context, the very name of the academy suggests inversion and reversibility. But here again metaphysics begins to creep, like the deserts JM reads about (where else but in *Time?*), into adjacent fields.

Each of the three sections turns on its set of lessons, and the sets of lessons come at nicely judged different points. In "Yes," discussions in the wake of Michael's entrance and then the introductions of the angels precede "The First Lessons," which are followed only by the brief postmortem the students customarily conduct among themselves after a seminar ends. "The Middle Lessons" in "&," in contrast, prefaced by "Samos" and assorted extracurricular shenanigans, and succeeded by some socializing and "The House in Athens," come precisely in the middle. "No" completes the pattern by turning around the arrangement in "Yes." Introduced only by a verse paragraph of stage directions, "The Last Lessons" come early and then give way to a series of postgraduate activities (including the time-honored trip "abroad" and a grand "Finale").

This balanced structure has to be considered along with the internal organizations of the three sets of lessons. Each trimester builds to what seems a high point in the penultimate lesson and then continues to a second sharply different but more truly climactic point in the last. In "Yes," for example, a festive party attended by the most distinguished shades culminates in the ninth lesson in a miniature silver jubilee (which recalls Queen Elizabeth's gala in 1977), during which the otherworldly guests get to see themselves wondrously multiplied in different colors by means of "'sense / Prisms' conferred on them by Michael" and to hear a fifth "Last Song" by Strauss (who when living composed four such songs) sung by the great soprano Kirsten Flagstad. Lesson 10 of "Yes" contrasts powerfully with this celebration; there the mediums abruptly discover WHA and MM adrift in a "*bitter-black and vast*" sea of absence, "RISING RISING INTO . . . A VOID & HOWL" we soon understand to be poor God B's own dark night of the soul. This fascinating episode appears to echo Dante's warning to the reader in the *Paradiso,* II to those who would follow him further in his voyage "beyond humanity":

O voi che siete in piccioletta barca,
　desiderosi d'ascoltar, seguiti
　dietro al mio legno che cantando varca,
tornate a riveder li vostri liti:
　non vi mettete in pelago, ché forse,
　perdendo me, rimarreste smarriti.

O you that are in your little bark, eager to hear, following behind my
ship that singing makes her way, turn back to see again your shores. Do
not commit yourselves to the open sea, for perchance, if you lost me,
you would remain astray.[3]

While WHA and MM undergo their ordeal, DJ and JM, at their board, pick
up a transmission from a "galactic radio"—an eerie ten-line message in de-
casyllabics, addressed to his brothers in the Pantheon by God B himself,
who proclaims repeatedly and enigmatically that "I AND MINE HOLD IT
BACK AND WE SURVIVE." Their experience of "THE BLACKNESS" so shocks
WHA and MM that they must be revived by Mirabell, who has "STOOD
BRAVELY BY WITH SMELLING SALTS & ST / BERNARD FLASK."

　　Similarly, in "&" the astonishing appearance in Lesson 4 of the Muses
(who perform a sort of anti-masque that parodies the festivities in "Yes," 9
and "No," 9) pales beside the entrance in Lesson 5 of the triple goddess Na-
ture/Psyche/Chaos in the second, most demure of her aspects:

Enter—in a smart white summer dress,
Ca. 1900, discreetly bustled,
Trimmed if at all with a flowering black bow;
Black ribbon round her throat; a cameo;
Gloved but hatless, almost hurrying
—At last! the chatelaine of Sandover—
A woman instantly adorable.

There follows one of the most important revelations in *Scripts*, as Psyche discloses God B's thoughts on "DUALITY" at the time of the creation. Finally,
Lesson 9 in "No" presents a glorious fête *cum* masque for which Nature
orders that the grounds at Sandover be utterly transformed:

MICHAEL, FROM YOUR BOREALIS
MAKE FOR US A SHINING PALACE!
ON THIS CLAY GROUND, EMMANUEL,
A SHIMMERING LAKE, A WISHING WELL!

NOW GREEN TREES HUNG WITH UNCUT GEM,
YOU RAPHAEL, SEE TO THEM!
AND FOR FANCY'S SAKE A CHANDELIER,
GABRIEL, HANG UP HERE & HERE!

Soon MM enters on an ecstatic unicorn, Yeats delivers an encomium, and Nature grants selected wishes out of hand. (She commands that DJ and JM never be separated, gives Ephraim back his vision, and quenches the "nuclear fire-ache" in Mirabell's eyes and installs him henceforth in her own garden.) Nothing could rival such revelry—except a visit by God B. So in Lesson 10 God B speaks directly to the mortals for the only time.

These three twin pinnacles, symmetrically situated, each set affording a grander view than the last, provide for much of the "PROPORTION" and "SPLENDOR" in the last book of the trilogy. The different locations of the lessons within the sections serve other structural ends as well. Just as the delay of the introductory lessons until late in "Yes" keeps that first climax from coming too soon after Michael's initial, awe-inspiring appearance, so the placing of the concluding lessons early in "No" separates their epiphanies from the denouement of the plot which the poem has been developing.

The plot that I have in mind involves the fortunes of those spirits whom DJ and JM knew as people. In addition to Maria Mitsotáki and Auden, these spirits now include Robert Morse and George Cotzias. Although Maria Callas, Vladimir Nabokov, Robert Lowell, and other notables also drop in shortly after their deaths, these two are the only other shades admitted to the little class. Cotzias (or Kotzias, in stricter transliteration) is the Greek-American research biologist to whom the poet's sister introduced him. Toward the end of *Mirabell* JM feared that Cotzias, who had become "Gravely ill" in the course of developing a hormone to prevent aging, might be among those "CERTAIN HIGHLY CLONED / SCIENTIST SOULS forced back from the frontier" by the overseeing powers, loath to let humanity advance too quickly. Exactly so. When JM last sees him in the hospital early in *Scripts,* Cotzias assures him that he will "Turn up" in Athens—but it is only thanks to the board that he does so. Meanwhile, owing to a high-level black bag job, his theorem for immortality, which he recklessly gave to JM, gets stolen and "FILED SAFELY" in the other world until its time has come. Like MM, who we were told in *Mirabell* would return to Earth in some vegetable form, and like WHA, who we learn early in this poem will come back in mineral form, GK spends his vacation preparing for reentry, when his energies will somehow be distributed among "18 LABS THRUOUT THE WORLD." Until then, he eagerly pursues his work ("WE'RE SETTING UP A LAB!"), joins the seminar, and, lest the world go up in flames, helps the others try to justify the dubious ways of man to the angels.

So does Robert Morse. Back in *Mirabell,* in the "elegy" touched on earlier, he foresaw the course that DJ and JM would follow. He took his leave of them on the Feast of the Assumption with a blend of impish blasphemy, coy self-deprecation, and good advice all his own:

> "Today
>
> We celebrate Maria's Himmelfahrt
> And yours. You're climbing, do you know how high?
> While tiny me, unable to take part,
>
> Waves you onward. *Don't look down.* Good-bye."

What RM, as he was shortly to become, did not foresee was that he would play a part in the ascent.

Not that he has really been "unable to take part" before. As the elegy constrained to appear in disguise discreetly attested, Morse has an intricate relationship to Merrill's poetry, a relationship that illustrates the way in which the work and the life have both fed the fire that Merrill once called "the consuming myth." An amateur pianist with a gift for wordplay as well as a penchant for the baby talk that E. F. Benson parodies in his Lucia novels, RM can be traced back to Andrew in "The Summer People"—or rather Andrew can be traced back to Morse, one of the people to whom *Water Street* was dedicated. In *Mirabell,* 8.8 JM called him "Closest of summer friends in Stonington" and gave him anew a witticism that Andrew had coined in the ballad: "'Ah lads,'" he says of the stack of transcripts that brought forth that poem, "'it's taxed / My venerable beads'" ("'Me giddy fwom / Uppercut of too much upper case'"). JM confirms this connection later in *Scripts* when he records a meeting in the other world between RM and Andrew Marvell ("I called *you* Andrew in 'The Summer People'") and perhaps implies that his friend's wit had suggested the fictional name in the first place. Morse also contributed to *Ephraim,* as Merrill hinted in 8.8 when he referred us to a poem that Auden collected in *A Certain World* under "Spoonerisms" and that Merrill included when he collected, after his friend's death, the latter's *Nineteen Poems.* That poem, "Winter Eve," concludes with lines whose elegiac overtones (though not their bawdy) harmonize with Merrill's purposes in 8.8:

> I'll hash my wands or shake a tower
> (a rug of slum? a whiskey sour?)
> water my pants in all their plots,
> slob a male hairy before I seep—
> and dropping each Id on heavy lie,

with none to sing me lullaby,
slop off to dreep, slop off to dreep.[4]

Ephraim's "figure in the mirror" (section T), naturally given to reversing things, not only uses this Morse code (coarse mode, he must have said someplace) but even borrows this excerpt's first phrase. For such reasons, one imagines, Merrill cast their brief last encounter in a dramatic terza rima reminiscent of one of Dante's meetings with some dead "master."

When RM reappears in *Scripts* on the other side of the mirror, he has lost none of his puckish wit, as his sulky response to a run-in with an overbearing Pythagoras proves: "HAVE WE A SLASH MARK? LET HIM TAKE THAT / ." He has, however, gained a certain single-mindedness, a capacity for what Ephraim (in his passionate speech in section Q) called "DEVOTION." Hence, perhaps, his close association with another new character, Uni, a sweet, hornless unicorn (a descendant of the centaurs destroyed by Mirabell's race), who virtually embodies constancy. Hence, too, after an orientation period during which he is excluded from discussions of top-secret matters, RM's emergence as a great composer to be (who will come back to Earth after MM, WHA, and GK). Thus when he joins the seminar, the class gains a musical genius, as well as a gifted scientist in the person of GK. The ghastly convenience of it all provokes Merrill to poignant musings on

> The buffeting of losses which we see
> At once, no matter how reluctantly,
>
> As gains. Gains to the work. Ill-gotten gains . . .
> Under the skull-and-crossbones, rigging strains
>
> Our craft to harbor, and salt lashings plow
> The carved smile of a mermaid on the prow.

But those losses become gains must turn back into losses, more final losses—for once their friends have returned to this world, DJ and JM can no longer establish contact with them. They cannot, that is, unless we take seriously the rendezvous they schedule with Maria for 1991—a rendezvous possible only because she is to be reborn, not "AS A TREE" after all, but as a Punjabi male who will invent, twenty-seven years later, "A POLLUTION-EATING ANTIGAS." Indeed, it is one of the trilogy's most startling revelations that Maria is "OF THE FIVE," who, we now discover, are no less than "GODS" themselves. Specifically, she is Plato, Nature's "DARLING," and "NEAREST THE ANGELS."

Someone has laid the groundwork carefully but unobtrusively. As early as *Mirabell*, 1.3, where she suddenly snatched control of the teacup from the still-intimidating bats (probably, in retrospect, because they momentarily arrogated the angels' powers to themselves), MM had about her a curious air of authority. When Mirabell held forth in 5.8 on the continuous mining of "PLATO'S POWERS" and the "GOLDEN / CONTAINERS" that he presumed the Muses to be, she kept so quiet—"eyes / Lowered while the menfolk theorize"—that DJ and JM thought she had left. Now one can see that she was biding her time, for as she asks rhetorically in "No," "HOW . . . WD YOU HAVE TAKEN IN THE TRUTH?" Throughout *Scripts* DJ and JM are subtly prepared for the disclosure. In "&" JM regrets that his "chronic shyness / Vis-à-vis 'ideas'" has kept him from seeking out Plato, and something inspires DJ to guess that "*Wystan is Plato.* Has been all along." While they debate whether to tell their friend that they have guessed his secret, WHA tries to steer them in the right direction by letting slip that he is on to something himself: MM "HAS THE (M) SPECIFIC GRAVITY / OF A CULT FIGURE   PUREST GUESSWORK   BUT / NO   I'LL PUZZLE IT OUT." (Since DJ and JM miss the point, they cannot detect the gentle irony in his later regret, provoked by reflections on Plato's "PEARLS" of wisdom: "& ME / WITH NO THREAD TO MAKE MM A CHOKER.") Such "TWINKLING CLUES," even though overlooked, justify MM's contribution to the varied refrain in "No"'s beautiful ballade, JM's "SONG OF . . . MISGIVINGS" in response to the upsetting discovery that the mortal being they loved was only a disguise: "Was anyone prepared for it? U WERE." We all were—as the ballade form, with all of *its* economies, helps to indicate. As WHA asks much earlier, "IS GOD GEORGE ELIOT?"

Dismaying as it is to DJ and JM, MM's unmasking cannot diminish their ultimate loss, especially since (except for one moment during Nature's masque in which she appears proleptically as a "chubby brown young man we've never known, / Dressed in white *Nehru* jacket and puttees") she stays in character for the rest of this volume. Their grief becomes both harder and easier for them to bear when they realize that they themselves—by smashing a mirror, the symbol of communication between the two worlds—will have to break the connection and dispatch MM and their other two friends to earth. This discovery so unnerves them that WHA offers a means of cushioning the blow: "TAKE A BOWL / OF WATER WE CAN SLIP INTO & OUT / WITH A GREAT SPLASH INTO A PLANTED POT." But JM immediately spots the aesthetic problem: "No. Back to flames, back to the green / Rhine go the rings in Wagner and Tolkien. / The poem's logic, though I hate to say, / Calls for the shattering of a glass."

So in the end they adopt DJ's compromise, break a small looking glass into a bowl of water (the "Marble wedge" they use to break it appropriately "stops a door downstairs"), then pour the water into a potted, blooming cassia, which MM discovered in the wild and which was (also) "transported by her." Merrill has already described, in "Glimpses of the Future," the few events that follow this incident, and consequently he avoids an anticlimax. These lines come from a set of quatrains, once more rhymed ABBA, near this volume's conclusion:

> Giving up its whole
> Lifetime of images, the mirror utters
>
> A little treble shriek and rides the flood
> Or tinkling mini-waterfall through wet
> Blossoms to lie—and look, the sun has set—
> In splinters apt, from now on, to draw blood,
>
> Each with its scimitar or bird-beak shape
> Able, days hence, aglitter in the boughs
> Or face-down, black on soil beneath, to rouse
> From its deep swoon the undestroyed heartscape
>
> —Then silence. Then champagne.

Thus the relationship with MM, WHA, and GK ends. After a few more lines Merrill and Jackson, forced to survive their friends once more, sign off with a three-line reprise of God B's own proud, lonely, survivor's message, first heard in Lesson 10 of "Yes," to his brothers in space:

> HERS HEAR ME I AND MINE SURVIVE SIGNAL
> ME DO YOU WELL I ALONE IN MY NIGHT
> HOLD IT BACK HEAR ME BROTHERS I AND MINE

❭ ❭ ❭

God Biology's relationships to his brothers in the Pantheon and to the "IT" he opposes or withstands are central mysteries. We learn from MM and the angels that "THE GALACTIC COUNCILS" gave God B, the "'YOUNGEST BROTHER,'" a charter to create life on Earth. According to the angels, the other gods stipulated only that he regard his creation as "'ONE WITH ALL. NOTHING IN IT WILL BE ENEMY TO OUR REALMS.'" As soon as he descended from the Pantheon, however, another, potentially destructive force, "THE BLACK" or "THE MONITOR," also entered the world. Whether God B brought this "FOREIGN GERM" with him or it arrived under its own power, whether his brothers had deceitfully sprinkled it along with the sand onto "THE SEALS OF THE COMPACT" he carried with him or were ignorant of it, whether God B knew that he had received a "TWO-EDGED GIFT" as WHA speculates or did not: these issues baffle even the angels. We get no closer to an answer than in Lesson 10 of "No," where God B summarizes the school year for DJ and JM thus: "MY SON MICHAEL LIT UP YOUR MINDS   MY SON / GABRIEL TURNED THEM TO THE DARK FORCE WE / CONTAIN."

This dark force sometimes seems to be an invading power, as when Gabriel recalls God B's warning that they are "'HARD PREST'" by "'GODS AS POWERFUL'" as he from "'OTHER GALAXIES.'" JM equates it with a continuous bombardment of antiparticles that would extinguish life on Earth except that "our Lord of Light / Darts promptly forward to annihilate" them. The dark force is "kin," he suspects, to "that insane / Presence beyond our furthest greenhouse pane" which we heard about in *Mirabell*, 3.7. More often (especially when viewed as the Monitor) this "GREAT OPPOSING FORCE TO MATTER" seems to reside in the heart of the Earth. As Gabriel warns, "BENEATH US . . . IS THE CAPPD VOLCANO." On their field trips to the underworld, the shades in the class approach the raging center of things (at one point identified with the planet's molten core, at another with a subterranean nuclear explosion) and return with harrowing reports. To complicate antimatters even further, while they sometimes associate the dark force with "EMPTINESS," they sometimes believe that "NOTHING" itself paradoxically shields us from "THE OTHER." We cannot even be certain that the dark force is flatly evil. True, Michael says early on that God B "KNEW THE FORCES ARRAYED AGAINST HIM: THE NEGATIVES, THE VOIDS" and "NAMED THEM EVIL." But the term "EVIL" stands out because it occurs so rarely in this volume, and much later Michael argues that the Monitor is "NOT OUR ENEMY," that it is "NOT AS EASY AS THAT." It is instead "THE REFLEXION, THE UNDOER TO DOING." At another juncture the Black seems tantamount to "the screen / Of self which forms between God and His creature," and elsewhere it takes the form of Time.

Obscure though this force is, the necessary response to it is nonetheless clear: it must be "contained," as God B puts it in a term reminiscent of the cold war, or "resisted," to use the word that JM and the others resort to time and again. God B's message to his brothers—that eldritch "Song of the blue whale / Alone in space"—assures them simply that "I AND MINE HOLD IT BACK" and that therefore "WE SURVIVE." "MATTER'S VERY / NATURE & ORIGIN ARE THIS RESISTANCE," GK postulates, and JM guesses that "The Greenhouse from the start had been / An act of resistance." Resistance even seems to be the essence of progress, whether in time, space, or thought. "Friction made the first thin consommé / Of all we know" (that is, the original chemical soup), and MM reveals that the apparent hostility between Michael and Gabriel in the opening lessons was a necessary deception, "MICHAEL'S INSPIRATION: / 'ALL GOOD DISCOURSE MUST, LIKE FORWARD MOTION, / KNOW RESISTANCE.'" But then the principle of the value of resistance generates *its* contrary. The impulse to oppose, which JM once glosses as "Nature's gift to man," cuts two ways—as Nature confirms when she answers his question about the role resistance will play in the "Alpha" period, or Paradise: "THE RESISTANCE? NONE." The post-human creature "WILL, YES, SWIM & GLIDE, / A SIMPLER, LESS WILLFUL BEING. DULLER TOO? / IF SO, IS THAT SHARP EDGE NOT WELL LOST / WHICH HAS SO VARIOUSLY CUT AND COST?"

Interpreted that way, this impulse seems a manifestation of the dark force, as it does when WHA identifies one of the 00, Mirabell's master and the blackest of the bats, with "RESISTANCE." That paradox is the whole problem in small, for the Black contaminates everything. GK links it with "THAT IDEA OF DESTRUCTION WHICH RESIDES / BOTH IN MAN & IN THE ACTINIDES." If at the level of human life it shows itself most flagrantly in "THE DULLWITTED, THE MOB, THE IDIOT IN POWER, THE PURELY BLANK OF MIND," at the level of the angels it takes the form of Gabriel, who claims to "SIT ON A BLACK THRONE AT MY FATHER'S RIGHT." JM wonders whether Gabriel is not "Lord of Antimatter," and GK suspects that he might be "THE MONITOR ITSELF," since "IN G'S VOICE I HEARD / THE HUM   THE SUCK   THE CONTRADICTING WORD." When Emmanuel boasts that he and his twin buried the two earlier species that succumbed to the darkness (a race of creatures on the Chinese plain antedated *Mirabell*'s centaurs), and that they still strive to "HOLD IT BACK," Gabriel rejoins with a cool, nonplussing "IT?"

Mirabell looks forward to escaping the "BLACK" he comes from when given the run of Nature's garden—but she too has touched pitch. One of her aspects is Chaos, a term that Michael uses for Gabriel, and GK thinks that she might be Gabriel's mother. In view of WHA's hypothetical distinction "Between NATURAL (PSYCHIC) & UNNATURAL CHAOS," one might presume Nature and Gabriel innocent—but the distinction is so tenuous as to be legalistic. Besides, his later verdict on this relationship is that while Gabriel is "GOD'S," he has inherited "HIS MOTHER'S ONE / BLACK OR 'RESISTANT' GENE AS LIAISON / WITH THE CHAOTIC FORCES." Gabriel, who nevertheless aligns himself with the powers that "HOLD IT BACK" in the eighth lesson of "No," refers to the "TWO SIDES OF MATTER" and makes it clear that one is the dark side; and "MATTER," according to Mirabell's unchallenged proposition, is "MATER" or Nature.

Like Gabriel, then, whose ambivalence projects itself as "*Fire fighting itself—fire its own screen*," she works in conflicting ways. As Melville's Old Miser puts it in *The Confidence Man:* "'Look you, nature! I don't deny that your clover is sweet and your dandelions don't roar; but whose hailstones smashed my windows?'" It is she who insists on the "THINNING" process, the reduction by any convenient means, however repugnant to us, of lives on the increasingly overpopulated Earth. Compare with the charming figure in "&" *this* harridan, who appears just before MM, WHA, and GK are to return to this world:

CITIES, FORESTS, THESE WE KNOW ABOUT, MUCH THINNING TO
    COME IN THE FORMER, BUT JUNGLES!
WHO CAN COUNT THE LIVES THERE? CAN I? NO, IN A WORD. O
    THERE'S MUCH TO BE DONE!
POET, THINK ON THAT WHEN YOU GO LIKE A FOX TO EARTH, HAH! &
    REPORT TO ME, ME!
NOW COME ALONG MY DEAR, SO SORRY ABOUT INDIA BUT WE CAN'T
    ALL HAVE DISHWASHERS & ELECTRICAL GADGETS I'M SURE!
BEAT YOUR SERVANTS, THEY'LL WORSHIP YOU!
YOU OTHERS, LOOK ALIVE! MUCH TO DO! THE SUMMER TO GET
    UNDER WRAPS!

Granted, this is less the point of view of the Monitor than of the frenetic, tyrannical mistress of the plantation—and her "THINNING" might be justified in terms of some quasi-Augustinian theodicy—but her eagerness for such decimation inevitably associates Nature with the dark force.

So, even more dramatically than *Mirabell*, *Scripts* presents us with a Manichean universe, throughout which light and darkness resist each other. GK tells us that the atom comprises a "BLACK VOLATILE HALF" and a "WHITE HALF, DEPENDABLE," and JM earns his instructors' praise when he asks this fundamental question: "When we suppose that history's great worm / Turns and turns as it does because of twin / Forces balanced and alert within / Any least atom, are we getting warm?" What he calls an "innermost dichotomy" lay at the heart of God B's blueprint, as Nature discloses when she recalls one early tête-à-tête:

'SISTER, BEFORE I CALL FORTH INHABITANTS OF THIS PLACE, LET US
    PLAN.
WHAT POINT IS THERE IN AN IMMORTAL BEING (THOUGH LESS,
    MUCH LIKE OURSELVES) IF HE CONTAINS NOTHING NEW, NO
    SURPRISE, TO CALL HIS OWN?
LET US DIVIDE THE FORCE OF HIS NATURE, JUST AS WE WILL MAKE
    TWO SIDES TO ALL NATURE,
FOR IN DUALITY IS DIMENSION, TENSION, ALL THE TRUE
    GRANDEUR WANTING IN A PERFECT THING.
SISTER, TAKE COMMAND OF HIS . . . RESISTANCE? HIS 'UNGODLY'

SIDE. MAKE HIM KNOW DARK AS WELL AS LIGHT, GIVE HIM
PUZZLEMENT, MAKE HIM QUESTION,
FOR WOULD WE NOT LIKE COMPANY?' I AGREED.

This crucial passage itself creates a certain "TENSION," since if any god must be judged by his creations, God B must also fall short of "A PERFECT THING." GK raises this last possibility when he toys with the idea that the creation was an act of "DISOBEDIENCE   GOD AS PROMETHEUS"—and so does WHA, when he argues that the "DESCENT" from the Pantheon was actually a "F A L L" from "THE GALACTIC / PRECIPICE."

Whether or not God B has fallen, the poem leads us to believe that he includes his own opposite—that even he incorporates duality. His allusion to "THE DARK FORCE WE / CONTAIN" is after all as Delphic as anything here, since it might mean not only that he and the angels limit or confine it but also that it exists *within* them. Early in "No," GK asks provocatively whether it was really God B that DJ and JM heard in Lesson 10 of "Yes." Mightn't it have been "the Black God? God A / For Adversary?" Or the voice of a blindingly "WHITE REASON" that has driven the truly creative powers into exile in the universe's black holes? Ostensibly, GK still distinguishes one god from the other, but his theorizing, with its sleight-of-hand transposition of black and white imagery, has the effect of yoking them together, and we must wonder whether God B and God A are not different names for the same power. Every elementary particle, modern physics teaches, has a corresponding antiparticle: electron and positron, neutron and antineutron, and so on. In the case of the photon, however, the particle is its own antiparticle; and while God B sheds the "*Light*" at the beginning of "No," the Monitor itself later appears to WHA as "A PURE / WHITE LIGHT, THE NEGATIVE OR 'EYE' OF BLACK." In other words, B might also stand for Black—and God B refers to Gabriel as his own "'DARKER SIDE.'"

Consider too that name the angels use among themselves for God B: "ABBA." Now "Abba" is New Testament Aramaic for "Father" (that is, God), but it suggestively combines the two significant initials. A palindromic word, it mirrors itself. Because this is the sort of linguistic event that enchants both Islamic mystics and the poet of "Syrinx" and "Dreams about Clothes," it is no surprise to find Merrill intrigued by the notes on symbolic calligraphy which WHA has picked up from a "SLOEEYED SUFI (13 CENT)." Meditating just before the fourth lesson in "No" on an ornate version of the Arabic phrase "*Bismillah* ('in the name of Allah')," JM points out that the non-Arabic or "backward reader" of the script will find "*Ism* (world of names, empty phenomena) / Within the broadly tendered palm of *ba*," its first letter. Its "Initial meaning," he continues, is "God B knows what." Exactly—not only because God B is that palm, but also because *ba* combines B (Biology or Black) with A (Adversary or Allah).[5]

No matter which of the elements in Merrill's universe we analyze, we end up fumbling with contraries. As "Abba" can be simplified to *ba*, so *ba* can be reduced to that letter's diacritical mark, to which JM's lyrical explication of *bismillah* pays special attention. A mere subscript dot, it is also God's protective hand in the form of a "fist" closed on all existence. According to the Sufi tradition that is surely behind JM's lines, this dot "symbolizes Divine Essence itself, the Mystery, the abysmal darkness. It is single in itself but embraces all phenomena. With the Sufi, it corresponds to the Heart's centre; it is that to which desire is directed," "the Divine Source," and "the Prototype of the world."[6] In JM's double pun, this "inky star," a tiny synecdoche, is "the Whole Point."

In his essay on Dante, Merrill notes that, because he is "Concise and exact," the Italian poet is "partial to points."[7] Merrill draws our attention to a number of them in the *Commedia,* where they recur often enough that "A children's book comes to mind—*Adventures of a Hole* or whatever—where the small round 'hero' piercing the volume from front to back serves as a focus to the picture on every page." Now it is apparent throughout this essay that he is alert to parallels between his work and Dante's, as when he describes the cast of the latter, which includes "saints, philosophers, emperors, angels, monsters, Adam and Ulysses, Satan and God. To these [Dante] added a poet he revered, a woman he adored, plus a host of friends and enemies whose names we should otherwise never have heard." So too his comment on Dante's "points" reminds us of their importance in *Sandover,* from the ellipses in *Ephraim*'s Z through the "black eye-hole" in the physician's mirror that GK wears on his forehead in *Scripts.* Merrill emphasizes two especially important points in the *Commedia:* one a virtual "black hole" at the nadir of hell in the *Inferno,* the other the "infinitesimal, intensely brilliant point" that is God in the *Paradiso.* If his own epitome of a "Point" in the lyric on the calligraphic *bismillah* (so strikingly reminiscent of the "blind spot" in section seven of "From the Cupola") is "Whole," that is partly because it combines these other two. Like the atom—"in our day, the point on which all nature and its destruction depend," as Merrill says in his essay—it unites the positive and the negative.

At exactly this point, duality can hardly be distinguished from unicity. If all things share duality, mightn't they all be the same thing—or the same indivisible but double force differently manifested? At the same time that dark and light mingle within God B, he pervades existence. It is he "Whose body is Earth. Whose eye—the glowing sun— / Upon the sparrow also is the sparrow," in JM's tentative formulation in "Yes." The angels also seem to be his emanations, as their private name for him perhaps confirms. If we take A and B as symbols, "ABBA" stands for the four brothers, with the twin major angels separated, as though by buffers, by the twin minor angels.[8] "DAZZLING TO SET FORTH INITIALLY / THE WHOLE DESIGN," WHA quips— although he has in mind four other initials that represent the angels: "M E E K," where "K" is "G" because they are "TWINS / PHONETICALLY." He needn't have gone so far afield. Or he might have gone further, since if the meek are to inherit the Earth they must inherit it from their father, Abba.

"Maddening the way / Everything merges and reflects," JM reflects— and his complaint anticipates that of the reader searching for even the ghost-liest demarcations. God B turns out to be Innocence itself, while his "star-twin" Nature embodies Idea, but they blur in unexpected chiasmatic ways into Michael (who shares God B's light yet speaks for Idea) and Gabriel (who merges with Chaos but takes the part of Innocence). Then, too, Gabriel's fire gives Michael's light. Other sets of twins include GK and RM ("TWINS SCIENCE & MUSIC"), WHA and JM ("TWIN SCRIBES"), MM and DJ ("MADAME SECRET WEEDER & TWIN SECRET HAND"), not to mention such odd couples as Nefertiti and Plato, and Eurydike and Calypso (the Muses, in this novel version, of tragic and comic drama respectively, who combine to create "LAUGHING GRIEF"—which would be one way to de-scribe the tone of this volume's conclusion). Just as JM suspected that the instructors in *Mirabell* were Ephraim in disguise, so now he imagines that Ephraim might have been "our quick-change / Michael." "St. Agatha," the mysterious figure whom Maria has assisted all along in cultivating night-mares to be implanted in the minds of politicians, seems in the end to be another name for Nature—but then "Maria" is another name for Plato, and he (or she) turns out astoundingly to be "ALL NINE" of the Muses, whose mother is Nature (not Mnemosyne, who is instead one of the Muses her-self). WHA and MM, *Mirabell*'s "Father of forms and matter-of-fact mother," reflect God B and Nature (MM's initials even condense the matter/mater pun), and they also tend to merge. At least twice, camping it up, WHA re-fers to himself as "YR MOTHER," and since it is Maria, the mother figure, who emerges as Plato (hitherto associated, like WHA, with mind), one has to wonder whether there was not something to DJ's inkling about WHA after all. It begins to look as though the angels and the shades leave such incipient identifications undeveloped simply out of respect for the depen-dence of human understanding upon *some* distinctions.

Such insistent fusions and doublings, that is, imply a single, compre-hensive union, which gets one of its most explicit and yet compressed treat-ments in Lesson 9 of "Yes," where Strauss improvises a clever "*four-note theme, / BDEA,*" for Michael's fête. Perhaps inspired by Bach's famous

BACH motif (in which, according to German terminology, H is the note B-natural while B is B-flat), Strauss's little theme works out as IDEA (since in our notation B and I would be identical). It follows that "*I come to Be, is the Idea.*" And indeed, as *Ephraim* first suggested, it is the idea of the trilogy that humanity and divinity come to themselves through each other, that the race is God B in the process of evolving. That is one aspect of the idea anyway—the Jungian aspect, or even Gnostic, for in some Gnostic thought one of God's secret names is man. The other aspect recalls Spinoza or Whitehead, for Strauss's theme further intimates, as the two earlier volumes did on occasion, that if humanity is one name for God, Nature is another.[9] Nature embodies Idea, we remember. Moreover, Strauss's B (or I) makes sense only when joined with the easily translatable DEA. Using the other letter motif, WHA similarly encodes the identity of God and Nature when he refers to the latter, whom he often calls "QUEEN MUM" or "QM," as "QUEEN M(AB)." It is as though M(AB), BDEA, ABBA, *ba*, B (or A), and the diacritical dot itself were different ways of writing the one name. "Thy word is all, if we could spell," Herbert admits in "The Flower" to the Word who is All.

Not that *Scripts* testifies to the unity of things any less equivocally than to their duality. Like *Ephraim* and *Mirabell*, it everywhere bears witness to Evelyn Underhill's observation that "The Unconditioned One . . . cannot of itself satisfy the deepest instincts of humanity: for man is aware that diversity in unity is a necessary condition if perfection of character is to be expressed. Though the idea of unity alone may serve to define the End—and though the mystics may return to it again and again as a relief from that 'heresy of multiplicity' by which they are oppressed—it cannot by itself be adequate to the description of the All."[10] JM seems to make the same point in his sonnet on *bismillah*, when he notes that his "characters, this motley alphabet, / Engagingly evade the cul-de-sac / Of the Whole Point," even as he finds himself "drawn by it." If diversity's ineluctability helps to account for JM's view of God B, Nature, and the others as entities, its counterpart—the attraction of the One—helps to explain why God B must nonetheless be God A and thus why Nature, who has at least as much say in this matter as he, must balance "Yes" and "No."

Ever since *Ephraim*, the crucial question has been whether humanity will survive, in God B's words, to "CREATE . . . A PARADISE," whether we can achieve, in Michael's phrase sung by Flagstad, "THIS HEAVEN IT IS GIVEN YOU TO WIN." The ampersand at the center of the only possible response is the Gordian knot, or Whitman's "old knot of contrariety"—or the untied naught, the "CIPHER" we might still make of ourselves. It is also that bridge that can be crossed both ways, as JM muses just before setting foot upon it, and the subsequent revelations bear him out. Just after the last lesson in "&," as the class moves inexorably toward "No," Nature, in response to the students' anxious pleas, seems to tip "THE SCALE" to "Yes"— to decide to give humanity another chance. To move into "No" is to negate its negation. Or so it seems at first. Anyone who recalls JM's earlier reminder of the positive "meanings / The word 'negative' takes on in *Ephraim*" will be prepared, however, for the mirroring affirmation with negative overtones in "No." It comes at the end of Nature's masque, as the sun sets:

NOW MARCHING TUNES!
MICHAEL YOUR RAINBOW LINE, IT IS OUR WISH
YOU REEL US IN LIKE FLOPPING FISH,
BUT LET ME CRY A LAST RESOUNDING YES
TO MAN, MAN IN HIS BLESSEDNESS!

WHA teases out the ambiguity, as sly as that in God B's containment speech, a couple of pages later:

Nature said Yes to man—the question's settled.
SHE SAYS DEAR BOY E X A C T L Y WHAT SHE MEANS
LOOK IT UP   "A last resounding Yes."
LAST? The fête was ending. JM: Or
Because man won't be hearing Yes much more?
AH SHE SETS MEANING SPINNING LIKE A COIN.
HEADS UP? You're asking us? TIP SCALE TO YES
& ALL'S THE GLINT OF QUEEN M(AB)'S ALLEGRESSE.
LEAN TOWARD NO, & NO AMOUNT OF SKILL
WILL KEEP HER IMPS LOCKED UP IN GABRIEL'S SCHOOL.
We do the judging? Everyone? INDEED.

In this soteriology God proposes, at best, and man disposes. WHA has said of the angels that "I BELIEVE WE SHALL DISCOVER / THEIR POWERS ARE IN US QUITE AS MUCH AS OVER," and MM's "Sermon at Ephesus" has much the same message: "'PREPARE TO WEAN / YRSELVES OF THE FATAL DELUSION OF ALLPROVIDING / HEAVEN. MAN MUST PROVIDE.'" At another point, defending humanity's dangerous "CURIOSITY," she infers that it must have been inculcated because "WE, MANKIND, MUST DO / IMMORTAL WORK" and argues that one day when "EARTH BECOMES / PARADISE" we will emerge as "THE ELDERS IN A RACE OF GODS." The theme goes back to *Ephraim,* along with the image that occurs to JM when he guesses at humanity's purpose: "To feed the earthward flow / Of Paradise? That final waterfall . . ." Late in "No" RM advances his "THEORY . . . THAT PARADISE / ON EARTH WILL FLOOD EACH EMPTY PIGEONHOLE / OF THE BUREAUCRACY

WITH RADIANCE," and MM and the other two return to their V work on Earth by means of that "mini-waterfall" at the end. Yet for all the hopeful predictions, precisely because the future is in human hands, the scripts must remain plural and the drama's outcome uncertain. Doubtless because she knows all too well that the future hangs in the balance, Nature—Queen *Mum* indeed!—refuses to read two of her lines in the masque: "'NOW LET US BAN-ISH GLOOMY DREAMS / FOR HEAVEN ON EARTH MOST LIKELY SEEMS.'"

Frustrated by such paradoxes and intricacies, and in spite of the richness of formulas such as those noted above, JM finds himself after Lesson 3 of "No" despairing of "Language's misleading apparatus" and sympathizing with Pound, "Who 'said it' with his Chinese characters— / Not that the one I need here could be found." But two such figures do turn up. Gabriel dictates one of these in Lesson 8 of "No" and draws it in chalk on his blackboard while JM puts it down in pen, element by element, on his white page.

The finished product is shown above. The upper X, we learn, represents at once the "IT" of God B's message, and humankind reaching for enlightenment (the figure stands on the earth), and an hourglass or Time. The angels do not say, although they might have, that the X is itself a reflected V, as though it signified the combined V work of heaven and Earth, with the point of each V indicating the direction or focus of the labor. The horizontal line between the "ARMS REACHING UPWARD" represents the sand in the hourglass, which symbolizes "ANY SURFACE FUEL" that humankind converts to energy ("NATURAL POWER," as GK has called it earlier). In the "DOWNWARD ENIGMA" or reflected X, the "SAND RUNNING UP" represents "DEEP FUELS TAPPD," an "UPWARD VOLATILE FORCE" ("UNNATURAL" power, especially petroleum and atomic power) that threatens to destroy the world and that we and the angels try to hold back even as the ground bulges with the pressure from beneath.

The "SAND RUNNING UP," we gather from Lesson 3 of "No," also indicates "TIME SET RUNNING BACK," or evolution inverted. If souls like Jesus and Buddha urge us on toward utopia, those like Caligula and Hitler, hearing "ANOTHER SIREN SINGING," lure us toward self-annihilation. By taking to an extreme the task of "THINNING" which is part and parcel of the creation of Paradise, the latter have gone over to the Monitor or God A, whose name we could put beneath the ideogram (the triangle with legs at the bottom *is* an A), just as we could put God B's name above it. And there we are: one with a symbol doubled against itself, using all the fuels at our disposal to create Paradise and simultaneously developing the means to bury ourselves, with time running out and nuclear warheads piling up.

God B supplies the other of these ideograms in this volume's last lesson. Taking over the cup himself, he traces out a "Quincunx," the salient points of which are Yes, No, A, and Z. The very crux of the matter, this figure elegantly abstracts Gabriel's reflected hourglass, as God B implies in his gloss:

MY UPRIGHT MAN
FULL OF TIME   HE STRUGGLES TO HOLD IT BACK
AND CREATE FOR ME A PARADISE I
IN MY OWN UPSTRETCHED ARMS WILL SHOW CRYING
SEE BROTHERS WE HAVE HELD IT BACK SEE SEE
I AND MINE BROTHERS IN OUR DAY SURVIVE

"FULL OF TIME": with time to spare, that is? Or handicapped by it? As JM sees immediately, the closed St. Andrew's cross that God B draws might represent either "the mark / That cancels, or the letter writer's kiss," a "Twin-bladed axe" or a "Fulcrum and consort to our willowy &." "Thy word is all, if we could spell." Because we cannot spell, "God B His Mark" also forms "The X / Of the illiterate." Being humanity, that is, God B can hardly *read* his own nature before completing its *creation*. Paradoxically, however, his mark must also be one way of writing the All. If the X stands for the unknown, as in algebra, it also stands for the conjunction of divinity and humanity, as in Christianity, and for the intersection of the other world and this one. The various meanings of it all have been there from the outset, then, latent in the board's layout. As a Sufi says of an analogous synecdoche, "The meaning of the four sacred books / is contained in a single *alif*" once its ramifications have been understood. It almost seems inevitable that the nearest tropic relative of God B's diagram would be chiasmus, the figure of "crossing," which rhetoricians sometimes represent by the letters ABBA.[11]

So the hourglass is our glass, which perforce reflects opposite images at once. The hourglass's sand itself serves this volume much as the "current"—continually fluctuating between creative and destructive power—served *Ephraim*, as the relationship between Raphael and Emmanuel could suggest. To the extent that the "THINNING" process facilitates the creation of Paradise, the sand falling into the "RISING DUNE" contributes to the "FLOOD" of "RADIANCE" that RM and Ephraim envision. But Gabriel uses that dune as a metaphor for a reservoir so dangerous that he likens it to "ATOMIC WASTE"—a "RESERVOIR OF SPENT TIME." (This phrase gives RM's cute Bensonian version of "au revoir," "AU RESERVOIR," a menacing ironic edge— especially when Nature, in a peevish mood, adopts it herself.) Water and sand, auspicious and sinister foreshadowings, combine in JM's touching anticipation of his friends' return to Earth:

> (. . . The ninth moon setting—at whose full
> Enormous turtles, barnacled like moons,
> Eggs buried in the lap of silver dunes,
> Regain the ebbing world they mustn't fail.)

While his treatment of Earth in terms of the sea and his fine choice of "lap" blur the distinction between the realms of sand and water, the boundary between Yes and No becomes just as indeterminable. The "eggs" in the "silver dunes" point in one direction, "the ebbing world" and "buried" in the other.

As in *Ephraim*'s section V, "the ebbing world" that Earth is takes shape as the "drowning, dummy paradise" of Venice, which Merrill—now rhyming with the flair of Byron, now brushing in a scene in shimmering, translucent colors—describes once more in terza rima. And here again, as in section M of *Ephraim*, an account of a film by Maya Deren summarizes some chief concerns. Merrill's art and Deren's converge during the trip to Venice when DJ discovers that some students are showing her film as "Part of some sort of anti- / Biennale." The same documentary that MD happens to have compared early in *Scripts* to JM's project, it records a voodoo ceremony that she participated in while in Haiti, which would have been about the same time that DJ and JM first made contact with the spirit world ("How many years ago now, twenty? thirty?"). As the "Credits flicker" and the camera takes in "A bare beach" and "Glinting wavelets," Merrill's opening in *Scripts* flashes to mind: a list of "Speakers" and the "Sun [that] dwindles into Sound." Deren shot her film in "dialectic whites and blacks" reminiscent of this volume's interacting forces, and "the soundtrack's / Treacherous crosscurrent" that seems to slow the action ironically recalls Merrill's own mode. Because of its age, the film sometimes threatens to be "swept clean / Away by particles that . . . bombard . . . [and] flay an image to the bone-white screen," a "flak fired outward from time's core" that calls up Gabriel's "CAPPD VOLCANO" with its "UPWARD VOLATILE FORCE." Any anxieties that Deren might have shown during her induction, JM surmises, "have been cut, or never filmed," just as he himself prefers, as he has told us a few pages earlier, "the happy ending":

> Weren't the endings
> Always happy in books? Barbarity
> To serve uncooked one's bloody tranche de vie . . .
> Later, if the hero couldn't smile,
> Reader and author could; one called it style.

The film ends—interrupting JM's meditation on "'Paradise' impending"— with "One last shot: dawn, the bare beach," which takes us back to its beginning, as *Sandover* will eventually return us to its point of departure. "'Happy ending?'" DJ asks with a smile—and he makes the ending happy *by* smiling.[12]

If we ask his question about JM's documentary, the answer must also be yes—and no. Yes, on the emotional level, because MM and the others return to the world so eagerly, as do DJ and JM. (DJ, echoing Merrill's sentiments near the end of "From the Cupola," impatiently concludes one philosophical discussion with the shout "Look! This whole world's *a place to live!*" and a rebellious plunge "Into the blue depths of Emmanuel." Even JM, for his part, feels a growing urge "to put / These headlong revelations finally / Between the drowsy covers of a book.") Yes, too, on the eschatological level, because Nature and God B leave the gate to Paradise ajar. But also no, on the emotional level, because the relationships with Maria, Wystan, and George have finally ended, and DJ's and JM's world is the poorer without the spirits of these loved ones. And no again, because that "bare beach," the sand over all, the sand even in the ampersand at this volume's center, prefigures a world blasted clean of all life as easily as it does Paradise. Whether our ending proves happy depends on whether it is also a beginning, on whether it turns into the Alpha period—and on the nature of that brave new world. Since the issues cannot be resolved except in time, Merrill's last sentence, when it comes several pages later, remains incomplete, and God B's concluding message begins and ends *in medias res:*

> And should elsewhere
> Broad wings revolve a horselike form into
> One Creature upward-shining brief as dew,
> Swifter than bubbles in wine, through evening air
>
> Up, far up, O whirling point of Light—:

HERS HEAR ME I AND MINE SURVIVE SIGNAL
ME DO YOU WELL I ALONE IN MY NIGHT
HOLD IT BACK HEAR ME BROTHERS I AND MINE

❯   ❯   ❯

The final rhyme in *Scripts*—"Light" with "NIGHT"—once more interlocks the positive with the negative and the human voice with the divine. The last three lines themselves might as well be JM's address to his now silent friends—or to the reader, or to posterity. "It's almost as if *we* were dead / And signalling to dear ones in the world," DJ has realized earlier. During Deren's film, watching DJ's face "going white" in the light of the projector, JM thinks "*We* are the ghosts, hers the ongoing party." He refers to Deren, but the larger party is hosted by someone else, the third aspect of his Trinity, who appears here, as the result of our tuning in to God B's incessant transmission in the middle of the word "BROTHERS," in the message's startling first word. Even as JM's voice merges with God B's, the term "HERS" implicitly, dramatically assigns all existence, from the Pantheon down, to Nature. Beginning and ending with its reciprocal, all-inclusive possessives, revolving around the ambiguous "I" at the middle of its central line, this last message tries one last time to say it all at once, to frame the Word, the single symbol, of which the ornate Arabic phrase, Strauss's ingenious theme, the angels' ideogram, and God's mark are all translations.

In any form, that symbol must be a "*twinned / Emblem,*" simply because, grounded though it is in an intuition of unicity, Merrill's experience of the world, the "plus and minus signs" of its "vast evolving formula," demands expression in ambivalent terms.[13] Perhaps no other contemporary American poet would respond as sympathetically to Karl Abel's thesis in "The Antithetical Sense of Primal Words," the pamphlet made famous by Freud's review. Abel argues that since "everything on this planet is relative," and since "every conception is thus the twin of its opposite," it should not surprise us that primal words often said opposite things at once. He cites the parallel thesis of Alexander Bain, the Scottish philosopher, that all mental life must be pervaded by something like that very "DUALITY" that God B instilled in nature. According to Bain, "The essential relativity of all knowledge, thought, or consciousness cannot but show itself in language. If everything that we can know is viewed as a transition from something else, every experience must have two sides; and either every name must have a double meaning, or else for every meaning there must be two names."[14] If Merrill were to formulate a language doctrine, it would surely involve fraternal propositions like Bain's and Abel's. (And what he mightn't do with *those* names!) Merrill's favorite rhetorical and prosodic devices—the pun, the paradox, the oxymoron, the couplet, the ABBA quatrain—either spring from or comport with an intuition of "the essential relativity of all knowledge" and the consequent necessity of two-sided expression. We might even think of his metaphysics as his rhetoric and his prosody writ large, ramified, and reinforced by a physics that seems sometimes to rhyme with them. Unity in duality (or in multiplicity, since dualism propagates) constitutes the poem's fundamental principle, metaphysical and aesthetic alike. The Word is a pun, as Heraclitus and others have suspected.

Merrill delicately reminds us that we must look elsewhere for theological dogma when he echoes, in the lines on the "horselike form" in his conclusion, this fable, which Mirabell has recounted in "&":

> CIRCA 3000 BC A WIND
> SWEPT DELOS   THE MALE POP RUSHING TO PUT STONES ON THEIR
> ROOFS
> WERE SWEPT UP UP UP THEN IN A CYCLICAL FREAK MANNER
> RETURND, SET DOWN. ONE CASUALTY: A FAT TEMPLE SCRIBE
> WHO, LEFT ARM BROKEN, DECIDED IT MEANT THEY HAD BECOME
> TOO SOBER TOO WITHOUT LYRIC JOY   SO HE INVENTED
> GREAT PAEANS TO WEIGHTLESS LOFTY & PURELY COMIC LIFE.
> DELOS SET UP A SHRINE & THE SCRIBE'S WORDS 'WE RODE THE AIR,
> WE LAUGHD DOWN AT THE DOMESTIC EARTH' CAUSED A HORSE
> FIGURE
> TO BE WORSHIPT THERE BY ALL WHO ASPIRED TO THE WORD.
> NOTE THAT THE 'GOD' RESPECTED THE SCRIBE'S RIGHT HAND

The fable replays the trilogy: JM and DJ have also been swept up and returned to earth; JM too is a scribe (whose left arm will have felt the effect of long hours with the cup); these volumes are comic paeans. The "HORSE FIGURE" celebrated by the Greek scribe is a version of Pegasus, the Muses' horse. Trying to ascend to heaven on his back, Bellerophon fell to earth, like the scribe, and Pegasus went on alone to install himself among the stars, like the "horselike form" in this volume's conclusion, in turn a stylized representation of Mirabell riding Uni. If Merrill's own ascent fails, it fails just as it must, because it is finally "only" a fable itself. Asked why he put "GOD" in quotes, Mirabell replies "I BELIEVE U KNOW" and thus hints at the "PURELY COMIC LIFE" of the poem, its inevitably fictional or provisional nature, its essential agnosticism.

JM also obliquely acknowledges the fiction involved immediately after the last lesson, when he recasts the angels' story of the descent of God B and Nature from the Pantheon in these knowing terms:

> Yet here
> In their New World, this branch at least, these two
> Have fallen on hard times. Their *Mayflower*
> Long run wild, they bend to the poor lamplight,
> Her deft hands full of mending, His roughened ones
> Forming letters which the flame, tipped blue
> As if with cold, breathes fitful life into:
> *I've found work, we get on, Sister keeps house.*
> *Stay well, and please do not abandon us . . .*

To this canny translation MM responds, as though with a proud but sad smile, "ALAS ENFANT THERE'S NO DECEIVING U"—which is as much as to say that they have all been treated to an old story tricked out in a new fashion. The angels' cosmogony is no more, if no less, than the New World myth, one more variation on a venerable theme.

Merrill reveals yet another analogue to and possible source for the trilogy a few lines later, when he smoothly turns cosmogony into autobiography (or does so more explicitly, since "these two" with their "mending" and writing look a good deal like our boarders). His readers will recognize elements of the autobiography from "The Broken Home," "Lost in Translation," and other earlier work. The opening sentence provides the transition, as the primordial broth becomes both the amniotic fluid and a remembered stock; thereafter the personal narrative dominates, though it is always shadowed by the myth:

> Friction made the first thin consommé
> Of all we know. Soon it was time for lunch.
> Between an often absent or abstracted
> (In mid-depression) father and still young
> Mother's wronged air of commonsense the child sat.
> The third and last. If he would never quite
> Outgrow the hobby horse and dragon kite
> Left by the first two, one lukewarm noodle
> Prefigured no less a spiral nebula
> Of further outs. Piano practice, books . . .

If Nature and "DISTANT-MINDED" God B, as she has called him earlier, stem from Merrill's own level-headed mother and "absent or abstracted . . . father," humanity's predecessors derive from the poet's older siblings, here given attributes that link them with the centaurs and the creatures of the Chinese plain. JM's early experiences foreshadowed even Maria's fate, as we know it from the trilogy:

> A woman speaking French had joined their sunstruck
> Looking-glass table. Fuels of the cup
> Lowered to her lips were swallowed *up*.
> The child blinked. All would now be free to shatter,
> Change or die. Tight-wound exposures lay
> Awaiting trial, whose development
> Might set a mirror flowing in reverse
> Forty years, fifty, past the flailing seed
> To incoherence, blackout—the small witness
> Having after all held nothing back?

Like the governess in "Lost in Translation," MM speaks French and (having drunk her bitter cup to the dregs) appears at JM's table, "sunstruck" at least since Michael's entrance—which, the "Coda" reveals, was as Ephraim himself. First Maria's death and then her return to Earth repeat the childhood catastrophe, and these later losses also leave behind them impressions whose poetic "development" entails recollection. Thus JM's different "exposures" to disaster might have given rise to the trilogy, whose very hourglass in which the sand runs up to obliterate the world seems a translation of memory's "mirror flowing in reverse" until it meets the point of its own origin, the intersection of beginning and ending, "incoherence, blackout"—the dark force in yet another form.

By candidly exposing those relationships, Merrill has "held nothing back" in the sense that he has once and for all confessed the possible autobiographical sources of his revelations. Are we perhaps to read the whole poem, this "spiral nebula," merely as a wild elaboration of personal experiences? But "by now we know / Where that will get us," as JM says after he has asked whether he and DJ were "Literally" *in* the mirror-world during Michael's fête: "Tutti: Y E S & N O." The suspicion itself that he has "held nothing back," for instance, turns his self-analysis back into analogy, since it is identical with the fear that his V work has failed, that his poem will have altered nothing, that we will give in to the dark force. The brilliantly equivocal phrase insists on the importance of the otherworldly communications at the same time that it challenges their authenticity.

This paradox pays its double tribute to "resistance," one name for the power at the heart of Merrill's trilogy. On the one hand, he withstands the temptation to believe that the séances have put him in touch with the Truth; but on the other, he resists the perhaps stronger inclination to see the revelations as chimerical projections. These two forms of resistance, to credulity and to skepticism, coexist in the early comment on the nature of the schoolroom settings, where "*Real and Ideal study* much as we / Good luck to them! *compatibility.*" But we will not be able to write Merrill off as a Janusian skeptic who trifles with mystical notions. That last couplet verges on an understanding of the Real and the Ideal as "*two floating poles / Of color*" that "*Undulate and intertwine like snakes.*" The other side of this motivating force known as "resistance" is a vision of existence as a fabric in which contraries weave together. Speaking of JM's father and mother, or of God B and Nature, MM cautions that "NO MAN'S MIND CAN REACH / BEYOND THAT HIM & HER   THEIR SEPARATION / REMAINS UNTHINKABLE." But she could be speaking of the actual and the fictive, the living and the dead, God and humanity, or A and B. Merrill's vision of things embodies what Stanley Kunitz has called "the supreme awareness [that] we can have," the awareness "that all existence is a continuous tissue, a gigantic web of interconnected filaments, so delicately woven that if touched at any point the whole web trembles."[15]

This volume's most magical and extended formulation of that awareness is "Samos," the poem at the beginning of "&." MM seems to introduce it by way of a bilingual pun at the end of "Yes," where she endorses DJ's proposal that they at least include a bowl of water in their last rites: "BRAVO ENFANT   OUR EAU DE V WORK   SMOOTH / SEAS TO SAMOS." "Samos" is, at any rate, a sort of ode to V work, written in the fascinatingly recursive form of Auden's "Canzone." As in God B's "Quincunx," the "ghosts of Five and Twelve," two of Mirabell's favorite numbers, rise up here, since "Samos" has five stanzas of twelve pentameter lines each, plus a coda of five lines; it also uses only five end words (and ingenious variants on them): "water," "fire," "land," "light" (the angels' four elements) and "sense" (which points to both the apprehension and the interpretation of these elements). Because of the recurrence of these end words, the poem recombines the elements and the sense it makes of them much as the sea it describes reticulates the refracted sunlight. Take this second stanza, whose shimmering tissue both imitates and extends the web of existence:

Fire-wisps were weaving a string bag of light
For sea stones. Their astounding color sense!
Porphyry, alabaster, chrysolite

Translucences that go dead in daylight
Asked only the quick dip in holy water
For the saint of cell on cell to come alight—
Illuminated crystals thinking light,
Refracting it, the gray prismatic fire
Or yellow-gray of sea's dilute sapphire . . .
Wavelengths daily deeply score the leit-
Motifs of Loom and Wheel upon this land.
To those who listen, it's the Promised Land.

In its own way, the canzone's luminously intricate rhyme scheme also spells out God's name.[16]

As "the Promised Land," Samos is a possible future world in small, a foretaste of the Paradise that V work aims at. At the same time it is a part of this world, and the canzone is a dazzling amplification of Emily Dickinson's "Fact that Earth is Heaven— / Whether Heaven is Heaven or not." So "Here we are" again, as Merrill insists in this set piece's change (one of many in *Scripts*) rung on that motif from *Ephraim,* studying the sense of the rhyme of Real and Ideal. From one perspective, "Samos" sees through the surface of things to a unity comparable to that sensed by certain Western mystics and enshrined in much Oriental metaphysics. As Douglas Hofstadter reminds us, for example, "The Buddhist allegory of 'Indra's Net' tells of an endless net of threads throughout the universe, the horizontal threads running through space, the vertical ones through time. At every crossing of threads is an individual, and every individual is a crystal bead. The great light of 'Absolute Being' illuminates and penetrates every crystal bead; moreover, every crystal bead reflects not only the light from every other crystal in the net— but also every reflection of every reflection throughout the universe."[17] If this outlook has striking affinities with propositions in Leibniz's *Monadology,* it shares much too with Romantic mysticism. The light of Absolute Being has its analogue in Wordsworth's

> sense sublime
> Of something far more deeply interfused,
> Whose dwelling is the light of setting suns,
> And the round ocean and the living air,
> And the blue sky, and in the mind of man.

Merrill most nearly approaches Wordsworth's "something"—"A motion and a spirit, that impels / All thinking things, all objects of all thought"— and "the great light of 'Absolute Being'" at his canzone's climax:

Blood's least red monocle, O magnifier
Of the great Eye that sees by its own light
More pictures in "the world's enchanted fire"
Than come and go in any shrewd crossfire
Upon the page, of syllable and sense,
We want unwilled excursions and ascents,
Crave the upward-rippling rungs of fire,
The outward-rippling rings (enough!) of water . . .

He comes as close here as he did in section X of *Ephraim* to "grasping the naked current" of the immanent "absolute." The "Eye that sees by its own light" and that is itself seen through the "monocle" of the blood cell is clearly not just the sun but the essence of things, the connecting force tantamount to Indra's Net, of which the page's shrewdest "crossfire" of pun, etymological ramification, homophone, and allusion (as in this case to *The Rake's Progress,* act 1, scene 2) is a crude representation. Like Heraclitus the Obscure, that philosopher of paronomasia and paradox, Merrill tries to come to grips here with "the tremendous energy that flows through reality," with the "living fire that supplies the driving force of a universe in endless change."[18]

At such moments unity takes precedence, and Merrill virtually replicates the thought of the Sufi who considers Allah "at once seen, seeing eye, and thing seen." Again, "God becomes the mirror in which the spiritual man contemplates his own reality and man in turn becomes the mirror in which God contemplates His Names and Qualities."[19] But the actual world, the historical world that the members of our little band hope will be a phase in the evolution of Paradise, the world of division and diversity, gets its due here as throughout *Sandover.* Yeats takes up a similar sleave of distinctions in *Anima Mundi:* "There are two realities, the terrestrial and the condition of fire. All power is from the terrestrial condition, for there all opposites meet and there only is the extreme of choice possible, full freedom. And there the heterogeneous is, and evil, for evil is the strain one upon another of opposites; but in the condition of fire is all music and all rest."[20] Having had his own encounter with fiery reality, Merrill, with a light, self-deflating touch, avails himself in the fifth stanza of a "fire / Escape," conveniently attached to the hotel, to descend to the cooler, problematic, transitory world of things. "(Now some details—how else will this hold water?)" After bringing himself back to "Trifles," to "things that fade," he reprises the other world in the middle of his envoi:

Samos. We keep trying to make sense
Of what we can. Not souls of the first water—

Although we've put on airs, and taken fire—
We shall be dust of quite another land
Before the seeds here planted come to light.

The reader could hardly be blamed for thinking of these "seeds" as *Sandover*'s details, which will be disclosing their meanings for a long time to come, but Merrill must have in mind the canzone's inkling of the Promised Land. I wonder whether among those seeds there might not also be that of the cassia that blooms at the end of *Scripts*. There DJ and JM break the symbolic mirror, and its "splinters" fall into the shrub, where some lie "aglitter in the boughs" and others lie "face-down, black on soil beneath" the shrub— an image that betokens mundane duality, opposition, and destruction. Still—the poem will not let us think the one thought without thinking the resisting other—any of those splinters will be "Able, days hence . . . to rouse / From its deep swoon the undestroyed heartscape." These interlocked claims of Real and Ideal shape even the dust jacket of the one-volume edition of *Scripts,* where the hole in a broken mirror gives like a jagged window onto an idyllic shore scene. The shore could well be that of a Greek island. Jutting into the scene, in the foreground just beyond the mirror's plane, is a flowering bush, its blossoms plausibly an "oracular yellow" and thus almost certainly a cassia—the tree of life in one Chinese paradise. Just as the broken mirror corresponds to the actual world, this scene corresponds to the ideal, unified world.

In this paradisiacal future, Nature admits near the end of *Scripts*, there will be no resistance. And "IS THAT SHARP EDGE NOT WELL LOST / WHICH HAS SO VARIOUSLY CUT AND COST?" Though that question must remain unanswered, it gives one pause to recall, as the opening "sonnet" in *Scripts* tells us, that "light's / Comings and goings" themselves "in black space remain / Unobserved . . . Until resisted." Moreover, it is quite clear that Merrill's art depends upon the cutting and the cost. In the end, his poem must resist itself in the name of life. At the moment when it most dramatically does so, Merrill implicitly calls into play *The Tempest*. Just as Prospero breaks his staff, drowns his book, and releases Ariel, so JM and DJ break the mirror, pour out the water, and free WHA and MM (who will be addressed as Ariel in the song that opens the "Coda"). Although JM does not altogether abjure his "rough magic," which has given him too grounds to say that "Graves at my command / Have waked their sleepers, oped, and let 'em forth," he turns in the direction of the actual world at the end of the third part of *Sandover.* The mirror, "thirsty for the wine- / Green slopes" of Mount Lykabettos "where sobbing couples intertwine," is surely metonymic not only for MM and WHA, but also for DJ and JM, who sip the celebratory champagne after their friends have been launched "and are melted into air, into thin air." But then these "couples" also include poetry and life. As the "insubstantial pageant" in Shakespeare is both the Globe and "the great globe itself," so the *Pageant* that Merrill's *Scripts* are written for is both the work and the world. The consuming myth—the tale that takes us up completely.

As its relationship to the epigraph to *Scripts* suggests, the very shattering of the looking glass stands for an eternal and sacred union. The epigraph, from *Jean Santeuil*, recounts an incident in which Jean confesses to his mother that in a fit of rage he broke a vase of Venetian glass which she had given him. He expects her to be furious, but she responds by comparing the vase to the glass ritually broken under the heel in the Jewish wedding ceremony: "'Ce sera comme au temple le symbole de l'indestructible union.'"[21] In the trilogy, the broken glass unites DJ and JM and their friends and also humanity, divinity, and Mother Nature, the goddess for whom Merrill has built this later version of Plenorios' temple. For better and for worse, whether we end up saying Yes or No and thus completing the transformation into either God B or God A, we are "HERS."

❭ ❭ ❭

It would be wrong, musically, for the "Coda: The Higher Keys" to reveal anything utterly unanticipated. Musically, too, however, something in the way of a conclusion seems indispensable. As the last lines of *Scripts* swept us "Up, far up" so that we could hear God B one last time, so we, like the scribe in Mirabell's story and like the two mediums in their lives, should be returned to earth in the "Coda." If God B is the provisional end of the process that the trilogy is—the summit that is *au fond* a *cul-de-sac*—the "Coda" can keep the process going. So this last part concerns itself with returns and beginnings of different kinds. Here is the opening lyric, an apostrophe to MM, a study in rhyme and stanza break:

> O Ariel who from a golden
> Lidded compact beamed DJ's
> And JM's profiles into heaven blazing
> Above their tables where the cups grew cold,
>
> > Then snapped it shut: once more a lightly
> > Made-up presence all in black
> > To leave us, mind on her last-minute packing—
> > Now to what destination does one write?

Down to Earth a ray slants true as birdsong
Through boughs in sparkling bloom too high to pluck.
This onionskin the shower puckered
Will soon be dry enough for words.

As Merrill inverts the last stanza, beginning with the longer instead of the shorter lines, he brings us "Down to Earth" as gently as he might raise a curtain, and the "Coda" gets under way. Here we learn more about MM and her new life. His new life, I mean. Not that he has forgotten the one just shed, I suspect, because Ephraim reports that his first word (the pronunciation of which is one of the nine "miracles" he has performed so far) is "MOO." An appropriate if shockingly precocious response to the sight of a cow, that first word is perhaps also a covert, affectionate signal that he remembers his former name and the significance of the initial M (*mu*, in Plato's Greek). In a similar vein his second word, "B R O T H E R S," ostensibly an address to some attendant priests, encodes his relationship to the angels. His third word, and the last that we hear him speak, "GO," by virtue of its Japanese meaning in *Mirabell*, signifies his continued pursuit of V work. At the same time it is a benediction, a sort of "ave atque vale" beamed off the satellite Ephraim to DJ and JM.

"G O" is also the last otherworldly word addressed to RM, who likewise returns to Earth—though the ceremonies marking the rebirth are tinged with sadness (as though the grief that DJ and JM felt at the time he died had been recreated by this event). In a variation on the stripping process in *Scripts*, the image in RM's "full-length self-portrait," hung in the schoolroom, disappears little by little, while the fetus he becomes acquires his senses. Just before his rebirth, "A pinch of dry, used color dusts the floor" beneath the canvas. "Faint sanguine plots a newly primed expanse. / DUST   DUST TO DUST   GO, G O." Raphael, "OLD GRANDFATHER CLAY," who speaks these last words, also reveals RM's new name. It might almost have been predicted. His V work will be to compose the music of the future, "'A MUSIC TO / CLEAN UP & THIN OUT THE WESTERN SCENE' . . . SOMETHING   THIN   NONREPETITIVE," a "'SWEET REVEILLE / FOR THOSE STILL LEFT TO WAKE'" after Nature has completed her millenarian gardening. He is to be a sort of new Adam, then—and "Adam," we found out in *Mirabell*, is a variant of "atom," which WHA disclosed in *Scripts* is a Tom: Tom Rakewell of *The Rake's Progress*, to be specific. So RM is reborn as Tom, a moniker that, mirrored, spells "mot" and might therefore have been especially welcome to his old self. (It now appears that the self, as distinct from a certain quantum of energy, does not endure the transition to a new life except in extraordinary cases, such as MM's). But the name is ambiguously prophetic in view of the original

Rakewell's fate: he is saved from damnation by love, but he loses his mind. Like the "dawn" and "the bare beach" in Maya Deren's film in *Scripts*, the "Faint sanguine" hue and the "newly primed expanse" radiate conflicting meanings.

These Earthward movements and the broken connections they necessitate have a counterpart in the death and induction into the other world of another longtime friend, Mimí Vassilikós, the wife of the Greek novelist Vassilis Vassilikós. While she and her husband are in Rome, Mimí dies suddenly and unexpectedly—though the dress that he had just bought for her in retrospect seems premonitory. A "dress / Costing the earth, a web of light and frost / Unthinkable to ever really *wear*," it is the dress that Mimí appears in on the other side of the mirror. Vassilikós returns to Athens and goes to DJ's and JM's house just in time, as it happens, for the last session recorded in the "Coda"—a session during which august presences from the other world convene to hear JM read the beginning of the trilogy. Anguished, distraught, Vassilikós unintentionally reminds DJ and JM of the comparative frivolity of their transactions with the dead, and DJ starts to put away the Ouija board, "Because, just as this life takes precedence / Over the next one, so does live despair / Over a poem or a parlor game." Vassilikós, however, whose very initials remind us doubly of V work, welcomes the diversion; and as he was meant to do, for there is no accident, he takes the last empty chair in the audience, the only one reserved for a living person.

There are twenty-six chairs, one for each letter of the alphabet, and the guests (Austen, Bewley, Congreve, and so forth) make up an alphabet (with some doublings and omissions). Like Mimí's appearance in the other world in a white dress, this arrangement is a little reminder of devices in *Ephraim*, as the trilogy begins to bend to its beginning. This last section is a "Coda," a tail for the tale JM finds in his own mouth when, with the "Coda"'s last word, he begins *Ephraim*: "'Admittedly . . .'" So the word that derives from roots meaning "to send in" again sends us into this epic written (JM claims in the last part) "for the dead." Not that it is any longer clear who the dead are. "*We* are the ghosts, *hers* the ongoing party," he has imagined in the changing light of that film projector. In any case, we are also now prepared to see this "undertaking," as he calls it in the poem's first line, in a different light. He is right to end with *Ephraim*'s first word, to send us back to reconsider the origin, because the trilogy has been such a dialectical process—a process, that is, like the one Hegel describes in the *Phenomenology*, "this way that generates itself, leads itself on, and returns into itself" and that "makes of itself what it is implicitly."[22] As Northrop Frye perhaps implies when discussing Dante's own "'polysemous' meaning" and the dialectic, and as M. H. Abrams explains, the natural geometrical form for such a dialectical progression is the spiral.[23] Hegel himself verges on saying so when he observes at one juncture that "we have now returned to the notion of the Idea with which we began" and that "this return to the beginning is also an advance."[24] As we have noticed, DJ and JM have followed a spiral course, and it is suitable that the reader—along with JM, now a "reader" of his own work—continue to do so.

Having read the trilogy, we are prepared to read the trilogy.

When we return to the figure with whom the trilogy began, we are prepared to see what Michael, in the "Coda," points out to us: that he himself was (in a sense) Ephraim. WHA's pun back in *Mirabell*—that E is "ANY EMCEE'S EQUAL, EVEN SQUARED"—is even more apt now, since E equals M (or Michael) times C (the velocity of his light) squared. "MUCH HERE IS PURE & SIMPLE MYSTERY"! This revelation also accounts for the new office of "Mister E" in the "Coda," that of "secretary." As JM leads us to discover (in the *Oxford English Dictionary*), that last term comes from *secretus* and denotes "one privy to a secret" and thus applies to those "entrusted with the secrets or commands of God, or a god." The same root that gives us "secretary" also gives us "scribe," "script," and "scripture." Secret "AIRY MICHAEL" is consequently even more closely linked with the author of *Scripts:* both are members of the same "mystery," the old term for a profession or calling, especially a craft or art. Indeed, the phrase "art and mystery" was once "a formula usually employed in the indentures by which apprentices are bound to a trade" (*OED*). The more one considers him, the more implicated Michael seems to be in the trilogy's mesh, this network that so often bears out Valéry's thought: "Etre humain, c'est sentir vaguement qu'il y a de tous dans chacun, et de chacun dans tous." Michael is implicitly there, for instance, in the song that prefaces the "Coda," where the "Ariel" whom we must identify first with Maria holds "a golden / Lidded compact" that beams the reflections of DJ and JM "into heaven blazing / Above their table." This is the Hermès compact that JM gives to Teddy, who plays Mrs. Smith, whose "maiden name" is Psyche, one of whose other names is Santofior. This last name means something like "sacred flower" and thus confirms Nature's connections with the divine.

Who, then, "is" this multivalent Ariel? A Secretary of Nature, in the charming antique phrase? The Secretary who *is* Nature? The Changing Light itself? The smart little compact links all these figures and forces—as it should, since a compact, like an indenture, is what binds, if anything does.

chapter eight

A SHUTTER OPENS

Late Settings and *The Image Maker*

> Nature
> Is dead, or soon will be. And we
> Are well out of it, who in the tempest—
> Exultantly baring through coppery
> Lips the carnivorous silver—
> Knew best how to throw around weight
> And go overboard.

>)))

Divides and rejoins, goes forward and then backward.

    Heraclitus (trans. Guy Davenport)

"What next? What next?"

    Manuel in *The Image Maker*

THE SUN SETS, and songs are set, and lines of type, and precious stones. "Setting" also signifies surroundings, and scenery—and on the one hand an ambush, on the other a table laid for guests. "Late" too has its range of meanings: "toward the end," yes, but also "very recent," as in "late developments." So while *Late Settings* can indicate compositions done late in life, or the world's last twilights or suppers, it can also refer to recent contexts, or to newly mounted gems—or to full summer days. The phrase creeps up on the present like dawn itself and looks to the future. A setting is a placed bet, as well as the direction a current flows in. When fruit sets, it begins to develop from the flower. We might well remind ourselves, when we settle down with Merrill's first volume to be published after the completion of *Sandover,* of such anticipatory glimmerings of his title, along with its darker shadings.

Merrill has usually constructed his volumes with an eye to the skyline that the poems create on the reader's mental horizon, and *Late Settings* is no exception. Its thirty-six poems are divided into three parts, each of which contains a splendid long work. The first and last poems, captivating lyrics both, give us a sense of the scale of the large efforts they abut: "Clearing the Title," the second poem, which purports to discover in its course the title of *The Changing Light at Sandover,* and "Santorini: Stopping the Leak," the penultimate poem. The book's most imposing work, "Bronze," 352 lines in eight sections, comes at the end of the central part. Among these major achievements shorter poems—which include a ballade, a shaped poem, and "Ideas," an exquisitely comic poem for two voices that is a study in variety of diction—form shifting alliances.

One hears throughout an elegiac tone. Like *Sandover,* this volume faces squarely the possibility that Earth is dying. "World without end?" Merrill asks near the end of "Radiometer," which plays with the notion that the solar-driven toy portends the perpetual revolution of Yin and Yang in our existence. But then he completes the couplet darkly: "Not this one. Look: the setting sun, my friend." "Developers at Crystal River," which deplores the pitiless mutilation by Florida entrepreneurs of manatee cows (sweet "Muses of sheer / Indolence"), retuns to the crucial problem, mind's betrayal of nature. "Think Tank" ingeniously interprets our covert oligarchy of experts as prolicidal fish and our faceless corporate censorship and sanitizing of information as "the Snail / Our Servant, huge and blind."

None of Merrill's incomparable technique is sacrificed to his outrage. In a poem published recently in *The New Yorker,* in much the same vein as these poems in *Late Settings,* the twentieth-century United States is seen from the vantage point of a time after the melting of the polar ice cap, when the country has come to be a huge Venice: the "once young republic tasseled / sea to sea with golden wit," in Merrill's adaptation of "America," has "tattered to a / wrack of towns, bubble / domes unpricked on the lagoon's / fogged mirror."[1] In the concluding list of items imported to this world power turned "tourist / mecca," the last is

> a fine-gauge
> 20-karat wire, from which
> our morose goldsmith
> on the Bridge of Smiles
> has already fashioned this
> shimmering, cereal wand.
> Wear it, Milady,
> in your frosted hair.

That "morose goldsmith" is behind this wiry syllabic elegy, a metaphorical hair ornament for Lady Liberty (who suddenly looks a good deal like a blighted Ceres, offered this piece of "golden wit" instead of a sheaf of wheat or an ear of corn in a fertility rite), and he is no less behind *Late Settings.* "Channel 13" works out its point with touching formal precision. Even as it tracks our hard-pressed wild creatures through ever smaller arenas of activity, from "Grassland to circus to Roman floor mosaic to / TV room," and finally to that room's "snug electronic ark of / What has been," each stanza chokes its lines down three times from thirteen syllables to three. After pairing internal rhymes like Noah's animals in each stanza's first two long lines, Merrill dismisses them from the third. Like other political poems here, it is written in a chilling past tense, as though nature had already vanished down the black hole at the center of the dying tube. We hear future ghosts as well in "Popular Demand" (one of the coldly bitter, poignant mini-sequence entitled "Topics"), where "the worst / Has happened," and the only survivors are the politicians in their "deep strongholds." Merrill's keen ear picks up "a first, uncertain laugh": "Spirits reviving, as life's bound to do? / Not from dead land, waste water, sulphur sky."

These poems are the more affecting for the steadfast eschewal of scapegoats and simplification that we have come to expect of Merrill. "Channel 13," seeming to discover the origin of "our ultimate 'breakthrough' lenses" in Adam's naming of the animals, implies that the extinguishing of other species is inextricable from our pursuit of knowledge. "The Pier: Under Pisces," a poem as metrically flexible as its fisherman's "bamboo diviner . . . Vigorously nodding / Encouragement," unfolds a conceit with a Möbius twist, by virtue of which the poet—a Pisces—joins those who take the irresistible bait of their own "minced kin." After describing in flamboyant metaphor the landing of the catch, Merrill imagines certain fish left in the sea and recalls a first experience of his own:

> far and wide and deep
>
> Rove the great sharkskin-suited criminals
> And safe in this lit shrine
> A boy sits. He'll be eight.
> We've drunk our milk, we've eaten our stringbeans,
>
> But left untasted on the plate
> The fish. An eye, a broiled pearl, meeting mine,
> I lift his fork . . .
> The bite. The tug of fate.

But the boy is not "safe." As surely as the poet is the boy ("I lift his fork"), the boy and the fish are one (the "eye" meets the "I"). This is The Peer, then, too, and twice: as he and the fish peer at each other, he sees that he is the fish's peer. So it is that the boy's "bite" joins him with the fish who takes the bait, as well as with the fisherman. They are all of the fallen world, and a part of the boy's maturing is realizing his complicity with the fisherman—and thus with the "sharkskin-suited criminals." If the latter are almost more people than they are fish, as earlier the "floozy fish" have been so vivid as to seem actual streetwalkers, the point is that the natural and the human are threads in the same material.

Inspired by the discovery several years ago off Riace, Italy, of two Hellenic statues, "Bronze" too involves ecological themes. A "QUEENS / MAN" killed by his sons is a New York artist, but he can also be thought of, in the wake of *Sandover,* as QM's favorite, God B himself, and in one riveting section the statues impart certain "*cold lessons,*" the gist of which is that "*hard on the heels of God's death*" we must acknowledge that "*Nature / Is dead, or soon will be.*" But "Bronze" fends off epitome. It is also about a stunted love affair, an Italian friend's trek through enemy territory in the closing days of World War II, his mysterious parentage, and other things. The Greek bronzes, a bust of King Umberto I, Merrill's sculpted portrait, childhood games of statues, a vivid internal "figure" of Eros: the poem's lines of force play among these and related images—as they do among shells, armatures, fortresses, and retreats. On each reading its loopings and interloopings and -lopings all become more closely knit and more diverse. Of the many things one might say about this undertaking, which like its railroad timetable is "Dense . . . with station and connection," one is that it moves away from art and toward an embracing of life—and all the while makes it clear that it is the poem that accomplishes the movement.

The relationship between art and life frames itself first in terms of a quarrel between Merrill and his traveling companion, a painter. Finding themselves in Tuscany, not long after the restored statues have gone on display in nearby Reggio Calabria, these two differ as to whether they should make the trip to the museum. The friend demurs, as he has resisted a closer relationship with the poet. As one would expect, Merrill in part sympathizes with his friend's feeling that "'Close connections . . . harm the soul.'" He has often portrayed himself as a "cold man," after all, and he is quickly "Half resigned" to his friend's recalcitrance—if "Half fuming" as well. These two halves of the self (characteristically projected in the poet's "Notebook and cigarette" and in an owl and a "twittering dither" of starlings) he figures as duelists, as he walks beneath the trees in his host's garden and wrestles with his frustration.

The poem's burden, however, is less the opposition between aesthetic detachment and affective bonds, or between the contemplative and the active lives, than the desirability of combining the two. Thus one of its heroes, his host, Umberto Morra, is at once the former confidant of Montale, Berenson, and Edith Wharton and the man who risked his life to provide the liaison at War's end between Italian anti-fascists and the Allies.[2] True, the poem superficially discounts the value of art: a seagull fouls Merrill's portrait bust, and a friend spills beer on it. Moreover, if "Umberto first intended the estate / As a 'retreat for scholars,'" in the end he has "left it intact to Mario the butler, / So long devoted and his brood so great." Time and again the poem stresses the primacy of "Close connections"—of the "social fabric" and the ecological network, rather than "the Work of Art." Yet all these details belong *to* the poem, which is an elaborate version of a friend's T-shirt, emblazoned with the motto "*Clean Air / Or Else.*" No wonder that Merrill's title denotes an alloy. The Greek bronzes, "*Exultantly baring through coppery / Lips the carnivorous silver,*" are both stunning works of art and Nature's fierce spokesmen, who warn that "*the Mediterranean will in / Another few decades have perished, / And with it those human equivalents, / Memory, instinct, whatever / In you the first water so joyously / Answered to.*" Since it is through the poet that we know what they have to say, it is appropriate that he too "exist in bronze," in the form of the bust, a copy of which is on the deck of the Stonington house, that one Laszlo made when Merrill was a child.

It is because his poems constitutionally resist themselves that *Late Settings* will not resolve into elegy. His "Island in the Works" claims to be "Jaded by untold blue / Subversions," and just as one sub-version of "Jaded" is something like "turned viridian," so this volume's mourning weeds have their greener side. Likewise its "Grass":

> The river irises
> Draw themselves in.
> Enough to have seen
> Their day. The arras
>
> Also of evening drawn,
> We light up between
> Earth and Venus
> On the courthouse lawn,
>
> Kept by this cheerful
> Inch of green
> And ten more years—fifteen?—
> From disappearing.

The ominous and the whimsical are one in this example of what the newly risen "Island" has in mind when (speaking from the vantage of a poet who has just finished an epic) it promises to "trick / Out my new 'shores' and 'bays' / With small craft, shrimpers' / Bars and rhetoric." Among *this* small craft's appointments (in addition to the tiny echo of the twenty-year-old poet's wish as reported more than two decades earlier in "A Tenancy") are the delightful rhymes, not just "irises" and "arras" but their light rhyme across the stanza break with the second syllable of "Venus," which rhymes its first syllable with the middle lines in stanzas one and three (which in turn rhyme consonantally with the enveloping rhymes in stanza two). The final rhyme, hidden in "cheerful" and "disappearing," is cheerfulness itself, as it comes and goes, peering and disappearing, like the joint's glow. All flesh is grass, Isaiah teaches, but to smoke pot on the courthouse lawn is to thumb one's nose at that law too.

"Santorini" converts its valedictory drift into a paean to the dogged perseverance of things. Though it weaves in as well the various light of Marvell and Blake, it takes its fire from Yeats, and its first octave concludes with a wry revision of that earlier master's embarkation for Byzantium: "Whereupon, sporting a survivor's grin, / I've come by baby jet to Santorin." If Yeats thinks to have abandoned a country of "sensual music," Merrill imagines that in leaving a home in Greece and a lover he is also leaving a way of life. The intricacies of the reversal are formidable. But how to persuade the reader with mere excerpts that this wonderful renunciation of renunciation springs convincingly from the removal of a plantar wart? Or that the radiation treatment and the wart's return repeat perfectly the destruction and the resurgence of the volcanic island itself, the Turkish suppression and the eventual renaissance of Greek culture, the repression but persistence of a belief in vampires, the loss of the ancient *gymnopaediai* and their resurrection by Satie? The poem itself is "one throbbing multiplex," by way of which a principle in Merrill's work resurfaces. As he put it in "Lost in Translation": "Lost is it, buried? One more missing piece? / But nothing's lost. Or else: all is translation / And every bit of us is lost in it / (Or found . . .)." Merrill's friend and traveling companion, Nelly (or Nelláki, in the Greek diminutive), has long ago lost her twin (Plato tells us that we have all done so), but his place is taken, for the moment at least, by the poet himself.

His own attempts to achieve "an oblivion / That knew its limits" (to give up both his Greek bed and "what was done in it," for instance) can only prepare the way for a countervailing experience, a bizarre dream vision in which he is virtually possessed by a life "Utterly not my own," by the teeming memories of an "olive-skinned Iraqi" and perhaps others. It is as though the willed rift in his emotional life, the counterpart to the hole in his sole, were an opportunity for the dead or the uncreated to rush in, for Nature to prove her abhorrence of a vacuum. As he lies on his rejected bed on his last evening in Athens, vignettes run in "A cinéma-mensonge" before his mental eye, "Swifter now, churning down the optic sluice, / Faces young, old . . . all random, ravenous images / Avid for inwardness, and none but driven / To gain, like the triumphant sperm, a table / Set for one." This waking nightmare drives him from bed to mirror, where he prays to a "Queen" we will recognize as Nature/Psyche/Chaos that he "*Be made whole.*" As though in response to this "petition," and heralded by "the peevish buzz" of a fly at the windowpanes, "From some remotest galaxy in the veins / A faint, familiar pulse begins," as the wart makes itself felt anew. At just this point Merrill resumes his recollection of the Santorini sojourn (which has preceded this harrowing experience in Athens)—and with good reason, since the wart is in effect his past, his memory, his very life. "Certain things die only with oneself," as the poet learned in "Friend of the Fourth Decade."

Against other poems in this book, "Santorini" asserts the possibility of continuity through renewal. (So it is, by the way, that he and Nelly are unable to meet in Santorini "three old maiden sisters," famous hostesses to whom she has hoped to gain entrée. "The ladies must be met," no doubt, as surely as the Fates must, but since that meeting is not yet to be, though "Things just aren't what they were," they are not radically different either.) One likely reason that Empedocles figures here—in the poem's most difficult passage, which summarizes by way of its legends Greek history from the beginning to this philosopher—is that he envisioned a world cycle in which the two opposing forces, Love and Strife, which produce unity and chaos respectively, alternate dominance, with Love having the last word. So this poem, after a brush with "the hole," ends with an emphasis on "a deep fault made whole"—much as Santorini's major volcanic eruption was succeeded by new islands, new vineyards, a new life. Perhaps "catastrophe" cannot "long be lulled" by our variously propitiatory creations, from the original Greek dances performed in honor of Apollo Karneios through Satie's compositions to this poem, but so far the world has endured, like the poet and Nellie at poem's end, where, after their excursion to "Prophet Elias' / Radar-crowned monastery" and other sites, they return to what is probably Kamari: "We made on sore feet, and by then *were* made, / For a black beach, a tavern in the shade."[3]

Empedocles also figures here because, in the legend that he flung himself into Mount Etna, "that primal scene / And deafening tirade," Merrill has an analogue for the consuming myth, "The mother tongue / At which his blood boiled, his brain kindled," that he confronted in *Sandover*. The issue of renewal thus has a personal dimension, and his question as to whether Empedocles actually met his death in the volcano is also a question as to his own fate after the epic. But even the framing of the question supplies the answer, for Empedocles has become this new Oedipus (his foot swollen after the x-ray removal of the wart), just as the original "Oedipus became Empedocles" in Merrill's version of Greek history. Everything changes; nothing does—a principle consonant with Empedocles' doctrine of the elements, which taught that underlying all things are immutable elements which combine in different proportions to produce all the different phenomena. To the extent that this philosophy celebrates metamorphosis, it comports with much of Merrill's recent work. "From the Cutting-Room Floor," which nonetheless salvages a few passages omitted from *Sandover*, characteristically concludes with Michael bidding farewell lightheartedly to the epic's cast and looking forward to a new day's revisions. His light *is* change:

> BUT THEY HAVE HAD THEIR DAY (& SAY). THEREFORE
> CHANGE AND CHANGE, O SCRIBE! COME UP TO THIS
> INSTANT (FOR YOU INKY) AT MY HEIGHT
> AS TOUCHING THE HIMALAYAS I DEFINE,
> MORE, REFINE THEM, FOLD ON FOLD, FOREVER
> GETTING AT THEIR BONE OF MEANING. CHANGE!
> REVISE, RISE, SHINE! GOOD AH MY CHILDREN NIGHT!

"Clearing the Title" reverses the structure of "Santorini." Here Merrill is at first reluctant to take up a new life, this time defined in terms of the new second residence which he and David Jackson established in Key West at the beginning of 1979 and which has come to replace the home in Athens. It seems to him that to embark on this new life is to "cast / Three decades' friendships and possessions out"—and also somehow to distance himself from *Sandover* (so much of which had its roots in Athens), for it is not only real estate that he has in mind when he asks "What happens next? Behind a latticework / Of deeds no one has time or patience to undo / We cultivate our little lot, meanwhile / Waiting companionably for kingdom come?" But even as he resists, he begins to like the idea of the change (to the degree that it *is* a change, for he spent much of his youth in Florida, and he sees old friends everywhere, in trumpet vine and "cracked pavement"—as will the reader of "From the Cupola"). After he surmises that "what at first appall precisely are the changes / That everybody is entitled to," his poem ends with a refusal to end, with the thought that "tonight we trust no real / Conclusions will be reached" and with "the changing light." "Island in the Works" even mocks the idea of real conclusions. The island has no sooner located itself by latitude and longitude ("This dot, securely netted / Under the starry dome") than "this page" on which the monologue has been drafted is wafted out of the poet's hand (as we learn in a parenthetical last stanza) and into his pool's "cool glares, ever / So lightly swayed, or swaying . . . / Now who did that?" To which one answer is, the eminently irreverent processive principle itself.

Being now a part of the past, an episode in the story of his life, *Sandover* itself changes from Merrill's point of view. Its characters now appear as background figures, diminished by distance, who can be alluded to rather than presented, and who thus contribute to the depth of the recent poems. To be sure, the new work can be admired in isolation, and there are everywhere independent felicities. In "Days of 1941 and '44"—a sonnet sequence that strikes notes rarely heard hitherto in Merrill's work, as the embarrassed and the vindicated, the resentful and the sorrowful jostle one another in a crowd of tones—he turns an adolescent tormentor's taunt of "Rich boy" to this dazzling advantage: "Remember, though, how untrained eyes subtract / From the coin-glint of a summer glade / The adder coiled to strike." In another poem Gertrude Stein offers Elvis Presley—in heaven, on a brief sojourn between loves—a Lethean "CUP OF NULLITY." In another a bad trip ends with the victim, fallen asleep, producing "a suite for solo pharynx / Clumsily bowed and scraped." There is perhaps no better snoring in our poetry. Merrill writes lines as abrasively witty as the bearded bronzes' self-description: "*men in their prime / With the endocrine clout so rebarbative / To the eternally boyish / Of whichever sex.*" And lines as deftly lovely as "I hear the ferrous, feather-light diluvian / Lava clink at a knife-tap from our guide."

Still, many of these poems will ripen more fully in the changing light of *Sandover*. During the excursion on Santorini, "a toy chapel to St. Michael" helps to set the stage for the relationship between radiance and radiation, or "whole" and "hole," in the poem's antithetical rhyme. If the colorful clown of "Clearing the Title"—who "rides unicycle" and juggles firebrands—makes us think first of the poet, that is partly because Merrill treats *Sandover*'s hottest issues so playfully.[4] But in his role as militant solicitor for the Salvation Army, the clown is also a genial parody of Gabriel: "'Y'all give!' our deadpan clown / Yells brandishing a hammer fit for Thor, / 'Give or Ah'll clobber yew!' and *grunt* go the trombones." "After the Ball," this volume's last poem, treats the changing light itself in miniature. In what we might think of as a Merrillian remake of "In a Station of the Metro," the Muse or Sandover's chatelaine takes the form of a date dressed in "magic / Change-making taffeta" who, by evening's end, has helped the poet to take "Such steps in dream logic / That the Turnstile at Greenwich / Chimed with laughter— / My subway token." This little poem is borne along by its own dream logic—as "taffeta," for instance, coming from a root meaning "to twist, to spin," involves itself with the "Turnstile" at the Greenwich Village station. The Turnstile in turn is a style that turns, as from epic to lyric, and that turns one thing into another, as its taffeta turns (suitably, for Rosamund Smith) from "Old rose to young spinach / And back."

Whatever its elegiac undertones, then, this closing lyric chiefly celebrates change in a "Changemaking" style—a style that finds the spin in "spinach," and the spinach's color in "Greenwich," and a crepitant rhyme for "taffeta" in "laughter." Once more "A shutter opens" (to borrow from "Trees Listening to Bach" a phrase in which Merrill lets us hear the latent paradox), and it is not surprising to discover him most recently at work anew in an old field. *The Image Maker,* a one-act verse play, was first produced in Los Angeles in May—the month in which the action is set—of 1986. If *The Birthday,* the short verse drama that Merrill wrote at Amherst in 1947, now seems a sketch for *Sandover* (four strange characters who look remarkably like God B, Nature, Michael, and Gabriel meet the protagonist, Raymond, in a room with red walls and inform him that "We are you"), *The Image Maker* rings light changes on the epic's devices and themes. Here too Merrill provides an array of verse forms, though they are comparatively simple, ranging from a basic tetrameter line through a pair of sonnets for two voices to a chain of quatrains in which Manuel, the image maker, alternately prays to God and talks to himself about his craft, which consists of carving and restoring wooden icons of household saints, or *santos.* Manuel is a *santero,* a practitioner of Santeria, the Caribbean mystery religion that syncretizes Yoruba folklore and Catholicism.[5] Santeria would be especially interesting to Merrill not just because of his acquaintance through Maya Deren with voodoo, but also because the figures venerated by its followers are essentially double: any given santo is outwardly a Christian saint but underneath an *orisha,* or pagan deity (who represents both a natural force and a human concern). Although Manuel can touch up the saint's features and repaint the costume, the much less tractable Yoruba god, the basic resisting force, is incorrigible.

In the santos Merrill has found a telling trope for humanity, with all its cross-purposes and contradictions. The most important santo in his play is Barbara, the virgin martyr, whose Yoruba self turns out (surprisingly but rightly) to be the strife-loving, philandering Changó, who most evidently resembles his Christian counterpart in that he has power over thunder, lightning, and fire—*and* likes to dress in women's clothes. St. Barbara as Changó, taking the tone of Queen Mum at her most irascible, foments a rebellion of the santos in Manuel's workroom. One of the santos, Miguel, who naturally has affinities with *Sandover*'s Michael (and even uses the latter's signature rhyme), is closer in temperament, when the Yoruba element is awakened, to Gabriel. The "great angel" of light and balanced judgment, he becomes a wild, petulant bantam terrorist, the very wedge of chaos and anarchy, who is responsible for a minor conflagration, a reprise of the *Götterdämmerung* motif, when at the play's climax he focuses his light on a wall calender—the temporal world—and makes it catch fire. Under Changó's influence, Francisco, the gentle saint who "knows how to speak / With birds and wolves and fish," causes a pet dove's death, and the human lovers Juanita and Antonio are nearly separated. Although the santos work "to dispel / The dark within us," they also serve it. "We are you," they might as well say to Manuel—and with all the more reason since the play hints that their rebellion (which blurs into his dream) enacts the santero's own "fears and fantasies."

In the first place, however, Manuel is engaged in V work. As his name suggests to an English speaker, his task as artist is to try to make man well. He is also a rendering specifically of James Merrill, and like Merrill, he must confront the issue of having had "no time for child or wife." He calls a santo a "figure," and this *is* an apt figure, this icon represented on stage by a puppet, for this diminutive play. Manuel is at the same time a type of the deity, as Merrill makes clear when he has his woodcarver pray that God take us in hand as he himself does his errant saints. But Manuel—and here too he is like God, as well as like the author of, say, "Island in the Works"—cannot strictly control his creations. They unfailingly "surprise" him, and often trick him, and he can keep any one in line only "for a while." He would understand fully the Rilke who (besides appreciating puppets) saw so clearly how the world "fills us. We arrange it. It breaks down. / We rearrange it, then break down ourselves."[6] And the Heraclitus who proclaimed (in a different version of the fragment quoted in *Ephraim*): "History is a child building a sand-castle by the sea, and that child is the whole majesty of man's power in the world."[7] And the poet who ended his first novel with children building a sandcastle.

His santo Miguel, as an orisha, goes so far as to claim that "I make the Image-Maker"—a boast that translates readily into *Sandover*'s Delphic proposition that humankind is the god-making animal. It also reformulates Merrill's statement about his poetry: "It created me." It will have been doing so since at least as early as 1937, when he and his Mademoiselle were staging those first puppet plays—and assembling that jigsaw puzzle, whose palm-shaped piece is now the more fitting because the palm is Changó's residence. Indeed, when lightning strikes the tree it is Changó—who has remarkable affinities with St. Theodore—returning home.[8] Not that James Merrill has more in common with changeable Changó than with that dwelling place itself. The palm, in Merrill's superb rendering of Valéry's last lines, is "Like one who, thinking, spends / His inmost dividends / To grow at any cost." As Manuel—whose name (like Miguel's) shares its bounding sounds with the poet's—tells a voice that is and is not his unseen, imperious, needful mother's: "My work, Mamá. That's *my* whole life."

)   )   )

Works by James Merrill
Notes
Acknowledgments
Index

"And over here's Miguel
Who cast the devil down
From Heaven's citadel."

Works by James Merrill

Poetry, Fiction, and Drama

Jim's Book: A Collection of Poems and Short Stories. New York: Privately Printed, 1942.

The Black Swan. Athens, Greece: Icaros Publishing Company, 1946.

The Birthday: A Play in Verse. [1947.] (Mimeographed copies.)

"Rose." *The Glass Hill*, 1, Oct. 1949, unpaginated.

First Poems. New York: Alfred A. Knopf, 1951.

The Bait. In *Artists' Theatre: Four Plays*, ed. Herbert Machiz. New York: Grove Press; London: Evergreen Books, 1960. Originally in *Quarterly Review of Literature*, 8, no. 2 (1955), 81–98. (First produced in New York in 1953 by The Artists' Theatre.)

The Immortal Husband. In *Playbook: Five Plays for a New Theatre*. New York: New Directions, 1956. (First produced in New York in 1955 by John Bernard Myers in association with The Artists' Theatre.)

The Seraglio. New York: Alfred A. Knopf, 1957; New York: Atheneum, 1987.

The Country of a Thousand Years of Peace. New York: Atheneum, 1959; rev. ed. 1970.

Selected Poems. London: Chatto & Windus, 1961.

Water Street. New York: Atheneum, 1962.

"Driver." *Partisan Review*, 29 (Fall 1962), 491–506; reprinted in *The Poet's Story*, ed. Howard Moss. New York: Macmillan, 1973.

The (Diblos) Notebook. New York: Atheneum, 1965; London: Chatto & Windus, 1965.

Nights and Days. New York: Atheneum, 1966.

The Fire Screen. New York: Atheneum, 1969.

"Peru: The Landscape Game." *Prose*, 2 (Spring 1971), 105–114.

Two Poems: "From the Cupola" and "The Summer People." London: Chatto & Windus, 1972.

Braving the Elements. New York: Atheneum, 1972.

The Yellow Pages. Cambridge, Mass.: Temple Bar Bookshop, 1974.

Divine Comedies. New York: Atheneum, 1976.

Mirabell: Books of Number. New York: Atheneum, 1978; London: Oxford University Press, 1979.

Scripts for the Pageant. New York: Atheneum, 1980.

The Changing Light at Sandover. New York: Atheneum, 1982.

Late Settings. New York: Atheneum, 1985.

The Image Maker. New York: Sea Cliff Press, 1986. (First produced in Los Angeles in 1986 by the Los Angeles Theatre Center in association with UCLA.)

Recitative. Ed. with intro. by J. D. McClatchy. San Francisco: North Point Press, 1986. (This collection of short fiction, nonfiction, and interviews includes many of the items listed separately in this bibliography.)

Nonfiction

"The Transformation of Rilke." *Yale Poetry Review,* 1 (Spring 1946), 22–27.

"*A la Recherche du Temps Perdu:* Impressionism in Literature." Honors thesis, Amherst College, 1947.

"Notes on Corot." In *Corot 1796–1875: An Exhibition of His Paintings and Graphic Works.* Chicago: The Art Institute of Chicago, 1960.

"Robert Bagg: A Postscript." Review of *Madonna of the Cello,* by Robert Bagg. *Poetry,* 98 (July 1961), 250–252.

Comment on "The Country of a Thousand Years of Peace." In *Poet's Choice,* ed. Paul Engle and Joseph Langland. New York: The Dial Press, 1962.

"Foreword" to libretto for *Le Sorelle Bronte: Opera in Quatri Atti,* by Bernard de Zogheb. New York: Tibor de Nagy Editions, 1963.

"Foreword" to libretto for *Phaedra: An Opera in Two Acts,* by Bernard de Zogheb. [n.d.] (Mimeographed copies.)

"Object Lessons." Review of *The Voice of Things,* trans. Beth Archer Brombert and *Things,* trans. Cid Corman, by Francis Ponge. *The New York Review of Books,* 30 Nov. 1972, 31–34.

"Marvelous Poet." Review of *Cavafy,* by Robert K. Liddell, and *C. P. Cavafy: Collected Poems,* trans. Edmund Keeley and Philip Sherrard. *The New York Review of Books,* 17 July 1975, 12–17.

"Elizabeth Bishop (1911–1979)." *The New York Review of Books,* 6 Dec. 1979, 6.

"Divine Poem: Dante's Cosmic Web." *The New Republic,* 29 Nov. 1980, 29–34.

"Foreword" to *Nineteen Poems,* by Robert Morse. [U.S.A.:] The Temple Press, 1981.

"Condemned to Write about Real Things." *The New York Times Book Review,* 21 February 1982, 10–11, 33.

"The Clear Eye of Elizabeth Bishop." Review of *The Complete Poems, 1927–1929,* by Elizabeth Bishop. *The Washington Post Book World,* 20 Feb. 1983, 2–3, 14.

"Foreword" to *The Evolution of the Flightless Bird,* by Richard Kenney. New Haven: Yale University Press, 1984.

"Foreword" to *Navigable Waterways,* by Pamela Alexander. New Haven: Yale University Press, 1985.

"Foreword" to *Terms To Be Met,* by George Bradley. New Haven: Yale University Press, 1986.

Translations

With Ben Johnson. "The Eel," by Eugenio Montale. *Western Review,* 18 (Autumn 1953), 50–51.

"Selections from Chamfort" [ten maxims and anecdotes]. *Semicolon,* I, no. 1 [n.d.].

With Ben Johnson. "New Stanzas," by Eugenio Montale. *The Paris Review,* 12 (Spring 1956), 60–61.

"In the Greenhouse," "In the Park," "The Shadow of the Magnolia," and (with Irma Brandeis) "Café at Rapallo," by Eugenio Montale. In *Selected Poems* by Eugenio Montale, intro. Glauco Cambon. New York: New Directions, 1965.

With Joop Sanders. "The Malleability of Sorrow," "The Water," and "For My Father," by Hans Lodeizen. In *Translations by American Poets,* ed. Jean Garrigue. Athens, Ohio: Ohio University Press, 1970.

"Second Rose Motif," "Vigil," "Ballad of the Ten Casino Dancers," "The Dead Horse," and "Pyragyrite Metal, 9," by Cecilia Meireles. In *An Anthology of Twentieth Century Brazilian Poetry,* ed. Elizabeth Bishop and Emanuel Brasil. Middletown, Conn.: Wesleyan University Press, 1972.

"The Three T's," by Vassili Vasilikos. *Shenandoah,* 27 (Fall 1975), 44–48.

"In Broad Daylight," by C. P. Cavafy. *Grand Street,* 2 (Spring 1983), 99–107.

Interviews

Sheehan, Donald. "An Interview with James Merrill." *Contemporary Literature,* 9 (Winter 1968), 1–15; reprinted in *The Contemporary Writer: Interviews with Sixteen Novelists and Poets,* ed. L. S. Dembo and Cyrena N. Pondrom. Madison: University of Wisconsin Press, 1972.

Brown, Ashley. "An Interview with James Merrill." *Shenandoah,* 19 (Summer 1968), 3–15.

Kalstone, David. "The Poet: Private." *Saturday Review of the Arts,* 60 (December 1972), 42–45.

Vendler, Helen. "James Merrill's Myth: An Interview." *The New York Review of Books,* 3 May 1979, 12–13.

Labrie, Ross. "James Merrill at Home: An Interview." *Arizona Quarterly,* 38 (Spring 1982), 20–36.

McClatchy, J. D. "The Art of Poetry XXXI." *The Paris Review,* 24 (Summer 1982), 185–219. Reprinted in *Writers at Work: The Paris Review Interviews,* Sixth Series, ed. George Plimpton. New York: Viking Penguin, 1984.

Lunn, Jean. "A Conversation with James Merrill." *Sandscript,* 6 (1982), 2–22.

Bornhauser, Fred. Interview with James Merrill. In entry for Merrill in *Contemporary Authors,* New Revision Series, 10. Detroit: Gale Research Company, 1983, 322–329.

McClatchy, J. D. "DJ: A Conversation with David Jackson." *Shenandoah,* 30, no. 4 (1979), 23–44.

Bibliographies of Works by Merrill

Hagstrom, Jack W. C., and George Bixby. "James Merrill: A Bibliographical Check-list." *American Book Collector,* NS, 4, no. 6 (November/December 1983), 34–47.

Hall, Holly. *James Merrill, Poet.* St. Louis: Washington University, 1985. (Catalogue of extensive exhibit of printed materials and manuscripts drawn from the Merrill papers in the Modern Literature Collection of Washington University Libraries.)

Notes

1. Backward-Looking Figures

1. Quotations from Merrill's trilogy are from the one-volume edition, *The Changing Light at Sandover* (New York: Atheneum, 1982), rather than from the component volumes published separately and earlier. Similarly, except when otherwise indicated, a quotation from a poem included in *From the First Nine: Poems 1946–1976* (New York: Atheneum, 1982) is from that collection rather than from the book in which the poem first appeared. Because my discussion usually identifies the source of a quotation from Merrill's work and, when the information is essential, its approximate location, I have omitted reference to page numbers and the apparatus that such reference would entail.

2. Friedrich von Schlegel, *The Philosophy of Life, and Philosophy of Language, in a Course of Lectures,* trans. A. J. W. Morrison (London: Bohn, 1847), 389.

3. "The Poet: Private" (interview by David Kalstone), *Saturday Review of the Arts,* 55 (December 1972), 44.

4. "The Art of Poetry XXXI" (interview by J. D. McClatchy), *The Paris Review,* 29 (Summer 1982), 215.

5. Frederick Buechner, the novelist, Merrill's close friend and classmate at Lawrenceville, briefly recalls that period and their relationship in his memoir, *The Sacred Journey* (San Francisco: Harper and Row, 1982), 65–72.

6. From some verses in a letter to Thomas Butts, 22 November 1802, in *The Complete Poetry and Prose of William Blake,* ed. David V. Erdman with commentary by Harold Bloom, rev. ed. (Berkeley: University of California Press, 1982), 722.

7. Ralph Waldo Emerson, *Journal of Ralph Waldo Emerson,* ed. Edward Waldo Emerson and Waldo Emerson Forbes (New York: Houghton Mifflin, 1910), IV (1836–1838), 248–249.

8. Lewis Thomas, *Late Night Thoughts on Listening to Mahler's Ninth Symphony* (New York: Viking, 1983), 23.

9. "Condemned to Write about Real Things," *The New York Times Book Review,* 21 February 1982, 33. He also comments on the phrase "heavenly colors and swell fish" in "Days of 1941 and '44" in *Late Settings.*

10. "The Poet: Private," 45.

11. Marcel Proust, *A la Recherche du temps perdu* (Paris: Gallimard, 1969), VII, *Le Temps retrouvé,* 348. The English is from *Remembrance of Things Past,* trans. C. K.

Scott Moncrieff and Terence Kilmartin; and by Andreas Mayor (New York: Random House, 1981), III, 1086.

12. Roland Barthes, *A Lover's Discourse,* trans. Richard Howard (New York: Hill and Wang, 1978), 138. See also Barthes' pithy essay, "From Work to Text," in *Textual Strategies: Perspectives in Post-Structuralist Criticism,* ed. Josué V. Harrari (Ithaca, N.Y.: Cornell University Press, 1979), 73–81. The idea of the Text, Barthes suggests, implies an author whose "life is no longer the origin of his fables, but a fable that runs concurrently with his work. There is a reversal, and it is the work which affects the life, not the life which affects the work: the work of Proust and Genet allows us to read their lives as a text. The word 'bio-graphy' reassumes its strong meaning, in accordance with its etymology." Barthes suggests that the metaphor that properly describes the Text is the "network" (*réseau*).

13. *A la Recherche,* VII, 213–214. *Remembrance,* III, 931.

14. Merrill's unpublished honors thesis, "*A la Recherche du Temps Perdu:* Impressionism in Literature" (Amherst College, 1947), is in the Merrill papers at Washington University in St. Louis. In *The Fields of Light* (New York: Oxford University Press, 1951), 43, note, Brower acknowledges his borrowing of a term Merrill employed in his thesis. On p. 116, in a note to his discussion of *The Tempest,* one of the sources Merrill most frequently alludes to, Brower acknowledges a further debt to the thesis. Brower's comments were brought to my attention by Kathleen Bonann Marshall.

15. One remembers Merrill's remark about his "host in a remote farmhouse" in Greece who told "Aesop's fables as if he had made them up; that they had made *him* up was closer to the truth." See "Marvelous Poet" (review of Robert Liddell, *Cavafy: A Critical Biography* and *C. P. Cavafy Collected Poems,* trans. Edmund Keeley and Philip Sherrard), *The New York Review of Books,* 17 July 1975, 14.

16. "The Art of Poetry XXXI," 212.

17. Merrill's remark is in "The Poet: Private," 45. The original version of Valéry's *mot,* quoted as an epigraph to this chapter, is in "Eupalinos, ou l'Architecte," *Oeuvres de Paul Valéry* (Paris: Bibliothèque de la Pléiade [Gallimard], 1957), II, 142.

18. Northrop Frye discusses dialectic in these terms in *The Great Code: The Bible and Literature* (New York: Harcourt Brace, 1982), 221.

19. In *From the First Nine,* in addition to omitting poems published in the original volumes, Merrill has juggled the order of a few others. But these changes are rarely dramatic, and indeed the only other one of much import is the shifting of "For Proust" from an undistinguished seventh position to the penultimate position in the selections from *Water Street.* In no case except that of "Lost in Translation" does he change a volume's concluding poem.

20. Charles Merrill, *The Walled Garden: The Story of a School* (Boston: Rowan Tree Press, 1982).

21. "An Interview with James Merrill" (by Donald Sheehan), *Contemporary Literature,* 9 (Winter 1968), 7. Cf. "An Interview with James Merrill" (by Ashley Brown), *Shenandoah,* 19 (Summer 1968), 12. The "Waldstein" rondo form is different from the second rondo form outlined here.

22. This structure is pointed out by David Lehman, "Elemental Bravery: The Unity of James Merrill's Poetry," in *James Merrill: Essays in Criticism*, ed. David Lehman and Charles Berger (Ithaca: Cornell University Press, 1982), 60.

23. *A la Recherche*, VII, 209. *Remembrance*, III, 926.

24. *The Fields of Light*, 37. Cf. also p. 29: "Our whole aim in analysis of tone is to delineate the exact speaking voice . . . but we can succeed only by attending to the special, often minute language signs by which the poet fixes the tone for us." In "An Interview" (by Donald Sheehan), 7, Merrill says of Brower's course at Amherst that "it was chiefly a course in tone, in putting meaning and the sound of meaning back into words."

25. Valéry's original, accompanied by a translation by David Paul, can be found in Paul Valéry, *The Collected Works*, ed. Jackson Matthews, I: *Poems*, Bollingen Series XLV (Princeton: Princeton University Press, 1971), 228–235. Rilke's translation of the poem into German is included in Rainer Maria Rilke, *Übertragungen* (Frankfurt am Main: Insel Verlag, 1975), 281–283. Merrill's translation originally appeared in *The New York Review of Books*, 18 March 1982, 10, before it was included in *Late Settings*.

26. Rainer Maria Rilke, *Letters to a Young Poet*, trans. Stephen Mitchell (New York: Random House, 1984), 23–25. In "An Interview" (by Ashley Brown), 9, Merrill touches on the influence of Rilke: "What I got from Rilke was more than literary; that emphasis on the *acceptance* of pain and loneliness. Rilke helps you with suffering, especially in your adolescence." One thinks of those capitals in Rilke's translation, "lonelier than life." Merrill had written about Rilke as early as "The Transformation of Rilke," *Yale Poetry Review*, 1 (Spring 1946), 22–27.

27. *A la Recherche*, VII, 217–218. *Remembrance*, III, 935–936.

28. *A la Recherche*, VII, 214–215. *Remembrance*, III, 932.

29. "Idiosyncrasy and Technique," in *A Marianne Moore Reader* (New York: Viking, 1961), 171.

30. On Mademoiselle and her background, see "Condemned to Write about Real Things."

31. The puppet show flyer is in Merrill's possession.

32. "Foreword" to Bernard de Zogheb, *Phaedra: An Opera in Two Acts* (New York: n.p., n.d.), 3–4. The sensibility behind these librettos is close enough to Merrill's that it has been thought that Zogheb is a pseudonym for the poet. For the report of Merrill's correction of this rumor, see Jack W. C. Hagstrom and George Bixby, "James Merrill: A Bibliographical Checklist," *American Book Collector*, 4, NS (November/December 1983), 44, under *Le Sorelle Bronte, Opera in Quattri Atti*, a work by Zogheb to which Merrill contributed a similar foreword.

33. *Letters on Poetry from W. B. Yeats to Dorothy Wellesley*, introduction by Kathleen Raine (London: Oxford University Press, 1964), 22.

34. *The Selected Poetry of Rainer Maria Rilke*, ed. and trans. Stephen Mitchell (New York: Random House, 1982), 194–195.

35. Indeed, Rilke wrote poems in French, and the title of one of his collections of French poems is *Vergers*. In "The Transformation of Rilke," in discussing Rilke's

poetic evolution, the young Merrill speculates that the "German idiom, rich as almond paste," would not let him wholly renounce "'things,'" and that he could do so only in French, whose "airiness" was conducive to the spiritual essences he sought. Merrill's own translations from three languages include "Selections from Chamfort," *Semicolon,* I, no. 1 (n.d.; 1955?), unpaginated; "The Three T's," by Vassili Vasilikos, *Shenandoah,* 27 (Fall 1975), 44–48; "In Broad Daylight," by C. P. Cavafy, *Grand Street,* 2 (Spring 1983), 99–107; and four poems (one with Irma Brandeis) in *Eugenio Montale: Selected Poems,* introduction by Glauco Cambon (New York: New Directions, 1965).

36. Helen Vendler, "Chronicles of Love and Loss," *The New Yorker,* 21 May 1984, 127.

37. John Hollander points out that Stevens's line itself might echo Valéry's "Le Cimetière marin," where "Midi le juste y compose de feux / La mer, la mer, toujours recommencée." (He goes on to note wisely that in "all phenomena of this sort, we must always wonder what our contribution was—how much we are always being writers as well as readers of what we are seeing." The poem also is "toujours recommencée.") See *The Figure of Echo* (Berkeley: University of California Press, 1981), 99.

38. Published in *The Atlantic Monthly,* 250 (November 1982), 68. "Word golf," the game that John Shade and Charles Kinbote play in *Pale Fire,* was invented by Lewis Carroll, who called it "Doublets." It involves changing one word into another, usually its opposite, by way of intervening words, each of which differs from its predecessor in only one letter, as in Merrill's example. For more information, see Tony Augarde, *The Oxford Guide to Word Games* (Oxford: Oxford University Press, 1984), 184–189.

39. Northrop Frye, *Fables of Identity* (New York: Harcourt Brace, 1963), 222. A very interesting discussion of Merrill's characteristic unfolding of detail is David Kalstone, "Persisting Figures: The Poet's Story and How We Read It," in *James Merrill: Essays in Criticism,* 125–144.

40. "The Art of Poetry XXXI," 208.

41. "Notes on Corot," in *Corot 1796–1875: An Exhibition of His Paintings and Graphic Works* (Chicago: The Art Institute of Chicago, 1960), 15.

42. "Divine Poem," *The New Republic,* 29 November 1980, 29–34 and "Marvelous Poet," 14. One thinks also of his honors thesis, in which he discusses, *à la* Joseph Frank's *Spatial Form in Modern Literature,* the connections among passages widely separated in Proust's novel.

43. Merrill made this comment in a class he visited at UCLA in March 1983.

44. The factitiousness betrayed by this correspondence of form and alliterative titles, which would become anathema to Merrill before long, manifests itself on several occasions in *First Poems.* It derives in part, I think, from a willingness to repeat what has been successful. When this willingness afflicts individual poems, they are likely to be what Richard Howard has called poems in which "everything is given from the start, nothing allowed to happen or become." See *Alone with America: Essays on the Art of Poetry in the United States since 1950* (New York: Atheneum, 1971), 328.

45. "An Interview" (by Ashley Brown), 10.

46. Randall Jarrell quotes Eliot's remark—"The only method is to be very intelligent"—in *Poetry and the Age* (New York: Vintage, 1959), 81. Merrill touches on the relationship between simplicity and intelligence as early as *The Birthday* (1947), an unpublished verse play in the Merrill papers at Washington University. There, a character named Max, "supposed to be rather naive," speculates that "The really brilliant people never think."

47. William Smith, *Smith's Bible Dictionary* (New York: Pyramid Books, 1967), 79.

2. Breaking and Entering

1. *Staying on Alone: Letters of Alice B. Toklas,* ed. Edward Burns (New York: Liveright, 1973), 287.

2. There are two editions of *The Country of a Thousand Years of Peace:* New York: Knopf, 1959 and New York: Atheneum, 1970. The latter omits one poem included in the first edition ("At Mamallapuram") and includes three previously unpublished poems: "Saint," "The Day of the Eclipse," and "Power Station." Only the latter appears also in *From the First Nine.*

3. *Poet's Choice,* ed. Paul Engle and Joseph Langland (New York: The Dial Press, 1962), 241.

4. "The Art of Poetry XXXI" (interview by J. D. McClatchy), *The Paris Review,* 29 (Summer 1982), 208.

5. Among the enlightening discussions of "Mirror" are those in J. D. McClatchy, "Monsters Wrapped in Silk: James Merrill's *Country of a Thousand Years of Peace,*" *Contemporary Poetry,* IV, no. 4 (1982), 24–29; and John Hollander, "A Poetry of Restitution," *The Yale Review,* 70 (Winter 1981), 163–171.

6. Cf. the discussion of the Marsyas story in Emmanuel Winternitz, *Musical Instruments and Their Symbolism in Western Art: Studies in Musical Iconology* (New Haven: Yale University Press, 1979), 152. According to Winternitz, this story is "a poetic condensation of an eternal conflict, the antagonism between two musical realms, between string and wind instruments. This means not only the difference between the serene and silvery sound of plucked gut strings and the bleating, shrill, guttural, exciting sound of a reed pipe . . . It means in the rationalized form of the Greek myths the realm of inhibition, of reason, of measure . . . as opposed to the realm of blind passion."

7. Merrill is quoted in Judith Green, "More Truth in Poetry," *The Virginian-Pilot,* 23 April 1983, A16.

8. On the dramatic element in his lyric poetry, see Merrill's comments on the poet and the playwright in "An Interview with James Merrill" (by Donald Sheehan), *Contemporary Literature,* 9 (Winter 1968), 7.

9. "James Merrill at Home: An Interview" (by Ross Labrie), *Arizona Quarterly,* 38 (Spring 1982), 29.

10. "James Merrill at Home," 28.

11. "The Art of Poetry XXXI," 212. Merrill's mature work frequently bears out W. B. Yeats's pronouncement in "Per Amica Silentia Lunae": "We make out of the quarrel with others, rhetoric, but out of the quarrel with ourselves, poetry. Unlike the rhetoricians, who get a confident voice from remembering the crowd they have won or may win, we sing amid our uncertainty; and, smitten even in the presence of the most high beauty by the knowledge of our solitude, our rhythm shudders." *Mythologies* (London: Macmillan, 1959), 331.

12. W. H. Auden, *The Dyer's Hand* (New York: Random House, 1962), 338.

13. "An Interview" (by Donald Sheehan), 10.

14. Letter of 18 November 1920 in *Lettres françaises à Merline 1919–1922* (Paris: Editions du Seuil, 1950), 38–39. The translation is from *Letters to Merline 1919–1922,* trans. Violet M. Macdonald (London: Methuen, 1951), 47–48.

15. See David Lehman, "Elemental Bravery: The Unity of James Merrill's Poetry," in *James Merrill: Essays in Criticism,* ed. David Lehman and Charles Berger (Ithaca: Cornell University Press, 1983), esp. 30–38 and 44–48; and Willard Spiegelman, "Breaking the Mirror: Interruption in Merrill's Trilogy," in *James Merrill: Essays in Criticism,* 186–210.

16. "Object Lessons" (review of Francis Ponge, *The Voice of Things,* trans. Beth Archer Brombert and *Things,* trans. Cid Corman), *The New York Review of Books,* 30 November 1972, 31. Merrill's wittiest and most extensive treatment of "Ideas" is in the poem by that title (*Late Settings*), a consummate comic dialogue between the latest avatars of Xenia and Charles.

17. Cf. Merrill's discussion of things and essences in "The Transformation of Rilke," *Yale Poetry Review,* 1 (Spring 1946), 22–27, especially the observation that "the paradox in [Rilke's] poetry is that he has made things infinitely real to us at the same moment that he proclaims them insubstantial."

18. "Object Lessons," 31.

19. Wallace Stevens, *Opus Posthumous,* ed. Samuel French Morse (New York: Knopf, 1977), 158.

20. Robert Graves, *The White Goddess,* enlarged ed. (New York: Vintage, 1958), 539. The two poems are on pp. 540–541.

21. Marcel Proust, *A la Recherche du temps perdu* (Paris: Gallimard, 1969), I, *Du Côté de chez Swann,* 72. *Remembrance of Things Past,* trans. C. K. Scott Moncrieff and Terence Kilmartin; and by Andreas Mayor (New York: Random House, 1981), I, 51.

22. It is remarkable, then, that this line was not in the version, different in no other respect, that was published in *Partisan Review,* 27 (Winter 1960), 62–65.

23. "An Interview with James Merrill" (by Ashley Brown), *Shenandoah,* 19 (Summer 1968), 12.

24. David Kalstone has written about Merrill's association of poetic work and house in *Five Temperaments* (New York: Oxford University Press, 1977), 88–90. See also J. D. McClatchy's rich essay "On *Water Street*" in *James Merrill: Essays in Criticism,* esp. 79–88.

25. Gaston Bachelard, *The Poetics of Space,* trans. Maria Jolas (Boston: Beacon Press, 1958), 6–7.

26. Sigmund Freud, *Civilization and Its Discontents,* trans. James Strachey (New York: Norton, 1961), 38.

27. Bachelard, *The Poetics of Space,* 15.

28. "Condemned to Write about Real Things," *The New York Times Book Review,* 21 February 1982, 11.

29. In *Poetry,* 98 (June 1961), 167, the pertinent lines are as follows: "Its leaner veteran will rise to face / Partners not recognized / Until drunk back to youth and beauty; / The bone-tipped index lifted, / Music more rapid will explode / From passing cars, from my depressions."

30. William Gass, *Fiction and the Figures of Life* (New York: Knopf, 1970), 287.

31. Louise Bogan, "Verse" (review of *First Poems* and other volumes), *The New Yorker,* 9 June 1951, 110.

32. "Object Lessons," 32. In "An Interview" (by Donald Sheehan), 12, Merrill notes that he "might have discovered [the novel's technique] much earlier from, say, that edition of Keats' letters where the deletions are legible; and, of course, from letters one receives oneself: the eye instantly flies to the crossed-out word. It seems to promise so much more than the words left exposed."

33. Merrill names the island in "James Merrill at Home," 27. Certain important elements in *The (Diblos) Notebook*—Poros and the Sleeping Woman, the wealthy couple with a yacht, the *zeybékiko* as a rite of union—occur also in Peter Mayne, *The Private Sea* (London: John Murray, 1958), which Merrill might well have read.

34. "An Interview" (by Ashley Brown), 11.

35. Cf. "Dream (Escape from the Sculpture Museum) and Waking," *The Country of a Thousand Years of Peace:* "You called me cold, I said you were a child. / I said we must respect / Each other's solitude. You *smiled.*" This Rilkean theme recurs with surprising frequency in Merrill's work.

36. Letter to Lady Elizabeth Pelham, quoted by Richard Ellman, *Yeats: The Man and the Masks* (New York: Dutton, 1948), 285.

37. "James Merrill at Home," 26.

38. "An Interview" (by Donald Sheehan), 5.

39. Finley has been discussing an affinity between hero and poet, "a natural bond between the heroic temper and a gaze that sees the world with sharp and bright particularity." This bond exists too between *cravache* and pen—or bow and lyre, in Heraclitus's famous phrase. See John H. Finley, Jr., *Four Stages of Greek Thought* (Stanford: Stanford University Press, 1966), 28.

40. Marilyn Aronberg Lavin, *Piero della Francesca: The Flagellation* (New York: Viking, 1972), esp. 45–51, 74–80.

41. Philip Guston, "Piero della Francesca: The Impossibility of Painting," *Art News,* 64 (1965), 38–39, quoted in Lavin, 13.

3. Double Burdens

1. Cyril Connolly, *The Unquiet Grave: A Word Cycle by Palinurus* (New York: Viking, 1945, 1966), 120–121. Merrill surely knows this dense, sad, charming work—which could almost be the "book of words" he leafs through in "Last Morn-

ings in California" (*Late Settings*), though he means to refer in the first place to a dictionary (*Wörterbuch*). That poem's lemur, Paulette, who begins "high up / In eucalyptus uttering her sun cry" and later somehow merges with a figure sleeping under a patchwork quilt, seems to descend from Connolly's marvelously evoked companions, Whoopee and Polyp, "ring-tailed lemurs with their reverence for the sun" who would "worm their way down to sleep in the bottom of the bed." See especially pp. 95–96 and 117–119 in *The Unquiet Grave*. (Connolly also quotes from and discusses Chamfort, some of whose maxims Merrill has translated, as I have noted earlier.)

2. W. H. Auden, *New Year Letter* (1940), in *Collected Poems,* ed. Edward Mendelson (New York: Random House, 1976), 176.

3. Wallace Stevens, *The Palm at the End of the Mind* (New York: Vintage, 1972), 233. Merrill's comment is in "An Interview with James Merrill" (by Ashley Brown), *Shenandoah,* 19 (Summer 1968), 7.

4. Jonathan Bishop, *Who Is Who* (Ithaca, N.Y.: Glad Day Press, 1975), 93.

5. C. P. Cavafy, *Collected Poems,* trans. Edmund Keeley and Philip Sherrard, ed. George Savidis (Princeton: Princeton University Press, 1975), 409.

6. Connolly, *The Unquiet Grave,* 102–103.

7. "James Merrill at Home: An Interview" (by Ross Labrie), *Arizona Quarterly,* 38 (Spring 1982), 20.

8. "An Interview with James Merrill" (by Donald Sheehan), *Contemporary Literature,* 9 (Winter 1968), 6–7. Cf. the sixth sonnet in "Matinees," where Merrill recalls the effect of his first operas in much the same language.

9. "An Interview" (by Donald Sheehan), 3.

10. "The Art of Poetry XXXI" (an interview by J. D. McClatchy), *The Paris Review,* 29 (Summer 1982), 214.

11. "An Interview" (by Donald Sheehan), 6.

12. Donald Sutherland, *On, Romanticism* (New York: New York University Press, 1971), 196.

13. Louise Bogan, "The Pleasure of Formal Poetry" (1954), reprinted in *The Poet's Work: 29 Masters of 20th Century Poetry on the Origins and Practice of Their Art,* ed. Reginald Gibbons (Boston: Houghton Mifflin, 1979), 205.

14. "An Interview" (by Donald Sheehan), 6.

15. David Lehman, "Elemental Bravery: The Unity of James Merrill's Poetry," in *James Merrill: Essays in Criticism,* ed. David Lehman and Charles Berger (Ithaca: Cornell University Press, 1983), 46.

16. A. R. Ammons, "Summer Session," *Collected Poems: 1951–1971* (New York: W. W. Norton, 1972), 248.

17. On poems written "against" others, see "The Poet: Private" (an interview by David Kalstone), *Saturday Review of the Arts,* 55 (December 1972), 45.

18. It seems the more likely that Merrill is thinking of "Le Cimetière marin" since earlier, in "A wind rising," he virtually translates "Le vent se lève!", which immediately precedes the famous imperative. But effort is a persistent theme in Valéry's writings.

19. "The soul . . . came with age to resemble *a body one no longer had*" harks

back to some lines in "A Tenancy": "The body that lived through that day / . . . is now not mine. / Would it be called a soul?"

20. The quotations come from Jacques Derrida, *Of Grammatology,* trans. Gayatri Chakravorty Spivak (Baltimore: Johns Hopkins University Press, 1976), 167 and 187, but the whole of part II, chapters 2 and 3 has some bearing on the matter. On "differance" see Spivak's preface, xliii–xliv.

21. William Gass, *Fiction and the Figures of Life* (New York: Knopf, 1970), 287.

22. Sutherland, *On, Romanticism,* 102.

23. *The Portable Thoreau,* ed. Carl Bode, rev. ed. (New York: Viking, 1964), 386.

24. Erich Neumann, *Amor and Psyche: The Psychic Development of the Feminine,* trans. Ralph Manheim (Princeton: Princeton University Press, 1956).

25. H. J. Rose, *A Handbook of Greek Mythology, Including Its Extension to Rome,* rev. ed. (London: Methuen, 1953), 286–287.

26. Joseph Campbell, *The Hero with a Thousand Faces* (New York: Meridian, 1956), 97–98.

27. "An Interview with James Merrill" (by Ashley Brown), 14.

28. John Berryman's *Homage to Mistress Bradstreet* (New York: Farrar, Straus & Giroux, 1956) was first published in *Partisan Review* in 1953.

29. Eileen Simpson, *Poets in Their Youth* (New York: Random House, 1982), 226.

30. Ibid., 228.

31. Friedrich von Schlegel, *The Philosophy of Life, and Philosophy of Language, in a Course of Lectures,* trans. A. J. W. Morrison (London: Bohn, 1847), 389.

32. Neumann, *Amor,* 143.

33. "James Merrill at Home," 29–30.

34. "An Interview with James Merrill" (by Donald Sheehan), 9.

35. Neumann, *Amor,* 76.

36. Neumann, ibid., 82, n.9, mentions the Artemis in connection with the Great Goddess.

37. Ibid., 74.

38. Ibid., 80.

39. Quoted in *Letters on Poetry from W. B. Yeats to Dorothy Wellesley,* introduction by Kathleen Raine (London: Oxford University Press, 1964), 174.

40. "Notes on Corot," in *Corot 1796–1875: An Exhibition of His Paintings and Graphic Works* (Chicago: The Art Institute of Chicago, 1960), 15. The work papers in the Merrill papers at Washington University indicate that this crucial "NOON" section went through an extraordinary number of drafts—extraordinary even for Merrill, who is a tireless reviser. It seems at first to have been an independent poem, perhaps the seed of "From the Cupola," and was tentatively entitled "A Temptation," "The Celibate," and "Self-Denial."

41. On these very parsnips, see the amusing entry under "Reward" in Eleanor Perényi, *Green Thoughts: A Writer in the Garden* (New York: Random House, 1981), 187–188.

42. Neumann, *Amor,* 81–84.

43. Merrill's punning use of "still" perhaps pays tribute to Berryman's *Homage*, where it appears in identical rhymes with double meanings in the first and last stanzas.

4. At the Web's Heart

1. See "James Merrill at Home: An Interview" (by Ross Labrie), *Arizona Quarterly*, 38 (Spring 1982), 23. He is alluding to an entry in *Adagia*, in *Opus Posthumous*, ed. Samuel French Morse (New York: Knopf, 1977), 171.

2. Ludwig Wittgenstein, Proposition 6.4311, *Tractatus Logico-Philosophicus*, trans. D. F. Pears and B. F. McGuinness (London: Routledge and Kegan Paul, 1961), 147.

3. Hans Jonas, "Gnosticism," *The Encyclopedia of Philosophy*, III (New York and London: Collier-MacMillan, 1967), 340.

4. "The Poet: Private" (interview by David Kalstone), *Saturday Review of the Arts*, 55 (December 1972), 44.

5. Joseph Campbell, *The Hero with a Thousand Faces* (New York: Meridian Books, 1949), 40.

6. An influential presence in Merrill's work at least since *Nights and Days*, Yeats figures especially often in *The Fire Screen*. In one way or another, he might be glimpsed in the background of "The Friend of the Fourth Decade," "More Enterprise," "Flying from Byzantium," "Last Words," and "Matinees." In this last poem Merrill alludes to "Sailing to Byzantium," "Byzantium," and "Dialogue of Self and Soul," as well as perhaps "Cuchulain Comforted," "The Circus Animals' Desertion" and "Meditations in Time of Civil War." Indeed, Yeats seems to be the "'father'" figure and dentist who has "'tampered with [Merrill's] mouth'" so that "'From now on, metal, music, myth / Will seem to taint its words.'" Since one form this figure takes is that of a Dr. Scherer, Yeats might be thought of as Merrill's secret Scherer in this sonnet sequence (though that title could also go to Wagner, whose own fire and gold recur throughout).

7. Stéphane Mallarmé, *Oeuvres complètes* (Paris: Bibliothèque de la Pléiade [Gallimard], 1945), 882.

8. John Porter Houston, *French Symbolism and the Modern Movement: A Study of Poetic Structures* (Baton Rouge: Louisiana State University Press, 1980), 115.

9. "Object Lessons" (review of Francis Ponge, *The Voice of Things*, trans. Beth Archer Brombert and *Things*, trans. Cid Corman), *The New York Review of Books*, 30 November 1972, 32.

10. "The Parnassians," *The New York Review of Books*, 27 October 1983, 4.

11. Mallarmé, *Oeuvres complètes*, 368 and 386. The translations are mine. There is a brilliant analysis of "the idea of a *double language*," with its first clear articulation in Mallarmé and its elaboration in Valéry, in Gerard Genette, "Valéry and the Poetics of Language," trans. Josué V. Harari, in *Textual Strategies: Perspectives in Post-Structuralist Criticism*, ed. Josué V. Harari (Ithaca: Cornell University Press, 1979), 359–373.

12. Mallarmé, *Oeuvres complètes,* 366. My translation has benefited from those by Bradford Cook in *Selected Prose Poems, Essays, and Letters* (Baltimore: Johns Hopkins University Press, 1956) and Mary Ann Caws in *Stéphane Mallarmé: Selected Poetry and Prose,* ed. Mary Ann Caws (New York: New Directions, 1982).

13. Umberto Eco, *The Role of the Reader* (Bloomington: Indiana University Press, 1979), 78. Eco elaborates on his "regulative hypothesis of a semiotic universe structured as a labyrinth" in *Semiotics and the Philosophy of Language* (Bloomington: Indiana University Press, 1984), chap. 2, esp. pp. 80–82.

14. William Gass, *In the Heart of the Heart of the Country and Other Stories,* with a Revised and Expanded Preface (Boston: Godine, 1981), xxxiv.

15. Geoffrey Hartman, *Saving the Text: Literature/Derrida/Philosophy* (Baltimore: Johns Hopkins University Press, 1981), 45. Hartman himself—like Derrida, the Saussure of *Words upon Words,* Michel Foucault in *Death and the Labyrinth: The World of Raymond Roussel,* the Gass of essays such as "Gertrude Stein and the Geography of the Sentence" in *The World within the Word*—implicitly urges what has been called "narrative allegory," as distinct from "allegoresis." In Gregory L. Ulmer's summary, the latter "'suspends' the surface of the text, applying a terminology of 'verticalness, levels, hidden meaning, the hieratic difficulty of interpretation,' whereas 'narrative allegory' (practiced by post-critics) explores the literal—*letteral*—level of the language itself, in a horizontal investigation of the polysemous meanings simultaneously available in the words themselves—in etymologies and puns—and in the things the words name . . . In short, narrative allegory favors the material of the signifier over the meanings of the signifieds." See "The Object of Post-Criticism," in *The Anti-Aesthetic: Essays on Postmodern Culture,* ed. Hal Foster (Port Townsend, Wash: Bay Press, 1983), 95. Ulmer is quoting from Maureen Quilligan's heuristic study, *The Language of Allegory* (Ithaca, N.Y.: Cornell University Press, 1979). Merrill's symbolist work often invites such a "post-critical" approach.

16. Mallarmé, *Oeuvres complètes,* 869. My translation.

17. See Jean Starobinski, ed., *Les Mots sous les Mots: Les Anagrammes de Ferdinand de Saussure* (Paris: Gallimard, 1971), trans. Olivia Emmet, *Words upon Words: The Anagrams of Ferdinand de Saussure* (New Haven: Yale University Press, 1979). For the influence of Saussure's zany, brilliant notebooks, unpublished in his lifetime, see Hartman on Derrida in *Saving the Text,* 82–83, and Michael Riffaterre, *Text Production* (New York: Columbia University Press, 1983), 75–89.

18. Hugh Kenner, *The Pound Era* (Berkeley: University of California Press, 1971), 171. It is not altogether clear why such words should be thought of as "rare," however.

19. Albert Thibaudet, *La Poésie de Stéphane Mallarmé* (Paris: Gallimard, 1926), 311.

20. Paul Verlaine, *Oeuvres complètes,* I (Paris: Albert Massein, 1925), 295. My translation.

21. Kenner, *The Pound Era,* 171.

22. Ibid., 130.

23. Merrill perhaps has another source that might be invoked at this point.

I quote the summary in Jorge Luis Borges, *Seven Nights,* trans. Eliot Weinberger (New York: New Directions, 1984), 66–67: "Among the stories of the Buddha, there is one that is particularly illuminating: the parable of the arrow. A man has been wounded in battle, but he does not want them to remove the arrow. First he wants to know the name of the archer, to what caste he belongs, what the arrow is made of, where the archer was standing at the time, how long the arrow is. While he is discussing these things, he dies. 'I, however,' said the Buddha, 'teach that one must pull the arrow out.' What is the arrow? It is the universe. The arrow is the notion of I, of everything to which we are chained. The Buddha says that we shouldn't waste time on useless questions. Is the universe finite or infinite? Does the Buddha live after Nirvana or not? All this is useless. What matters is that we pull the arrow out. It is an exorcism, a law of salvation."

24. On the Black Mesa of San Ildefonso, the site of the seige mounted in 1694 by the Conquistador De Vargas against the Tehua and Tanos natives who had ensconced themselves there, see Ralph Emerson Twichell, *The Leading Facts of New Mexican History,* I (Cedar Rapids: The Torch Press, 1911), 393–394. The poem's speaker also thinks of himself as the "desert father" who "falls for" the courtesan in *Thaïs.*

25. Hartman, *Saving the Text,* 80.

26. An excellent discussion of "18 West 11th Street" is in Richard Saez, "James Merrill's Oedipal Fire," *Parnassus: Poetry in Review,* Fall/Winter 1974, 159–184. For contemporary accounts of the explosion, see "Bombing: A Way of Protest," *Time,* 95 (23 March 1970), 8–10 and "Terrorism on the Left," *Newsweek,* 75, pt. 2 (23 March 1970), 26–28. "18 West 11th Street" is one of the poems objected to by Judith Moffett, one of Merrill's most sympathetic readers but one of his most severe critics when it comes to "obscurity." In *James Merrill: An Introduction to the Poetry* (New York: Columbia University Press, 1984), 122, provoked by poems such as this one, she complains that "not to care whether one communicates effectively . . . with one's genuinely committed average reader may arguably be the one capital crime a good writer can commit." She presents her case in more detail in an essay, "Sound without Sense: Willful Obscurity in Poetry," *New England Review,* 3 (Winter 1980), 294–312.

27. Cyril W. Beaumont, *The Complete Book of Ballets* (Garden City, N.Y.: Garden City Publishing Company, 1941), 565.

28. "The Clear Eye of Elizabeth Bishop," *The Washington Post Book World,* 20 February 1983, 1–2, 14. Judith Moffett writes interestingly about this kind of metaphor in Merrill and his distance from "nature in the wild" in *James Merrill: An Introduction to the Poetry,* 8–13.

29. *Mauvaises pensées,* in *Oeuvres de Paul Valéry* (Paris: Bibliothèque de la Pléiade [Gallimard], 1957), II, 862.

30. Stéphane Mallarmé, *Correspondance,* I: *1862–1871* (Paris: Gallimard, 1959), 224–225. The translation by Bradford Cook, from *Selected Poems, Essays, and Letters,* by Stéphane Mallarmé, is in *Stéphane Mallarmé: Selected Poetry and Prose,* ed. Mary Ann Caws, 85.

5. *The Fullness of Time*

1. See Stéphane Mallarmé, *Correspondance, I: 1862–1871* (Paris: Gallimard, 1959), 225, n. 1. Mallarmé reverses the emphasis when he remarks, in a comment Merrill alludes to at the end of section P in *Ephraim*, that "Au fond, voyez-vous, le monde est fait pour aboutir à un beau livre." See Mallarmé's interview with Jules Huret in the *Echo de Paris,* reprinted as "Sur l'Evolution Littéraire" in "Réponses à des Enquêtes," *Oeuvres complètes* (Paris: Bibliothèque de la Pléiade [Gallimard], 1945), 872. (He glosses the point in "Le Livre, Instrument Spirituel," in the same volume, 378–382.)

2. Merrill quotes Ephraim's reference to Caligula, "THE MONSTERS NEPHEW," and then adds a "(sic)." Caligula was actually the great-nephew of Tiberius—as well as a sort of legal grandson.

3. An immigrant from Russia (like Sergei), Deren was a dancer and founder of the Creative Film Foundation as well as a director and author. There is a good deal of confusion about her birth date, which JM gives in D as 1917 and which the *Oxford Companion to Film* lists as 1908. It seems to be a confusion that she fostered, and JM reports in G that Ephraim, to Deren's consternation, told them that she was born five years earlier than the date she claimed, which must have been 1922, since DJ and JM found out at the time of her death in 1961 that Ephraim "had been correct."

4. The excerpt comes from Peter Quennell, *Alexander Pope: The Education of Genius 1688–1728* (London: Weidenfeld and Nicholson, 1968), 185–186.

5. This passage, and the next quoted, occur in a section JM later refers to as a "net of loose talk," since it is in hendecasyllabics, this poem's approximation of prose. The switch from pentameter corresponds to his attempt "to say outright" what he feels about "the absolute," and he returns to it presently, just after noting that "The twinkings of / Insight hurt or elude the naked eye, no / Metrical lens to focus them." Meter, in other words, is to insight what the "neutral ground" of the lost novel would have been to his themes.

6. Merrill's sections often begin with key words, but even when they do not do so (as in T, U, W) their initial letters sometimes coincide with the first letters of words that are especially important in their sections (Time, Unconscious, Wendell). Not just a witty device, the alphabetical division is also a convenient mnemonic one.

7. The review of Robert Liddell's *Cavafy: A Critical Biography* (London: Duckworth, 1974) is in *The New York Review of Books,* 17 July 1975, 12–17. Liddell quotes Cavafy's note, which is essentially a paraphrase of a passage in Ruskin's *A Joy Forever,* on p. 118.

8. Spenser describes the Garden of Adonis in *The Faerie Queene,* book III, canto vi. Merrill quotes stanzas 41–42. Spenser's version of the garden troubled by time, Heraclitus's image of time as a child playing checkers, and T's figuring of time as a reflection combine in the rather sour song in L, in which a global garden mirror tosses the surrounding "crudities" (also *crudités*) like a salad. That Spenser's Adonis as presented in III.vi.47—"eterne in mutabilite" and "the Father of all forms"—would be of special interest to Merrill seems apparent. Cf. the discussion later of the Proteus passage in V.

9. The excerpt from Heraclitus is fragment 52 in *Die Fragmente der Vorsokratiker, Griechisch und Deutsch*, I, ed. H. Diels and W. Franz, 10th ed. (Berlin: Weidmann, 1961), and fragment 93 in M. Markovich, *Heraclitus: Greek Text with a Short Commentary* (Merida, Venezuela: Los Andes University Press, 1967). The "board game" here must be related to the "checkerboard linoleum" over which Sergei and Time pick their way toward each other in T. The "board game" is often translated as "checkers" or "dice," but for obvious reasons Merrill would want the broader term. The "checkerboard linoleum" might owe something to Henry James's story "The Jolly Corner," where Brydon meets *his* alter ego on a floor of "black-and-white squares," and perhaps more to the floor in the music room of Merrill's house in Stonington. (See J. D. McClatchy's headnote to "The Art of Poetry XXXI," *The Paris Review*, 29 [Summer 1982] for a fine description of that room.)

10. Merrill's source is Nancy Thompson de Grummond, "Giorgione's 'Tempest': The Legend of St. Theodore," *L'Arte*, 5, no. 18–19/20, 5–53. Later in the trilogy, he admits that this essay has not laid to rest all the questions raised by the painting.

11. Cf. the quotation from John Michell in Q in which it is (falsely) intimated that the folk hero, Lambton, must kill his father and Merrill's treatment of his own father in this poem and in *The Seraglio*.

12. It must be said, however, that the dragon is not easily pinned down and that the passage might accommodate other views of it. For example, if one took the "hill" in Y that disguises some horror, such as a crematorium or a nuclear testing site, to be parallel to the "landscape" that conceals the presence of the dragon, the dragon might be associated with evil. JM himself, apparently following Jung on the anima, tentatively links the dragon to his mother—and then discreetly retracts that view.

13. Michell, *The View over Atlantis* (London: Sago Press, 1969), 58–59.

14. JM says that the names of his novel's chief characters were meant to associate them with the four Evangelists, "Plus the beast familiar to one." The others are Matt (Matthew), Lucy (Luke), Sergei Markovich (Mark), and Leo (Mark's symbol is the lion).

15. See Martin Green, *Children of the Sun: A Narrative of "Decadence" in England after 1918* (New York: Basic Books, 1976), 316, for a report of the incident. The finely tuned details are Merrill's.

16. *The Penguin Dictionary of Saints*, ed. Donald Attwater (Harmondsworth, England: Penguin Books, 1973), 116–117.

17. Wilde, "The Critic as Artist (Part II)," in *The Writings of Oscar Wilde* (New York: Gabriel Wells, 1925), 203.

18. Henry James is connected with the poet in both O and D (where he is the "past master of clauses" who, in Eliot's phrase, has a mind so fine that "'no idea violates'" it). James might also be somewhere behind the last sentence in *Ephraim*, "For here we are." *The Ambassadors* concludes with Strether's response to Maria's attempt to sigh it "at last all comically, all tragically, away. 'I can't indeed resist you,'" with "Then there we are!"

19. The first clause paraphrases a proposition in *Adagia*, in *Opus Posthumous*

(New York: Knopf, 1957), 178, and the second alludes to "The Noble Rider and the Sound of Words," in *The Necessary Angel* (New York: Random House Vintage, 1951), 36.

20. Jung, "Answer to Job," in *The Portable Jung,* ed. Joseph Campbell (New York: Viking, 1971), 647.

21. Ibid., 638–639. Cf. the passage in F in which JM compares man's position to that of a particular chimpanzee that has been learning sign language: "Weren't we still groping, like Miranda, toward / Some higher level?"

22. See George Duckworth, *Structural Patterns and Proportions in Vergil's Aeneid* (Ann Arbor: University of Michigan Press, 1962) for the use of the golden section by Vergil and others of his time. Bartók employs the golden section in several works including the *Sonata for Two Pianos and Percussion* and the first, second, and fourth movements of the *Fifth Quartet*. For a brief history of its use in the visual arts and a bibliography, and this translation of Book 6, Proposition 3, see *The Oxford Companion to Art,* ed. Harold Osborne (New York: Oxford University Press, 1970), 488–489.

23. Jung, "Answer to Job," 632. Merrill also alludes to *Götterdämmerung* in W, X, and Z, and twilight pervades the poem.

24. Ibid., 523.

25. Ibid., 648.

26. Ibid., 523.

27. Ibid., 650.

28. The play's young hero, said to his surprise to be Mrs. Crane's son, is Raymond, whose name has an obvious similarity with Rosamund's. Are they not very early versions of the figures in Giorgione's painting as it is interpreted in X? When Mother Nature shows her other side, in the following books in *Sandover,* we might well recall her name in *The Birthday*—and its overtones in light of the "crane" in "A Tenancy" and in *The White Goddess*. See the discussion of "A Tenancy" in Chapter 2. *The Birthday* is included in the Merrill papers at Washington University.

29. Stevens, "Three Academic Pieces, 1," in *The Necessary Angel,* 80–81.

30. Indeed *Ephraim* is a Venetian poem, and the whole of *Sandover* is a Venetian work, if we have in mind Michel Beaujour's rich essay, "The Venetian Mirror." In this essay, published even as *Ephraim* was being written, Beaujour reflects on Venice as a "commonplace" and on the variants that it has generated, including "self-reflection, doubling, and multiplication." He points out that "a durable transience" and "an evanescent solidity" have always been features of a "literary Venice" and that the tropes most often used in its service are oxymoron, chiasmus, and antithesis. "Venice," he argues, "teaches the writer to do away with the identity principle, and to discard Being in favor of Passage." On his definition, "all Venetian texts are in some respect fragmented or unresolved texts." One of his key examples is Jules Vuillemin's *Le Miroir de Venise,* in which we find the narrator musing thus on that city: "Everywhere, I find things, ideas, and more memories; vainly, I espy myself, dissolved and broken up myself among the reflecting mirrors which I perceive." See Beaujour, "The Venetian Mirror," *The Georgia Review,* 29 (Fall 1975), 627–647. Cf.

also the discussion in Chapter 7 of the breaking of the mirror at the end of *Scripts for the Pageant.*

31. "Rose" appeared in *The Glass Hill,* no. 7 (1949), unpaginated.

32. Zimmer, *The King and the Corpse,* 2nd ed., ed. Joseph Campbell (New York: Pantheon, 1956), 4–5.

6. The Nature of Mind

1. Merrill's reference to Rilke is to the ninth of the *Duino Elegies,* lines 32ff.: "Sind wir vielleicht *hier,* um zu sagen: Haus, /Brücke, Brunnen, Tor, Krug, Obstbaum, Fenster— / höchstens: Säule, Turm . . . aber zu *sagen,* verstehs, / oh zu sagen *so,* wie selber die Dinge niemals / innig meinten zu sein." Stephen Mitchell translates as follows: "Perhaps we are *here* in order to say: house, / bridge, fountain, gate, pitcher, fruit tree, window— / at most, column, tower . . . But to *say* them, you must understand, / oh, to say them *more* intensely than the Things themselves / ever dreamed of existing." *The Selected Poetry of Rainer Maria Rilke* (New York: Random House, 1982), 199–201.

2. See *A Vision of the Last Judgment* (Rossetti ms.) 71–72, in *The Writings of William Blake,* III, ed. Geoffrey Keynes (London, 1925), 146, quoted in Northrop Frye, *Fearful Symmetry: A Study of William Blake* (Princeton: Princeton University Press, 1969), 40, and the letters to John Butts, dated 25 April 1803 and July 1903 in *The Complete Poetry and Prose of William Blake,* ed. David V. Erdman with commentary by Harold Bloom, rev. ed. (Berkeley: University of California Press, 1982), 728–730.

3. Cf. the remarks on light and serious verse by Louise Bogan, "The Pleasures of Formal Poetry," in *The Poet's Work: 29 Masters of 20th Century Poetry on the Origins and Practice of Their Art,* ed. Reginald Gibbons (Boston: Houghton Mifflin, 1979), 205, quoted in Chapter 3.

4. Martin Gardner tells this anecdote in *The Ambidextrous Universe,* rev. ed. (New York: New American Library, 1969), 243.

5. Donald Sutherland, *On, Romanticism* (New York: New York University Press, 1971), 133. Perhaps I should add, however, that Alfred North Whitehead, who should know, has written that "If Shelley had been born a hundred years later, the twentieth century would have seen a Newton among chemists." See *Science and the Modern World* (New York: The Free Press, 1967), 84.

6. Friedrich Schiller in a letter to Korner, 1 December 1788, quoted in Sigmund Freud, *The Interpretation of Dreams,* trans. James Strachey (New York: Avon, 1967), 135.

7. See "James Merrill's Myth: An Interview" (with Helen Vendler), *The New York Review of Books,* 3 May 1979, 12. Merrill associates two rooms in the Stonington house—the "domed red one where we took down the messages, and a blue one, dominated by an outsize mirror" and containing the bat wallpaper—with the brain's two hemispheres, as explained by Julian Jaynes.

8. Julian Jaynes, *The Origin of Consciousness in the Breakdown of the Bicameral Mind* (Boston: Houghton Mifflin, 1977), 117–118.

9. Friedrich Schiller, quoted in Freud, *The Interpretation of Dreams*, 135.

10. Friedrich von Schlegel, in an excerpt from "Dialogue on Poetry," printed as "Modern Mythology," trans. Irving Wohlfarth and the editors, in *The Modern Tradition: Backgrounds of Modern Literature*, ed. Richard Ellman and Charles Feidelson, Jr. (New York: Oxford University Press, 1965), 662.

11. C. G. Jung, *The Collected Works of C. G. Jung*, XII, *Psychology and Alchemy*, trans. R. F. C. Hull, 2nd ed., Bollingen Series XX (Princeton: Princeton University Press, 1953), 292–293.

12. John Armstrong, *The Paradise Myth* (London: Oxford University Press, 1969), 72–73. For the following quotations from this book, see pp. 86–87.

13. Friedrich von Schlegel, *Atheneum Fragments*, 53, in *Lucinde and the Fragments*, trans. Peter Firchow (Minneapolis: University of Minnesota Press, 1971), 167.

14. Dante Alighieri, *The Divine Comedy*, II: *Purgatorio, Text and Commentary*, trans. Charles S. Singleton, Bollingen Series LXXX (Princeton: Princeton University Press, 1982), 249. For the gloss, see 546–547.

15. Randall Jarrell, *Poetry and the Age* (New York: Vintage, 1959), 198.

16. See "Number Symbolism" in the *Harvard Dictionary of Music*, ed. Willi Apel (Cambridge, Mass.: Harvard University Press, 1970), 583.

17. Francis Bacon, quoted in M. H. Abrams, *Natural Supernaturalism: Tradition and Revolution in Romantic Literature* (New York: W. W. Norton, 1971), 61.

18. The quotations and Abrams's comments are in chapter 1 of *Natural Supernaturalism*.

19. Lewis Thomas, *The Lives of a Cell* (New York: Bantam, 1974), 1. DJ leafs through the book in 1.4, and Merrill refers approvingly to Thomas in "James Merrill's Myth: An Interview" (with Helen Vendler), 12.

20. Alfred North Whitehead, *Process and Reality: An Essay in Cosmology* (New York: The Free Press, 1969), 411.

21. Gregory Bateson, *Mind and Nature: A Necessary Unity* (New York: Bantam, 1979), 14, and David Bohm, *Wholeness and the Implicate Order* (London: Routledge and Kegan Paul, 1981), 208.

22. Bohm, *Wholeness*, 203–204, 210.

23. See Julian Jaynes, *The Origin of Consciousness*, 269.

7. The Names of God

1. In the first lesson in "&" however, MM calls Michael "GOD'S OLDEST CHILD." The following discussion should suggest the reason for this characteristic blurring of identities.

2. The description of Artemis comes from *The Oxford Classical Dictionary*, ed. N. G. L. Hammond and H. H. Scullard, 2nd ed. (Oxford: The Clarendon Press, 1970), 126–127. Merrill's retrospective comments on the "design" of *Scripts* are

somewhat riddling. "With *Scripts*," in contrast to *Mirabell*, "there was no shaping to be done. Except for the minutest changes, and deciding about line-breaks and so forth, the Lessons you see on the page appear just as we took them down. The doggerel at the fêtes, everything. In between the Lessons—our chats with Wystan or Robert [Morse] or Uni . . .—I still felt free to pick and choose; but even there, the design of the book just swept me along." "The Art of Poetry XXXI" (interview with J. D. McClatchy), *The Paris Review*, 24 (Summer 1982), 190–191.

3. Dante Alighieri, *The Divine Comedy*, III: *Paradiso, Text and Commentary*, trans. Charles S. Singleton, Bollingen Series LXXX (Princeton: Princeton University Press, 1982), 15.

4. Robert Morse, *Nineteen Poems* ([U.S.A.:] The Temple Press, 1981), 21, and W. H. Auden, *A Certain World* (New York: Viking, 1970), 358.

5. The symbolic import of the letter *ba* is discussed in Frithjof Schuon, *Understanding Islam*, trans. D. M. Matheson (London: George Allen & Unwin, 1963), 61, and Annemarie Schimmel, *Mystical Dimensions in Islam* (Chapel Hill: University of North Carolina Press, 1975), 420. The significance of the *a* and *b* in the transliterated *ba* would of course be original with Merrill.

6. For the Sufi interpretations of the diacritical mark, see Laleh Bakhtiar, *Sufi Expressions of the Mystical Quest* (London: Thames and Hudson, 1956), 68, 28, and Schuon, *Understanding Islam*, 61, n. 4.

7. Merrill's essay is "Divine Poem: Dante's Cosmic Web," *The New Republic*, 29 November 1980, 29–34.

8. Sufism has a rough analogy. According to one authority, "the four angels Gabriel, Michael, Seraphail, and Azrail correspond to four aspects of the name *Allah*. The four letters ALLA correspond to the mystic's Heart, Intellect, Spirit and Soul." See Shah Ni'matullah Walli, quoted in Bakhtiar, *Sufi Expressions*, 89.

9. On Gnosticism, which has several analogies with the system in the trilogy, see Hans Jonas, *The Gnostic Religion*, 2nd rev. ed. (Boston: Beacon Press, 1963), and Jonas, "Gnosticism," in *The Encyclopedia of Philosophy*, vol. 3 (New York: The Free Press, 1967), 336–342. Spinoza's "Deus sive Natura" has its analogue in Whitehead's view that God and the World are different aspects or phases of each other. See Alfred North Whitehead, *Process and Reality: An Essay on Cosmology* (New York: The Free Press, 1929, 1969), esp. 403–413.

10. Evelyn Underhill, *Mysticism: A Study in the Nature and Development of Man's Spiritual Consciousness* (New York: Dutton, 1911, 1963), 107.

11. The Sufi is Yūnus Emre, quoted in Schimmel, *Mystical Dimensions in Islam*, 418. On chiasmus, see, for example, Richard A. Lanham, *A Handlist of Rhetorical Terms* (Berkeley: University of California Press, 1968), 22–23.

12. Which of Deren's films could this be? The version that I have seen of her documentary on voodoo rites, entitled (like her book) "Divine Horsemen," neither begins nor ends with "a bare beach." Did Merrill see another film or another version? It is interesting that the end of *Scripts*, with its water and broken mirror, harks back to the last frames of another of Deren's films, "Meshes in the Afternoon," in

which the sea washes over pieces of a broken mirror lying on what we might indeed think of as an otherwise "bare beach."

13. "The Art of Poetry XXXI" (interview by J. D. McClatchy), *The Paris Review*, 24 (Summer 1982), 215.

14. Freud quotes Abel's excerpt from Bain's *Logic, Deductive and Inductive* in "'The Antithetical Sense of Primal Words': A Review of a Pamphlet by Karl Abel, *Über den Gegensinn der Urworte*, 1884," *Collected Papers*, trans. Joan Riviere (New York: Basic Books, 1959), vol. 4, 189.

15. Stanley Kunitz, "The Life of Poetry," *Antaeus*, 37 (Spring 1980), 153.

16. As in a sestina, the end words in a canzone follow a set order. In the first stanza, they appear in this order: ABAACAADDAEE. The second stanza begins with a linking E and repeats the pattern: EAEEBEECCEDD. And so on, until the coda's lines end ABCDE. That is, as the end words in a sestina's main stanzas recur in the order 615243, so the canzone's end words recur in the order 12, 1, 12, 12, 2, 12, 12, 5, 5, 12, 8, 8.

17. Douglas R. Hofstadter, *Gödel, Escher, Bach: An Eternal Golden Braid* (New York: Vintage, 1980), 258.

18. Robert S. Brumbaugh, *The Philosophers of Greece* (New York: Thomas Y. Crowell, 1964), 48–49.

19. Mahmūd Shabistarī, trans. E. H. Whinfield, quoted in Bakhtiar, *Sufi Expressions*, 15; and Ibn 'Arabi, paraphrased by Seyyed H. Nasr, *Three Muslim Sages* (Cambridge, Mass., 1963), 116, quoted in Schimmel, *Mystical Dimensions in Islam*, 270–271. The eye and the mirror are nearly interchangeable metaphors for the Sufi concept of the unity of Allah and creation. It is interesting that Bakhtiar summarizes the gist of the mirror metaphor by means of a diagram virtually identical to the one that God B traces on the board. Commenting on the diagram, she tells us that mankind "polishes" the mirror that is the macrocosmic universe so that there will be a "place for all the particular forms to gather into a unity," a "place for the Divine Self to see Self." I do not mean that Merrill must have read Bakhtiar; the closed X or double triangle appears in diverse writers, and many mystics use the mirror and the eye as metaphors. Moreover, Merrill's "Eye" magnified by the blood cell has just as much in common with Boehme ("If thou conceivest a small minute circle, as small as a grain of mustard seed, yet the Heart of God is wholly and perfectly therein") and Blake ("a World in a Grain of Sand"). And that is the point: Merrill's tropes, sometimes superficially esoteric, have venerable precedents.

20. W. B. Yeats, "Per Amica Silentia Lunae," in *Mythologies* (London: Macmillan, 1959), 356–357.

21. *Jean Santeuil précédé de Les Plaisirs et les jours* (Paris: Gallimard [Bibliothèque de la Pléiade], 1971), 423. (George D. Painter discusses the biographical origin of this incident in his *Marcel Proust: A Biography* [New York: Random House, 1959], vol. 1, 214–215.) Proust's note to this passage tells us that after his confession, Jean went to his room to revise his will, in order to leave most of his furnishings to his father and mother. While he was doing so, his mother came to his room and asked

him to go out. Proust concludes, "il cessa de songer à la mort pour jouir de la vie." Just as the bequest might serve indirectly to dedicate the trilogy to God B and Nature, so that last sentence might serve as an oblique farewell to the other world. At the same time, however, since the hero goes off with his mother, that sentence could vicariously imply, once more, the bond between humanity and Nature and thus between the trilogy's two worlds. "Pour jouir de la vie": the trilogy's V work is "vie" work, a work in the service of life, a life's work.

22. G. F. W. Hegel, quoted in *Hegel: Texts* and *Commentary,* trans. and ed. Walter Kaufmann (Garden City: Doubleday Anchor, 1966), 98.

23. Northrop Frye, *The Great Code: The Bible and Literature* (New York: Harcourt Brace, 1982), 220–226; M. H. Abrams, *Natural Supernaturalism* (New York: W. W. Norton, 1971), 183–187.

24. *The Logic of Hegel,* trans. William Wallace, 2nd ed. (Oxford, 1982), 379, quoted in Abrams, *Natural Supernaturalism,* 184.

8. A Shutter Opens

1. "Icecap" appeared in *The New Yorker,* 16 December 1985, 40.

2. William Weaver, in "Literary Tuscany," *Vanity Fair,* October 1984, 57–62, 119, recalls and collects other reminiscences of Count Umberto Morra's villa. The accompanying photographs by François Halard include one of "a portrait of Umberto I, second king of Italy and friend of the Morra family."

3. Background for this poem's details can be found in Stuart Rossiter, ed., *The Blue Guide to Greece* (Chicago: Rand McNally, 1973), 625–630.

4. It is partly too because the clown, with "a bright cerulean tear / On one rouged cheek," mirrors the bust of the young Merrill in "Bronze," with "a streak / Staining bluegreen my cheek."

5. See Migene Gonzalez-Wippler, *Santeria* (New York: The Julian Press, 1973). (The spell for bringing back a lover that Merrill's characters discuss at the end of the play seems to be the one described in *Santeria,* p. 157, and the Yoruba invocation to Changó that Manuel uses in his exorcism is similar to an invocation quoted on p. 43.) Merrill's first indication of his interest in this subject is his poem "Santo" in *Late Settings.*

6. *The Selected Poetry of Rainer Maria Rilke,* ed. and trans. Stephen Mitchell (New York: Random House, 1982), 195.

7. This translation is fragment 24 in Guy Davenport, *Herakleitos and Diogenes* (San Francisco: Grey Fox Press, 1979), 15.

8. See Gonzalez-Wippler, *Santeria,* 93.

Acknowledgments

James Merrill, to put first things first, graciously responded to certain questions that I had about his work and graciously refrained from asking many that he must have had about mine. Mary Bomba has been my tireless reader and faithful critic. I have learned from the advice of Calvin Bedient, Mary Kinzie, and David Lehman and from suggestions made by Eric Gans, Shusi Kao, and Karen Pennau. Holly Hall, Head of Special Collections at the James M. Olin Library of Washington University, was a solicitous guide to the James Merrill papers in the Modern Literature Collection. I could hardly name all of the former students who have contributed to this project, both by way of specific information and by way of general enthusiasm, but I must single out Lee Zimmerman and Reed Wilson. The others are represented in my mind by a woman in one of my classes who proposed a reading of a passage near the end of "From the Cupola" that was so surprising that I resisted it as ardently as I later came to endorse it. University of California Faculty Research Fellowships have facilitated this project, and I have been fortunate to have had exemplary research assistants in different phases of it: Dawn Morais Menon, Caroline Fraser, Harbour Fraser Hodder, Barbara Guarino, and Susan McCabe. For their careful typing of the manuscript I am indebted to Jeanette Gilkison, Nora Reyes-Elias, and especially Conni Lund.

David Jackson generously presented me with a copy of his sketch of the house in Athens and allowed me to reproduce it here. The superb photograph of the interior of the house in Stonington is by Rollie McKenna (copyright © Rollie McKenna) and is reproduced with her permission. Nikos Tombazi took the photograph of the Sleeping Woman, which is reproduced here with the permission of Alexandros N. Tombazi. The Garraway Company's photograph of the Merrill house in Southampton is reproduced by permission of The Slide Center, Rutherford, New Jersey. The photographs of the following works are from Alinari/Art Resource, New York, and are reproduced by permission: Piero della Francesca's "The Flagellation of Christ," in the Galleria delle Marche, Urbino; Giorgione's "The Tempest," reproduced by permission of the Galleria dell'Accademia, Venice; the Artemis of Ephesus, in the Villa Albani, Rome; and the head of Warrior A in the Museo Nazionale, Reggio Calabria. The photograph of San Miguel, by David Bowen, is reproduced by permission of Helene Brack. I am grateful to Christopher Spillers of the Getty Center for the History of Art and the Humanities for his courteous assistance in locating photographs. Eugeni S. Nesterov of UCLA Photographic Services was meticulous in his work with the reproductions. The Arabic calligraphy is by Bijan Samandor. Craig Smith kindly redrafted the angels' pictograph.

Harvard University Press has been consistently helpful and accommodating. I am especially grateful to Margaretta Fulton for her sympathetic tact and to Mary Ellen Geer for her painstaking editing of the manuscript. Gwen Frankfeldt, the book's designer, has been tolerant and inventive.

I am pleased to acknowledge permission to quote the following material: Lines from the letter to Thomas Butts in *The Complete Poetry and Prose of William Blake,* edited by David V. Erdman with commentary by Harold Bloom, revised edition, copyright © 1965, 1981 by David V. Erdman, are reprinted with permission of the University of California Press. Extracts from Marcel Proust, *Remembrance of Things Past,* translated by C. K. Scott Moncrieff and Terence Kilmartin, and by Andreas Mayor, copyright © 1981 by Random House Inc. and Chatto & Windus, Ltd., are reprinted with permission of Random House, Inc. and Chatto & Windus, Ltd. Lines from "Notes toward a Supreme Fiction" from *The Palm at the End of the Mind: Selected Poems and a Play,* by Wallace Stevens, edited by Holly Stevens, copyright © 1967, 1969, 1971 by Holly Stevens, are reprinted with permission of Random House, Inc. and Faber and Faber, Ltd. Lines from W. H. Auden, *New Year Letter* (1940), from *Collected Poems,* edited by Edward Mendelson, copyright © 1976 by Edward Mendelson, William Meredith and Monroe K. Spears, executors of the Estate of W. H. Auden, are reprinted with permission of Random House, Inc. and of Faber and Faber, Ltd. Excerpts from *Homage to Mistress Bradstreet* by John Berryman, copyright © 1956 by John Berryman, copyright renewed © 1984 by Mrs. Kate Berryman, are reprinted with permission of Farrar, Straus and Giroux, Inc. Excerpts from *The White Goddess* by Robert Graves, copyright 1946, renewed copyright © 1975 by Robert Graves, are reprinted by permission of Farrar, Straus and Giroux, Inc. Excerpts from Marcel Proust, *A la Recherche du temps perdu,* I, *Du Côté de chez Swann* and VII, *Le Temps retrouvé,* copyright © Editions Gallimard, are reprinted with permission. Lines from "The Circus Animals' Desertion" and "Lapis Lazuli" are reprinted with permission of Macmillan Publishing Company and A. P. Watt, Ltd. from *The Poems of W. B. Yeats,* edited by Richard J. Finneran, copyright 1940 by Georgie Yeats, renewed 1968 by Bertha Georgie Yeats, Michael Butler Yeats, and Anne Yeats. Lines from "Vacillation" are reprinted with permission of Macmillan Publishing Company and A. P. Watt, Ltd. from *The Poems of W. B. Yeats,* edited by Richard J. Finneran, copyright 1933 by Macmillan Publishing Company, renewed 1961 by Bertha Georgie Yeats. "The friends that have it I do wrong" is reprinted with permission of Macmillan Publishing Company and A. P. Watt, Ltd. from *The Poems of W. B. Yeats,* edited by Richard J. Finneran, copyright © 1983 by Anne Yeats. Lines from "Winter Eve" from *Nineteen Poems,* by Robert Morse, copyright © 1981 by Daniel Morse, are reprinted with permission of Daniel Morse. The lines from "Summer Session" from *Collected Poems, 1951–1971,* by A. R. Ammons, are reprinted by permission of W. W. Norton & Company, Inc., copyright © 1972 by A. R. Ammons. Excerpts from Dante Alighieri, *The Divine Comedy,* translated with a commentary by Charles Singleton, Bollingen Series 80, vol. 2: *Purgatorio,* copyright © 1973 by Princeton University Press, excerpts, pp. 248–249 and vol. 3: *Paradiso,* copyright © 1975 by Princeton University Press, excerpts, pp. 14–15 are reprinted with permission. Lines from Yūnus Emre, *Divan,* translated by and quoted in Annemarie Schimmel, *Mystical Dimensions in Islam,* copyright © 1975 by the University of North Carolina Press, are reprinted with permission. Lines from "The Eighth Elegy" from *The Selected Poetry of Rainer Maria Rilke,* edited and translated by Stephen Mitchell, copyright © 1982 by Stephen Mitchell, are reprinted with permission of Random House, Inc. The quotation from T. S. Eliot's letter to William Force Stead, copyright © 1978 by Mrs. Valerie Eliot, is reprinted by her permission and that of Faber and Faber Ltd.

Quotations from the following works are reprinted by permission of James Merrill: *Jim's Book,* privately printed, copyright 1942 by James Ingram Merrill; *The Black Swan,* published by Icaros, Athens, Greece, 1946, quoted poems from which are included in *First Poems,* published by Alfred A. Knopf, copyright 1946, 1947, 1948, 1949, 1950 by James Merrill; *The Seraglio,* published by Alfred A. Knopf, copyright © 1957 by James Merrill.

Quotations from *The Bait,* published originally by *Quarterly Review of Literature* and then in *Artists' Theatre: New York* by Grove Press, copyright © 1955, 1956 by James Merrill, are reprinted by permission of Grove Press, Inc. Quotations from James Merrill, *The Immortal Husband,* copyright © 1956 by New Directions, are reprinted by permission of New Directions Publishing Corporation.

Quotations from the following works are reprinted by permission: "Processional," copyright © 1982 by James Merrill, originally in *The Atlantic Monthly;* "The Parnassians," copyright © 1983 by James Merrill, originally in *The New York Review of Books;* "Icecap," copyright © 1985 by James Merrill, originally in *The New Yorker;* and *The Image Maker,* copyright © 1986 by James Merrill, published by Sea Cliff Press.

Quotations from the following works are reprinted by permission of Atheneum Publishers: *The Country of a Thousand Years of Peace,* copyright 1951, 1952, 1953, 1954, copyright © 1957, 1958, 1970; copyright renewed © 1979, 1980, 1981, 1982 by James Merrill; *Water Street,* copyright © 1960, 1961, 1962 by James Merrill; *The (Diblos) Notebook,* copyright © 1965 by James Merrill; *Nights and Days,* copyright © 1960, 1961, 1962, 1963, 1964, 1965, 1966 by James Merrill; *The Fire Screen,* copyright © 1964, 1966, 1967, 1968, 1969 by James Merrill; *Braving the Elements,* copyright © 1969, 1970, 1971, 1972 by James Merrill; *The Yellow Pages,* originally published by the Temple Bar Bookshop, Cambridge, Massachusetts, 1974, copyright © 1970, 1972, 1974 by James Merrill; *Divine Comedies,* copyright © 1976 by James Merrill; *Mirabell: Books of Number,* copyright © 1978 by James Merrill; *Scripts for the Pageant,* copyright © 1980 by James Merrill; *The Changing Light at Sandover,* copyright © 1980, 1982 by James Merrill; *From the First Nine: Poems 1946–1976,* copyright © 1980, 1981.

Quotations from *Mirabell: Books of Number* are reprinted also with the permission of Oxford University Press.

Acknowledgments

Diverse passages from *Selected Poems* by James Merrill and "From the Cupola" and "The Summer People" from *Two Poems* by James Merrill are reprinted by permission of the author and Chatto & Windus, Ltd.

Excerpts from "The Art of Poetry XXXI," an interview with James Merrill by J. D. McClatchy, from *The Paris Review,* reprinted in *Writers at Work: The Paris Review Interviews,* Sixth Series, edited by George Plimpton, copyright © 1984 by The Paris Review, Inc., are reprinted by permission of The Paris Review, Inc. and Viking Penguin, Inc.

Chapter 5 originally appeared in a different form in *Canto.* A bit of Chapter 6 was first published in *The Yale Review,* copyright © 1979 by Yale University, and is reprinted with permission. An earlier version of Chapter 7 appeared in *James Merrill: Essays in Criticism,* edited by David Lehman and Charles Berger, pp. 246–281, copyright © 1983 by Cornell University Press, and is used here by permission of the publisher. A part of Chapter 8 is reprinted with permission of *The Boston Review,* where it was first published.

Index